Preserving and Enhancing Communities

Preserving and Enhancing Communities

A Guide for Citizens, Planners, and Policymakers

Edited by   Elisabeth M. Hamin, Priscilla Geigis, and Linda Silka

University of Massachusetts Press   Amherst

LC 2007006701
ISBN : 978-1-55849-564-7 (paper); 563-0 (library cloth)

Designed by Dennis Anderson
Set in Minion Pro and Myriad Pro
Printed and bound by Hamilton Printing Company

Library of Congress Cataloging-in-Publication Data

Preserving and enhancing communities : a guide for citizens, planners, and
policymakers / edited by Elisabeth M. Hamin, Linda Silka, and Priscilla Geigis.
    p.   cm.
   Includes bibliographical references and index.
   ISBN 978-1-55849-564-7 (pbk. : alk. paper) — ISBN 978-1-55849-563-0 (cloth : alk. paper)
   1. City planning. 2. Community development, Urban--Government policy.
3. Cities and towns—Growth. 4. Cultural property—Protection.
I. Hamin, Elisabeth M., 1961– II. Silka, Linda. III. Geigis, Priscilla.
TD160.P74 2007
307.1′216—dc22

2007006701

British Library Cataloguing in Publication data are available.

Dedicated to leaders everywhere who inspire us
through their actions and commitment to preserve and
enhance our communities for the well-being of all.

Contents

Section I. Gathering Perspectives and Getting Involved

Section II. Developing a Vision

Section III. Preserving Natural Resources

Section IV. Enhancing Community Strengths

Section V. Keeping the Best

Color plates follow page 98.

Acknowledgments

First, the editors would like to thank all the contributors to this book who patiently responded to our suggestions and developed what we humbly consider truly valuable contributions to better communities. The principles and policies behind Community Preservation were developed by Robert Durand while he was Secretary of the Executive Office of Environmental Affairs (EOEA) in the Commonwealth of Massachusetts, and we salute his vision and leadership. From start to finish, this book was a collaborative process and would not have been produced without the support and assistance of many people at EOEA and the University of Massachusetts. In addition to the authors, the editors wish to thank Bob Durand, Chuck Anastas, Arthur Bergeron, and Jack Ahern. The initial idea of this book was developed in close collaboration with the Community Preservation Working Group established through the Commonwealth Partnership between EOEA and the University of Massachusetts, and we gratefully acknowledge their support and dedication. The co-chairs of the Community Preservation Working Group are Betsy Shure Gross, EOEA, and Linda Silka, UMass Lowell. The members include: from the EOEA, Commissioner David Balfour, Kurt Gaertner, Priscilla Geigis, Christian Jacqz, Sara Miller, and Commissioner Peter Webber; and from UMass, Leslie Ackles, Jack Ahern, Robert Bowen, John Bullard, Mary Grant, Jody Hensley, John Mullin, Gisela Walker, and Jack Wiggin. The authors would particularly like to acknowledge chapter author Bob Kuehn, who truly was one of the good guys. While his unexpected passing in 2006 has left us all poorer, his life's legacy leaves our communities enriched indeed.

Last but not least are the family and friends who helped us in uncountable ways to complete this work, and the University of Massachusetts Press's Bruce Wilcox, Carol Betsch, and Jack Harrison, who helped us to bring it to fruition.

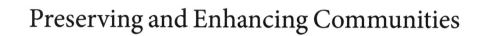

Preserving and Enhancing Communities

Photo: Nedim Kemer

Introduction

Preserving and Enhancing Communities

Elisabeth M. Hamin, Linda Silka, and Priscilla Geigis

GUIDING the growth and development of our communities in the twenty-first century will be complicated, challenging, rewarding, and necessary—just as guiding communities in the last century was. Our communities, the ways they have grown, and the ways they have stayed the same, say something about who we are as a nation. Since the founding of our country, land development has shaped our civilization. We often built communities by clustering houses and institutions of commerce around town and city centers, and these centers made our communities come alive, congregating people and bringing life to our neighborhoods. As transportation advanced, these same communities expanded, often pushing people away from these vital centers that were once the heart of our communities. As a result, throughout the country the landscape is now dotted with haphazard development patterns that unnecessarily consume land and isolate residents from traditional centers of commerce and activity.

Each of our communities, through the decisions of its local leaders, has chosen a path that has shaped it—whether outlined in a specific growth strategy or the result of unplanned circumstances, or, most usually, some combination of the two. As citizen leaders, we are challenged with preserving what is special about our communities as they continue to develop and evolve. We are further challenged to encourage growth that enhances our communities through its design, patterns, and locations. One approach to this is captured by the name "community preservation" which focuses on empowering residents to become involved in local decision-making in municipalities, and seeks to preserve what is best about existing towns and cities while also encouraging changes and development that enhance sense of place as well as providing homes and jobs for new and existing residents.

The fundamental philosophy of community preservation is that when individuals, organizations, and communities are empowered to work together to make growth decisions, the constituency for planning expands and the result is a better reflection of community values that contribute to the quality of life. Most land-use decisions in the United States occur at the local level—municipalities are where the rubber meets the road, metaphorically speaking. As a result, if we are to change development patterns to increase the choices available to residents, efficiently use resources, and preserve important natural systems, the local level is where this has to happen. Community preservation and enhancement is about this local level improvement in the built environment—our city centers, towns, villages, rural areas, and neighborhoods.

Most local land-use decisions lie in the hands of citizen volunteers, who often come from disparate backgrounds yet are asked to make critical decisions affecting the long-term health of communities and quality of life of current and future residents. While these citizen-planners may have professional planning staff to turn to for recommendations, it is typically up to the citizens as members of local planning, zoning, and conservation boards to make the final decisions. Even when residents are not on official boards, there are many opportunities for them to influence local planning. As a result, citizen-planners need the best information and ideas available in the field, presented in nontechnical language that is still sophisticated enough to respect the importance of the decisions local communities face. This need is what this book seeks to address.

The fundamental design ideas in this book, and in community preservation in general, share a great deal with what many places and people call "smart growth," and we hope this book contributes to that literature. According to the American Planning Association,

> smart growth means using comprehensive planning to guide, design, develop, revitalize and build communities for all that:
> - have a unique sense of community and place;
> - preserve and enhance valuable natural and cultural resources;
> - equitably distribute the costs and benefits of development;
> - expand the range of transportation, employment and housing choices in a fiscally responsible manner;
> - value long-range, regional considerations of sustainability over short term incremental geographically isolated actions; and
> - promotes public health and healthy communities.
>
> Compact, transit accessible, pedestrian-oriented, mixed use development patterns and land reuse epitomize the application of the principles of smart growth. (American Planning Association 2002)

An essential difference between smart growth and community preservation, and the reason that we prefer to use the latter term, is that, correctly or not, smart growth is often perceived as a top-down policy, where states tell local governments how they should plan. That sort of policy is often helpful, but in places such as Massachusetts and the many other states with a strong local orientation, such a policy is not likely to be politically successful. Thus, community preservation seeks to achieve many smart growth goals through empowering local leaders, and their municipalities, to realize stronger and better communities through action at the local level. Community preservation is thus both a philosophy of local planning and a state-level approach to empowering good planning at the local level. The main body of the book describes this approach to local planning, while the final chapter describes the Commonwealth of Massachusetts's Community Preservation Initiative in more detail.

This book is intended as a guide for local leaders, policymakers, citizen-planners, and anyone engaged in their communities. It will also be of use to students of planning. Our goal is to help readers learn not just about typical ways of doing things, but also about a range of current best and emerging practices for specific topic areas. Understanding those best practices, however, requires understanding how particular natural and social systems work; in other words, you can't know how to plan for water until you know where your water comes from and goes to, and what lives in your water. So each chapter lays out foundational principles of its particular topic, then presents some of the typical current ways of addressing the issue, as well as some more innovative techniques which have not yet had as broad an application, but appear likely to be influential and helpful in the coming years. The topics of each of these chapters could be, and are, topics for whole books; as a result, each chapter should be considered just an introduction to its subject. Most chapters conclude with a set of references readers can turn to when they need guidance of greater depth on any particular issue. A set of indicators for the topics is also presented, a point to which we will return below.

The backgrounds of the authors vary. Some authors are traditional academics whose practice is teaching, research, and occasional studio or outreach projects. Others were engaged in the development of particular aspects of state-level policy and thus bring to the chapters both advocacy and a deep understanding of the issues and reasons for that particular policy. Still others are local professionals and consultants with experience in implementing existing policy as well as in trying to "push the envelope" of existing regulations and practices. It was our intent to bring together a diversity of views, and as a result many chapters are co-authored by individuals of different backgrounds and orientations. The result is a unique book that integrates and reflects the perspectives of researchers and practitioners. Massachusetts is the focus for many of the examples used throughout, not only because this is the home territory for the editors and many of the authors, but also because Massachusetts brings together in one place so many of the challenges other states are now confronting. We have also included examples from across the country and anticipate that the book will be relevant in many states, when adjusted for local circumstances as well as state government patterns and land-use case law.

Within this diversity, specific themes link these chapters into a whole. Taken together, they identify some of the key aspects of good planning in the twenty-first century.

Policy Development through Partnerships

In a world where power is widely distributed and groups of engaged members of the public are many and fluctuating, the only way to implement change successfully is through engaging many actors in the process. Bringing in multiple perspectives opens the way for better policies by tapping the breadth of local knowledge and expertise as well as by making clear how particular actions will affect different groups. Developing buy-in from multiple parties is often necessary if political support is to be created. As a result, the issues of developing consensus and buy-in permeate the chapters. At the local level, these issues form the focus of the first section of the book ("Gathering Perspectives and Getting Involved"), with many other chapters suggesting likely coalitions for change on individual topics. At the state level, the issue of consensus building is the heart of the book's final chapter, which describes Massachusetts's Community Preservation Initiative in some detail.

Community = Diversity

To be politically effective, it is important to reach out to key powerbrokers in the community. But to be equitable, one must also reach out to populations who may not traditionally have had access to public processes. And reaching out may also be necessary to achieve implementation, as a policy developed without the perspective of diverse members of the community is likely to run into opposition as it moves forward. As chapter 3 suggests, involving diverse community members can yield a wealth of expertise and knowledge. The challenges are great, however, as lower-income groups may face more competition for their time (like getting enough pay to make the rent) than higher-income groups, may not use English as a first language, and may have a cultural history of distrust and disempowerment vis-à-vis government. Engaging diversity requires a commitment of time, resources, and creativity, but yields better and fairer policy.

Building from the Best

Community preservation suggests that each city and town has positive aspects. These might be in the built environment —the town common, landmark buildings which give a place a sense of place; in the social relations in the town— the ethnic and income diversity, the culture of volunteerism and neighborliness; or in the broader landscape—the ready access to countryside and local produce, the views of the shore, the frogs in the backyard. The point is to identify these best aspects and put into place policies which will assure that they continue. Then the town or city can look for other areas that can be improved.

Integration of Systems and Policies

A book such as this one has to break topics down into separate components to be manageable for readers as well as authors. Yet despite the fragmentation necessary in a chapter-based approach, an overall theme is that all natural systems are interrelated, and as a result the policy choices we make are interrelated with the resources and with each other. An example may clarify what we mean. Water quality and quantity affect biodiversity (fish need clean, flowing streams; frogs need vernal pools); water quantity affects economic development and land-use futures (bringing in industry or new homes requires adequate, clean water); water quality is affected by transportation (run-off from roads) as well as building codes (impermeable paved surface = lack of aquifer recharge) and engineering standards (is storm water piped directly downstream, or allowed to recharge the local aquifer? are green roofs—roofs with lawns on them—allowed in your town?); and assuring adequate water supplies for the future is directly related to protected lands (often land protection is for aquifer recharge areas or correlates to wetlands and streambanks), which is connected to recreation (much protected land is also recreation land), and planning and zoning (what will we allow to be built in flood zones? how will we zone land near the river?). This example shows why comprehensive planning, dealt with in chapter 5, is so important—it is the place where these connections are explicitly considered.

Natural and Cultural Systems as the Base

Much of the book is devoted to issues of biodiversity, natural lands, water, and historic buildings and landscapes. These conditions provide the base upon which communities plan. An ideal planning process remains the one proposed by Ian McHarg (1992); McHarg suggests that the land be analyzed for its environmental constraints, and he argues that human systems need to fit within the local natural systems, so that processes are mutually supporting. Land that is very important for biodiversity or water, land that has natural constraints such as steep slopes that limit its appropriateness for building, or land that is very important agriculturally should be put aside first, and development should be focused on the rest of the land, particularly those parcels near existing town centers. All land-use planning needs to be environmental planning. For all the land, implementing appropriate regulations is key, so that land appropriate for development is made easy to build on, while land that for one reason or another is deemed unsuited to development becomes hard to build on.

Making the Good Easy and the Bad Hard

This very obvious principle nevertheless bears repeating. Developers, as described in chapter 4, seek to minimize risk, and so will try to build whatever requires the least permitting, negotiation, and general uncertainty. This simple principle suggests that the place to start in understanding your municipality's current form and likely future is to review your town's existing regulations, and talk to a local planner and a local developer, to see what sorts of development the current regulations make easy. A buildout analysis, which

works from existing code and is described in chapter 7, is a good next step. Then you, and everyone else, can talk about whether the development that is permitted by your zoning codes matches your desired future for your town or city. If not, then you can start seeing what needs to be changed. In those changes, remembering the simple principle of making the good actions easy goes far in creating sensible, effective regulations.

The Need for Community Structures to Support Each Other

Municipal resources are usually too limited to engage in many single-purpose programs. And they are certainly too scare to allocate to conflicting purposes. Thus, another reason that comprehensive planning is so important is that it provides an opportunity to identify those points where the community may be working at cross-purposes and then determine which goals should take precedence. Perhaps, for example, a community wants to provide housing for the traditional working class that has long lived in that town, but the community has also adopted a zoning policy of allowing new homes only on one-acre lots; the zoning policy is likely to prevent meaningful accomplishment of the first goal unless extraordinary steps are taken. A clear vision and prioritization of goals will be needed. This example also suggests one of the criteria that can be used to decide which policies to implement: place a high priority on those criteria that enable your community to achieve multiple goals. Plan for open space in aquifer recharge areas, and put bike trails along the open space that connect people's houses to where they work or to the town center, thereby increasing transportation alternatives. Look for economic development opportunities that can occur on brownfield sites, and try to reuse existing structures for new job sites. Undertake historic preservation of structures, but adapt them for stores or small offices on the bottom floor and affordable housing in the upper stories. These sorts of initiatives not only make good financial and policy sense, they also bring coalitions, even partnerships, of support.

Best Practices

Rather than provide a single-fit guide for what all towns and cities ought to do, the following chapters instead describe a variety of practices which current research and experience suggest can be effective. In recent years important advances have been made in creative approaches for addressing current issues, so the range of available policies within cities and towns is now quite large. We share many of these ideas. Citizen-planners are unlikely to become expert in all of the techniques described, and our intent is not to suggest that citizen-planners should become experts. Instead, our goal is to point to the level of creativity now being unleashed as cities and towns become innovative in addressing municipal goals. With an overview of the range of tools and practices, citizen-planners can push for new approaches to existing problems and demonstrate that other towns have already taken the new path. Citizens can turn to their planner or regional planning agency for technical advice on which approaches work best where and which might be feasible and legal in their state. We hope in this book to push up the bar a bit in average municipal planning practice, by helping residents and policy-makers see what is possible.

Varied State Roles in Local Planning

U.S. state governments' degree of activism in local planning varies greatly from state to state. Some states, such as Oregon, are notably activist, dictating the general form and some of the policies that communities must use. Other states have adopted a more regional approach. Vermont, for example, focuses on having a regional-level review of major development projects and local planning. Still other states, such as Massachusetts, emphasize strong localist traditions, whereby neither state nor region has much influence on the content of local plans, and instead the culture is one of municipalities having fairly free rein in planning for their future. This book does not take a position as to which type of state role is best overall. Instead, our focus, and the focus of community preservation as a state policy, has been to respect both political reality and local traditions, and work within the universe of the possible. In Massachusetts and in many other states, that means that the state's primary role is to support and empower local planning to become better, rather than to mandate specific changes. Nevertheless, Massachusetts's example as described in chapter 17 shows that there are helpful actions states can take to encourage better local planning.

Indicators

Many communities across the nation are instituting indicators programs. Indicators, simply defined, are community-determined measurements of elements that are important to that particular place and those particular people. They are ways of seeing "how much" or "how many" or "to what extent" or "what size." The indicators movement started with groups working toward sustainability at the community level, and many indicators reflect the tenets of sustainability—that the best municipal policies achieve the intersection of improvements to the local and global ecology, economy, and equity. The best indicators are locally meaningful and are effective measures of the topic at hand. They are based on the awareness that what values we hold dear influence what data we collect, but also, what data we have at hand influences the policies we implement. Communities use a portfolio of indicators to benchmark, to measure, progress toward the goals identified in their comprehensive plan or other visioning document. The trends of specific indicators over time can suggest which policies are working and which need to be adjusted as the community evaluates its progress toward its goals. Indicators can suggest problems not foreseen in the comprehensive planning or visioning process, such as groups that are not being reached by local services. And the examination of indicators itself requires a reevaluation of the goals of the comprehensive planning or visioning process, thereby creating a way to keep the process alive, to make adjustments along the way, and to test the validity of goals and programs over time. At their best, indicators projects draw the community together in efforts to measure and achieve community goals over time, and can publicize those efforts as well, thereby encouraging public support. An overview of community indicators is provided in the Appendix, along with a list of suggested indicators that relate to different chapters in this book. These will provide a starting point for determining relevant indicators in your community.

THE LAST twenty years has seen significant increases in the range and types of policies and bylaws available to municipalities and their citizen activists to improve local land-use planning. Empowering local citizen-planners and their municipal staff to use these new tools is at the heart of community preservation and enhancement. We hope this book will assist residents, volunteers, staff members, planners, and policy-makers in many towns and cities in creating better communities during this early part of the twenty-first century.

References

Most of the following chapters provide specific references to sources that address their topics. Some of the more general sources we like best for follow-up reading include the following:

American Planning Association. 2002. *Policy Guide on Smart Growth*. http://www.planning.org/policyguides/smartgrowth.htm. Accessed on 1/21/04.

Campoli, J., E. Humstone, et al. 2001. *Above and Beyond: Visualizing Change in Small Towns and Rural Areas*. Chicago: APA Planners Press.

Conservation Law Foundation and Vermont Forum on Sprawl. 2002. *Community Rules: A New England Guide to Smart Growth Strategies*. Conservation Law Foundation and the Vermont Forum on Sprawl.

Daniels, T., and K. Daniels. 2003. *Environmental Planning*. Chicago: APA Planners Press.

Daniels, T. 1999. *When City and Country Collide : Managing Growth in the Metropolitan Fringe*. Washington, DC: Island Press.

Daniels, T., J. W. Keller, et al. 1995. *The Small Town Planning Handbook*. Chicago: Planners Press, American Planning Association.

Kelly, E. D., and B. Becker. 2000. *Community Planning: An Introduction to the Comprehensive Plan*. Washington, DC: Island Press.

McHarg, I. L. 1992, 1969. *Design with Nature*. New York: J. Wiley.

O'Neill, D. 2000. *The Smart Growth Tool Kit*. Washington, DC: ULI—the Urban Land Institute.

Randolph, J. 2004. *Environmental Land Use Planning and Management*. Washington, DC: Island Press.

I

Gathering Perspectives and Getting Involved

Courtesy of Town of Amherst, Massachusetts

1

Getting Involved

Local Residents and the Planning Process

Elisabeth M. Hamin and Jeff Levine

COMMUNITY preservation and enhancement are based on the idea that it is the residents of a municipality that, through their love of place and willingness to get involved, will decide the future of each town and city. For those who have not been extensively engaged in issues of local land use, the first question likely to arise is: how do I get involved? The second question, given limited time and energy and the desire to see outcomes from one's participation, is likely to be: how can I make my participation as effective as possible? This chapter introduces these two topics. We begin with a fairly general discussion of the local land-use process, including where and when residents can most effectively involve themselves in planning decisions.

The focus of this chapter is getting involved as an individual in the usual sort of town planning processes. Sometimes, one needs to create coalitions with other individuals and groups to try to get more major change implemented outside the usual planning procedures; this is the topic of chapter 2.

Pressure Points for Resident Influence

One of the amazing, frustrating, and wonderful things about local land use is that, while there usually is some professional staff, it is the residents of towns and cities that ultimately control it. That control is exerted in three ways. First is the issue of who gets elected as mayor or to city council or town meeting. Second is that the key decisions on land use, such as the comprehensive plan and the town's zoning, are made by volunteer boards of citizens. Third is the ability of residents to influence the decisions of those boards. Planning staff provide advice and information, but it is the municipality's volunteer boards and elected officials that decide. (Note that while we will occasionally use the term "citizen" in this discussion, for most situations citizenship *per se* is not important; the issue is whether someone is a resident of the town or region. Legal aliens have a right to participate in public hearings too, and in some instances those without papers can and should be involved as well, particularly when decisions will affect them.)

Some of the key areas for resident involvement include:

- Comprehensive planning: The comprehensive plan is a policy statement endorsed by the elected officials of a town about the directions for the town's future, its policies, and the ways those policies will be implemented. When a municipality draws up or revises a comprehensive plan, officials and their consultants will almost always engage in a significant effort to get residents to review the plan and comment. Because the comprehensive plan usually becomes the basis for future zoning and planning decisions, getting engaged in this process is crucial to shaping the "big picture" future of your town. At this stage there can be a lot of creativity, such as thinking about starting a historic district, limiting building in floodplains, or recommending design review for extra-large homes. In most states, comprehensive planning and changes to the existing plan are undertaken by the local planning board. Comprehensive planning is described more thoroughly in chapter 5.
- Public meetings: As a municipality considers its future, it often will (and should) hold public meetings to get a sense of the community's priorities. These may not have direct outcomes—in other words, they may not result directly in zoning or planning changes—but they often set the long-term direction for the town. Attending so that one can influence direction early, while the agenda for change is still mutable, can have a real impact. It can be difficult, however, to know which meetings will have real results and which are exploratory "fishing expeditions"; judgment and perhaps a call to the planning staff in your town will help sort out what meetings are really important.

  There are three basic types of public meetings: *informational meetings, public hearings,* and *workshops/charettes.* Each type has its own rules and norms. An informational meeting is designed to give the public news, not to take feedback from the public. Questions are appropriate at informational meetings, but feedback about whether ideas are good or bad is not the focus of the meeting.

  A public hearing is designed to both give information and take feedback on the information presented. This is either a formal chance to provide input or a less formal chance to discuss a proposal. If you don't know what to say right away, don't despair. Often times public input can be provided after the meeting in writing, by email, or in person, as long as you meet whatever deadline exists. A sub-category of these is the board or commission meeting, where a municipal board, such as the planning board, will hear from developers about a project, listen to comments from the public, and then take a vote among the board members to make a legal or policy decision. In these cases, you need to speak up before the board begins its voting in order to have an impact.

  Workshops and charettes tend to be sessions where those attending get to pick up a pencil and help actually design a place. Often a charette focuses on one site and asks participants to spend one to three days intensively collaborating to outline a design for the site. Workshops can be very similar but usually are at the neighborhood or community scale. Getting one's voice heard at these can help set the agenda for changes to the town's future, because future planning processes build on the results of these workshops.

- Zoning amendment hearings: A developer who needs to get a zoning change to undertake a project will go before a board, often called the zoning board of appeals (ZBA) or some similar name. Legally, the residents who live nearest the area of proposed change are required to be notified that a parcel is under discussion, although how that notice is delivered—letters to the nearby homes or just a notice in the paper—varies by state. Attending these meetings is crucial to getting your voice heard about specific projects. In principle, zoning changes should be hard for a developer to get, but if neighbors are not there to listen and comment, in many towns where development is popular changes in fact can be quite easy. A variant on this situation is that the municipality itself may want to revise its zoning, perhaps to match a new comprehensive plan. Again, resident input is crucial to the process. Zoning is explained more thoroughly in chapter 6.
- Subdivision proposals: If a project does not need a zoning change, the first official phase of project approval usually comes when a developer proposes that a large parcel of land be divided up into smaller lots to be built on. The developer will have to show a site plan, which indicates the number of units and their sort (townhouses? apartments? single-family houses?) and general size, as well as

the amenities the developer plans (sidewalks? retention ponds for storm water? a new park?). The planning board is usually the one that hears these requests. Subdivision design varies enormously, from the very good to the very bad, and while planning boards should be able to sort this out, more eyes on a plan are always better. Plus, your opinion may be very different than the planning board's! The municipality will have regulations about such things as setbacks (how far from the road and the lot lines a house must be) and lot size, and many have other standards that are legally binding. One of the strengths of local control (from the citizen's perspective, if not the developer's) is that planning boards are often very responsive to community concerns, so this is an excellent, really crucial place to get involved. Note, however, that if the project proposal fits in with the existing plan for the town and matches zoning and subdivision regulations, the board may be more receptive to the new development than the neighbors may wish. There are legal reasons for this—when a planning board disallows a subdivision, it is always at risk of a long and expensive legal battle. Also, what may seem like a bad idea to neighbors may be really needed for the overall town, such as higher-density affordable housing. This is why it is important to get involved in the upfront planning processes described above.

- Special permit review: Regular subdivision of property implies that the developer is going to use the land in the ways that the zoning code allows as by-right uses—you can check your zoning code to see which those are. Most towns and cities also have a category for "special permits"—for projects that are more complicated, ask for different uses (townhouses and retail instead of single-family houses, for instance), or are bigger. What qualifies for a special permit where in your city will be explained in the zoning code and accompanying map. Usually it is the planning board that has the responsibility for special permit reviews, although in some places it is the zoning board. An important point is that the relevant board has much broader authority to ask for concessions in the design or the public benefits of special review applications—this is the trade-off a city or town gets for giving permission for uses or designs outside the normal codes. So, public participation is crucial in telling the boards what sort of changes are needed to make these projects acceptable to the neighborhood and a benefit for the city and region.

- Building permit approval: When a developer is nearly ready to break ground on a project, they will apply for a building permit. Assuming the proposed project has the correct zoning, and either did not need subdivision approval or already has it, this becomes an engineering issue—does the project meet health, safety, and building codes? If so, it will get a building permit, although the town engineer, who is the one who deals with this phase of the approval process, may attach conditions to be sure the project meets code. This is *not* the right time to get involved; the process is a largely bureaucratic exercise at this point, and will not include public hearings. In other words, once a proposal gets to building permitting, the window of citizen opportunity to influence it— short of a starting a lawsuit—is pretty much closed.

- Specific commissions: Most municipalities also have specific commissions that examine development proposals. These vary state by state and town by town, but may include conservation commissions, which review the environmental impacts of projects; historic preservation commissions, which get involved when a property is of significant age or importance to the history of the town; and design review committees, which review the architecture of proposed projects, typically within specific areas of town or for projects of a certain size or type. Active involvement on these boards can be very rewarding, and attending their meetings gives you important input into proposed changes to the town.

- Budgets and capital improvement programs: Little is more important than how a municipality chooses to spend its money. Each year the city council or town meeting must vote to approve the budget. These meetings are often sparsely attended, so any citizen who has taken the time to really review the proposed budget and comment on it can often be very influential. The Capital Improvements Program (CIP) or some similarly named document is the municipality's five- or six-year plan for improvements to roads, schools, and public buildings. The first year of the CIP becomes incorporated into the town's official budget, while the projects described for the following years are more advisory (sometime more dream than reality). As with the budget, in most towns few citizens come to hearings on the CIP, so those who do attend and have thoughtful comments are often taken quite seriously.

- State agencies: When state agencies are acting on something local, they will hold local hearings. Examples include proposed state developments (like new office buildings or parks) and changes to state highways. It can be harder to influence these outcomes than more local decisions, but nevertheless state agencies have a responsibility to attend to how their proposed projects are received locally.

It should be clear that there is a wide variety of ways for residents to influence the public process. Indeed, one of the beauties of local land use is that this is often citizens' most direct experience of participatory democracy; in other words, it is your best chance to get your voice heard to influence the future. But these things vary from place to place and process to process, as we will see below.

The Realities of Public Participation

Some municipalities are very responsive to residents. In Amherst, Massachusetts, for example, the planning staff strongly encourage developers proposing a subdivision of any significant size to hold an "abutters'" meeting. This is a preliminary opportunity for developers to present their plans to neighbors, prior to the official public hearings. The meeting gives the neighbors the chance to preview a project and decide on their position about it before the public hearings begin, and also to put the developer on notice about what they are likely to object to most. Ideally, the developer makes changes in response to community comments even before the official hearings begin, although often enough little change happens and the neighbors still have to make their case in front of the planning board. Requests for changes to a site plan can be relatively minor, such as adding sidewalks or more landscaping, or more substantive, such as reducing the numbers of units or putting up different types of buildings. Either before or after such a meeting is a good time to try to develop some consensus among the neighbors about support, opposition, or changes to the plan. A consensus position will weigh much more heavily in planning board considerations than individual, often conflicting, comments.

Some towns, however, are much more responsive to developers than to neighbors, and influencing outcomes may be difficult. One of the main problems for residents is that by the time that neighbors hear about a project, the developer

How to Get Listened To

Getting listened to is actually pretty simple. If you've done your research and you're at the right meeting, don't blow it. Follow these rules:

- *Be Polite:* No one likes getting yelled at. Don't forget that the planner might agree with you, even if her bosses can't implement your idea because of factors such as money, politics, or the law. The nicer you are to people the more they will go to bat for your ideas with their superiors after the meeting.
- *Be Brief:* Everyone has been to a meeting where someone goes on for far too long about an idea, even if it is one you agree with. It is hard to listen to any one person for too long. State your main idea up front in one or two sentences, and try not to take more than a minute or two to finish your statement. There is no prize for using the most words!
- *Be on Topic:* We've also been to meetings where someone starts with one idea, breaks out sheets of notes, and then wanders from idea to idea without any real focus. The planner needs to know what your comment is, and the more comments you have, the less time she'll be able to devote to addressing each one, even if they all are somewhat pertinent.
- *Respect Deadlines:* If a meeting needs to be over by 9 p.m., don't hog all the time for public input. If you are providing written feedback, get it in by whatever deadline exists. Remember that the planner needs to get a job done like anyone else, and can't just sit at her desk waiting for people to get back to her months after the fact!
- *Again, Be Polite:* There's no point in insulting the person to whom you are giving comments, even if you think she is on the take. That person is most likely very nice and open-minded, even if she can't assure you that your idea will be implemented on the spot. Treat every public official as if you might meet her again at the soccer field where your children are teammates. Planners and public board members are people too!

Picking the Right Meeting

Many times a well-meaning member of the community will come to a public meeting, wait patiently for a chance to speak, and finally get up and speak his mind. Unfortunately, the dialogue often goes something like this:

Community Member: "Thanks for the chance to speak. I would like to see you put new bus shelters along the Number 88 Bus Route. I take that bus every day and I always get soaked waiting for your busses, which are often late. Thank you."

Transportation Planner: "I appreciate your input. However, this is a hearing about putting new bus lanes on Washington Street. If you are interested in new bus shelters you should come to the hearing next spring on the Capital Improvement Plan. And we have a committee on Service Standards if you want to express your concerns about late busses."

In other words, nice ideas, wrong meeting. The planner doesn't think the community member is stupid, it is just that the planner is focused on one planning issue and can't really change gears to effectively address the other issues. Even if she tries to do so, her power is often limited by the fact that she is not responsible for bus shelters, and if she tries to make it her business she might not get her own job done. She might even get a reputation for meddling in other people's business!

Going to public meetings can feel like playing the numbers, even if you think you are paying attention. If you go to the right meeting you might get a solid response to your comments, and they could make a difference. If not, you might have wasted your time. Upfront attention to the topic of the meeting and its agenda will save you time and make the most of your efforts.

has been working on it for some time, likely will already have met with the local planning staff, and may already have gotten general buy-in from the planning staff, board, or elected officials for the project. In these situations in particular, consensus and rapid proactive action by neighbors will be necessary to counter a culture that generally believes that any development is good. In the long term, your best option in this sort of town is to get elected to one of the key boards and begin to change that culture yourself.

In either sort of culture, some points are relevant. First, feel empowered to call your planning staff or whoever in your town is responsible for initial negotiations with developers. Planners generally go into their jobs because they are deeply committed to empowering citizens; it is their job to share information and be sure that residents have a say in the future of their hometown. They also have access to a lot of information, such as zoning maps, maps of critical habitat, parcel information, and in general what you will need to know to really judge and influence any proposed changes in town. They should share this with you, and explain any parts of the zoning code or other documents you don't understand. There may be some incidental charges for copying, but this is public information and you should feel free to ask for it. Second, having the right information is crucial. Arguments clearly based in facts are likely to weigh more heavily with board members. Know, however, that particularly in small towns, there may be few or no professional staff, which both limits the information that is likely to be ready at hand and also empowers you, because your knowledge and input are likely to be that much more valuable.

When a public board faces a subdivision proposal, for instance, that meets all the legal requirements of the zoning code, it will be difficult (potentially illegal) for them to turn it down. This is why it pays to read the zoning code and city plan before going to a hearing, so that you can argue why it doesn't meet code. Arguing that the code is wrong won't get you far, because it is a legal document that the town is bound to. While much of the discussion here is about how to react to specific proposals, this point demonstrates why it is so important to get the zoning right in the first place—the topic of chapter 6.

The job of the local commissions and boards, as well as of elected officials, is to weigh the possible negative effects of a project for one neighborhood against possible positive outcomes for the overall community and region. Say the town needs new soccer fields, or more affordable housing, or a new school. These have to go somewhere, and it may be that your neighborhood is in fact the best available location. In this case, the board members have a duty to weigh neighbors' desire that it not be in their backyards against the overall good of the project, and do the right thing—whatever that may be. As residents consider their positions on a proposal, it is important that everyone tries to sort out how much their opposition is about not wanting the project near them, and how much is a more objective view that it is in the wrong place or the design is wrong for it. Advocacy that is easily dismissed as NIMBYism (not in my backyard!) will be less persuasive than more solidly grounded positions that respect overall community needs.

With all of this in mind, remember that in point of fact, few residents ever get involved in local or state government. As a result, those who do may have great power to influence outcomes. You won't win every battle, but you should be able to win the ones on which you are right, and for which you follow the rules and get involved early.

The final, and most drastic, kind of citizen participation is the lawsuit. When a case goes to the courts, it is a sign of significant failure, likely on everyone's part. Lawsuits are expensive for towns and the residents pressing them, take enormous emotional and logistical energy, and have very uncertain outcomes. They can be useful, however, when a citizen group decides that their local cause is altogether lost and really believes that the town's decision is in *everyone's* worst interest. Often the main role of litigation is slowing the development process so much that developers will simply give up, and that occasionally happens. More often, the developer, who probably has deeper pockets than the neighbors, just waits it out, piles paper upon paper on the citizens group, and then, assuming that the process followed met local regulations, likely wins. Because of this, we encourage residents to do absolutely everything to avoid the drastic step of litigation, short of giving up when it is a project they believe will cause irreparable harm to the overall community or the environment.

THERE IS NO doubt that participation in local planning processes can be confusing and frustrating. It is also rewarding, exciting, and perhaps the best way to make a significant contribution to the long-term future of your community. This chapter has focused on the basics of the planning process and the right points at which to get engaged, and some items to remember to be sure your participation is effective. In the next chapter we turn to the question of what to do when a more major change is needed, one that requires getting support from a number of individuals and groups—in other words, coalition building.

Courtesy of Town of Amherst, Massachusetts

2

Building Consensus
Coalitions for Policy Change

Kathryn Leahy and Andrea Cooper

I**N OUR** democratic society a vital public process is key to accomplishing civic goals that meet the needs of as many constituents as possible, and also the more general environmental, social, economic, and infrastructure needs of a community. While these lofty aims may seem obvious, the reality is that all too often worthy initiatives fail because the public process is not fully understood and engaged from the very beginning through to adoption and implementation of a project. Implementing significant change in a community will usually require going beyond the boundaries of what already is, and building a coalition for change.

Critical steps that contribute to positive results from the coalition-building process include: creating and embracing a vision; setting goals and objectives for achieving the vision; developing an implementation plan; and establishing a strategy for long-term follow-through that includes monitoring for success. While every municipality depends on experts to help guide the community from identifying problems to crafting and implementing solutions, it is the vocal, and we hope, voting public that has the ability to help a project swim, or hasten its sinking. So, of equal importance to crafting a realistic vision, achievable goals and objectives, and a plan for follow-up, is building widespread community support. As we will see, crafting a plan and fostering support must happen simultaneously, and, most often, the path to success includes hearty doses of coalition- and consensus-building.

In this chapter, we discuss tools and strategies that can enable the general public and local officials to develop community master plans or move regional and statewide initiatives forward by building coalitions of diverse stakeholders to reach early consensus. We will examine two projects, one in Massachusetts and one in Florida, that exemplify the importance of coalition-building and engaging the public (which can also mean "users" or specific constituents) in helping shape the future of their community.

The Roles of the State, Its Agencies, and Municipalities

A state's general laws represent a collective vision of the state's citizens. For some topics, e.g., subdivision control in Massachusetts, the state legislature "enables" cities and towns to build on this legislative framework and adopt additional bylaws (ordinances in cities) that reflect the aspirations and needs of that community. These laws and bylaws can govern everything from zoning that establishes residential and commercial districts, through guidelines for subdivision development, to storefront sign-design regulations. A local bylaw or ordinance can increase protection measures established in many state laws, as for wetlands, floodplains, or viewsheds, among many other topics.

Under state law, municipalities have the authority to establish boards and commissions to review projects and ensure adherence to the laws of the state and the bylaws/ordinances of the municipality. These boards and commissions may also adopt regulations that add details and clarification to a bylaw/ordinance. In many states, this system of governance has led to a strong and fiercely protected system of local control. State agencies provide the bridge that connects state general laws as promulgated by the legislature and the executive branch, and their implementation at the local level. The agencies are responsible for crafting regulations to accompany state laws, guiding cities and towns through the regulatory process, and in some states, reviewing development projects that meet certain thresholds. Some agencies can issue enforcement orders to halt work that is not in compliance with the state regulations. In Massachusetts, for example, the Department of Environmental Protection (DEP) has this power if a project is found to be environmentally destructive, and can issue fines to a guilty perpetrator. The DEP can also hear and rule on appeals of locally made decisions.

Gaining a working knowledge of laws and the regulatory process may seem a daunting task, but fortunately nonprofit groups in many states have prepared citizen guides that provide the specifics for that state. Some conservation organizations have done so, and one can also look to the League of Women Voters or other groups. Another basic source of information in most states is the state and local governments' Web sites. The Massachusetts Audubon Society has prepared a citizen's guide that provides a thorough introduction to the federal, state, and local governments' role in land management.

Initiating and Implementing Change

In addition to having the opportunity to participate in the regulatory process, U.S. citizens have the democratic right to initiate and implement changes to the legal status quo and to propose, advocate for, and bring new laws to a vote. There are established methods for law-making and rule-changing, and sources of information to consult in order to learn how this process works. Although the task is challenging, at either the local or the state level, bringing about change is a rewarding venture.

Your initiative may involve a sweeping change to a state law, a modest addition to your town's bylaws, or raising funds to support a new project. Your challenge may be to gather a block of voters who will support your initiative at town meeting, convince a city council to vote approval, or mount a statewide campaign. Whatever the scope of the proposition, the strategies for achieving success remain the same. We first describe the steps that are needed for almost every initiative, and later turn to the coalition-building which will be necessary for more complicated and significant initiatives.

Town Meetings and City Councils

Imagine a group of residents or a committee who wish to gain approval through town meeting or a city council for the use of local funds to acquire land for preservation. Maybe the planning board has developed an innovative zoning ordinance that needs a favorable vote, or the conservation commission is trying to receive increased funding to hire a full-time agent. Whatever the cause, and however beneficial you may think it is, navigating the often rough political waters of a town meeting or a city council approval process can be daunting. The town meeting or city council hearing is nonetheless not where your initiative succeeds or fails. Many worthwhile initiatives fail simply because of improper preparation. Long before these events, you need to create a climate of success through a process of anticipating where your opposition may arise, educating, and building support. Strategies include identifying the important players in your community or region, such as reputable citizens, neighborhood or civic associations, businesses, or other governmental agencies. These are the local or regional "power brokers" who often wield influence and therefore should support your program. You should also reach out beyond these "usual suspects" and bring in as many members of the affected community as you can. For instance, if you are pushing for more affordable housing, recruit current residents of affordable housing to work with you and speak at hearings. Individuals making the case from their experience are often very persuasive to lawmakers.

Invite these politically influential people or representatives to informational and discussion meetings or hold an early public hearing. Do not miss this chance to truly listen to their concerns, prioritize key problems that you must address, and work on finding solutions to their concerns if possible. You may need to adjust your proposal to meet their valid objections. You do not want to arrive at town meeting or city council and be surprised by opposition or indifference to your initiative from an influential member of the local power structure or the affected public.

In addition to giving people an opportunity to voice their concerns, your outreach campaign should include writing letters to the editor or columns for local newspapers in which you address both the initiative's pros, as you and your supporters see them, and also the primary issues of concern. Do not belittle these concerns, but clearly state how your initiative will resolve the problems being raised. Hold another public hearing and prepare an opening statement that addresses concerns earlier expressed. You now have successfully launched an offense, preventing detractors from putting you in a reactive defensive position. In other words, you've already taken the wind out of their sails. Another effective tactic is to hand out or mail out fact sheets that clearly, briefly, and concisely answer questions and concerns that are likely to come up.

Prior to the town meeting or city council hearing when the vote will be taken, make sure key local boards and residents are prepared to vocalize their support to the voters. Many underestimate the power of persuasion. In most communities, for example, if the finance committee supports a fiscal proposal, it usually is adopted.

At the meeting, your strategy should essentially recap the lobbying efforts you have already accomplished. Hand out your flyers with the answers to the most frequently asked questions. Begin with a prepared statement that addresses primary concerns to reduce the likelihood that your opponents will express negative opinions, thereby backing you into a defensive corner. Bring your statement in writing or have notes. Don't trust your memory in an often nerve-wracking situation.

When you're being questioned or listening to negative comments, do not react as if you are being attacked personally (even if you are!). Always hold the high ground; answer questions, and never argue. You don't want to risk being seen as irrational. And finally, if you find that you are in over your head, consider asking for a postponement and bring your initiative back to another town meeting or city council hearing. Why risk defeat when you have an opportunity to regroup and win success later?

The State Legislature

It is a little-known fact that a dozen letters can influence the way a state senator or representative will vote on a matter of law or public policy. While professional lobbyists make it their business to stay attuned to the state law-making and fiscal process, often the general public and local governments are not aware of proposals and miss having their voices heard. You could potentially be the one constituent whose letter helped reach that magical number to influence a legislator's decision. After all, their political future depends on how well they represent their constituents—and that means you! A telephone call, a letter, or an e-mail expressing your views is a powerful tool. Whichever form of communication you choose, try to personalize your message, using your own words. Legislators will pay more attention to a message that indicates your genuine concern for the issue.

State governments have Web sites that help you find out about bills and budgets being considered by the legislature. The Web sites also contain information on the variety of ways you can contact your state lawmakers. Many reputable organizations such as conservation groups have regular e-mail newsletters that keep you up to date. For example, the Massachusetts Audubon Society's legislative office e-mails a Beacon Hill Weekly Roundup with the information useful for influencing state legislators and other government officials. Find out whether your local boards and associations know about the proposed bill or budget and want to join you in your advocacy effort. Finally, join an organization that represents your view and can advocate on your behalf.

Building Coalitions to Develop Master Plans or Promote Initiatives

For a more major policy effort or one that is likely to be very contentious, the key to success is building the right coalition at the right time. The best plan or strategy can be shelved or rejected because influential stakeholders and impacted groups are not part of the drafting process from the beginning. It is often the composition of a coalition or the timing of its inception that will make or break a community, regional, or statewide initiative. When a coalition of diverse interests develops an initiative collaboratively and achieves consensus, all members of that coalition feel that they are an integral part of the initiative's successful adoption and implementation and there is much greater likelihood of success. Your historic adversaries can become your most active advocates.

We tend to congregate with people who share our values, interests, or concerns. As a group with similar interests we define a problem and draft a plan for reaching our own idea of a solution and then attempt to sell this plan to those who may well have a very different set of interests and values. When differing interests react to a draft initiative or proposal, they are immediately skeptical and push to get all of their needs included. Having set up a reactive, usually negative, process from the start, we are left to constantly defend our work and to redraft the document to respond to each suggested change. At best, the draft becomes watered down and the core objectives may even be lost. In a worst-case situation the plan or strategy gets shelved or defeated. We've all seen this happen at town meeting, city council, and the county and state government level. In this scenario, consensus is not reached.

Before any plans are drafted, before any goals, mission statements, or objectives are formed, the most influential historically antagonistic factions need to gather at the table to agree, first of all, that a common problem exists, and eventually craft a solution that will have a broad base of support. "It will take forever," you say. Well, it may seem like that, but this process will actually save you time in the long run because when the plan or document is done, the "sales" process of advocating to all the groups in your community

(or state) is significantly reduced. After all, those groups helped draft the plan or project, and therefore they naturally take ownership for its success!

Coalition-building is an art. It begins with an identification of a problem that needs to be solved, and some idea of how this could happen. The next step is to develop a list of the priority organizations or individuals represented—the ones that have successfully gotten issues passed or blocked in the past whether at town meeting, city council, or county government. They are the power brokers, and if you don't know who they are, ask those who have been active in the community or region for years to help you identify them. Sometimes, it may be a group that is key—say, the chamber of commerce or a neighborhood association. Sometimes, it may be just a person who is so well respected that his or her opinions and support carry a lot of weight in your town or county. With this list in mind, think about those who will be affected by the proposal—would they feel represented by someone on the list? If there are groups who are affected but are not among the community's typical power players, bring them into the discussion anyway. This can be difficult, as such a group may not speak English, or may not be organized, but they nevertheless should be included. It is crucial that all those who are affected have some representation. This topic is addressed more fully in the next chapter.

Anticipate the needs and interests of each "player" when you first contact them. Be prepared to emphasize how important it is to address these needs and interests when you recruit representatives of organizations or groups. When you seek the representatives to be around the table, make sure that they can speak for their group. The "players" must have the backing of their interest group so votes can be taken at coalition meetings and agreements, negotiations, and consensus can move forward in a timely manner.

The best approach is to begin by drafting a coalition strategy, a set of ground rules the group agrees to adhere to, when the coalition first meets. Identify barriers that the group may encounter and state how you will address them. Because consensus requires each player to give and take, the strategy should discuss how the differing interests within the coalition will be managed. In other words, negotiation will be extremely important, but it must not get personal, and the more influential stakeholders should not use their position to bargain. Discuss how the differences will be handled. Some groups choose to work until everyone has reached consensus; this is admirable and sometimes necessary, but can also deadlock a process and make it excruciatingly slow. Usually a better plan is to allow for voting on stalemated topics, and then the majority wins and the group moves on. For important issues these sorts of votes should be avoided as much as possible, however, as voting opens the door to the losers leaving the table. Each player must specifically state his or her group's needs and interests —why is this issue important to them—so all players clearly understand one another. There has to be a balance between emotion and reason. The chairperson must have strong facilitation skills, but the group should also discuss how it will work to strike that balance.

You can expect that at the early meetings participants will want to vent their frustration at the status quo. This can actually be helpful, since you will learn what points of opposition you might face in the future, and you can search for places where your initiative can relieve that frustration. Very soon, however, players should be not be allowed to complain without also offering a positive suggestion for change. The group should clearly understand that each player will try to persuade but no coercion is acceptable. Finally, stakeholders should be allowed to be unconditionally constructive. In other words, provide time for brainstorming a free-flowing stream of thoughts. Criticism or approval can follow, but not during the brainstorming process, and comments must be aimed at furthering the overall coalition's objective—not at trying to change a stakeholder's values or "choosing sides."

Not everyone gets his or her way. The name of the game is consensus, and everyone must know and accept this fact from the start. This eliminates unnecessary concentration on fringe items and, at the same time, further bonds the participants as one group that speaks with one voice. If the coalition reaches a stalemate, be sure that all players have weighed in and have made an attempt to meet all needs. If the group cannot find a way out of the stalemate and a vote is too fraught by differences in power to be sustainable, it may be useful to bring in a professional facilitator who is unaligned with any of the parties.

While your initiative is extremely important and so is the proper building of the coalition and achieving consensus, you are probably not working on a plan for world peace. So, inject humor where appropriate and enjoy the camaraderie that will blossom eventually as the group moves forward and begins working together successfully.

Let's look at two case studies for coalition building. Both were successful, but one initiative "learned the hard way" while the other followed a coalition-building process. Note that each took time, patience, and long-term commitment; these processes are not for the faint of heart or for someone who wants instant gratification. If you cannot devote sufficient time and energy to a project, maybe you need to rethink your involvement. But if you do make that effort, you can expect that your chance of success will be high.

Green Neighborhoods Alliance Case Study

In 1996, the Massachusetts Office of Coastal Zone Management: North Shore Regional Office (CZM) and Mass Audubon North Shore Conservation Advocacy (MA:NS) finished reviewing data that showed sprawl to be one of the largest threats to coastal resources, including open space, wildlife habitat, and water quality. Although removing the sources of suburban sprawl would require many initiatives and changes in how development occurs, one obvious target was conventional zoning that actually promoted suburban sprawl by assigning a "one-size fits all" blueprint to subdivision design. CZM and MA:NS believed a new subdivision design approach was needed, as well as a willingness to support and use a new approach by all parties involved in growth management, from realtors to planning boards to developers to conservation organizations. At first, accomplishing this vision appeared to be a daunting challenge, with many barriers ahead. Who had the time and money to take on such an initiative? If an environmental organization was to embrace a new development design, would that be seen publicly as a promotion of growth rather than advocacy for conservation? How could the building community, environmental agencies, conservation groups, and local authorities ever come to agreement on one design concept?

CZM and MA:NS recognized that, if a new subdivision design process were to be created and accepted and if people were going to be asked to rethink residential development, each stakeholder in the land-use planning and development process had to be involved from the start. After hosting a well-attended seminar by nationally known land-use planner and innovative subdivision designer, Randall Arendt, CZM and MA:NS invited representatives from development companies, town and city authorities, conservation organizations, state agencies, regional planning councils, and realty businesses to meet and discuss the problems with the current subdivision design and permitting processes and needed changes. Many of the individuals on this diverse list had attended the seminar and expressed interest in the new approach, and the hosts reached out to other key individuals in the region. Other very important criteria used to compile the invitation list were that the invitees be credible stakeholders who could influence change and that they have the ability to speak for their organizations.

The first few meetings were contentious, with everyone venting their anger at "the system" and pointing fingers as to which stakeholder was the troublemaker. It was an "us against them" mentality. Stereotypes flourished: The environmentalists want to halt all growth; the developers want to destroy all land; the towns want too much control and make the system cumbersome and expensive. Out of these discussions, however, emerged the realization that the group could agree on one thing: the existing regulatory system was declared unworkable, with no stakeholder getting his or her needs meet, whether economically, environmentally, or socially. "I think the most important thing we accomplished in the first three years was getting beyond staring suspiciously at each other across the table; often treating each other with less than courtesy," one developer remarked later during a press interview. In fact, just by agreeing that the system wasn't working for anyone, the group had reached its first consensus, and it began to move along a path that led to forming a real coalition.

With funding from the Massachusetts Executive Office of Environmental Affairs awarded to the regional planning agency, the Metropolitan Area Planning Council (MAPC), the coalition began the arduous process of drafting a new subdivision design and an accompanying regulatory model that was a "win-win" for all. At first, each member wanted all his or her needs met without compromise, but little by little, stakeholders began to advocate for their primary issues and concerns while letting go of former "must haves" that were actually lower priority. Naturally, the developers and realtors were most interested in financial gain—bottom-line profits. The conservation organizations wanted assurance of no negative environmental impacts. Town planners wanted local control of the process with no hidden loopholes. Slowly each stakeholder began to realize that the process

could work only if the core of the new design concept was mutually beneficial to all interests.

The group decided that the core of the new subdivision approach would be conservation subdivision design's four-step process, developed by Randall Arendt many years ago while he was at the Center for Rural Massachusetts at UMass–Amherst.[1] This approach is widely beneficial: it protects open space, provides creative profitable incentives to developers, and makes the community an equal partner in the subdivision design. With this milestone, each member began to work as part of the group, and the coalition, now focused on creating its own version of conservation subdivision design, named itself the Green Neighborhoods Alliance. Although the alliance still faced tough negotiations to work out the details, a committed membership worked as a team and moved forward toward developing the core concept into a fully drafted regulatory model.

This stage, too, was an evolving, sometimes contentious, but flexible process. Although everyone clearly stated his or her interests and knew the ground rules for handling differences, emotions ran high at times. As the group reached consensus on each individual concept of the regulatory model, persuasion won out over coercion and positive suggestions replaced whining. Perhaps most important, when a certain route did not work in the best interests of the entire coalition, it was tossed out, but each time the group stayed with the core four-step process, which grounded the coalition. When disputes erupted, the conversation was directed to whether the issues brought to the table furthered the four-step process, which had been declared mutually beneficial to each stakeholder. Opinions were valued, and humor often broke an impasse.

After four years and some setbacks, the core concept blossomed into the Open Space Residential Design model ordinance, a new regulatory tool, providing cities and towns, developers, environmental protection advocates, and realtors with an opportunity to reach their individual goals in a less contentious and more creative manner. With consensus achieved, and a tool to promote, the alliance launched an outreach campaign. Because all stakeholders had worked collaboratively to develop the model, each individual wanted

---

1. See Randall Arendt, Robert D. Yaro, Harry Dodson, and E. Brabec, *Dealing with Change in the Connecticut River Valley: A Design Manual for Conservation and Development* (Amherst: Massachusetts Department of Environmental Management and the Center for Rural Massachusetts, 1988).

Open Space Residential Design

Using the 4-Step Process

The 4-Step Process is the key to creating an Open Space Residential Design (OSRD) subdivision. OSRD flips the conventional subdivision planning and permitting method by prioritizing open space protection and allowing for flexibility in road design, house sites, and lot lines. For more information about the Massachusetts OSRD model bylaw, including the 4-Step Process, visit www.greenneighborhoods.org.

OSRD: The Four Step Process vs. Conventional Process

1. Set Aside Resource Areas	1. Draw the lot lines
2. Locate House Sites	2. Align Roads
3. Align Roads & Trails	3. Locate House Sites
4. Draw the Lot Lines	4. Open Space?

Figure 2.1. Green Neighborhoods four-step process.
Source: www.greenneighborhoods.org. Adapted from Randall Arendt, *Growing Greener: Putting Conservation into Local Plans and Ordinances* (Washington, DC: Island Press, 1999).

to see the project succeed and therefore was willing to take on the important role of advocating to his or her respective constituencies. The outreach strategy incorporated a team approach with developers, CZM and Mass Audubon, MAPC, and other alliance members sharing the stage and speaking with one united message. The new regulatory tool is proving to be a popular addition to zoning toolkits in municipalities throughout Massachusetts. While the idea of conservation subdivision design had existed for many years, the coalition brought it to the political forefront, and provided towns with a model they could easily and directly adopt.

Open Space Residential Design is increasingly accepted statewide as an alternative to the conventional subdivision design approach. In addition to the improvements it brings to the planning process, it is also recognized as a model that can help communities achieve social, environmental, and economic goals by balancing preservation and profit.

Florida Keys Marine Sanctuary Case Study

Today the Florida Keys Marine Sanctuary is one of the country's great management plan success stories, resulting in the global marine ecosystem bounding back from near extinction, while the fisheries and tourism industry reap enormous financial benefits. But it didn't start very successfully according to Billy Casey, superintendent of the sanctuary. The process began very typically with the experts, Casey and his National Oceanic and Atmospheric Administration (NOAA) colleagues, drafting a management plan to restrict access to the sanctuary area, and then bringing their plan to the public and area businesses to receive their approval. But what they received was just the opposite: backlash.

Outside town halls and public buildings where meetings were being held, marine sanctuary staff was hung in effigy. Signs and newspaper cartoons made it abundantly clear that NOAA had taken the wrong road to coalition-building. Leaders involved in the $1.2 billion annual tourism-based economy felt threatened. Businesses representing the second largest commercial fishery in the United States thought this plan would quickly drive them out of business. All made their feelings abundantly clear.

What happened and how did the various parties finally achieve success? First, they threw out the draft plan that was developed solely by NOAA staff. Then, they formed a coalition to draft a new management plan involving all stakeholder leaders in the process. The coalition included representatives from hotels, marinas, chambers of commerce, dive and bait and tackle shops, parks, realtors, boat rentals, airports, and commercial fishermen, as well as the environmental agencies and governments. They were careful to use the best available natural and socioeconomic science, but also incorporated the best available anecdotal information when necessary. They were able to overcome perceptions of social and economic injustices by incorporating socioeconomic data.

The process assured protection of areas representing a wide variety of habitats that maintain ecosystem functions but enhance the very viable economic interests. The coalition developed a plan that encouraged activities compatible with resource protection and helped reduce user conflicts, which had been a problem in the past. The group moved forward with mutually beneficial goals of reducing stresses on sensitive wildlife populations by dispersing heavy concentrations of uses while concurrently assuring minimal adverse socioeconomic impacts.

Casey believes that the keys to their success were involving all stakeholders and jurisdictional partners (local, state, federal, and tribal), disregarding jurisdictional borders when drafting boundaries, and assuring that those at the table could speak for their agency. After the plan was adopted and implemented, the number of spiny lobsters has increased during open and closed lobster seasons, and the mean size of the lobsters is larger. Reef fisheries are showing a dramatic comeback, including yellow tail snapper. This is good news for both conservationists and the tourist and commercial fishing industries. In addition, with the support of all stakeholders and the success of plan implementation, the Marine Sanctuary Program received grant funding to use a global position system (GPS) to record sites of coral reefs of global significance. Today, for the first time, these reefs are included on global navigation maps used by operators of tankers traveling through the reef areas in the shipping channel, who formerly dropped anchor unaware of potential damage to these renowned marine ecosystems. Thanks to the commitment of all stakeholders, outreach materials are located in almost all commercial operations, recreations facilities, and conservation and governmental offices within the Keys region. The people who once hanged the NOAA staff in effigy are now an integrated part of the success story.

There are many people who have experience in effective coalition-building, and good advice can often push a process forward. We suggest some sources here. Also, speak to others with experience in initiating change and those representing diverse interests before developing a coalition-building strategy and moving ahead. It's a good reality check. And remember, the turtle won the race, not the hare.

References

American Planning Association. 2002, 2004. *Policy Guide on Smart Growth*. Washington, DC: American Planning Association.

Arendt, R. G. 1996. *Conservation Design for Subdivisions: A Practical Guide to Creating Open Space Networks*. Washington, DC: Island Press.

Chrislip, D. D. 2002. *The Collaborative Leadership Fieldbook*. San Francisco: Jossey-Bass.

Fisher, R., W. Ury, et al. 1991. *Getting to Yes: Negotiating Agreement without Giving In*. 2nd ed. New York: Penguin Books.

Fulton, W. 1989. *Reaching Consensus in Land-Use Negotiations (pas 417)*. Chicago: APA Planning Advisory Service.

Ricci, E. H., L. Armory, et al. 2006. *Shaping the Future of Your Community: A Guide to Involvement in Growth Management and Land Protection in Massachusetts*. Lincoln: Massachusetts Audubon Society.

Susskind, L., and J. Cruikshank. 1987. *Breaking the Impasse: Consensual Approaches to Resolving Public Disputes*. New York: Basic Books.

Courtesy of Karen Mendrala and the City of Holyoke Planning Department

3

Diversity
Multiple Cultures Forming One Community

Linda Silka and Veronica Eady

M OST OF the decisions that are made about community preservation and planning have the potential to affect a community's diversity (e.g., in income, occupation, class, age, and family composition). Such effects often happen unwittingly because inadequate attention is being paid to the impact that decisions are likely to have on diversity. The goal of this chapter is to help communities bring the focus of diversity to their discussions so the decisions are made consciously and with foresight and so that unwanted effects on diversity are minimized. We hope to expand readers' understanding of what represents diversity in the context of community preservation, show where information about a community's diversity can be found, and provide examples of the ways in which the consideration of diversity can strengthen community-planning discussions.

Many communities face the challenge that growth has the potential to alter who is able to live in the community and what kinds of conflicts are likely to emerge between groups. The three examples below suggest just how varied the cases are where changing conditions bring new challenges to a community's decision-making:

- In Maine, coastal populations are booming. Affluent people "from away" are retiring to the Maine coast to build their dream homes at the ocean's edge. At the same time, traditional engines of growth in this area, including military bases and large segments of the fishing industry, are disappearing. Those who grew up in coastal Maine are discovering that they can no longer find well-paying jobs and that they are being priced out of the increasingly expensive real estate in their communities. The plans for the coast's future endorsed by long-term Mainers versus newly arrived retirees—plans about growth, about zoning, about which industries should be recruited for economic development (Anderson 2000)—are often at odds. The diversity of views shows up around such issues as whether marine aquaculture should be pursued, how to weigh the need to create jobs against the inevitable changes resulting to the ocean viewscape; or whether zoning should be modified to increase required lot sizes to maintain the value of newly purchased properties. And discussions such as those recommending that more trailer parks be built as a way to increase the amount of affordable housing bring out deep differences in perspectives.

- In Iowa, bedroom communities are springing up in order to support new industries and take advantage of new economic opportunities (Probasco-Sowers 2003; 1000 Friends). Some of these developments are being built directly downwind from farms—in some cases "century" farms that have remained in the same family for a hundred years or more. New neighbors are in conflict with those farms over odors, noise, and the potential contamination of water from farm runoff.

- Lowell, Massachusetts, within commuting distance of Boston, is caught in a squeeze (Center for Family, Work, and Community 2001). The city stands in danger of losing its economic diversity. Long an economically depressed community, Lowell has achieved a recent economic renaissance that has increased the community's appeal to those who once would not have considered it as a place to live. The resulting influx of newcomers is leading to rapid increases in housing costs as too many people compete for too few homes. In addition, most new housing is high-end single-family homes rather than apartments and condos, and zoning changes that now mandate larger lot sizes are further exacerbating the affordable housing squeeze felt by Lowell's working families. The makeup of the community itself has also changed dramatically; Lowell now has the second largest Cambodian community in the country and is home to thousands of newly arrived African, Brazilian, Caribbean, and Colombian residents. The shifting character of the city is uncovering deep differences in the ways that people use public space and plan for housing, economic development, public transportation, and the development of other resources that are key to preserving the character of a community.

In each of these cases, diversity—whether it be income, ethnicity, age, race, length of residence, use of land—is deeply tied to both the opportunities and the challenges that arise with development. Communities are finding that decisions about growth and development fall unevenly on different residents. Those who are retired, for example, are affected differently from those seeking out their first jobs.

Those who depend on public transportation and the availability of nearby jobs, small shops, and other amenities bring a very different set of concerns to discussions than do those with ready access to reliable cars. Those with young children or who must locate childcare near their work have worries that differ from those with grown children or no children at all. Those who have a tradition of living in extended families with homes near one another likely want to preserve very different community characteristics from those of interest to young singles who arrive from throughout the United States. In short, diversity is at the heart of many issues underlying community preservation.

The Many Faces of Diversity

Communities are finding that once they turn their attention to diversity they run headlong into key issues, such as what makes a community vibrant or what accounts for the fact that teachers, police, and other civil servants are being priced out of the very towns in which they grew up and now work. A focus on diversity points community attention to the obstacles that are in place for individuals who want to remain in the same community as they go through different life stages, achieve different income levels, and experience different levels of need for services such as public transportation. Diversity is at the heart of difficult issues, and groups that are not alike cannot count on a shared agenda or common ground. In the small town of Postville, Iowa, long-time residents of Scandinavian background welcomed Hassidic Jews from New York City who came to reinvigorate an abandoned packing plant; only later did the two groups discover just how deep the differences were in their views about practices of decision-making, taxation, community development, and the like (Bloom 2001). Views about whether the need for open space or housing is greater may not be shared, with advocates for affordable housing pointing to one and proponents of parks arguing for the other. Perceptions of how community development should proceed may differ. In New York City, new development has sometimes taken such forms as locating a large number of diesel-emitting bus transfer stations within one small area (Harlem), resulting in a concentration of environmental risks from particulate pollution in the very part of the community that has the least voice (Northridge 2002).

As these examples are intended to indicate, diversity

Environmental Justice Leadership

Ground-breaking work on environmental justice over the last decade has brought into stark relief the extent to which some neighborhoods are especially impacted by environmental contamination, often as a result of poor, fragmented decisions in the past that include laxness in zoning and other inequities of urbanization. The problems within communities are not evenly distributed, and thus environmental problems are often concentrated within certain areas, frequently those where residents have had the fewest opportunities and resources to assert control of their surroundings or fend off developments that are destructive to the health and well-being of their neighborhoods. Low-income, minority neighborhoods are more likely to have substandard housing, poor air quality, poor transportation, undesirable polluting industries, *and* toxic waste sites that are a legacy of past industrial processes that were poorly monitored.

Decisions about zoning, affordable housing, open space, historic preservation, and economic development are far from neutral. Community preservation advocates can deepen their approach by incorporating environmental justice into their discussions and initiatives. Environmental justice leaders provide three important resources: First, this work indicates how the different community preservation topics such as housing, transportation, and economic development can be considered together in a justice context. Second, this approach provides us with useful, concrete examples of the ways in which communities have successfully come together to address these issues. Third, environmental justice leaders provide us with important tools and resources for ensuring that community decisions are made in ways that do not exacerbate injustices. Further information about environmental justice can be found in chapter 14.

comes in many forms, and subtle forms can have as much impact as those forms that are more easily discernable. In Lewiston, Maine, a largely Anglo community has been confronting salient differences between themselves and newly arrived Somali refugees, who wear traditional African dress and are moving into neighborhoods, starting businesses, and becoming a very visible part of the small city (Powell 2002). Yet differences in views about growth, zoning, and the like have been just as sizable among the non-Somalis, that is, between Mainers who are second- or third-generation French Canadian mill workers and Bates College faculty members who have recently moved from urban centers to teach at this rural elite college. Because community preservation represents community-based decision-making, this approach calls attention to the need to incorporate diversity or certainly to avoid traditional planning where development decisions are placed in the hands of the few.

Communities are also finding that as they attend to diversity they more fully recognize the degree to which the processes they use for advancing community preservation have the potential to reduce the degree to which diverse voices are heard. For example, diversity includes wide variation in interest in or time to devote to questions of community planning. Too often those who have the leisure to pursue questions of community preservation represent one small segment of the community; those not at the table may face a daunting array of obstacles to participation. In an egregious recent case in western Massachusetts, those most involved in community planning took it upon themselves to develop a plan that would most affect those who weren't a part of the planning process. This plan called for replacing an "unsightly" trailer court with permanent apartment housing that the decision makers confidently assumed would have much greater appeal to the trailer owners. Unfortunately, the residents of the trailer court would never have been able to afford the new permanent housing, and thus would have been pushed out of town.

It is worth noting that most people go about their business without devoting a great deal of attention to issues of community life. Although there are those who become ardently involved in community preservation, many others come to the discussion only when directly impacted by pending decisions. The rolling farmlands in Dracut, Massachusetts, are no longer in production as elders in the community reach an advanced age where active farming is no longer an option. Whether these lands should be developed for high-end housing, affordable housing, or should remain open space has suddenly become a topic of great urgency in this municipality for which past identity and pride were tied up in being the breadbasket for Boston. Residents who were previously uninvolved in questions of community preservation have become much more interested as change is contemplated for large swaths of land that have long been central to their community's identity

To sum up, diversity that can be affected by community-preservation decisions includes a range of characteristics: whether people have cars, what kind of house they can afford, how they use their land, whether they have young children, whether they are retired, whether they are in ill or in good health, as well as many other constraints such as whether people need to live within walking distance of shops and other amenities. Although there will be similarities across communities, what represents diversity in one community won't be identical to that which represents diversity in others. Decisions about zoning, transportation, open space, housing, and other aspects of community preservation can greatly reduce diversity or have the potential to increase it. Those people who are most affected may not be at the discussions; not everyone will automatically feel that they are welcome or that their opinions will be heard. Efforts beyond publicizing meetings need to be made to ensure that all people enter into discussions.

Resources for Gathering Information about a Community's Diversity

So, how do you know what sort of diversity exists in your community? Communities are increasingly finding that the gathering of information about the degree of their diversity is a key starting point if deliberations are to take into account who could be impacted by decisions, what might be preserved, and what may change. Measuring diversity has the benefit of ensuring that an assessment of where things stand takes place *before* particular planning decisions are made, thus allowing communities to work through the likely consequences of specific decisions on growth or community preservation (e.g., will a community lose its income diversity if zoning requirements are changed to require increased lot sizes? is a community likely to alter its age

diversity if certain decisions about public transportation are made?).

A variety of resources are now available that communities can use to identify the types of diversity among their residents. An excellent starting point is the U.S. Census Web site (www.census.gov). The census Web site contains a wealth of facts relevant to who lives in a particular community and thus what kinds of diversity currently characterize a town. From the results of the census "long form" it is possible to learn about the distances that residents typically drive to work, typical kinds of occupations, types of housing, educational and income levels, race and ethnicity, numbers of children, and even how long the typical person has lived in the community. The information is organized geographically and aggregated at different levels, including by census tracts or "chunks" of a community, so communities are even able to analyze the characteristics of particular neighborhoods that might have a high abundance of people without cars and families with children.

There are many reasons that the neighborhood level of analysis has become an increasing force for shaping discussions. It turns out, as environmental justice leaders have eloquently demonstrated, that public health risks often co-occur. People who live in neighborhoods that have substandard housing also often face more polluted environments, poorer transportation options, little nearby open space, and other kinds of substandard community infrastructure. Where one lives carries with it a variety of consequences, and census data helps communities better understand the ways in which community characteristics and resources cluster. The census data can thus assist the community preservation approach in allowing for the identification of some of those co-occurrences and thereby providing clues for how changes being contemplated in something like housing or transportation are likely to have multiple, cumulative effects in particular neighborhoods.

If a city is growing rapidly, the census information is likely to be outdated. One might want to investigate whether the city's municipal office has collected more recent data. Some states and municipalities carry out their own annual census that includes more limited information relevant to services or growth, such as ages of children in each household. Diversity data relevant to specific components of community preservation such as housing can be discovered on housing

Web sites such as the Citizens' Housing and Planning Association (CHAPA) Web site (www.chapa.org). Some of these Web sites are specific to particular states or regions, while others provide community-level information for cities across the country. A Web site such as CHAPA's can be used to develop estimates of the amount of affordable housing that currently exists in a community. Web sites developed by local or regional planning agencies can also include useful information about the characteristics of communities in their region. The local school system also might provide relevant data. The number of school children of various ages, for example, is public information generally available through the local school system and updated annually in many states. From publicly available school data, one may even glean information about other community characteristics, such as the percentage of families in poverty. Many communities report the percentage of youth in the system eligible for free or reduced school lunches, and this information, used by schools to gauge level of need, can be yet another indicator providing important data about families that may be impacted by decisions about community preservation.

Despite one's best efforts, sometimes needed data is not readily obtainable. In our recent work on housing in Lowell, Massachusetts, for example, we found that before any planning on community preservation could take place there was the need to know more about the current state of housing (that is, its availability and cost), yet no group or individual had been able to bring the needed information together. Some of the essential information remained in private hands whereas other needed facts were available only through a bewildering array of federal, state, and local agencies. And some of the most important information, such as types of housing permits being approved, was available only in handwritten form. The process of pulling together this information, carried out by a community-university partnership, gave residents an opportunity to begin to see firsthand how housing pressures were impacting groups in different ways and how the community's character was being affected by rapid and unexpected changes in the cost and availability of housing. Through the development of a manual that gathered this information into a baseline (available at www.uml.edu/cfwc/), the community had in its hands a set of materials to inform discussions about community preservation.

Using Diversity Measures

Once communities have facts about diversity in hand, there are a number of ways in which this information can be incorporated into considerations of the impact that particular planning decisions could have on different families. Again, excellent resources are available to assist you in approaching these issues. As just one example, the Orton Family Foundation in Vermont (www.orton.org) is working to put tools in the hands of communities—particularly rural communities—that will assist groups in examining these issues. The Orton Foundation has developed geographic information systems tools that enable local leaders to work through different scenarios when their community is faced with rapid growth that could alter its character in ways that make it more or less diverse. The Orton tools are not free to communities; other sites offer tools that are. In Massachusetts, the Executive Office of Environmental Affairs has developed a highly informative Web site (http://commpres.env.state.ma.us/) that puts existing but often scattered information into a usable form for community decision-makers. The EOEA site includes, for example, a buildout analysis for every Massachusetts municipality. This buildout analysis contains four to five GIS maps that visually lay out a community's development patterns and show what it will look like in the future if its current zoning ordinances remain unchanged. (See chapter 7 for more on GIS and buildout analysis.)

The EOEA Web site includes many questions that communities should consider as they discuss growth and its impact—questions that call attention to the diversity that already exists as well as to how that diversity will be impacted by particular decisions about growth and community preservation. An important goal of the Web site is to enable communities to think about balancing various issues that are related to diversity, such as "strong businesses, a robust local economy and housing opportunities for people of different incomes . . . and a balance of the necessary transportation options to support a multitude of lifestyles." The Web site goes on to note that community preservation and community planning include four core elements:

- Location, type, and quantity of new housing units, including housing affordable to individuals and families across a broad range of income;

- Location, type, and quantity of open space to be protected, including identification and prioritization of environmentally critical unprotected open space, land critical to sustaining surface and groundwater quality and quantity, and environmental resources;
- Location, type, and quantity of commercial and industrial economic development;
- Location and description of any improvements to transportation, e.g., bridge work, road widening, revised intersections, commuter rail stop, traffic calming.

As these core elements are examined, communities can use this information to assess how diverse families, such as families with young children, families with limited incomes, retirees, or families who depend on public transportation, will be impacted by the community-planning decisions that are contemplated. They can consider the likely consequences for families that currently live in the community as well as for the types of families that could be expected to move there in the future. By combining a concern for diversity with the complex dimensions of community preservation, communities are finding that they can be more certain that they are not making decisions in ways that fail to consider the complex effects of diverse groups.

Communities have also begun to consider innovative ways by which the measurement of diversity can be combined with the measurement of other characteristics linked to preservation and growth. The Sustainable Measures Web site (http://www.sustainablemeasures.com) and the Guide to Sustainable Community Indicators (1999), for example, provide tested ideas for how communities can measure sustainability. Using the sustainability measures as starting points, communities can then build in diversity and consider the impact that various steps will have on sustainability and diversity. Communities around the country have begun using these sustainability indicators to assess where they are and where they might go with regard to their environmental and economic health. (See the Appendix for more on indicators.)

Yet another way that communities are finding to bring diversity information into discussions is to incorporate it into geographical information systems or computerized maps of one's town. Mapped displays of information made possible by geographic information systems (GIS) can prompt thorough discussions of which neighborhoods and

Examples of CP Questions That Can Be Considered from the Perspective of Impact on Diversity

What growth patterns does current zoning dictate?

What long-term impacts does that growth create, on areas such as traffic, water quality and quantity, and education?

What is the maximum potential growth possible under existing zoning?

What are likely impacts on municipal services from that growth?

Is there an alternative, more favorable future and what would that look like?

What can be done now to enhance the pattern of new development?

neighbors will be affected by community preservation decisions being contemplated on housing, open space, location of public transportation corridors, or the development of new businesses. Many communities are exploring ways of making all relevant information available in visual form.

At the University of Massachusetts–Lowell's Center for Family, Work, and Community, we have used GIS not only to display information about diversity but also to bring diverse groups together to address tough issues (www.uml.edu/centers/CFWC/). As noted earlier, Lowell is a city of very diverse income and educational levels. Many residents speak a primary language other than English. Large numbers of refugees living in Lowell have limited formal education because they experienced educational interruption in their war-torn home countries. We have found GIS or community mapping very helpful in working across these levels of diversity. Census data can be displayed in color-coded ways that assist the community in making decisions that take into account where large numbers of children or the elderly live and in what proximity they live to public transportation, open space, hazardous waste sites, and the like. People do not need to know English to enter into discussions of information that is mapped. We often included community-generated information about locations (e.g., Buddhist temples, African churches) that oriented people from diverse backgrounds to familiar locations on the map. We also sometimes created customized, confidential maps on the spot at meetings: interested participants could provide their home address and have a map printed out to take home that showed where they lived relative to various open space and housing sites being discussed as a part of community preservation. We have found that community mapping can be an important way not only to convey information about diversity but also to involve diverse groups in the complex decision-making that is very much a part of community preservation.

The Lowell Example: Celebrating Diverse Traditions of Community Preservation

Too often it is assumed that diversity must end in divisiveness: "Why do you want more public transportation going through my neighborhood?" "My grown children won't be able to afford to live in this community if the zoning changes you are proposing go through." "Why don't you see the need for affordable housing in our community?" Such discussions are often organized so as to emphasize differences rather than common ground. They provide insufficient opportunities for diversity to serve as a means of moving forward discussions of community preservation by asking groups to illustrate best practices. There is another possibility, whereby opportunities can be set up to learn about one another in ways that are asset-building and link directly to community preservation. Again, we will use the example of Lowell, Massachusetts, to suggest how such an approach might be begun.

Lowell is a mid-sized city of a little over 100,000 residents, where the focus is strongly on neighborhoods, with many residents readily identifying themselves as living in particular neighborhoods, such as Pawtucketville, or the Acre, or the Highlands. Lowell is one of the earliest industrial communities in the United States, and this history can still be seen in old brick mills, canals, and, unfortunately, in the environmental contamination that remains after long years of industry. The Merrimack River flows through Lowell, and for decades this major eastern water artery was too polluted for fishing and swimming. Lowell also is a community with a mix of interests and concerns: there is a strong focus on historic preservation, there is an affordable housing crisis, and the city continues to struggle with the fact that little buildable land remains and much of what is available is classified as brownfields. Thus, Lowell shares many elements with many older, industrialized communities. In other ways, Lowell is remarkably different. Lowell is highly diverse. The community has changed dramatically over the last ten years or so. Over half of the youth in the schools now come from minority backgrounds. There are large African, Caribbean, South American, and Southeast Asian communities. Many of the small businesses are owned by newcomers who developed their business skills in other countries.

Discussions about community preservation naturally raise the concerns of many of the newest residents. What is being preserved? Is preservation about returning the community to what it was like before the latest wave of immigrants arrived from other countries? Is preservation about conserving what once was and about keeping people out?

In 2000, the Massachusetts Executive Office of Environmental Affairs and the University of Massachusetts–Lowell's Center for Family, Work, and Community came together to approach community preservation in a different way in Lowell (Silka et al. 2001). We knew from past experience that the concept of community preservation generally does not resonate with newcomers. In addition, new immigrants are often working multiple jobs during nontraditional hours and unable to come to an extended series of meetings that ask them to think about community preservation. Yet new immigrants are very important to the process and bring many new ideas and new strategies that they have used in their home countries. We knew that we needed to approach things in a different way. So we began a six-month process of events intended to help us learn about the best practices that Lowell's immigrant residents bring from their home countries—Brazil, Cambodia, many different parts of Africa, Laos, the Dominican Republic and Puerto Rico—on transportation, housing, open space, historic preservation, and environmental practices. These meetings were held in people's homes or at other locations where people felt comfortable. The meetings were translated, audiotaped, and videotaped. Many also included established leaders in transportation, housing, and the like there so that communication bridging would be begun.

The efforts produced a wealth of information about best practices in community preservation that are relevant to the decisions the Lowell community must consider. In the northeast part of Brazil there are important traditions of historic preservation that offer intriguing examples, and in southern Brazil a very advanced transportation system has been developed largely through the active involvement of teams of residents representing different occupations and perspectives (Horizon Solution Site). In Cambodia, a strong tradition of mixed land use has been followed in which stores and houses are built close to each other; examples of what has worked and what has not in Cambodia provide tantalizing ideas for the mixed usage that Lowell is considering. Lowell's residents reported that in some parts of Africa a strong tradition exists of building houses close together as a way to leave common open space for all to use. Such traditions provide intriguing examples of how density is managed. As a community we learned about best practices but we also learned about process. That is to say, we learned about the processes by which new immigrants would like to become involved in planning that deals with difficult issues.

This information-gathering concluded with a day-long

Community Preservation and Active Living

For some years, advocates for mixed usage and density in development couched their arguments within the framework of smart growth or sprawl avoidance. In the last few years, calls for traditional mixed usage of the sort more likely to be found in older cities have come from surprising sources: national leaders in public health. They have documented the emergence of a national obesity epidemic, one that threatens the health of Americans of all ages and one, they argue, that is largely the result of the ways that exercise has been "engineered out of our daily lives." They point out that patterns of development—those same patterns that also contribute to sprawl—make it very hard for people to build exercise into their lives by walking from their homes to stores, offices, schools, and other community sites.

The Robert Wood Johnson Foundation, a policy leader in raising concerns about healthy communities, has sparked a national discussion about the ways in which communities are being designed so that exercise is being "engineered out of daily life." The foundation points to decisions around zoning, economic development, transportation, housing, and open space that are all contributing to the difficulties of getting adequate exercise. The foundation is also quite explicit in calling for experts in different disciplines (transportation, economic development, and so forth) to come together and work with local leaders so that community redesign can be a force in bringing exercise back into our lives. The Robert Wood Johnson initiative is yet another reminder of the need to bring these different elements together in the analysis of our communities. More information on this initiative can be found at http://www.rwjf.org/index.jsp.Resources.

outdoor meeting, "Celebrating Diverse Traditions of Community Preservation," that brought together the groups that shared information, ideas, and approaches. A manual and CD were developed so that other communities might learn from this initiative (Silka et al. 2001).

The concept underlying all of this work was to approach diversity by recognizing how great the need is for multiple models if Lowell is to effectively pursue innovative approaches to meeting multiple goals. The method used also uncovered many untapped resources within the diverse communities in Lowell, people who had led planning initiatives, housing cooperatives, transportation planning, and the like in other cities and towns around the world.

Not all communities will be as rich in diversity as Lowell, but all can consider ways in which diversity can be a means of identifying and exploring multiple models for how a community can achieve its community preservation goals.

If Conflict Does Occur

We end this chapter with a few comments on the topic of conflict, the concern that is raised whenever discussions turn to diversity. Indeed, we have been surprised at the extent to which people we have talked with simply assume that community preservation discussions must inevitably end in conflict and position standoffs. Although disagreements are a natural part of discussions, conflict in many ways is increasingly understood as a by-product of poor process rather than an inevitable consequence of differences in perspective. In a community in central Massachusetts, conflict emerged after one group made decisions about how to mitigate the impact of growth on the educational system without bringing affected people into the discussion. A plan was developed for busing children from a neighborhood school in a poorer part of town to what was regarded as a better school in a better part of town. The families in question were not consulted about their preferences. The problem was the lack of an inclusive process.

Much of the discussion in this chapter has pointed to ways to build an inclusive process, not only so that more information is considered but also so that more people are involved in deciding how to use that information for community preservation. Many excellent resources are now available for building this kind of community process and addressing the disagreements that arise. The Community

Tool Box Web site, as just one example, includes a wealth of information for strategies that work, including:

- Analyzing your community and identifying assets;
- Locating good facilitators and instructing them about your goals;
- Identifying common ground;
- Bringing disparate groups together;
- Using multiple styles; and
- Using indicators to assess whether things are working.

All of the materials on the Community Tool Box are free and available to anyone with access to the Web. This site, useful as it is, is just one of many now available. Many other sites can assist communities in working through disagreements that might emerge in deliberations. Such sites can help in implementing many of the ideas presented in these chapters so as to strengthen attention to diversity. Consider the Environmental Protection Agency's site on Collaborative Problem Solving (http://epa.gov/compliance/ environmentaljustice/grants/ej-cps-grants.html). At this site, a complete model for community problem-solving is presented, ready to be customized to individual cases. EPA focuses on ways in which communities are affected by environmental problems, and although the site suggestions focus on assisting communities in working with their diversity to solve such problems, that focus can easily be extended to include the many other components of community preservation.

Final Thoughts: Exploring Opportunities

Diverse families are affected by the many different elements of community preservation: transportation, housing, economic development, and so forth. A great benefit of the community preservation approach is that these issues are treated as interlinked rather than as isolated phenomena. The interconnected consequences of development are brought to the forefront (e.g., a community may be working to attract new industries, but where will housing be located for residents of various incomes who will be drawn to the area by the new jobs? what will be the impact on the educational infrastructure? the transportation infrastructure?).

Communities should be aware as they contact experts to assist in these deliberations, particularly with diversity in mind, that many of the experts will offer advice based on their single area of expertise, be it housing, transportation, or economic development. Communities need to be alert to this single-minded focus among experts because it can exacerbate the same single-minded focus sometimes seen in community residents. If open space or historic preservation is of particular concern to an individual or group, the impact of community decisions on other areas may receive inadequate attention from this person or group. Such a single-minded focus has the potential to derail the very process of building consensus on community preservation. Community preservation is intended to keep such fragmentation at bay, and emphasizing diversity and the impact that decisions will have on different neighborhoods and parts of the community can be another important way to keep the various elements of community preservation equally at the forefront.

References

Anderson, Paul. 2000. "The Opportunities and Threats of Coastal Development: An MPR Roundtable Discussion." *Maine Policy Review* 9: 36–50.

Bloom, Stephen G. 2001. *Postville: A Clash of Cultures in Heartland Iowa.* San Diego: Harcourt/Harvest.

Center for Family, Work, and Community. 2001. *Meeting Lowell's Housing Needs: A Comprehensive Look.* Available at http://www.uml.edu/centers/CFWC/pastprojects.htm.

Hart, M. 1996. *Guide to Sustainable Community Indicators.* North Andover, MA.: Sustainable Measures. Available at http://www.sustainablemeasures.com/.

Horizon Solution Site. "Efficient Transportation for Successful Urban Planning in Curitiba." *Horizon Solution Site: Peer Reviewed Answers to Problems in Environment, Health, Population, and Development.* 28 Apr. 2003. Available at http://www.solutions-site.org/artman/publish/article_62.shtml.

Mullahey, Ramona, Yve Susskind, and Barry Checkoway. 1999. *Youth Participation in Community Planning.* PAS 486. Chicago: Planners Press.

Northridge, Mary B, Ilan H. Meyer, and Linda Dunn. 2002. "Overlooked and Underserved in Harlem: A Population-Based Survey of Adults with Asthma." *Environmental Health Perspectives Supplements* 110: 217–220.

Powell, Michael. 2002. "In Maine Town, Sudden Diversity and Controversy: Somali Influx Irks Mayor." *Washington Post* 14 Oct.: A01.

Probasco-Sowers, Juli. 2003. "Farmers Ask for Building Ban to Slow Urban Sprawl." *Des Moines Register* 29 Aug.

Silka, Linda, Cheryl West, Betsy Gross, and Priscilla Geigis. 2001. "Celebrating Diverse Traditions of Community Preservation." Oct. Committee on Industrial Theory and Assessment Conference on Diversity, Culture and Sustainable Development.

Web Resources

Citizens' Housing and Planning Association (CHAPA): www.chapa.org

Community Tool Box: http://ctb.lsi.ukans.edu

Environmental Protection Agency's site on Collaborative Problem Solving: http://epa.gov/compliance/environmentaljustice/grants/ej-cps-grants.html

Massachusetts's Executive Office of Environmental Affairs: http://commpres.env.state.ma.us/

Orton Family Foundation: www.orton.org

Robert Wood Johnson Foundation: http://www.rwjf.org/index.jsp

Sustainable Measures: http://www.sustainablemeasures.com

1000 Friends of Iowa, Citizens United for Responsible Land Use: http://www.kfoi.org

University of Massachusetts Lowell's Center for Family, Work, and Community: http://www.uml.edu/cfwc/

Photo: Nedim Kemer

4

Thinking Like a Developer

Partners, Adversaries, or Competitors?

Robert H. Kuehn Jr.

T HERE IS an old saying that "95 percent of all real estate developers give the other 5 percent a bad name." In this chapter, my task is not to apologize for the excesses of the majority or to comfort the unfairly maligned minority. Rather, my purpose is to explicate the thinking process of developers in order to more fully reveal their motivations and methods. With expanded insight, cities and towns may be able to fend off developers' advances in the event that such an unwanted apparition appears in one of their neighborhoods. Or better yet, communities may be able to use these insights to channel such incursions into a positive opportunity.

What Exactly Is a Developer Anyway?

Early in my career, I realized that a sure way to stop the conversation was to introduce myself as a developer. A friend suggested that I describe my career path as that of a "life-style facilitator," but that title seemed a bit awkward. So I started telling people I fixed up old buildings for a living, which suitably softened the image but often resulted in long, detailed discussions about home remodeling projects. Now I just say that I restore historic buildings for affordable housing, which still soft-pedals the message while avoiding impassioned debates about the best type of kitchen flooring to install.

The very word "developer" has a negative connotation—hard to even say out loud without adding a sneer. Nonetheless, the term springs from honorable roots. The dictionary defines *developer* as the agent for "unfolding more completely, evolving the possibilities, and promoting growth." In the context of photography, the *developer* is a chemical agent that makes the film's latent image visible. In the world of real estate, the *developer* is a change agent for transforming a latent opportunity—currently unused or underutilized land or buildings—into new uses that support our society and economy.

Practitioners of such change come in many forms. There is no professional accreditation for this calling or even many formal courses of study. Indeed, one of the attractions of this field is the relatively unfettered entrepreneurship it represents—put together some capital, commit the necessary time and energy, and, with more than a little luck, you too can be a developer. The problem is that not all self-selected real estate entrepreneurs also possess the skill and sensitivity to produce pleasing results without some encouragement. Some, however, can bring alive new opportunities that reinforce the character of a community and provide attractive places for people to live, work, and visit. Developers may be the professionals that the public loves to hate, but these are the guys that produce most of the built environment that we all occupy.

Who Are These Masked Men Anyway?

The universe of developers is drawn from a broad background, which in turn may influence their motivations, methods, and biases. At the risk of over-simplification, the range of professional credentials that may be encountered in a developer can be summarized as follows:

- *Business:* Some number of real estate entrepreneurs come out of a business background. Obviously, basic business acumen is required for the success of any enterprise. A command of finance is also critical to the often-leveraged world of real estate. The best of the business-oriented developers—whether smaller local companies or large national corporations—hire excellent design, construction, marketing, and management professionals to translate the numbers into well-conceived buildings. Others, unfortunately, get the business part right but fall short in terms of the built environment, forgetting that real estate is not a product on paper, but a real place that we all have to live with (at least visually).
- *Legal:* Some developers gravitate to the field from a legal background. Real estate law is a relatively complex specialty involving local, state, and/or federal permitting depending on the conditions of a particular site. A development opportunity often starts with a legal problem to be solved—assembling disparate parcels, rezoning a site, addressing an environmental issue, or otherwise resolving some legal impediment. But such legal gymnastics should be only the prelude to the development process, involving the engagement of other real estate professionals.
- *Contractors:* Some developers started as building contrac-

tors who then expanded their role to include the land assembly, design, and marketing. Many contractors take pride in their craftsmanship and live by their reputation for providing a good product. A common shortcoming, however, is a tendency to continue the status quo as to planning and design rather than exploring new alternatives with the input of allied professionals.
- *Designers/Planners:* Some developers come from an architectural and planning background. This is my own bias; I was trained as an architect and urban planner and turned to development in order to better control what I would have an opportunity to design and build. Our company focuses first on the quality of the living or working environment we wish to create and then tries to conform the business, financial, legal, and construction challenges to achieve this purpose. If there is a failing of design-based developers, it is that they try to stretch the bounds too far for public acceptance or that their business plans are not always sound.
- *Nonprofits:* Another more recent player in the world of real estate is the community development corporation and other nonprofit entities. Such nonprofits are often particularly focused on affordable housing but also engage in other economic development activities. These entities are often local or regional in nature, offering some comfort as to their commitment to the community. As a developer, however, a nonprofit is still subject to the same economic constraints and to the same need to exercise good judgment as to the planning and design. Sometimes the best of both worlds is to marry a local nonprofit to an experienced (and better capitalized) for-profit for the task at hand.
- *Property Owners:* Any development necessarily starts with a parcel of land or an existing building. The owners of such property can choose to sell their development rights to another developer, partner with an experienced development professional, or act as the developer themselves. Sometimes an owner has held a property for many years, and other times the owner is just holding it for speculation. Similarly, their motivations may range from wanting to see the right thing done to maximizing the profit realized. Since the control of the real estate is the necessary starting point for any opportunity, the negotiation with the property owner is critical, and the sale price and terms will often dictate the further course of the development.

A high price will also likely drive the density required to cover the fixed costs of the acquisition.

- *Miscellaneous:* Since there are no prescribed credentials for entering the field of development, there are any number of other developer types who might cross the threshold. On one end of the spectrum are those who think real estate is a "get rich quick" opportunity that requires little skill or hard work; these guys are definitely among the 95 percent who give the profession a bad name. Also be beware of the "ego developers," often individuals who have been very successful in some other enterprise and now want to try their hand at development; the results can be grand plans but clumsy execution. On the other hand, there are non-developers who take on a particular site out of a public or philanthropic motivation; these are often affirming impulses that can contribute to the well-being of a community if harnessed to a fully professional plan.

What Does a Developer Do?

Understanding the background of developers enables the public to better assess their capacities and limitations. But what is it that developers actually do? The answer is a little bit of everything. On one hand, that is part of the fascination with the business, involving a multifaceted process that combines design, building, finance, marketing, politics, and everything in between. The developer may have professional skills in one or more areas, or he or she may be only the impresario who organizes the skills of others. When I am perhaps in a grandiose mood, I liken the role of a developer to that of an orchestra conductor. The conductor should have an overall understanding of the score for a particular composition, but is dependent on the members of the orchestra to produce the music. Otherwise, the conductor ends up looking a bit silly, eagerly waving the baton but producing no sound.

In the context of real estate, the orchestra is the development team. A typical team includes an architect, a contractor, attorneys, and a marketing/management agent. A more complicated undertaking may also involve land planners, landscape architects, interior designers, environmental consultants, permitting specialists, public relation firms, accounting counsel, investment bankers, and any number of other specialized consultants for traffic and parking, historic or archeological resources, marketing focus groups, or a long list of other professionals. The team concept is critical to coordinate all of these inputs to produce the desired results. As the team leader, the developer has to weigh the often conflicting advice of the various professionals in order to find the right equilibrium. For example, the financial advisers may be saying that the economics dictate a minimum buildout of, say, 75 new homes, but the legal advisers may be counseling that it will be difficult to secure zoning permission for any greater density than 50 homes.

Another thing a developer does is bankroll this complex team effort. An undertaking of any size can involve many hundreds of thousands (if not millions) of dollars to pay professional fees to move a proposal forward. Given that the planning and approvals process can take years to complete, this can be a high-stakes commitment with no guarantee of success. The profits of a real estate developer often vacillate greatly from year to year, with significant outflows during the pre-construction process followed by more outflows during construction and marketing, which are then, one hopes, recouped by significant inflows at the end of the line. But the old rule is doubly true with development: "Time is money." Delays are the bane of existence that can erode potential profits.

If the process flounders along the way because of delays in obtaining approvals, changes in the economy, or any number of other pitfalls in the normal course of business, the result can be devastating. A few failures not balanced by offsetting successes can easily do in a developer—it is a singularly high risk/high reward business that requires not a little luck to go along with hard work and vision. I recall, for example, a colleague who specialized in small, well-planned subdivisions. At first he only did the land assembly, selling permitted lots to other homebuilders. After a few modest successes, he decided to also develop the homes himself to expand upon his enterprise. But then one day when he had maybe a dozen homes in inventory, low-level radon was detected in one of the basements. The local media erroneously ran a story about "radio-active homes," and my colleague's business never recovered.

Why Do They Say It's "Location, Location, Location"?

Real estate is not developed in the abstract, but is located on a specific site in a specific place. When I refer to "a site," this includes both vacant land and existing buildings. The land can be improved only through new construction, but an existing building can also be renovated and adaptively reused. The characteristics and conditions of a given site will have a lot to do with what can be accomplished, ranging from the cost of acquisition, the underlying zoning that determines the buildout potential, and any number of other physical conditions that create costs or cause constrains. Of course, the location of the site will also have a significant influence on the development potential in terms of market acceptance for a given use.

A site can be simply purchased, or the right to purchase in the future can be negotiated. Purchasing a property outright at the right price provides full control, but results in immediate carrying costs long before it is known with any certainty how the site can be developed. An alternative is to option the site, establishing a fixed price upfront but postponing the actual purchase on negotiated terms (usually involving periodic option payments). This approach allows the approval process to play out before fully committing the developer to purchase the property. Whether a developer owns the site or simply controls it under an option will sometimes dictate the tenor of discussions with local authorities, since there may be more desperation if the purchase is complete and the time clock is running. Of course, a developer may also have invested significantly in an option, which may be about to expire.

A key issue is whether the property to be developed was (or will be) acquired for a realistic price or not. If a developer stretches too far to acquire a prime property, this initial decision is likely to drive the density required to absorb the acquisition costs. For example, assume a ten-acre plot of land sells for $50,000 per acre and local regulations call for two-acre zoning. The math suggests only five homes could be built at a land cost of $100,000 per home. If this cost is difficult to absorb in the market, the developer may try to rezone at one acre, effectively halving the acquisition cost per home. Many of the tensions in the approval process emanate from the purchase of a site at an overly optimistic price in anticipation of favorable zoning. I have often passed on sites that I would have loved to develop because I knew the acquisition cost was excessive and would force subsequent design decisions that would be hard to justify.

Not all sites are purchased on the open market. Many of our development activities have involved publicly owned sites where the developer is selected through a competitive process. Responding to such "requests for proposals" (or RFPs) is an iffy proposition, involving a competitive process that requires a fair amount of time and money. But our company actively pursues such RFPs since at least the community has made some basic decisions about what it wants to see happen on a given site; we want to apply our skills and resources to building buildings, not arguing about whether to build anything or not. In other words, there is some likelihood that the proposal may actually result in a successful undertaking for the developer ultimately selected under the RFP process.

Another increasingly important consideration in site selection is the environmental condition of the site. Given that we live in Massachusetts, an older, urbanized state, many properties have been put to previous uses that have caused various levels of contamination. Environmental regulations create onerous liabilities for even the good guys who are trying to clean up such past sins, so many of these sites have lain fallow because of the costs and complications. Happily, the state's Brownfields Program provides new tools to deal with these compromised sites, offering technical assistance, limits on liabilities, and environmental insurance. Such insurance can be critical in bringing relative closure to contamination issues, which is otherwise difficult to accomplish under the state's environmental regulations. For example, we were asked several years ago to convert a derelict former post office in Chelsea for reuse as a campus for a community college. However, the undertaking was hung up over a low level of oil detected in the groundwater under this site (a not uncommon condition in urban locations). It could have taken years and tens of thousands of dollars to track down the source of this contamination (which nearly everyone agreed was of no consequence). But then environmental insurance coverage became available in the marketplace, which expeditiously solved the problem for relatively short dollars.

Finally, it should also be noted that developers acquiring (or optioning) a site may have a variety of endgames in mind. Some are anticipating a full range of responsibility, including planning, permitting, constructing, marketing, and ultimately owning and operating the property. Others are only looking to fully develop the site and/or improvements, but then sell the completed property to others who will assume long-term responsibility. Finally, some developers only assemble sites, permit the improvements, and then sell the site to others for the buildout. My company still holds most of the housing we have developed in our portfolio for the long haul, which provides some comfort as to our long-term commitment to manage the residential communities that we develop.

So Then It's Just Step 1, 2, 3 on the Way to the Bank?

The process of development is more art than science—it is definitely not a linear process but more like an obstacle course with many surprises along the way. But the normal steps that any particular proposal goes through include the following:

- *Assemble a Development Team:* After a site is under control, the developer starts to assemble a professional team to undertake the myriad of tasks necessary to translate preliminary ideas into a more tangible plan. I have already listed the range of development team members that may be involved depending on the complexity of the undertaking. In the case of competitive proposals for a public or private sale of a site, the primary members of the team may all be identified in advance since the credentials of the professionals involved are often an important part of the selection process.
- *Prepare a Preliminary Plan:* Once a site is identified, the next step is to conceptualize how the property might be developed. A land planner or architect usually prepares a schematic layout to approximate the level of buildout that can be accomplished on the site. The local zoning ordinances will be studied to determine the allowed uses, density, setbacks, and other prescriptions. This initial planning may also take an alternative look at the site from more of a "wishful thinking" point of view—what is the best design or the maximum density that might be reasonably proposed without strict compliance with existing zoning? Then it can be determined what level of variances or special permits would be required beyond the "by-right" zoning envelope.
- *Estimate the Costs:* Early on, the estimated costs for developing the site and improvements must be determined. A contractor and/or subcontractors may be added to the team, or such budgets might be prepared by an inde-

pendent cost estimator (especially if the final plans and specifications are going to be put out to bid rather than arranged by negotiated contract). Early budgets are likely to be only "ballpark" estimates based on past experience with similar proposals.

- *Assess the Market:* Simultaneous with preparing schematic plans and estimating costs, the potential market demand for the site must be assessed. Probably, the developer had a pretty good sense of the desired uses and demand for such uses when looking for sites. But now this general sense has to be updated and further quantified as to the rents or sales prices that can be achieved. A market study involves checking out comparable values and standards of the existing competition. If the site location is in an emerging development area without much guidance as to competition, the study may also look at economic and demographic data to divine the market trends. Any market analysis is inevitably imprecise, in part because one is comparing past practices and projecting these trends into the future, several years hence. Changes in the economy or other vagaries may easily cause a miscalculation.
- *Analyze the Economics:* The schematic design, cost estimates, and market analysis inform each other and must be optimized. Once a workable design is resolved which appears to meet cost estimates and to match up with the perceived market, the developer needs to put all this information together in a financial *pro forma*. First, a development budget is drawn up for the capital costs that are required to build the building. Second, an operating budget is devised, outlining the revenues and expenses for its management and maintenance. The link between these two budgets is the financing, which translates the capital costs into another component of operations through the debt service. Of course, if the property is to be sold, a marketing budget for the sales period replaces the operating budget. These budget estimates often need to go through numerous iterations before achieving equilibrium. Sometimes, however, the numbers simply cannot be made to work since the development costs exceed the net revenues anticipated in the marketplace.
- *Arrange Debt and Equity Financing:* After the *pro forma* is refined, it is time to start discussions with mortgage lenders and investor sources. Except for small undertakings, most developments run into millions of dollars, which most entrepreneurs cannot pay for out of their own

pockets. Rather, the developer anticipates borrowing as much of the cost as possible, at the most reasonable rates that can be supported. He or she may be able to cover the remaining costs, but often other equity sources will also be required. So early on, the developer will have to start warming up lenders and investors for the construction and permanent debt and equity. Usually, the developer is on the hook for all pre-construction costs, but often financial support is also needed during this phase.

So What's So Difficult about This Process?

Not included on the above list of what a developer does is perhaps the most difficult and time-consuming component of all: obtaining building permits. Unless a site can be developed "by right" under local zoning and other regulations, the developer is subject to an often lengthy review process before being allowed to start construction. This process typically involves the local planning board and sometimes the board of zoning appeals. Other municipal authorities also come into play, including the conservation commission, the health board, the historical commission, the building department, the fire and police departments, and a number of other boards and commissions depending on the circumstances. In larger cities like Boston, it is not uncommon to have to deal with over 20 separate agencies (all of whom, of course, want to be informed first and decide last). In some instances, regional commissions may also have a say, as on Cape Cod or the Islands. Other state and federal agencies may also have purview in certain circumstances.

Because Massachusetts is one of the oldest states in the country, frequently the only sites available to be developed are limited by various physical, environmental, and other constraints. The land that is still available is often not suitably zoned (especially for multifamily housing). Combine these facts with the strong tradition of "home rule" within the separate 351 jurisdictions that make up our Commonwealth, and the result has become virtual gridlock for the permitting of housing. Indeed, Massachusetts ranked 47th out of the 50 states according to recent Census statistics in terms of multifamily housing permits per capita (behind only North Dakota, Montana, and Wyoming, which do not suffer from a lack of available land). The mood in Massachusetts seems to be that we are becoming overdeveloped; the facts seem to suggest quite the opposite, with the lack of affordable housing quickly becoming both a social and economic limitation for our state.

Against this backdrop, our cities and towns generally rely on an antiquated set of zoning regulations to guide development. Indeed, the American Planning Association has listed Massachusetts as one of the states with the most outdated land-use laws. Although we talk "smart growth," we are hobbled by "dumb codes." Our state's zoning enabling law, Chapter 40A, is based on the "Euclidean" zoning model (named after a 1920s ordinance in Euclid, Ohio). These regulations first prescribe "zones" for various uses—single family, multifamily, commercial, industrial, and so on. The basic premise is that these uses are incompatible and should be kept separate. This premise may be sensible at the macro level—say, relative to locating factories away from homes—but this approach breaks down at the micro level when, say, a range of housing densities cannot be mixed in a town center or when the only retail units are located remotely so that one has to get into one's car to shop.

The other basic set of rules laid down under the Euclidean construct has to do with dimensional limits. This form of zoning prescribes various land/building area ratios, open space requirements, setbacks from the lot lines, heights of structures, and the like. Again, the premise is that each building should be suitably separated from the next. This makes sense at some basic level to avoid untoward encroachment of adjacent structures, but often breaks down when viewed from the perspective of the unified community design. For example, the typical suburban house lot subdivision requires houses to be placed in the middle of lots, set back from the street and abutting properties, squandering the open space left over into relatively small chunks. A clustering of houses would create more useful, real open space and perhaps allow the opportunity to conserve natural features, not necessarily at any greater density. These dimensional formulas are at best a crude tool to influence design, often producing clumsy results.

At a recent "smart growth" conference of the New England states, a prominent land planner commented that developers do not create our built environment out of whole cloth, they only implement the public policies embodied in our governmental rules and regulations. If you do not like what is happening in your own city or town—strip malls and big-box stores, sprawling subdivisions and McMansions, or a density of development out of scale and character—you probably do not need to look any further than your own local zoning ordinance. Unless development is being favored by variances under this ordinance, you are simply getting what you bargained for. The dreaded developer is only following the recipe that the community thought would produce the right results but now is only producing a bad taste.

But What's the Alternative to Zoning?

When I look back at our company's best work, one common thread is that all the usual zoning rules were set aside and the design was negotiated as some type of special permit. (In the case of the adaptive reuse of historic structures, we also rely on "grandfathering" under existing zoning; ironically, most of these reuse opportunities are buildings that most people like but that could never be built under current zoning). The special permit process was sometimes initiated by the city or town and sometimes initiated by us. But in either case, the two sides sat down and thought through the best approach for the site planning and architectural design in order to produce the most pleasing result. This strategy takes a bit more effort and requires a cooperative and collaborative attitude, but the proof is in the pudding as to the superior living or working environments that are created.

A companion piece to Chapter 40A, the state zoning enabling law, is Chapter 40B—also called "anti-snob" zoning since the purpose is to encourage communities to provide affordable housing equal to at least 10 percent of the total stock. This law has helped produce over 30,000 units of housing in 200 of the Commonwealth's cities and towns over the past 30 years. Recently, however, 40B has become controversial because of excesses on both sides of the equation. Communities feel put upon by developers looking to override local zoning, but take no initiative to address housing needs. Some developers abuse the process by threatening proposals that are out of scale and character with the community in order to leverage a permit. In the worst cases, housing is simply used as a means to another end, a circumstance that affordable advocates also decry.

What is being lost sight of in this debate is that Chapter 40B is also known as the "comprehensive permit law." By design, the process requires the various permitting agencies in a given municipality to convene to review the merits of a proposal. In effect, these agencies can create a special permit, which adapts zoning and other rules to the special circumstances. Moreover, the permit is negotiated in a coordinated fashion rather than each agency proceeding separately, sometimes with rules that even contradict each other.

But at the core of 40B is the ability to shape zoning for a particular site for a particular purpose without having to go through a general rezoning process. Many communities, for example, simply do not have much (or any) land zoned for multifamily housing. If a good proposal comes along—say, for elderly housing in the town center, youth lots for the next generation who want to stay in their hometown, or townhouses for the municipal workforce—how can this proposal be accommodated without reworking the zoning ordinance or granting extensive variances? The comprehensive permit provisions of 40B provide the tool that can tailor the solution like a special permit.

My company has done only two 40Bs, both "friendly" examples of how this law can work to everyone's advantage. The first was in the Town of Wayland, which had a surplus school that it wished to convert to elderly housing. The underlying zoning was for large lot, single-family homes. Rather than "spot zone" this site for the intended purpose, we entered into a cooperative negotiation to change the zoning rules to accommodate the shared objectives. I recall being tickled by how streamlined the process was since all the various boards and commissions met together (perhaps for the first time) to review the plans. For example, the fire department at first insisted on a paved roadway around the school building to provide emergency access while the conservation commission was equally insistent on non-impervious surfaces; a suitable compromise was reached without the developers being caught in the middle.

A more recent example is in the Town of Williamstown. My company purchased a derelict but historic mill complex near the town center and approached local officials about our vision for the site. The leadership was very receptive, looking to turn an eyesore into an asset. (They were also mindful that another mill had recently collapsed of its own volition after too long a debate about its future.) So we soon arrived at a mutually agreeable master plan for our site as mixed-income homeownership. The plan was then processed as a very friendly 40B, using this tool as it was intended, as a comprehensive permit in the absence of otherwise compliant zoning. This 40B was approved in less than three months without a single dissenting voice.

Density, Design, and Zoning

When people talk about development and developers, they often decry the density of new buildings that they think will adversely affect their communities. But density is not always as straightforward as it may seem. Instead, it is more the scale and character of the assembled buildings that really matter. An example is the traditional town center—these are often of moderate-to-high density and comprised of mixed uses, but the human scale of the buildings makes the neighborhood feel lively and pleasant, rather than crowded and uninviting.

But because not all design is equal and because bad buildings have been imposed in many places, most communities have implemented zoning laws to control future development. The basic purpose of zoning is to control building types, so that incompatible uses do not interfere with one another; e.g., an industrial use in a residential neighborhood. Hence the root word "zone." But zoning further regulates the design through a variety of controls on height, mass, open space, and setbacks that indirectly control the density of development.

Unfortunately, many zoning controls are blunt instruments that do not achieve the desired results. Indeed, the charming New England town centers we all treasure (and often pay a lot of money to visit on vacation) like Nantucket or Provincetown are all but outlawed under contemporary zoning. Somehow we continue to hold onto the hope that zoning laws will protect our communities against unwanted intrusions and, in particular, against unwarranted density. But the answer to creating great neighborhoods is not necessarily to reduce density (or diversity of uses). Rather, the answer is to insist on good design.

The foibles of our typical zoning laws and their effect on the perception of density can be readily illustrated. For example, my company built a new mixed-income cooperative about ten years ago on the last site in the Old West End of Boston (tragically cleared by urban renewal in the 1960s). If I do say so myself, the result is quite attractive and was honored by design awards from the AIA and the Masonry Institute. Observers have commented to me: "Boy, am I happy that you resisted developing big and tall like Charles River Park; the density of your West End Place is much more pleasing." But the fact of the matter is that our 7–10-story building is actually denser than the neighboring 40-plus-story Longfellow Towers. Our building computes to 114 units per acre versus about 97 units per acre next door. But West End Place is perceived as less dense because of its lower height and because the design more compactly covers the site. I also think that the average person can relate better to a design that respects the street frontage and is otherwise more human-scaled, as compared to the neighboring towers. The accompanying photographs (Figures 4.1–4.6) compare these similar densities in very different design wrappers.

The perception of density also plays out in the context of adaptive reuse of historic properties. A number of years ago, my company renovated a 100-year-old structure in Harvard Square for mixed-income apartments and offices, Chapman Arms. The result is quite handsome, and people frequently comment: "Why can't they build them like that any more?" The reason is that current zoning would clearly prohibit such an aberration: Our historic building has a density of about three times the land area (in a zone now limited to a fraction of that ratio); there is very limited

Figure 4.1. Longfellow Towers.
Photo: Keen Development Corporation, Inc.

Figure 4.2. West End Place.
Photo: Keen Development Corporation, Inc.

open space (much less than the 15 percent required); there are virtually no setbacks (in fact the cornice probably encroaches on the sidewalk); the height is about 55 feet (in a 35-foot zone); occupancy includes a mix of uses (which required a variance), and there is no parking on-site (another variance). Ironically, the controversial Fan Pier development in the South Boston Seaport District also has a density of about three times the land area (also known as a floor-to-area ratio or FAR). However, Fan Pier is perceived as too dense and too tall, probably because all the setback and open space requirements imposed by zoning rules and the public process reshaped the assembly in a way that critics decry.

This relationship between density, design, and zoning is also very clear when comparing older properties to new construction. Take, for example, two properties operated by Harvard University for married student housing. Shaler Lane looks like an English mews, with two-story dwellings arranged on an alley-like street with near zero lot lines in the rear. The result is quite attractive and

again, we hear positive comments about the scale and character. Less than a mile away, Peabody Terrace is a high-rise designed in the style of "towers in the park." Many people find this second site to be abrasive to the community, but it probably met zoning regulations. But guess what: both of these properties have almost the same density of 55 units per acre. It is the arrangement of the component parts that makes the difference in perception of density (and local zoning, with all the best of intentions, probably prohibits reproducing the one most people like better).

One way anyone can work on this in their own neighborhood is to find a streetscape or building that they really like, and then look at the local zoning code and see if it could be built again under current regulations (without time-consuming variances or special permits). If it can't, it is probably time to refine the zoning code. A second take-home point is not to be automatically afraid of higher density per se—instead, automatically insist on good design!

Figure 4.3. Peabody Terrace.
Photo: Keen Development Corporation, Inc.

Figure 4.4. Shaler Lane.
Photo: Keen Development
Corporation, Inc.

Figure 4.5. Fan Pier.
Photo: Keen Development Corporation, Inc.

Figure 4.6. Chapman Arms.
Photo: Keen Development Corporation, Inc.

A similar productive result was achieved in the Town of Lincoln. Through progressive local leadership, the town acquired a site and our company was selected as the developer. The decision was made, however, not to pursue a 40B process—the leadership was put off by the "anti-snob" sobriquet. But we mimicked the "comprehensive permit" procedures and negotiated a special permit, creating a master plan and architectural design cut from whole cloth. Ultimately, this permit had to be confirmed by a vote of town meeting (a step not required under 40B), but as I recall, there were only handful of dissenting votes. The result was Battle Road Farm, 120 mixed-income homeownership opportunities, 40 percent of which were affordable. Interestingly, there is a man-bites-dog story embedded here. I argued for a lesser density of about 100 homes while the town insisted on 120 homes; they were focused on achieving their 10 percent threshold of affordable housing—one of the first affluent suburban communities to do so.

The Town of West Tisbury on Martha's Vineyard followed a similar course. A group of residents joined together to design and build a "co-housing" community of 16 homes on a wooded lot. Their vision for a "sustainable design" of clustered cottages broke all of the local zoning rules. Chapter 40B provided a better mechanism than zoning variances, which would have had to be confirmed by town meeting. The results were so impressive that the zoning ordinance was subsequently changed to allow similar cluster housing design by right.

The Commonwealth has recently taken the 40B concept one productive step further as part of its broader "smart growth" agenda. Namely, cities and towns are encouraged to rezone land or buildings in town centers or near transit nodes for higher-density mixed uses, especially housing. This new set of incentives is known as Chapter 40R, providing more "carrots" than "sticks" to achieve the intended result. A community receives a density bonus payment, ranging upwards from $25,000, for the initial rezoning to help defray its technical costs. And then when the housing is actually developed, the community receives a payment of $3,000 per unit for each extra home or apartment built within the zone. A companion piece to the legislation, Chapter 40S, is designed to provide additional support for any incremental school costs resulting from the development. This state initiative has only recently been enacted, but holds considerable promise for positive results by making the approval process less adversarial.

How Can a Community Best Work with These Developers?

A developer can have a great site, a great concept, and a great team, but if the community does not accept the development proposal, all is for naught. Therefore, working through the local approval process is always the focus of successful developers. This includes not only technical zoning matters and related approvals, but also the critical public relations issues that ultimately dictate whether or not the community at large embraces the proposed development initiative.

Clearly, each unique site also has its unique set of abutters and other interested parties who will be impacted by the proposal and therefore are likely to weigh in during the permitting process. Most people are wary of change in any form, and their first reflex is to oppose development in any form. The more a given development proposal is in keeping with the character of the community and otherwise complementary to that community's own purposes, the more likely the proposal will be accepted. Therefore, the first decision about the site selection is a critical one for any development initiative. My company seeks out communities that have already thought through what they want to see happen within their borders, as evidenced by a master plan or other "good growth" guidelines. If on the other hand, a city or town signals that it wants to pull up the drawbridge, we are unlikely to attempt to swim across their moat full of alligators.

An experienced developer typically tries to test the waters early and often. I make it a point to ask a community even before I commit to a site whether what I have in mind is generally acceptable (although that is not always possible if an acquisition is confidential or competitive). Certainly after gaining site control, I like to introduce myself to public officials and interested residents to explain my general plans and to solicit ideas for the best way to proceed. Of course, the style of some developers is more of a stealth approach, holding back on public disclosures until their plans are more advanced.

I like to proceed incrementally, starting with broad concepts, which reference successful examples of completed properties that are similar in scale and character. I hope that this introductory process builds some confidence in the quality of our previous performance and creates a positive mental image of what could be accomplished on this new site. Unfortunately, such best intentions are not always rewarded. While some communities respond positively to an early dialogue, just as often the response is: "How can we react to your plans before they are fully fleshed out?" So, a developer is often caught in the Catch 22 of "damned if you do or if you don't."

I also try to be a good listener, cognizant that I am basically an outsider (and sometimes even an unwanted visitor). I realize that I cannot possibly know all the nuances and sensitivities of the city or town in which I hope to be working. I approach each new opportunity with an open mind and a willingness to consider all reasonable options; all I ask in return is a similar response from the community. An undertaking as important as building a new building or restoring an existing building should not be a contest of wills (or a legal contest). Rather, the most satisfactory results are usually achieved through a cooperative exchange of ideas that produces a common conclusion.

Too often, however, the dialogue never begins in many communities. Even a modest development proposal is viewed adversely, and "over my dead body" is the most common response before plans are even presented. As a developer, I fully understand that change is a scary thing—will the result be better for the community or a burden? Many jump to the conclusion that the status quo is the safer bet, even if the site is currently derelict or otherwise compromised. (I have found that the adaptive reuse of historic structures is often more readily accepted, in part because the building already exists, so there is less risk about what it will look like.)

My job as developer is to prove that our proposal for a site will be translated into an end product that will be a net benefit to the community. This is always a difficult task in that I can only show drawings and models (together with examples of our previous work) in order to communicate a vision for what could be. This task is often made even more difficult by the fact that the real issues are not always out on the table. For example, if the proposal is to build affordable housing, many people shy away from openly opposing it on the grounds that they fear less affluent people (or, gasp,

people of another race or ethnic background) living next door. So the opposition takes an indirect form like raising environmental issues regarding the site or expressing concerns about traffic and parking. There may indeed be environmental, traffic, or other collateral issues to be addressed, but too often such concerns are really ciphers for less politically correct reservations, which no one cares to directly articulate.

Recently, communities have started to raise fiscal defenses that are more direct and honest—that the city or town does not want any new development that does not cover its own costs, especially housing which could bring more children to the local schools. If a community chooses to close its borders to new residents, I really do not have a good antidote as a developer. These issues require a broader state policy resolution of local aid or real estate taxes to level the playing field and allow growth to occur in a fair and sustainable manner across the state.

In the face of opposition, direct or indirect, my company's response is to build public support by talking with those willing to listen, and then modifying plans to accommodate legitimate concerns. Once compromises are reached, I weigh the likely chances of success against the level of effective opposition. Ultimately, I will voluntarily withdraw a proposal rather than engage in protracted, unpleasant wrangling. But other developers—by dint of disposition or perhaps because they have become over-committed to a given site, financially or otherwise—are often willing to fight through the process to the bitter end. Before I exit, however, I will ask a community to consider a number of relevant questions: "Will this site remain undeveloped forever, or will inevitably something happen in the future? If the latter, how likely is it that someone else will do a better job than our company?" Sometimes, such soul-searching results in a second chance for reaching common ground.

Why Bother to Think Like a Developer?

So what have you gained from this journey through the thinking process of at least one developer? Some readers may come away only with new insights into how to oppose development based on a better understanding of how the process works and the leverages for derailing any proposal. Other readers, however, may use this understanding to help shape needed growth in their communities in a more thoughtful manner.

So next time a developer shows up on your doorstep, consider the alternatives to just saying no. Is the proposed site one that could be reasonably developed in the best interests of the community? Is the track record of the developer a good one in terms of producing at least as much as promised? If these two questions can be answered affirmatively, it then makes some sense to mutually explore two more questions: What is the best use of the site that will serve local purposes? What is the best design that will complement the scale and character of the community? If a consensus can be reached, there may be an opportunity for a non-adversarial plan that both sides can embrace and point to with pride as an example of positive community building.

II

Developing a Vision

Brookline

COMPREHENSIVE PLAN 2005-2015

TOWN OF BROOKLINE, MASSACHUSETTS

Courtesy of Town of Brookline, Massachusetts

5

Comprehensive Planning
Bringing It All Together

Steve Smith, Kurt Gaertner, and Glenn Garber

T HE PREVIOUS chapters have provided an overview of the process of getting involved in local planning as well a lot of substantive knowledge about the typical subjects that cities and towns need to address. In this next section of the book, we move beyond responsive or single-item topics, and discuss how to get municipal policy set up so that the right thing becomes easier and neighbors don't have to gear up for a fight each time a project is proposed. Instead, the idea is to have the community's goals and hopes for its future supported by the municipal plans and zoning. This chapter describes the comprehensive planning process, which sets community policy for the long term. The next provides a discussion of zoning, which is the legal realization of all the plans, hopes, and dreams developed previously by the community. The section concludes with an explanation of Geographic Information System technology and its applications in making decisions about current and future land use.

Comprehensive Plans: An Overview

A comprehensive plan (also known as a master plan or general plan) is a statement of the desired future physical growth of a community, specifying the policies and programs the community intends to implement to attain that future. True to the title, a comprehensive plan is intended to cover all the major aspects of a community's growth, change, and redevelopment, ranging from housing needs to infrastructure improvements, from economic enhancements to open space, historic preservation, and much more. It is both a broad vision for the community's future (whether a city, county, town, or region), and a slate of specific actions carefully thought through and designed to achieve that future state. Plans often have a twenty-year field of focus, but usually not longer, due to the difficulty of predicting beyond that point. Under ideal circumstances, a plan may be updated every five years, by either local decision or legislative mandate, but that is a goal not always attained, owing to the relatively high level of effort and expense inherent in comprehensive planning.

The goals, objectives, and actions involved in a comprehensive plan often result in major additions or changes to other community and regional policy documents, such as capital investment plans, zoning laws, subdivision control regulations, other laws and regulations, sewer and water improvement plans, and transportation initiatives.

Of course, not all communities have a plan. In their recent publication *Planning Communities for the 21st Century*, the American Planning Association found that in 10 states comprehensive plans are optional, 25 states require a comprehensive plan only when a local planning commission is created by the community, and 15 states unconditionally mandate the development of a plan. Additionally, approximately two-thirds of the states have some sort of requirement that plans be generally consistent with zoning laws.

While a plan is predominantly about the physical development of a community, it will of necessity reflect a community's social and economic goals, some of which will not have a directly physical expression. For example, the types of housing for which a community zones directly affect the affordability and desirability of housing. More than half the communities in Massachusetts allow only two-acre single-family houses as of right. Those who are not seeking such a home because they can't afford it, prefer to rent, or lack the car such development requires will be forced to look elsewhere to find a place to live. Under the topic of economic development, examples without a direct physical planning aspect could include recommendations to form a community development corporation, or create a training partnership between local industry and high schools and community colleges, or establish a business improvement district.

The typical comprehensive plan will include five types of information; often points 2 and 3 below are combined, but for our purposes it is helpful to consider them separately.

1. *Community vision or broad goals:* a general, conceptual agreement on what the community should be like at the end of the planning period, often up to 20 years.
2. *Analytical pieces by topical element:* existing conditions are documented, and then the collected data is employed in some detail to understand the problems and needs and point the way toward possible solutions.
3. *Strategic pieces by topical element:* policy options are considered and vetted; usually incorporated into the same topical element or chapter as #2 above.
4. *Implementation section, usually not by topical element:* the final set of policy recommendations is set out (usually in integrated form to assure that the recommendations work together in reasonable harmony), and implementation responsibilities are assigned.
5. *Compilation of remaining data:* statistics, maps, excerpts from other publications, and other useful information not used in the main body of the plan are compiled in appendices or sometimes a separate volume.

Different plans are organized differently and often include other things such as a "snapshot" of the community, which describes current conditions. Plans also come in very different lengths depending on the complexity of the community (a big city's comprehensive plan is obviously longer than a rural community's, for instance) as well as its goals and the budget available to make the plan. We briefly describe these main sections below.

The first section of a comprehensive plan will often be a set of visionary goals. These are usually broad, big-picture ideas, such as "increase the range of housing available in the community to match the needs of current and future residents," and attain the objective of a 10 percent affordable housing stock, or "assure balanced transportation options, including automobile, bus, bicycle, and pedestrian access," and new transit system connections. These are sometimes phrased as a "vision statement," which summarizes, generally in broad terms, the majority sentiments of a community and its visualization of itself in the future. An example might be: "Our town will continue to be a service and employment center for the region by providing a high quality of life and strong environmental protection."

By local decision, statute, or state policy, comprehensive plans are generally divided into elements by topic areas. The American Planning Association has found that a typical master plan contains eight elements and that as states update their planning legislation they tend to include more elements and to require additional detail within each required element. The American Planning Association (1999) reports that the elements most frequently included in a plan are, in order of frequency of occurrence:

- Land use, which should answer such questions as what are the major deficiencies in the community's regulatory structure, what lands have high biodiversity or water

Milford, Massachusetts's 2003 Comprehensive Plan Table of Contents

Reprinted courtesy of the City of Milford and Mark Lindhult, principal author.

---

recharge value, and what zoning changes are needed to achieve the community's goals.

- Transportation, focusing both on the needed improvements in the existing roadway system capacity, and on alternatives designed to reduce automobile dependency, such as transit, pedestrian and bicycle modes, and ridesharing programs.
- Community facilities and public services, such as libraries, fire stations, and public works, which again should support or constrain the directions for growth indicated in the land-use section.
- Agriculture (where applicable), including policies for protecting the best soils in the municipality and organizing development elsewhere to assure that farming continues.
- Recreation and open space, which includes both built facilities and often natural resource considerations, and

may indicate greenways and other lands that should remain undeveloped.

- Housing, suggesting what changes to policy are needed to accommodate changes in the population or currently underserved community members.
- Implementation strategies, or how the community will achieve the above goals (note that we treat this as a separate topic).
- Specific policies or action items, which typically include a wide array of recommendations for achieving the goals and objectives of the plan.

In the accompanying textboxes we present excerpts from a recent comprehensive plan prepared by the Department of Landscape Architecture and Regional Planning at University of Massachusetts–Amherst, with Professor Mark

Lindhult as the primary author. Milford, Massachusetts, is a fairly typical city for the Northeast, with a long industrial history bringing waves of immigration, and a variety of housing types and commerce and industry. Its 2000 population was just over 27,000, and it is located southwest of Boston. We chose this example both because we considered it to be a particularly well done comprehensive plan, and because Milford's challenges are relevant to many postindustrial communities across the country.

Within a plan element, a description of current conditions in the community is often included, along with data and conclusions about the future environment for the particular element. Development of a comprehensive plan generally involves the collection of pertinent data that provides a basis for understanding that element, and helps to identify future directions for policy-making. For example, a housing section often includes statistics about the current housing available in the community, demand for housing in the community and the region, and projections for future housing needs. From this data, the comprehensive plan will reach supportable conclusions as to unmet housing needs and glean from those conclusions the broad strategies for addressing the unmet needs, such as: increase rental housing supply, or enhance municipal capability in affordable housing implementation, or lower zoning barriers to constructing more modest dwellings. Specific action items might then include zoning amendments to permit multifamily housing in more districts and an inclusionary zoning provision. Other actions might include a proposal to create a local or regional housing opportunities agency. A cautionary note: the data included in the main body of the document should be sufficient only to make its analytical points. Beyond that level, data and analysis can bog down the reader in numbers and information, and so detailed data should be placed in appendices or separate volumes.

The implementation element (who is going to do what, when, how) has become an important part of a plan. Implementation sections list both long- and short-term measures to be undertaken to achieve the goals and objectives of the plan, and often assign tasks to boards and commissions, municipal departments, community organizations, and nonprofit service agencies, and suggest funding sources for the action. Progress should be examined annually against the goals of the plan in order to ensure that responsibilities are being met and to determine if additional actions are necessary.

Comprehensive plans are not exclusively in text and table format, but include other media, such as pictures and illustrative diagrams. Most plans include maps, such as land-use and zoning, and the trend is for additional maps to be included, depicting features such as natural resources and transportation infrastructure. Visuals are particularly important in helping a wide audience understand what the plan is trying to say. While older comprehensive plans were often focused on new growth, redevelopment in older communities and second-generation suburban reuse are increasingly present in newer plans. Also, plans for certain neighborhoods or sections of the community, often called functional or specific area plans, are often incorporated into the document.

Comprehensive plans must be internally consistent. For example, a call for affordable housing at the outskirts of town could conflict with a recommendation to put future transit links all in the center of town. In addition to internal consistency, plans are increasingly required to be consistent with the plans of neighboring communities, a regional planning agency or county, or even the state itself. In some cases, consistency with adjacent communities is addressed through a requirement for a "local coordination" element in the comprehensive plan. A situation where, for example, one community's plan calls for the creation of a business park that is adjacent to, and in the same watershed as the abutting town's water resources protection district suggests the need for compromises in the form of buffers, performance standards, or reductions in development intensity. Keep in mind as well that internal consistency also means that the division of a plan into topical elements, while allowing a more coherent and logically constructed document, is artificial. In reality, housing is not isolated from zoning, economic development from transportation, or public facilities from land-use changes. They are all integral parts of the same whole.

Roles and Responsibilities

The comprehensive planning process is typically led by either the local planning board or commission, or a specifically created master plan committee. The master plan committee often includes representatives from local boards, commissions, and departments. At a minimum, these boards should be asked for their input to and review of the

Milford, Massachusetts's 2003 Comprehensive Plan

Housing Recommendations

5.3 Recommendations

GOAL 1: Ensure that individuals and families in Milford have a full range of housing opportunities that include adequate ownership and rental options for low-, moderate-, and middle-income households and residents with and without disabilities.

Objective 1—Increase the amount of affordable housing in Milford, both under general affordability standards and Chapter 40B.

Action Steps:

1. Create an inclusionary zoning bylaw that requires all new residential developments to have 25 percent affordable units, or participate in a buyout option to help renovate existing units, which will be limited as affordable housing.
2. Create a Milford Housing Trust that will use CDBG funds and buy-out fees to purchase and renovate existing housing units that will be protected as affordable in perpetuity.
3. Continue to maintain a receiving area for affordable, multi-family units to direct residential growth to appropriate locations in mixed-use, mixed-income settings.
4. Create a linkage bylaw that establishes a fee for all new non-residential development to provide funds for new affordable housing.
5. Pass the Community Preservation Act to help fund the acquisition of affordable housing units.

Objective 2—Increase the variety of housing opportunities for low-, moderate-, and middle-income individuals and families.

Action Steps:

1. Continue to facilitate the creation of additional elderly housing that meets the needs of aging residents. As elder homeowners move out of their existing units, this strategy will make these units available for new homeowners.
2. Continue to allow for accessory housing and encourage smaller homes to ensure opportunities for households supportive of reduced resource consumption, elderly, disabled, and empty nester households in appropriate zoning districts.
3. Allow for multi-family housing in Milford 's zoning bylaws in appropriate areas. Consider creating a multi-family overlay district in the RA zone.

4. Continue preference for Milford residents in new affordable developments.

GOAL 2: Focus on the existing housing stock and its revitalization as a means to continue to attract new homeowners.

Objective 1—Encourage future infill development in a way that complements the existing character of neighborhoods.

Action Steps:

1. Encourage the development of housing on suitable vacant properties and promote infill development where appropriate.
2. Zone areas adjacent to the downtown for mixed-use to allow for small amounts of office and residential development, encouraging people to live near or where they work while preserving older homes.
3. Revise the dimensional requirements in the zoning by-law to allow infill units to meet the prevailing setbacks.
4. Expand areas for housing in proximity to the new senior center by rezoning appropriate areas of the IA zone for residential or mixed uses.

Objective 2—Work with private developers who can gain access to State and Federal programs that will allow Milford to address gaps in housing availability as identified in this study.

Action Steps:

1. Increase the number of single-family housing units participating in the Homeowner Rehabilitation (HOR) program.
2. Continue to encourage reinvestment in homes rather than relocating by providing technical assistance and incentives for those who cannot afford to maintain their homes on their own.
3. Offer incentives to landlords to improve their properties, including multi-family units.

Reprinted courtesy of the City of Milford and Mark Lindhult, principal author

comprehensive plan as it is developed. Neighboring communities, state agencies, regional planning agencies, and others are less frequently directly involved in the planning, but representation from such entities can be helpful. Once a general outline for the plan is developed, the committee often designates subcommittees to work on the various elements—for instance, an open space subcommittee, or a facilities subcommittee—to help in getting the work done more quickly.

In contrast to the historic practice of grand city designs prepared by renowned professionals, plan preparation since 1970 or earlier has moved gradually toward citizen-driven planning. Typically, a participation committee appointed by the chief administrative body, official, or planning entity lies at the heart of the process, acting in theory as a rough microcosm of the community, but sometimes consisting principally of citizens interested enough to become involved. Subcommittees may be spun off from the larger group. At a minimum, the group will act as an ongoing sounding board and partner to the consultants, professionals, and planning board. At the maximum, the committee will formulate, debate, and select all recommended strategies and actions. Broad public participation in developing a plan means it is more likely to get a favorable vote when it is time for its adoption, and then subsequently when zoning revisions are proposed to make the plan local law. This suggests a balanced role in the use of consultants to prepare plans. Goals should come from the community. A consultant can be very helpful in running public participation processes, but needs to have the input of the committee on how to reach people in that particular municipality. The consultant is often best placed to gather data and initially suggest policies to implement the community's goals, but final decisions on which policies to put in the plan need to come from the community. The importance of good public participation cannot be overstated, and it is a topic we return to in the section below.

Once a comprehensive plan is completed, in most states it must be adopted by the local governing body to have effect. Beyond local development and approval by the planning board or commission and/or the legislative body, increasingly regional and/or state review or approval is also required. These reviews will ensure that the plan is complete and that it conforms to planning objectives set by the state or region. Such reviews are often conducted under the premise that local interests do not necessarily conform to what is best for the region or state as a whole, as well as concern that local planning may exacerbate sprawling development patterns.

Public Participation

Planning is only a means to an end. We do not engage in a lengthy process for the sole purpose of producing a nice report of how we envision our community in the future. The comprehensive plan must be much more than that. It should be a road map to enable the community to reach a consensus vision of the future. Producing a document may be most expeditiously achieved by a small group of dedicated individuals working with professional planners, but completing a comprehensive plan that is a meaningful guide for achieving a community vision is a far different proposition. Producing a successful plan requires maximum participation of as many residents of the community as possible. If we are not committed to seeking out all perspectives and forging a broad consensus on our community's future, we will end up with the proverbial plan sitting untouched on the proverbial shelf.

Hundreds of citizens will turn out on short notice to protest a development that they deem unsuitable for their neighborhood, but we're often lucky if a dozen residents show up at a public meeting to provide input in the comprehensive planning process. Capturing the energy of those citizen protests in a comprehensive planning process is the challenge of our public participation effort.

There are techniques and gimmicks to capture the public's attention, ranging from traditional public meetings to Internet chat rooms about the community's future, but the essential ingredient in designing a successful public participation process is ensuring that the plan will be a real guide for implementation and that citizen input will truly make a difference.

It is important to spell out at the very beginning of the process the intent to follow through on the plan's recommendations in the form of zoning bylaw changes and other implementation techniques. Citizens should understand that the option of organizing a mass protest meeting against a proposed development is usually too late—most often a developer is simply following the laws, rules, and regulations that are already in place. And it will be through this planning process that those laws, rules, and regulations will be developed and modified by the community. The comprehensive planning process should anticipate those developments and engage the general public's energy in addressing their concerns before it is too late.

Technology has given us a great advantage in engaging the public in a comprehensive planning process. In addition to the traditional outreach tools, such as public meetings, hearings, and surveys, we have tools and techniques at our disposal that were unheard of twenty years ago. More innovative methods to engage the public might include the following:

- *Internet:* Chat rooms, Internet surveys, posting of issues and draft sections of the plan all can improve the public's access to the planning process. Remember, not everyone has access to this tool and not everyone is comfortable using it, so the Internet should not be an exclusive technique for public input. But it will give us broader access to the public, especially younger people most comfortable with this technology and often less apt to be engaged by a traditional planning process.
- *Community access television:* What could be better viewing than a TV show about the future of your community? Couple the medium of cable TV with visualization techniques (below), and you have a winner.
- *Visualization:* Computer software is available that will allow us to see (in the form of a computer simulation) what different development scenarios will actually look like. Using the "one picture is worth a thousand words" philosophy, these programs enable us to visually compare alternatives such as different streetscapes that would result from a strip mall with parking setbacks versus stores along the street with parking in the rear.
- *Buildout studies:* We can move beyond the usual tables of population, job, and traffic projections and get a much clearer view of where our community is headed by means of buildout studies. Theses studies project saturation development levels and associated impacts under different planning and development scenarios.

Invariably, the tried and true method of the public meeting or public hearing will be included as an outreach technique, often because it is written into state law as a requirement. In preparing presentations of community problems, alternative solutions, and final recommendations, remember that for the most part we are dealing with a subject that can be presented visually, and we should take advantage of that fact. Even though a zoning bylaw cannot be easily shown as a picture, the results can be, and undoubtedly there are numerous examples of those results available to us in neighboring communities. Use them. While a bylaw or planning objective seems dry and legalistic, a photograph of the desired result can speak volumes.

The Details of Comprehensive Plans

Great notions and inspired visions eventually encounter practical, financial, and political obstacles—usually near the conclusion of the comprehensive planning process. The discussion to this point has offered a broad overview of comprehensive planning. The sections to follow provide greater detail on plan-making, with the intention of helping communities create plans that have enhanced prospects for moving into real implementation, rather than remaining minimally used policy exercises.

The process of *data gathering* can be seductive—the temptation is to believe that surely more is better, and there must be one more piece of information out there that will prove the point. We must be careful to resist the temptation to gather and analyze data for its own sake; rather, we must make sure that the data serves our purposes. Data can tell us who we are as a community, where we are headed, and what the consequences are of alternative choices. If the data doesn't serve one of those purposes, we should probably bypass it.

A key role for data, however, is to sell the plan to skeptical local officials and residents. Nothing backs up your recommendations better than specific numbers. And if those numbers are in the form of dollars that can be saved by implementing the plan, then all the better.

In order to ensure that our data is useful to the comprehensive planning process, it is usually necessary to put it into a context of time and place.

- *Time:* Compare the most recent data sets with past years, and if possible, future years. This tells us where we are heading. For example, the median size of the households in our community is meaningless unless we know if it is growing or shrinking. The 2000 census shows that since 1990 the size of the average household in many

Table 5:1. Sample Data Sources

Data source	Useful data sets	Purpose
U.S. Census (Every 10 years)	Population Household size Age of population Racial/Ethnic profile Educational attainment Commuting destinations	Community growth trends Type and amount of needed housing Needs for services (schools, housing) Specialized needs Business development strategy Community's regional influence
State Environmental Agency	Public open space Air and water quality	Community's regional position Measure of quality of life
Regional Planning Agency/Metropolitan Planning Organization	Population projections Traffic counts Building permits Land use and zoning	Future needs Traffic analysis Housing growth rates Past and future growth trends
County business patterns (Census)	Economic data by industry	Economic growth trends
State employment office	Labor force/employment	Business development strategy
Area newspapers	Community circulation	Community's regional influence
State revenue agency	Tax rates	Community's competitive position

communities decreased by as much as 10 percent. This points toward patterns of a lower birth rate and an increase in single-head households.

- *Place:* Examine how your community fares when stacked up against comparable statistics for the region, state, and nation. If the average commute time for residents is much higher than those for the surrounding towns, it defines us as a classic bedroom community. Subscription data for area newspapers is also useful as an indicator of place. It will give us an idea of the residents' perception of the community's role in the larger region and aid us in knowing where residents travel to work, shop, and engage in cultural activities.

Data sources are more plentiful than ever, and the Internet makes them very accessible. Some of the best data sources, the types of data to be found, and potential uses for that data are shown in Table 5.1.

Remember that data is not solely numbers and tables. *Geographic Information System (GIS)* technology has revolutionized planning and data collection by allowing digital display of data in the form of computerized maps with accompanying tables of information. The cost of developing comprehensive GIS capability may be beyond the budget of many towns (due to both initial investment and ongoing operations), but fortunately, GIS data is available from an array of sources, including state agencies, regional planning agencies, utilities, and colleges and universities.

GIS information is organized in the form of data layers, or sets of information that can be displayed singly or together to provide us with a unique picture to answer a customized question. For example, we can produce a map that overlays public transportation routes with potential sites for housing for the elderly to evaluate the suitability of those housing sites. Or we may analyze the suitability of an area proposed for rezoning by overlaying it with a data layer of soil capability for onsite sewage disposal.

Typical GIS data layers that may be readily available from different sources include land use, environmental constraints (soils and wetlands), land ownership, transportation network, public open space, and the location of utilities. When converting paper maps to GIS maps, we refer to the new data that has been converted as digitized data. Many communities have all of their individually owned land parcels digitized for tax assessment purposes. (GIS is discussed more fully in chapter 7.)

Surveys can be another important tool in the planning process. Surveys of local residents and businesses can help set priorities in the comprehensive plan. There are many possibilities for distributing surveys, including household mailings, newspaper tear sheets, phone polling, the Internet, and high school or college class projects. All these methods have disadvantages—wide-spread mailings are costly while Internet options won't always reach a representative sample of the local population. But surveying local attitudes and priorities should give us useful data, and is an important step if for no other reason than giving residents a vested interest in the outcome of the planning process.

Design of the survey is of critical importance. In order to produce useful information, avoid simple yes-or-no questions such as "Do you favor lower taxes?" or "Do you want more preservation of open space in the community?" Respondents invariably answer in the affirmative, leaving us with no useful information. Ask residents to make choices or rank priorities.

Indicators are data sets that are popular methods for rating an area's quality of life or economic competitiveness. They are also often referred to as *benchmarks*. These are less traditional measures of community performance that are often undertaken by universities, newspapers, chambers of commerce, or regional planning agencies. Benchmarks or indicators may include an array of factors. Health statistics, natural species diversity, standardized school test results, acres of productive farmland, or measures of volunteer activity are some examples of widely used benchmarks or indicators. Example indicators are provided in Appendix A.

Evaluating Goals and Formulating Recommendations

The impetus for a community to prepare a comprehensive plan often comes in reaction to trends and developments that the residents don't like—loss of valued open space or excessive traffic or the desire for a broader property tax base. We have, to this point, developed a broad vision of what we want the community to be like in the future, we have analyzed statistical, graphic, and written data to gain an understanding of where the community has been and is

going if trends continue. Now we must turn our attention to what we want our plan to achieve. More specifically, we must ask if the visions and goals are supported by the analysis and recommendations from our work on the earlier sections of our plan. In other words, we have arrived at the critical juncture of translating our visions and goals into concrete actions. We may be in agreement that we want to preserve open space, create more affordable housing, revitalize our downtown, and expand our tax base—all while preserving our community character—but how do we accomplish these ambitious goals and realize these consensus ambitions?

Our first step is to review all visions and goals decided on throughout the planning process and develop specific objectives or strategies to accomplish each one—in the form of clear statements of what we hope to achieve. Here is where we take the broad concepts of the vision phases—the general community goals, what kind of community is desired—into a more specific realm, formulating approaches that will lead to a slate of particular action items. This is the critical interim phase linking the conceptual planning to implementation—the strategic thinking process that gets the plan set on its action-oriented course. We should apply three reality tests to objectives or strategies before making our action recommendations:

- *Consistency review:* Are the goals and objectives that have been developed throughout the planning process consistent with each other? Has the subcommittee working on water supply issues recommended development of a new municipal well where the recreation subcommittee wants ball fields? Are there recommendations for land uses along the community boundary that are in conflict with our neighbors? We are engaged in a comprehensive planning process (the key word being *comprehensive*), so we must resolve any conflict among the recommendations before proceeding.
- *Tools and techniques:* How do we expect to achieve our vision? We should match the recommendations with available methods to accomplish them. Sources of available tools and techniques are readily available, often tailored to individual states to conform to their laws. These tools may be in the form of laws and ordinances, rules and regulations, capital improvement programs, public

Milford, Massachusetts's 2003 Comprehensive Plan

Implementation Matrix, Section on Housing

In order to achieve this plan's goals and objectives, many Town boards, committees, and departments must be involved. The Planning Board will be primarily responsible for implementing this plan and updating it as necessary, but general consensus must be reached among all participants and the public. The matrix presented in this chapter identifies each action step recommended in the Plan, the board responsible for implementation, whether a town meeting (TM) vote is required, the general time frame, the type of action and the page where further background is provided. Responsible parties should report their progress in achieving progress to the Planning Board and Board of Selectmen on a regular basis.

Responsible Boards

BoH   Board of Health
BoS   Board of Selectmen
CC   Conservation Commission
CDO   Community Development Office
CIC   Capital Improvement Committee

HA   Housing Authority
HC   Historical Commission
HWY   Highway Department
IDC   Industrial Development Commission
MWC   Milford Water Company
OPE   Office of Planning and Engineering
OSAC   Open Space Advisory Committee
PB   Planning Board
PR   Parks and Recreation Department
ZBA   Zoning Board of Appeals

Time Frame

1 = Complete by 2006   2 = Complete by 2010
3 = Complete by 2025

Type of Action

R   Regulations   C   Continuing effort
F   Facilities and spending   P   Partnership
S   Study

Action Steps	Board	Town	Term	Type	Page
1 Create an inclusionary zoning bylaw.	PB	TM	1	R	51
2 Create a Milford Housing Trust that will use CDBG funds and buy-out fees to purchase, renovate, and limit existing housing units as affordable.	OPE, BoS		2	S	56
3 Continue to encourage new affordable housing under Chapter 40B to have its affordability secured in perpetuity.	ZBA		3	C	51–56
4 Continue to maintain a receiving area for affordable, multifamily units.	ZBA		2	C	51–56
5 Create a linkage bylaw that establishes a fee for all new non-residential development to provide funds for new affordable housing.	PB, BoS, TM		2	R	56
6 Pass the Community Preservation Act.	PB, BoS	TM			

Reprinted courtesy of the City of Milford and Mark Lindhult, principal author

education or investment in infrastructure and community amenities. Prepare a matrix of visions, goals, and objectives and the tools and techniques available to address them. This will help us to consolidate our ideas into a manageable set of recommendations.

- *Feasibility analysis:* Are the visions, goals, and objectives that have been developed throughout the planning process achievable? While we do not want to limit our vision by arbitrarily dismissing future goals for the community on the basis that "it's never been done before," we do want to separate those recommendations that need immediate attention from those that are less urgent. In structuring recommendations, we should divide them into short-term (0 to 5 years) and longer-term objectives. Cost is a relevant factor in evaluating objectives, but we must be careful not to constrain our vision simply because we think something is too expensive.

We have compiled our vision, goals, and objectives from the comprehensive planning process and examined their consistency, evaluated potential implementation techniques, and analyzed their feasibility. We have strategically organized our visions and goals into short- and long-term objectives. We have an idea of where we want our community to be and what route to follow to get there. But we are not finished.

The Policy Recommendation Process

Slates of action items need to be prepared—by either the consultant, professional staff, or members of the participation group—and vetted in a constant narrowing-down process in which recommendations (often, significant numbers of them) are eliminated, others are modified and qualified, and every proposed policy is debated, until consensus is finally reached.

Beyond this, action items need to be grouped by priority, in terms of importance to the community, or time frame, or, in some instances, relative ease of implementation, which gives approximately equal weight to the recommendations and then places the most readily attainable at the top of the list. Prioritizing acknowledges that only a small portion of the slate of action items can move forward in a given year or other time period, thus placing some kind of order on the many recommendations in the plan.

Following prioritization, it is important to assign implementation responsibility to the boards, committees, available professional staff, external service providers, nonprofit organizations, and other entities for every action item in the final plan. It is also usually a good idea to assign primary responsibility to one, or at the most two, parties in each instance. The purpose is to make the community aware that the plan will remain unachieved if the logical groups do not step up and take responsibility.

Examples of recommendations that are beyond the scope of local government—and who should be the responsible party—may include:

- Controls on access (curb cuts) to state highways—state highway department;
- Priority for funding for specified transportation improvements—regional planning agencies/MPO;
- Downtown façade improvements—local merchants association or downtown improvement association;
- Beautification at selected community locations—local garden club;
- Transportation demand management strategies—local employers.

When the policy recommendation process is completed, when the priorities, time frames, and responsible parties are identified and accepted by the participants group, the plan is ready for prime time. Getting to this point is almost always a negotiating process within the group, due to inevitable disagreement on particular recommendations. Priorities and time frames are often adjusted to attain consensus.

Comprehensive Plan Approval

If we have involved the public throughout the process and the final recommendations reflect their input and desires, approval of the plan should be achievable, but the form of that approval and the forums at which it takes place are important.

It is essential that those we are expecting to have a role in the plan's implementation sign off and agree to play their part—whether it's the chief elected officials, the planning board, or the local chamber of commerce. If they're being asked to take specific steps, ideally they should be asked to commit to them in writing.

In order to gain broader community acceptance, plan proponents may wish to conduct a post-planning public information campaign. It is usually a good idea to prepare a brief executive summary that contains the goals, strategic objectives and recommendations, and selected pieces of data and maps. A particularly effective format for a comprehensive plan summary is a fold-out map or satellite photo of the community depicting the plan's recommendations and their location. Visualizing recommendations in this manner is a particularly dramatic presentation technique (but also very expensive). The plan lays out the big picture, while zoning describes the exact borders involved. It may be helpful to use "fuzzy" borders or other ways to minimize arguments over the inclusion of a particular parcel in a proposal at this stage—otherwise community discussion can get very bogged down in details.

Comprehensive Plan Implementation

The key elements of implementation have all been discussed earlier, but cannot be emphasized enough. Many states require that all local laws and regulations be brought into conformance with the duly accepted comprehensive plan. This is an enormous advantage to the planning process, because it ensures that the process will not be ignored. Many states also require certification of consistency with state and regional plans and policies, which further ensures that the local process will not be an exercise in futility.

Regardless of whether or not your state requires bylaw conformity and regional and state consistency, these are the key elements of implementation—whether mandatory or voluntary. Because the plan is a road map, it must spell out how the visions, goals, and objectives are to be implemented. The most common methods recommended to implement a comprehensive plan are zoning and the capital improvement program, but general laws, subdivision regulations, non-regulatory initiatives, and other strategies are employed as well.

- *Zoning:* Matching our future and existing land uses to ensure compatibility is a prime goal of zoning. But it is a tool that can be used to address community character, vibrancy of neighborhoods, protection of natural resources, and even property values. (See the next chapter for more detail on zoning).

- *Capital improvement program:* No business can operate efficiently without a plan for scheduling investments to meet the needs of future growth. The same is true for a municipality. If the comprehensive plan tells us where we want to grow and the nature of the growth that we desire, the capital improvement program is a schedule of the infrastructure improvements to encourage and support that growth. Implicitly, by scheduling capital investments, it also serves to discourage growth where it is not wanted. Capital improvement programs should not be limited to roads, water and sewer investments, and schools, but should also include open space and recreation needs.

Other methods for plan implementation include historic preservation designations and districts, site plan approval laws, transfer of development rights programs, sign laws, farmland preservation programs, and designation of business improvement districts.

Very often, community members who get involved in local issues discover that their town's zoning is the problem, rather than the solution, as the existing zoning effectively prevents the sort of development that people want while making easy ugly, land-consuming, socially isolating development. Old zoning can significantly inhibit a municipality's ability to guide its future. Unfortunately, piecemeal corrections to zoning often don't address the underlying problems. When this starts to be the sense in the city, it is time to undertake a fundamental review of the city's vision and direction—it is time for a new comprehensive plan. The comprehensive planning process can be long, technical, and frustrating, particularly when the existing plan is significantly out of date. It is also the community's best chance to think strategically and long-term, to really envision what the community should be like in ten, twenty, fifty years, and to put in place the policies that will make that vision a reality.

This chapter has presented an overview of what is in a comprehensive plan and the steps that should be taken to prepare a meaningful new plan. Still, getting started can be daunting. Perhaps the best first step is to look around at communities in your general region that are similar in size and social makeup and find ones that you admire, ones that you would want to live in, ones that seem to be doing it right. Then call their planning board office and ask whether they have a comprehensive plan, and how you can get a copy. Gather up plans from several communities, and see what consultants worked with them on their plans, as well as what you like and do not like about the plans. You might also contact your local university. Planning programs often run studios with their students that can provide a good start to the planning effort (although studios cannot usually write the full comprehensive plan). Then, talk it over with the town planning staff, if you have them, or with your regional planning or county agency, if not. They will likely be familiar with funding sources for comprehensive planning and know local consultants. At that point you might want to turn to chapter 2 on coalition-building, because developing the municipal will for a new comprehensive plan will likely require good coalition-building skills. With a few good examples, the political will, and a good consultant or staff member on your side, the comprehensive planning process will be on its way.

References

American Planning Association. 1999. *Planning Communities for the 21st Century*. Available at: http://www.planning.org.

American Planning Association. 1998. *Growing Smart Legislative Guidebook*, Phase I and II Edition. September. Available at: http://www.planning.org.

Kaiser, Edward, David Godschalk, and F. Stuart Chapin, Jr. 1995. *Urban Land Use Planning. Chicago:* University of Chicago Press.

Kelly, Eric D., and Barbara Becker. 2000. *Community Planning: An Introduction to the Comprehensive Plan.* Washington, DC: Island Press.

Web Resources

American Farmland Trust: http://www.farmland.org/

American Planning Association: http://www.planning.org/

Citizens Planning Training Collaborative (Mass.): http://www.umass.edu/masscptc

Courtesy of Pictometry, MassHighway, and SRPEDD

6

Creative Zoning
Putting the Teeth in Your Planning

Jay Wickersham, Jack Wiggin, and Glenn Garber

F OR A LOCAL planning process to shape a community's future, it has to be given legal teeth. Citizens and local officials need to ensure that local regulations will reflect the goals of the plan. This, in turn, requires an understanding of zoning. Zoning is the most widely used and far-reaching form of land-use regulation in the United States. Through its zoning code, a community can define where residential, commercial, or industrial and other uses are located, the scale and extent of those uses, the size and shape of buildings, parking lots, and other physical features, and related aspects of the use of land.

The goal of this chapter is to help citizens and local officials employ zoning in a creative way to carry out community planning goals. The first part of the chapter provides an overview of how zoning evolved, and describes some of the shortcomings of conventional or "Euclidean" zoning. The second part describes the nuts and bolts of conventional zoning: the creation of uniform districts; the regulation of land uses; the bulk of buildings and density or minimum lot size; and the procedures through which zoning may be modified. This part also briefly examines the relationship between zoning and planning, and how zoning differs from other types of regulations affecting the use and development of land. The third part looks at a range of creative zoning tools that a community may employ to implement its planning goals: from protecting open space to redeveloping a town center to creating affordable housing. (Note: because the details of zoning laws vary widely from state to state and community to community, you should always consult an experienced lawyer before proposing specific changes to a local zoning code.)

Zoning: How Its History Challenges Us Today

In legal terms, zoning is an exercise of the police power: government's authority to regulate private property to protect the public health, safety, and welfare. Early precursors of zoning, enacted shortly after 1900 in Boston, Los Angeles, and other cities, capped building heights for fire protection purposes and set limits on the location of noxious industrial uses. In 1916 New York City passed the first comprehensive zoning ordinance, regulating both uses and building bulk on a city-wide basis.

Because in most states local governments do not have any intrinsic legal power, there must be a zoning enabling act passed by the state legislature, which delegates the power to zone to local governments. The first standardized State Zoning Enabling Act (SZEA) was developed by the U.S. Department of Commerce in 1924, under then-Secretary Herbert Hoover. The U.S. Supreme Court upheld the constitutionality of zoning in 1926, in *Village of Euclid v. Ambler Realty Co.,* 272 U.S. 365 (1926): hence the term "Euclidean zoning" to describe the standard model that still prevails today. The SZEA served as a national model, and by the 1930s some version had been adopted by nearly every state. Many zoning enabling acts today still resemble the SZEA.

A few states subscribe to the legal theory of home rule: cities and towns have independent legal power, including the power to zone. In those states the zoning law is not an enabling act, but rather an act that sets certain limits on how the local power to zone may be exercised. On a day-to-day basis, the practical difference between enabling act states and home rule states is small, since zoning is typically administered at the local level, with little or no direct state-level oversight. In court challenges, however, the enabling vs. home rule differences could be magnified.

Conventional or "Euclidean" zoning has changed relatively little since it was introduced in the 1920s. As the next part of this chapter will describe in more detail, zoning employs simple techniques that make it relatively easy for laypeople to understand and administer. As a result, zoning is a form of regulation that has largely remained under local control; it is not administered by expert agencies at the state or federal level. Zoning has remained politically popular because it maintains local control of land uses and their physical aspects and, thereby, of community character and growth patterns. Most important of all, because zoning provides predictability about allowable future uses to landowners, developers, and investors, it is widely seen as a form of government regulation that protects property values, particularly in residential areas.

But zoning's history means that conventional zoning is not always well suited to help communities face the challenges of today. The problems of rapidly growing cities in

Zoning and the Constitution

Government's authority to impose zoning restrictions arises from the police power: the power to regulate private property to protect the public health, safety, and welfare. The 1926 *Euclid* decision firmly established the legal power to restrict allowable land uses and the bulk and density of new development. More recent decisions have upheld the expansion of government regulation to such areas as visual appearance and historic preservation (*Penn Central Transportation Co. v. New York City,* 438 U.S. 104 (1978)), and the protection of open space (*Agins v. City of Tiburon,* 447 U.S. 255 (1980)).

The principal limit on government's regulatory power is the Takings Clause of the Fifth Amendment: "nor shall private property be taken for public use without just compensation." Since the 1920s, courts have applied the Takings Clause to require government compensation when a regulation deprives the landowner of all economically beneficial use of its land, unless such use would be barred on other grounds (for example, that it would pose a nuisance to neighboring landowners) (*Lucas v. South Carolina Coastal Council,* 505 U.S. 1003 (1992)). Note, however, that a severe diminishment in the value of the land will usually not qualify as a taking; courts rarely find that a taking has occurred unless the regulation is so restrictive that no development whatsoever—not even a single house—can be built on the property. Moreover, in measuring the impact of the regulation, the court will look at the value of the property as a whole (*Penn Central; Palazzolo v. State of Rhode Island,* 533 U.S. 606 (2001); *Tahoe-Sierra Preservation Council, Inc. v. Tahoe Regional Planning Agency,* 535 U.S. 302 (2002)). Thus, a regulation that renders one lot unbuildable in a multi-lot subdivision will likely not be viewed as a taking. Another controversial subject in takings law has been the increasing use of exactions in the regulatory process, which is discussed below in the text.

the early 1900s, in which factories, saloons, and boarding houses could be built within an existing residential neighborhood, are very different from the problems we face today: city and town centers trying to compete with suburban shopping malls, and large-scale suburban housing developments and office parks consuming natural resources without offering the lively mix of activities found in older communities. Conventional zoning has significant shortcomings: hence the need for the creative zoning tools described in this chapter. Some might argue that conventional zoning provides a (limited) degree of protection for farms, forests, wetlands, and other open spaces, while others would argue that zoning in the last half-century or more has been the primary vehicle for destruction of those resources. Conventional zoning often makes it difficult or impossible to recreate denser, mixed-use, pedestrian-friendly neighborhoods. Conventional zoning can exclude uses that are necessary to society as a whole—notably, affordable housing. And finally, conventional zoning is not necessarily based on a comprehensive planning process, and it perpetuates the disconnect between local land-use decisions and regional and state-level decisions on infrastructure investments and environmental protection.

The Nuts and Bolts of Conventional Zoning

Zoning codes are existing laws and, like all laws, are more easily modified than repealed and replaced. Citizens seeking to use zoning as a creative tool to shape their community's future must first understand the structure of conventional zoning codes, so that they can propose effective new techniques that will work within the existing legal framework. This section describes the basic techniques of conventional zoning: the creation of uniform districts and project-specific review procedures.

Uniform Zoning Districts and As-of-Right Entitlements

The basic tool of zoning is the division of a community into uniform districts, or zones. As a legal matter, uniform districts ensure that property owners will be treated fairly. Within each district, all property owners are subject to the same laws and standards, governing three principal factors: the allowable uses of the land and any buildings on

it, the allowable bulk (size and shape) of buildings, and the overall density of development, measured in square footage or housing units per unit of land area. District regulations define the "as-of-right" zoning entitlement for a property: the amount of development that the owner can presume without having to undergo a project-specific review process to receive a discretionary permit or other approval. Thus, uniform districts give property owners assurances as to what they, and their neighbors, will be permitted to do, thereby encouraging social stability and allowing confident financial investment.

Use Restrictions

Use restrictions apply both to buildings and to vacant land within the zoning district. Districts are generally classified as Residential, Commercial, and Industrial. There may then be further subclassifications of districts, such as: Single-Family, Two-Family, and Multi-Family Residential; Neighborhood and General Commercial; and Light and Heavy Industrial, or Mixed-Use zones. More specific designations have evolved as well, particularly in business zones, such as Office Park, or Research and Development, and for farmland protection.

The zoning code will generally contain a table listing the uses that are allowed within each type of district. These tables start with the "as-of-right" uses. The code will also list uses that are considered "accessory" to the allowed uses. For example, many Single-Family Residential zones will allow a limited home business, or a small apartment within the principal dwelling for a family member or a limited income renter, as accessory uses. Finally, the code may list certain uses that are "conditional" within a certain district, or in some way subject to further compliance tests before they can be permitted. (For conditional uses, see the discussion of special permits below.) Any use that is not specifically listed as allowed, accessory, or conditional is forbidden in that zoning district.

Most zoning codes, starting in the 1920s, initially used a system of cumulative or pyramidal use districts. (The term "pyramidal" refers to the way one can depict the system in a pyramid-shaped diagram: see Figure 6.1.) Under a cumulative system, the most restrictive use district is the Single-Family Residential, which is placed at the top of the pyramid because the principal allowable use is the single-family

District	Allowable uses

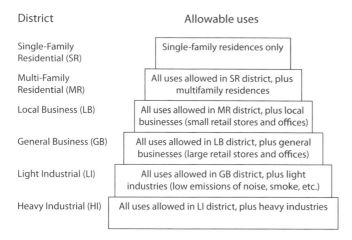

Single-Family Residential (SR) — Single-family residences only

Multi-Family Residential (MR) — All uses allowed in SR district, plus multifamily residences

Local Business (LB) — All uses allowed in MR district, plus local businesses (small retail stores and offices)

General Business (GB) — All uses allowed in LB district, plus general businesses (large retail stores and offices)

Light Industrial (LI) — All uses allowed in GB district, plus light industries (low emissions of noise, smoke, etc.)

Heavy Industrial (HI) — All uses allowed in LI district, plus heavy industries

Figure 6.1. Zoning pyramid.

house. As one steps down the pyramid, more uses are added in each district. The most permissive zone of all under the cumulative system is Heavy Industrial, where often anything goes.

Cumulative use districts are very restrictive at the top of the pyramid, but very permissive toward the bottom. This can give rise to conflicts, particularly when residential, commercial, and industrial uses are located close to one another. In response, some zoning codes have incorporated exclusive use districts. Under the exclusive use system, commercial and industrial zones, like residential, are limited to that particular set of uses. The result is a greater "sorting out" and separation of uses, of the kind that we observe in post–World War II suburban development, as opposed to the more fine-grained mixing of different uses that characterizes older urban areas (particularly those developed before the adoption of zoning in the 1920s). The down side of exclusive use is that it has tended to promote greater automotive dependency and more parking facilities, higher housing costs (because so much residential zoning has evolved only allowing single-family housing), and greater consumption of land and natural resources, because modern suburban densities are relatively low.

Dimensional and Bulk Restriction

For each district, the zoning code will set out restrictions on where buildings and other structures may be located within each separate parcel of land. The two basic restrictions consist of setbacks (also described as yard depths)—the distances that a building must be set back from the front, side, and rear lot lines—and maximum restrictions on building height, often expressed in both feet and number of stories. Combining these two sets of dimensional restrictions will yield the "maximum dimensional envelope": an imaginary three-dimensional volume of space within which a building may be located (see Figure 6.2). Refinements such as floor-to-area ratio, further discussed below, have evolved from these fundamental tools.

Density/Intensity Restrictions

Traditional dimensional restrictions may adequately control the level of development on a given lot. Sometimes, however, the maximum dimensional envelope may allow an overall amount of development that imposes significantly negative shadow (shade) and visual impacts on neighboring lots, or whose impact far exceeds the capacity of roads or sewers. For this reason, zoning codes also include density/intensity restrictions, aimed at regulating the maximum density of development within a district. (Density is the usual term for discussing residential development, while intensity is the term for industrial and commercial uses, but these are terms of art, not rigid terminology.)

For residential zones, the principal forms of density restrictions control minimum lot size, allowable units per lot, minimum street frontage, and maximum lot coverage. Minimum lot sizes for Single-Family Residential districts may vary from one-eighth acre to three acres or more. To prevent or limit the creation of "pork chop lots," in which one or more very closely spaced, narrow driveways lead off a street to a broader interior lot, codes may require that each lot have a minimum frontage on the street (minimum lot width requirements serve a similar purpose). Maximum lot coverage requirements limit the total amount of land area that may be occupied by buildings and other structures, thereby placing a ceiling on the total permissible building program on the site (see Figure 6.2).

In urban areas, the density of both residential and commercial districts is often controlled through the maximum floor-to-area ratio (FAR). FAR is calculated by dividing the total or gross square footage (of all floors) of the building by the total square footage of the lot. FAR has developed into a commonly used control that adds a multidimensional tool

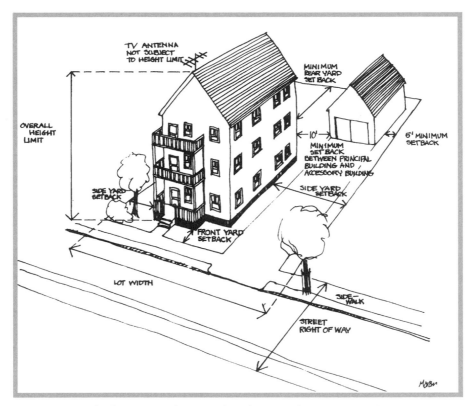

Figure 6.2. Example of a maximum dimensional envelope as set by zoning restrictions.
Source: *The Zoning Guide: A User Guide to the City of Cambridge Zoning Ordinance* by the Community Development Department, Community Planning Division, City of Cambridge, Mass. By permission.

to the kit, by relating the building program on a site, for however many stories there are, to the area of the lot. It is commonly employed in commercial/industrial districts. To fully understand the maximum zoning envelope for a particular parcel, therefore, one will need to look at both the dimensional requirements, which limit setbacks and heights, and at lot coverage, FAR, and other density restrictions.

Example: An FAR of 2.0 could permit a two-story building that occupies the entire lot, or a four-story building that occupies one-half of the lot, or an eight-story building that occupies one-quarter of the lot. (See Figure 6.3.)

Most zoning codes contain minimum requirements for off-street parking and loading areas. Instead of varying by district, these tend to vary by different types of uses, and to be applied uniformly throughout the entire community (except in some large cities). Parking requirements for residential districts are expressed as the number of required

parking spaces per dwelling unit. Parking requirements for commercial and industrial uses are often expressed as the number of required parking spaces per 1,000 square feet of development. (To avoid double-counting, parking garage space is usually not counted as part of the total building square footage for FAR purposes.) For commercial developments on suburban sites, off-street parking requirements often control the density on a lot, rather than setbacks, lot coverage, or FAR. While parking requirements are logical in an automobile-dependent society, widespread use of high parking ratios has produced the environmental degradation of excess paved area, the familiar "sea of parking" on sites everywhere.

Example: In a suburban zoning code, the parking requirement for retail development is six spaces /1,000 square feet. At a conservative calculation of 333 square feet per parking space (including driving lanes and access roads),

Creative Zoning

73

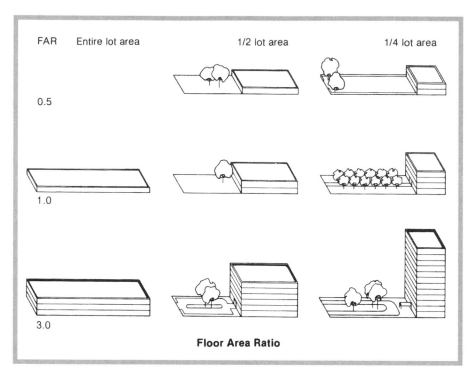

FAR   Entire lot area   1/2 lot area   1/4 lot area

0.5

1.0

3.0

Floor Area Ratio

Figure 6.3. Floor-to-area ratio examples.
Source: *The Zoning Guide*. By permission.

parking and roads will occupy two-thirds of the site, and the building can occupy no more than one-third— even before setbacks and other requirements are taken into account. Thus, this level of parking requirement effectively imposes a maximum FAR of about 0.3.

Overlay Districts

In addition to the basic use districts, a zoning code may define overlay districts that protect specific resources or encourage particular land uses. An overlay permits special protection or alternative development outcomes, while allowing the existing base zoning to remain in place, thus avoiding the difficulties and legal complexities of a wholesale district rezoning. The purposes of overlay districts may range from protecting environmental resources and public health and safety (such as an aquifer protection district, floodplain overlay district, or local wetlands protection law), to protecting historic resources and visual quality (a landmark or downtown business overlay district). The tool has often been used as a means of encouraging desired

redevelopment of deteriorating strip commercial areas. To determine the as-of-right zoning entitlement for a property within an overlay district, one compares the standards for the district and for the underlying zoning district, and applies the more stringent standard.

Grandfathering and Vested Zoning Rights

What about land uses or buildings or lots or setbacks that predate a zoning code, and do not comply with the current restrictions? Zoning codes universally have "grandfathering" provisions that allow the continuation of nonconforming uses and buildings and undersized lots. Some states freeze minimum lot sizes for a stipulated number of years, protecting a subdivider from more restrictive densities. In Massachusetts, some lots can enjoy such protection for up to eight years, with the filing of a simple preliminary subdivision plan, which usually ensures a boom in subdividing when zoning restrictions are proposed. The limit to grandfathering in the case of an existing use or structure typically comes with a full rebuilding, with any enlargement of a nonconforming structure, or a change from one nonconforming use to another type of use. These will typically require a variance or other form of zoning action to maintain the grandfathered condition, or the property will simply have to conform to the current code. Zoning codes also sometimes contain "amortization" provisions which require the termination of a nonconforming use after a certain period of time. Such provisions are typically not well enforced.

The general topic of nonconformity and grandfathering and related issues has historically presented a challenge in many states and has produced widely varying interpretations in case law.

Project-Specific Review Procedures to Increase Zoning Flexibility

Planners began to recognize the limitations of zoning and its inherent inflexibility beginning in the 1960s. This section describes a variety of project-specific review procedures that may be used to provide greater zoning flexibility than uniform district-wide rules. The first, site plan review, does not increase or reduce the as-of-right zoning entitlement for a property. When a property owner seeks to use a particular lot for a use that is not allowed as-of-right, or to construct or enlarge a building beyond the bulk and density requirements, the owner will have to undergo a procedure to obtain zoning relief: either a variance, an amendment, a special permit, or a planned unit development (PUD). This section concludes with a discussion of exactions: contributions of land or money that a property owner may be required to make as a condition of a project-specific review.

In crafting zoning reforms, citizens and local officials should consider the ways in which project-review procedures and exaction requirements may discourage desired forms of development. It may be preferable to provide incentives for desired development patterns by allowing them as-of-right, even at the cost of giving up some degree of control over project permitting and the exaction of public benefits.

Site Plan Review

Many zoning codes require projects of a certain size or type to undergo site plan review, usually by the planning board. Site plan review cannot be used to override the as-of-right provisions for land use, bulk, and density. Instead, it focuses more narrowly on the layout and design of structures, curb cuts and access drives, landscape buffers, parking, and other physical elements on a site, in order to reduce negative impacts from traffic, stormwater runoff, loss of greenery, and similar concerns. The zoning provisions should specify the size and/or use thresholds for projects that will require site plan review, and the standards by which they will be judged. Typically, site plan review is not a process for denying a project or causing its wholesale redesign, but it is a review where critical site "tinkering" can take place, to make a development more acceptable to or protective of the community.

Variances

Both the state-level zoning enabling act and the local zoning code will typically contain provisions for the granting of a variance, the narrowest standard of zoning relief. To obtain a variance from the as-of-right restrictions on a property, the owner appeals to the local zoning board of appeals (ZBA) or its equivalent. Both zoning codes and courts have made variances theoretically difficult to obtain, because of the fear that too many variances will undermine the uniformity and intent of the zoning district. Typically, the property owner must satisfy three tests: (1) strict imposition of the existing zoning requirements would constitute a substantial hardship—in effect, there would be a regulatory taking because there is no reasonable economic gain possible from the property, should the relief be denied; (2) there are special or unique circumstances pertinent to that lot (such as an irregular shape, steep slope, or poorly drained soils) that make strict compliance impractical; and (3) the variance would be consistent with the overall purpose of the zoning code. As a further limitation, in many jurisdictions only dimensional variances are allowed, and use variances are expressly forbidden.

Special Permits

A powerful and widely used portion of the zoning authority is the special permit. As previously noted, certain uses within a district may be classified as "conditional." A conditional use is allowed only upon the grant of a permit, known variously as a conditional use permit, a special permit, and an exception. We use the term "special permit" because special permits may also be employed to allow a greater intensity of development for certain uses within a district, such as cluster development or affordable housing in an otherwise single-family zone. In such instances, a special permit process can be seen as a kind of zoning relief.

Special permits (SP) are usually granted by the local planning board or commission, although the zoning code may specify otherwise (for example, having the town or city council grant the permit). Often, SP authority may be divided between the planning board or commission, the ZBA, and sometimes the chief executive or legislative board, such that commercial special permits go to the ZBA, residential permits go to the planning board, and public property privatization goes to the governing body, but the system varies greatly from community to community. The permit process will involve a public hearing and the submission of plans and studies by the property owner, demonstrating that the proposed project will not impose undue impacts on neighboring properties or public infrastructure. In addition to any preexisting standards, the local SP authority will typically impose case-specific conditions on a special permit, including measures to mitigate the project's impacts. These discretionary conditions may involve specific site planning constraints (such as an increased setback or reduced height in certain locations), physical road or sewer improvements, or the payment of mitigation money into a dedicated fund.

Example: The as-of-right requirements for an office building in a General Business District are defined as maximum height of 150 feet and maximum FAR of 3.0. Through the grant of a special permit, the zoning code allows a mixed-use development containing at least 50 percent residential uses, a maximum height of 250 feet, and a maximum FAR of 4.5. The planning board may impose permit conditions, including dedication of public open space and financial contributions to transportation mitigation improvements and a bikeway.

Amendments and Rezoning

Zoning may be changed by vote of the body that originally adopted it. Such modifications may be minor, such as clarifying the setback requirement for corner residential lots. Other modifications may be major, such as changing a remaining residential district on a roadway that has since developed as an intensive commercial strip, to an appropriate business designation. Sometimes the former action is referred to as an amendment, while the latter might be called a rezoning, but there is nothing hard and fast about those two terms. When a rezoning is applied to a single property, some caution is in order. Courts have placed certain restrictions on rezonings, particularly where they increase the intensity of use to benefit a specific property owner (these are called "up-zonings," as opposed to "down-zonings," which are amendments, typically sought by neighbors, to reduce the allowable intensity of use). A court will sometimes disallow a narrowly focused zoning amendment as improper "spot-zoning" when it appears solely to benefit a private individual and not to serve the common good.

Planned Unit Developments (PUDs)

The most far-reaching technique for project reviews is commonly known as the "Planned Unit Development," or PUD, a tool that evolved by the 1970s. A PUD is a set of highly site-specific zoning regulations which may be authorized either through the issuance of a special permit, or through the adoption of a zoning amendment, or both. PUDs often mix different housing types (single-family houses, townhouses, and apartments) and different types of uses (residential, office, and retail). In return for the wider mix of uses, greater densities, and more flexible dimensional restrictions, PUDs typically provide greater public benefits, both on-site (such as increased open space) and off-site (contributions to infrastructure improvements). The mechanism of a PUD offers landowners the chance to work with local officials and citizens to develop a more imaginative project design that meets both development and community goals, without being limited by the tight confines of Euclidean zoning. However, it is not good practice for the creation of PUDs to be entirely discretionary on a case-by-case basis. The zoning code should set out minimum land areas for projects to qualify as PUDs; many codes also cap the allowable height and density standards for such projects, and set minimum open space requirements and other parameters.

Exactions

Exactions are public benefits that a property owner must provide as a condition of a project-specific review procedure, to offset the potential impacts of the proposed development.

There are two principal types of exactions: land and money. Sometimes the developer may be required to dedicate a portion of the site for a public use to serve the new development: a park; a right-of-way for a road, transit line, or bicycle path; or a site for a fire station or school. More commonly a developer is required to pay for improvements to public infrastructure, such as roads, water supplies, sewers, or stormwater management systems, that will accommodate the increased impacts of the project. Such payments should be set aside in a dedicated account, to ensure they are used for their intended purpose.

Exactions have become widely used by cities and towns over the past thirty years, but the practice remains controversial. Developers often claim that requiring exactions imposes unequal costs upon new projects to provide public services that should be paid for by all taxpayers. Some citizens have argued that exactions may distort the development review process in the other direction, enabling the permitting of over-scaled projects. Where there is housing involved, some are concerned that mitigation fees or off-site subdivision improvements only add to the cost of dwellings. There has often been wrangling between applicants and regulators in regard to how distant from a site a capital improvement may lawfully be demanded when required as a site-specific mitigation.

In practice, local communities, particularly where there is a large project, will attempt to "exact" all manner of capital improvements, services, and fees from major developers, even when a nexus between the impact of the project and the desired improvements is not clearly present. Requesting excessive exactions creates a risk to the community. If challenged, such exactions could be found to be impermissible taxation, or the courts could void all or part of the exaction. In some locations, usually larger cities, the concept of spreading public benefits more equitably among other neighborhoods has led to linkage laws, which unquestionably broaden the range of the developer exaction issue. An example is requiring downtown office developers to pay into a fund for affordable housing in outlying neighborhoods. However, linkage is a limited technique not suitable for most communities or encouraged by statute.

Courts and legislatures have set some limits on the use of exactions. The U.S. Supreme Court has twice ruled on the constitutionality of land dedications under the Takings Clause of the Fifth Amendment. In *Nollan v. California Coastal Commission*, 483 U.S. 825 (1987), the Court held that there must be a "nexus" or relationship between the impacts of a project and the site area that it is required to be set aside for public use. In *Dolan v. City of Tigard*, 512 U.S. 374 (1994), the Court held that even where a nexus exists, the local permitting agency must show evidence that the exaction is "roughly proportional" to the project impacts. Although the U.S. Supreme Court has never ruled on the constitutionality of financial exactions, many state courts and legislatures have imposed similar rules on both land dedications and financial exactions, to ensure fairness and predictability for property owners. The lesson for communities is that exactions requests should be clearly related to the cost or scale of mitigations for the actual impact of the project. Many cities and towns have developed schedules that set predictable formulas for exaction payments, tied to the amount of the predicted cost of infrastructure improvements and proper study and documentation of these capital facilities needs. These systems are sometimes referred to as impact fees.

The Relationship of Zoning to Planning

The original SZEA stated that local zoning codes must be adopted "in accordance with a comprehensive plan." However, in the early years of zoning the practice of local land-use planning lagged behind zoning. When judges were asked to interpret the phrase "in accordance with a comprehensive plan" in situations in which no plan existed, they generally looked to the zoning code itself to determine whether an amendment or other change was consistent with the overall intent of the code.

Even today, legal requirements for the consistency of local zoning with local planning vary considerably from state to state. At one extreme are states such as Oregon, which requires the preparation of local plans, reviews those plans for their consistency with state-wide planning goals, and will strike down provisions of local zoning that are inconsistent with the approved plan. At the other extreme are states such as Massachusetts, which normally requires local planning, but then gives the plans that have been prepared little or no legal weight in the establishment or review of local zoning and other regulatory components. Most states today fall somewhere in between; at least two-thirds of the states either require local plans, or provide financial incentives to prepare plans, and they require some measure of consistency between local plans and zoning.

Other Regulations Affecting Land Development

In addition to the local zoning code, other forms of government regulation may shape the character and pace of future development. These include subdivision regulations, historic preservation regulations, and various environmental laws and regulations. It is important to note that these controls are legally distinct from zoning, although they may all apply to the same property involved in a zoning or subdivision action. For both landowners and citizens, this complexity underscores the importance of a local planning process, which can identify community-wide goals and then examine the most appropriate regulatory methods to put those goals into practice.

Subdivision Regulations

In every state there is a subdivision control law, distinct from the zoning enabling act, that authorizes local regulation of the process of subdividing land into multiple lots, prior to their development and sale. In the subdivision approval process, the local planning board will review the layout or upgrading of roads, stormwater facilities, and utilities, to ensure that they meet engineering and planning standards. Emerging nationally in the mid-twentieth century, subdivision control was seen as a means of protecting local communities from being burdened with the costs of infrastructure from new development, as well as assuring the engineering quality of that infrastructure, linking lot frontage on a street to the required improvements, avoiding nuisance conditions such as stormwater running from one property to another, and helping to assure an orderly pattern of development. In actuality, the subdivision has always been a "two-headed monster" in planning: by compelling high improvement standards, such as 50-foot-wide residential street rights-of-way, subdivisions tend to look overly improved and accommodate the automobile at the expense of common amenities and public domain. Some localities in recent years have countered with more modest street standards or an open viewpoint toward granting design waivers in the public interest, and requiring, where

allowed, public amenities and open space. Planning boards typically are empowered to create all subdivision regulations, requiring only a public hearing, rather than a vote of the chief legislative body.

Some large, multi-building commercial developments are leased rather than sold, so they do not have to undergo the subdivision review process. For these projects, the site plan review process, discussed above, is employed to afford some public control.

Historic Preservation Regulations

Depending on the state enabling laws, historic preservation restrictions may be implemented, either through local zoning or through other preservation laws and regulations administered by a separate historic district commission or historical commission.

Historic district regulations apply only to specific properties that have been designated as significant, either as an individual historic site or as part of a larger historic district. Once a property has been locally designated as historic, then approval will be required for exterior alterations. This is essentially architectural façade regulation. In some communities, review may be limited to major changes to a building; in others, it may regulate details as specific as window mullions or paint colors. Historic preservation regulations do not regulate the use to which a building or property is put, and they rarely extend to portions of buildings not visible from the street, or to the interior. Most regulations incorporate a variance procedure that allows a landowner to prove that strict compliance would impose an unsustainable economic burden. An entirely different preservation strategy employed in some places is to administer a demolition delay bylaw, which is further discussed below.

Environmental Controls from Higher Jurisdictions

Distinct from zoning, there is an enormous body of federal, state, and local environmental regulations that also dictate how land can be used and developed. Laws and policy initiatives such as the National Environmental Policy Act, the Clean Water Act and its amendments, the Safe Drinking Water Act, the EPA Stormwater Regulations, the Endangered Species Act, and other federal programs have led to reciprocal, directly connected laws and initiatives through- out the fifty states, administered by state environmental agencies and covering specific development projects and local governments. Some of these laws and regulations may be even more restrictive than zoning, at least with respect to certain properties—notably, environmental regulations pro- tecting wetlands, beaches, and endangered species. Many of these laws are further discussed in Section III of this book. These federal and state requirements in no way, however, preclude the need to engage in strong planning and regula- tion at the local level, with a comprehensive local planning process that can identify key environmental resources to be protected, and then specify the best regulatory tools to carry out those goals.

Creative Zoning: A Toolbox of Solutions

Over time, planners and designers have developed a wide array of new zoning tools to address the specific problems that arise with conventional zoning. We have grouped these creative zoning tools into categories, based on the problems they seek to correct:

- Providing better protection for farms, forests, wetlands, and other open spaces.
- Creating denser, mixed-use, pedestrian-friendly neigh- borhoods rather than single-use zones.
- Assuring that housing is available for most members of the community.
- Regulating the location and pace of development.

Preserving Open Space and Protecting Natural Resources

Cluster Development

Cluster development emerged in the 1960s, with roots in the earlier Garden Cities movement in England and the Green- belt movement in the United States. It has also been termed in its more recent incarnations a conservation or open space residential subdivision, which implies a more site-sensitive and qualitative design process, rather than a reliance upon quantitative formulas alone to set standards. These processes offer an alternative to the conventional subdivision of a par- cel of land into uniformly sized building lots that adhere strictly to the lot area and other dimensional requirements

of the zoning code and subdivision regulations. A cluster plan, by contrast, locates development on only a portion of a site, preserving the remainder in its natural condition or as common (or usable) open space. In this way, less of the site is disturbed by development, environmental impacts are reduced, and something of the pre-development site character is retained. Cluster design accomplishes this by reducing individual lot sizes and allowing flexibility in road standards, while allowing at least the same total number of lots as would be allowed under the conventional as-of-right entitlement. The landowner still realizes significant devel- opment potential, the costs of road and utility construc- tion often are less, open space is preserved at no cost to the public, and homeowners enjoy a permanent amenity. Some newer cluster bylaws determine the amount and location of land to be preserved based on site ecological characteristics rather than set formulas.

There are a number of options to consider in designing a cluster development regulation:

- Cluster design may be authorized as-of-right (although this is a rarity, due to the complexities of review) or through the granting of a special permit.
- Zoning may require cluster design (either as-of-right or through the special permit process) or provide for it as an option for developers.
- Cluster development may be applicable in all districts, only in certain districts or natural resource areas, or on a case-by-case basis. Mandatory clustering is usually sup- portable from a legal standpoint only in environmentally sensitive areas.
- Cluster provisions often, though not always, include a density bonus, procedural relief, or other incentive mech- anism as an inducement to cluster, or they might require a community benefit such as affordable housing.
- Regulations may specify permanent legal protection of open space through deed covenants or conservation restrictions, along with acceptable stewardship arrange- ments for control and maintenance of these spaces, often employing a local conservation board or a private non- profit to play this role. Ideally, this open space will include provisions for public access to it.
- Minimum dimensional requirements for lots and roads and other features may be specified in the zoning code or left to the project review process.

Agricultural Protection Zoning

An agricultural protection zone is intended to preserve existing farmland or land that has potential for agricultural production. In some places, this means requiring very large minimum lot sizes, usually in excess of 10 acres, and in a few places, 100 to 160 acres, usually reflecting local conditions of what is necessary for successful farming. It often involves limiting or even forbidding uses other than agriculture. The number of dwellings is typically limited; and sometimes new dwellings are required to be located on soils least suitable for agriculture and clustered on small lots whose development will not interfere with the efficient farm use of the rest of the land. This maximizes the amount of contiguous land still available to farm, while allowing farmers some profit from the residential development value of their land.

Agricultural zones have most commonly been successful, politically and legally, in areas where there is widespread recognition of the importance of agriculture to the local or regional economy and where farmland has not come under significant development pressures. It is important to differentiate true agricultural zoning from suburban large-lot zoning. Courts in some states, particularly more populous and urban ones, have not been supportive of large minimum zoning lots. The 1997 Massachusetts high court case in 1997, *Johnson v. Edgartown, 425 Mass. 117*, upheld three-acre zoning on the basis of fragile ecology, and the necessity to maintain community amenities in a tourism economy. This is effectively large-lot zoning, since even in Massachusetts a typical working farm requires more than three acres. True agricultural zoning typically exists on much larger acreage and is justified on the basis of encouraging agricultural retention by limiting development value of properties in the district or overlay. Many communities use large-lot zoning as a way to limit population growth in a community and the resultant impacts on public services, such as education costs, and to prevent construction of more modest homes. While there may be particular situations where large-lot zoning is appropriate, more often it maximizes land consumption, ensures sprawl, and adds to the affordable housing deficit. The cost of public services, from roads to sewer lines to school bus routes, increases with large-lot zoning. Wildlife habitat is fragmented into lots that are "too large to mow, too small to hay."

There are other tools and techniques that can be used to lessen development pressure and infringement on farming. Right-to-farm laws have been around for some time but are increasing in use. These laws acknowledge that "the farmer was there first" (before the subdivision), and establish a mediation process either to halt lawsuits against the farmer or to ameliorate perceived nuisance conditions from agricultural activity.

Another technique that is used in Pennsylvania, Maryland, Virginia, Michigan, California, Washington, North Carolina, Ohio and a number of other states is area-based allocation zoning. This technique creates dwelling entitlement formulas that compute the permitted number of non-farm dwellings in a way that is designed to encourage retention of larger parcels for agriculture, forestry, or natural resources protection. Area-based allocation zoning typically requires not only that the non-farm dwelling units be limited in number, but that they be built on relatively small lots; as a result, large areas of farmland are left intact.

Sometimes these formulas have a fixed-area basis: although the entitlement always stays at one dwelling unit per gross parcel, the overall parcel size varies and thus changes the allowable dwelling-to-parcel ratio.

Example: A zoning code allows one non-farm dwelling unit for every 15 acres of an agricultural parcel. A 15-acre parcel would permit the building of one non-farm dwelling, while a 75-acre parcel would yield 5 non-farm dwellings. The actual houses built would be located on lots that either front on an existing road, or are sited on the worst soils on the property.

Sliding-scale formulas are a variation on this theme, where the allowable maximum density of development is reduced proportionally as parcel sizes get bigger.

Example: A 10-acre lot under sliding-scale zoning might lawfully be subdivided into 2 lots, but a 50-acre parcel might have allowable dividing rights of only 4 lots, while a 200-acre tract would be divisible only into 8 lots. The relative entitlement or proportion of non-farm dwellings decreases as the parcel size increases.

When a ceiling is placed on the amount of lot creation in inverse ratio to the usual development entitlement, large tracts for open space, forestry, or agriculture are preserved. In addition, the houses that are built can be sited in the more developable areas of the parcel, removed from the best resource land.

Agricultural and area allocation-type zoning can be powerful techniques in areas where there are significant blocks of farming or active forestry (and, to a lesser degree of applicability, natural resources), but they can be open to legal challenge. Stringent density limitations could be deemed to be an uncompensated taking by the public regulatory authority. There have also been concerns raised that a control which promotes nearly exclusive use in a district is not a uniform standard, and that it prevents a fair share allocation among other reasonable uses. At the local legislative level, area allocation laws have been challenged by landowners: once they have built out their allowed number of units, they bring rezoning petitions to the local government to change or relax the applicable density limits.

Common Drives

A common drive is a private travel way providing access to multiple residential lots. It can serve as an alternative to a conventional road that would otherwise be necessary to meet the lot frontage requirements of the zoning code and the roadway standards of the subdivision rules. It is not meant to circumvent the adequate and safe access provisions of subdivision regulations; rather, it reduces the amount of landscape alteration that would be involved to build a full roadway or multiple driveways to serve a small number of lots. A common drive may better protect natural resources, in places where multiple individual driveways or a fully built cul-de-sac or subdivision street would alter the character of a scenic road or landscape.

Zoning and subdivision regulations need to include provisions defining the circumstances under which a common drive will be allowed. The regulations should specify parameters for such drives, such as length, width, geometry, quality of construction, and number of houses allowed on the drive. Since a common drive is not built to the subdivision standards for a public roadway, the lot owners are responsible for its maintenance, repair, and reconstruction; this should be noted in the regulations and stipulated in recorded covenants and easements.

Creating Walkable, Transit-Friendly, Mixed-Use Communities

Perhaps the greatest challenge in zoning reform is modifying an existing code to encourage the creation or preservation of walkable, transit-friendly, mixed-use communities. Conventional zoning responded to the ills of gritty, rapidly growing industrial cities by strictly separating different land uses, particularly residential from industrial, and in the post–World War II era, by promoting the "healthy" non-urban virtues of low-density single-family suburban lots. However, conventional zoning (loosely defined here as widely prevalent suburban land-use patterns) fails to address many of the qualities of site and building design that give a community its distinctive character. Parking requirements and roadway standards respond more to the needs of the automobile than the comfort, convenience, or safety of pedestrians. In general, a return to more compact and denser developments is one of the central tenets of the current smart growth movement.

This section starts by describing three situations in which alternative zoning approaches may produce more pedestrian-friendly results: village center or traditional neighborhood design zones; transit-oriented development zones; and urban overlay districts in existing centers. The section then discusses four specific sets of zoning techniques that may be used in all of these areas to achieve the planning goals: minimum density and mixed-use zoning; design guidelines; maximum parking requirements; and standards for walkable streets.

Village Center or Traditional Neighborhood Design

Whether called village center zoning, traditional neighborhood design (TND), or mixed-use zoning, this alternative to conventional zoning aims to produce a mix of residential, commercial, and civic uses at a relatively high density, reduce dependence on automobiles (or at least the typical length of auto trips), and create a safe, efficient, and pleasant pedestrian environment. Achieving some degree of design consistency is also a common objective. Typically, these guidelines are informed by the scale, densities, and mix of uses of the center's earlier, pre-zoning history.

The mechanism for achieving this outcome could be a new zoning district, but it is more commonly either specific amendments or an overlay zone covering the village/

town center area, in order to avoid the political challenge of wholesale elimination of zoning that might have been in place for decades. Village center zoning can be as simple as allowing multifamily residences as-of-right above first-floor retail stores, as a way to return a resident population to the center. In some communities, it might entail the addition of a few new or restored commercial uses to encourage more diverse investment in the area, or placing limitations on some uses ("we have too many banks, and no hardware stores"). If a sufficiently broad array of uses is already allowed in the district, relaxing rigid dimensional standards might be enough to produce the desired pattern. Alternatively, the bylaw can prescribe dimensional requirements for site coverage, height, setbacks, and parking requirements and location that better support the intended density and development pattern. Building, sign, and site design standards are often included. Minimum sidewalk and streetscape design standards, shared parking, and traffic calming measures can reinforce the overall objective. Local government should target its capital improvements to catalyze private investment, and consider public purchase of strategic parcels for redevelopment or public open space or other compatible public purposes.

Transit-Oriented Development

Transit-oriented development (TOD) describes areas that are designed and developed with a mix of uses and at a density to support and encourage the use of transit. TOD districts are centered on transit stops and extend out a walking distance of one-quarter to one-half mile. Development must be at a moderate to high density to produce sufficient transit ridership. A mixture of retail, commercial, and residential uses further supports transit use, and the related goal of an active and varied street life. The residential mix should include housing types suitable for and affordable by the elderly, students, and others who tend to rely on transit. Streets and sidewalks should be designed to be attractive and safe for walking and bicycling. Off-street parking requirements can be reduced and even capped, to further discourage automobile use and encourage denser development by reducing costs.

Urban Overlay Districts

In many older areas of a community that were developed prior to the era of modern zoning regulations, existing development patterns—lot size, setbacks, on-site parking, uses, and so forth—do not conform to current zoning requirements. As a result, unused second-floor office space may not be legally convertible to housing; efforts to establish new businesses in existing buildings may be thwarted by excessive on-site parking requirements or other zoning requirements. This may result in abandonment of the project or demolition of a viable building to create the required parking. The nonconforming status of such properties, which triggers additional review procedures, can also discourage property owners who are interested in redevelopment. Through the creation of an overlay district, the regulations can be adjusted to better accommodate existing conditions and provide incentives for redevelopment (such as as-of-right housing uses, and reduced setbacks and parking requirements), without compromising public health and safety.

Minimum Density and Mixed-Use Zoning

Creating or preserving a vital neighborhood, town center, or downtown may require a certain level of density and the intermingling of shops, restaurants, workplaces, and residences. But developers may not always choose maximum buildout, preferring instead to conform to an existing pattern of development or respond to a perceived desire for suburban-style development. To address these issues, zoning codes can define minimum densities in appropriate areas, and contain provisions that encourage mixed-use development.

Minimum density zoning carries out the goals of a community plan by establishing a threshold for development density below which the objectives for the area would not be achieved. The minimum density requirement may be expressed as a minimum floor-to-area ratio (FAR) for commercial development, and as a maximum lot size or minimum number of units per acre for residential development. For multiple lots, minimum density can be averaged over the entire development, allowing the mix of larger lots with smaller lots. This technique can be very helpful in increasing the supply of moderately priced housing in the community. The increase in zoning flexibility can make such projects economically viable.

Example: For an area targeted for multifamily residential development around a transit station, the zoning code defines a minimum density of 15 units per acre and a

Managing New Residential Development to Preserve Community Character, Protect Natural Resources, and Encourage Affordable Housing

Westwood, a suburban community outside of Boston, witnessed steadily increasing residential growth during the 1990s which threatened to consume all remaining undeveloped and unprotected land. During the process of preparing a new comprehensive plan that was issued in 2000, townspeople expressed concern with the effects of this development—specifically, the impacts on natural resources and scenic landscapes and the loss of open space. Further, there was the desire to have any new residential development contribute to the town's social and economic diversity.

The planning process and the plan's recommendations led to the drafting and adoption of an innovative technique for better managing new residential development. A new section of the zoning bylaw, Major Residential Development (MRD), gives the planning board greater involvement in *how* land is developed into residential lots and provides flexibility, creativity, and incentives to encourage superior design that is responsive to the characteristics of the site.

The MRD provisions require a special permit from the planning board for land divided into four or more lots (with a few exceptions). At least two substantially different schematic development plans for the site must be submitted for review. The plan which the planning board determines better responds to the bylaw's purposes and decision criteria proceeds through to approval.

To encourage better site design, dimensional regulations are relaxed, allowing lot area and frontage to be as little as is necessary to provide adequate access, meet board of health requirements, and provide a lot area (exclusive of wetlands) equal to five times the habitable floor area of the dwelling to be built on the lot (maximum allowable floor area is recorded on the plan). In other words, maximum habitable floor area is limited to one-fifth the lot area. Each residential lot on the plan must show potential building envelopes covering no more than 40 percent of the lot area or 20,000 square feet, whichever is greater. No yard setbacks constrain the location of the building envelope, but it cannot encompass wetlands, flood plain, slope greater than 25 percent, or areas of critical environmental importance or visual sensitivity. Density bonuses are awarded for units included in the plan that are legally reserved for the elderly, for moderate income, or for affordable housing.

The town's experience illustrates not only innovation in managing development, but also the importance of the planning process as a catalyst for action and for building community and leadership support for implementation.

---

maximum density of 25 units per acre. For a single-family transition zone located near the transit station, the code establishes a minimum lot size of 5,000 square feet and a maximum lot size of 7,500 square feet.

A publicly beneficial mixture of uses can be encouraged by offering density bonus incentives, through a special permit or PUD process. For example, to encourage residential development in a downtown area, projects containing at least 50 percent residential uses could be allowed greater height and FAR. Alternatively, the use of "split" zones can encourage mixed uses on an as-of-right basis. Split zones define the maximum density of both commercial and residential uses on a lot, and define the total FAR for the project. Thus, a developer has flexibility to respond to market forces in deciding whether or how to combine different project elements. But the developer cannot take advantage of the maximum buildout without developing a mixed-use project.

> *Example: Within a mixed-use zone along a commercial corridor that is targeted for greater residential uses, the zoning code sets a maximum FAR for commercial uses of 1.5, a maximum FAR for residential uses of 1.5, and a combined-use maximum total FAR of 2.0.*

Design Guidelines

Particularly but not exclusively within downtowns and neighborhood centers, design guidelines try to ensure that new construction has a character appropriate to its context. A community plan may determine that the massing, scale, height, roof form, window and door styles, materials, lighting, and other external features of new buildings should share or complement characteristics of existing development, respecting their scale, size, and features. Design review may also address site design, landscaping, driveways, and parking. Design guidelines should allow designers to exercise flexibility and creativity, rather than imposing a rigid uniformity of appearance.

Since the particular aspect of building appearance and materials is essentially architectural "skin" control—and therefore not within the domain of traditional zoning authority in most states—design review boards are often advisory in nature, rather than having statutory and final authority. Historic district commissions, by contrast, possess specific power in the area of architectural control. Design standards are often expressed and depicted in manuals, which are not ordinances or even regulations, but merely guidelines. However, a clearly constituted and active design review board can, in fact, have powerful influence over community redevelopment. In some places, its role is so strongly acknowledged that advisory authority effectively blurs into full regulatory power.

Guidelines for both site layout and building design can be made part of development reviews under zoning, both for projects allowed as-of-right and those subject to special permits or other project-specific procedures. The local authority has the discretion to apply the guidelines during its review of a project. The zoning code should specify the areas of the community and the types of projects to which design guidelines will apply, such as all projects in the town center, and large-scale commercial, mixed-use, or multi-family projects in other areas.

Maximum Parking Standards

Conventional zoning typically sets minimum parking standards, designed to ensure that all cars attracted by a certain use can be accommodated with on-site parking. This has had the effect of lowering development densities, producing large tracts of impervious pavement, and increasing area-wide traffic problems. To address these problems, some urban communities are establishing maximum, rather than minimum, limits on the number of parking spaces to be provided as part of a new development. Limiting the number of available parking spaces discourages automobile trips and provides incentives for a greater use of transit, bicycles, and walking, thereby relieving traffic congestion and improving

air quality. Reducing the amount of land dedicated to paved parking lots allows on-site development densities to be increased, while still preserving open space. It also reduces flooding and water pollution. Developments that need not invest in as much parking may be able to provide greater support for affordable housing.

Standards for Walkable Streets

Conventional roadway standards in zoning codes or subdivisions regulations respond more to the needs of the automobile than the comfort or convenience of pedestrians. Wide pavement, multiple lanes, large radius curves, and prohibitions against on-street parking tend to produce a car-dominated landscape and discourage walking. A pavement width of 20 feet (or even slightly less) is adequate for most two-lane neighborhood streets while still allowing access for public safety and maintenance vehicles; it also tends to serve as a traffic-calming measure, increasing neighborhood safety. Tighter radius turns at street corners require vehicles to slow down and shorten the distance that a pedestrian must walk across the street. Parking lanes slow traffic and serve as a physical and visual barrier between street and sidewalk.

Many suburban subdivisions are developed around cul-de-sacs. This pattern evolved because the construction of neighborhood streets to conventional standards facilitated their use as high-speed alternative routes. Cul-de-sacs may reduce the number and speed of vehicles on these roads by eliminating through traffic, but they also chop up neighborhoods into isolated units, at a cost of physical mobility and sociability. A network of connecting streets, properly designed, can better serve the community. Where cul-de-sacs are still desired or justified, they should be connected by paths for pedestrians and bicycles.

Inclusionary Zoning to Create Affordable Housing

Many communities have provisions in their zoning bylaws requiring the construction of affordable housing, or promoting it by offering incentives. The requirement to include affordable housing can be made part of special permit review. The zoning code would stipulate that a minimum percentage of the total number of units—10 to 20 percent are common levels—be made affordable in new housing

Rezoning to Transform a Railyard into a Transit-Oriented Neighborhood

In Cambridge, Massachusetts, 60 acres of abandoned railyards in the eastern part of the city offered an opportunity to create a new mixed-use neighborhood adjacent to an existing transit stop. The city placed a moratorium on new development while it undertook an 18-month public planning process. The process successfully brought together landowners and neighborhood representatives to develop a new vision for the area.

To implement the planning process, the city adopted new zoning for the area. Major projects require approval of a Planned Unit Development (PUD) by the planning board, through a special permit process. The new zoning requires an active mix of uses. PUDs cannot contain more than 35 percent non-residential development. While the maximum density is generally capped at an FAR of 2.4, densities may increase to as much as FAR 3.0 adjacent to the transit station, or for purely residential projects. At least 20 percent of the land area must be publicly usable parks, plazas, or sidewalks. A series of height zones ensure that taller buildings will be located away from existing neighborhoods, and where they will not cast shadows on public open space. So that new residents and workers will rely on transit and not driving, on-site parking is capped at a ratio of 0.4 to 0.5 spaces per 1,000 square feet of development. Design guidelines, applied through the PUD review process, strongly encourage the location of ground-floor shops, restaurants, and other active uses along major public streets.

Following the adoption of the new zoning, the planning board approved one 767-unit residential project in 2002, and a 4.5 million-square-foot mixed-use project, with 2,400 housing units, in 2003.

developments above a certain size. Some bylaws permit the developer to create affordable housing off-site or to make a financial contribution of equivalent value into a mitigation fund. There is sometimes controversy over these options, particularly with use of cash payments, which can in some instances lie unexpended in an escrow account if the designated entity fails to take the lead in housing initiatives, or if the fund lacks critical mass to achieve any real benefit. Inclusionary requirements may also be applied to large commercial developments which create demand for more housing. A requirement to provide affordable housing can also be imposed as a condition on projects seeking more density, floor area, or height than normally allowed.

As an incentive, the zoning code can provide density bonuses for developments providing affordable housing, both in multifamily projects and single-family subdivisions. In the latter case, flexible standards for lot dimensions and layout are necessary to accommodate the additional density and help reduce development costs.

Regulating the Location and Rate of Development

Growth Rate Controls

Growth rate controls seek to ensure that growth (usually residential) occurs in a gradual manner, so that the municipality can plan to provide and maintain public services commensurate with the demands of the new growth. A community can impose an annual town-wide cap on the issuance of building permits for new dwelling units for a stipulated period of time, or it can require the inclusion of a phased development schedule as a condition of individual project approvals. Some local codes include both provisions.

In the case of a growth cap, the zoning code limits the maximum number of building permits to be issued in a one-year period, usually based on recent local trends. For example, the number could be set at either the average number of permits issued over the last five years or at a level no higher than the highest number issued in any of the past eight years. The number can serve as either a cap or a threshold: in the latter case, once the maximum number of permits is exceeded, a phasing requirement is triggered for individual project reviews. A required phasing schedule can limit annual construction within an individual project either to a set number of units or to a percentage of the total—often on a scale graduated inversely to the magnitude of the project.

Example: Under a local phasing requirement, if an approved project contains five dwellings or less, the developer is allowed to develop 50 percent of the units in a year. For a project of six to ten units, the annual cap decreases to 40 percent; for a project of greater than ten units, it decreases to 30 percent.

The code may exempt from the growth controls certain types of projects, including renovations, single units on existing lots, and accessory dwellings. Other exemptions can be offered as incentives to achieve community-planning goals, such as exempting all affordable housing units. An exemption could be granted for each lot in a development for which one or more acres of open space or farmland is preserved. The phasing of a development could be accelerated if it utilizes a cluster site plan, village center provisions, or Transferable Development Rights, or if it is served by existing infrastructure. To provide fairness and predictability, some codes include a point system for rewarding these desirable attributes, with the number of points awarded or deducted based on a series of clear criteria (affordable housing, cluster, open space provisions, village center development, and so forth).

Community-wide rate-of-development laws offer something of a "breather" for local governments and residents when development pressures are significant. However, a considerable body of case law in the states has set limitations on these laws. They must be temporary in nature, must be proposed and adopted on the basis of a legitimate and demonstrable public need that justifies their use, and must be put into place to allow study and action that address that public need. For example, they can usually be justified while a community undertakes a new comprehensive planning and rezoning process. Phasing of units within a development has been less legally problematic.

Transferable Development Rights (TDRs)

A TDR program reduces development pressures on resources that need protection, like farmlands or historic properties, and allows denser development in appropriate locations, all the while trying to ensure financial equity so the process does not create winners and losers. TDRs are often used instead of significant rezoning which would reduce by-right development in some areas (down-zoning) and encourage higher density in others (up-zoning). Such wholesale rezoning creates big financial gains for landowners in up-zoned areas and big financial losses for those who had hoped to develop in down-zoned areas.

TDR is a regulatory technique that allows transfer of some or all of the development rights from one property to another. TDR is based on the legally supportable concept that the rights associated with property ownership are divisible and can be marketed. A TDR regulation delineates "sending areas," in which the allowable density of development is reduced, and "receiving areas," where increased density or intensity of development is permitted. Landowners in a sending area can sell their development rights to landowners in a receiving area, who are allowed to build at greater density as a result of buying those rights. Once development rights have been transferred from a sending property, its as-of-right buildout is permanently reduced.

TDR programs may be expressly enabled by state statute or be based on municipal authority. In some of the most successful programs, like the one in the New Jersey Pinelands, a publicly funded bank has been created to make a market. The bank purchases development rights from willing sellers and holds them until a buyer is found.

Example: In Massachusetts, Chapter 40A, section 9 of the General Laws authorizes municipal zoning ordinances to provide for TDR by special permit. The statute requires such ordinances or bylaws to "include incentives such as increases in density of population, intensity of use, amount of floor space or percentage of lot coverage, that encourage the transfer of development rights in a manner that protects open space, preserves farmland, promotes housing for persons of low and moderate income or furthers other community interests."

TDRs are not a simple technique to adopt or implement. Challenges occur in terms of determining the value of the TDRs to ensure financial equity, in public opposition to up-zoning in the receiving areas, and in the complications offered by the extra layer of the real estate transaction. However, with optimum conditions—a strong resource in the sending area, a receiving zone that is fully suitable, and a minimum of public opposition or other complications—

Using Demolition Delay to Preserve Affordable Housing

Nantucket's demolition delay ordinance dovetails with the local housing authority's program to salvage and move existing homes for affordable housing. The bylaw mandates a delay and requires the applicant to place an advertisement in the newspaper seeking anyone who would be willing to "adopt" the housing. Dozens of structures, including a number of modest cottages without historic significance, have been salvaged. Often the houses have been turned over to the new owner simply for the price of moving the structure. Another benefit of the program is the reduced amount of demolition material sent to the local landfill.

their use can be a highly effective tool for both protecting important natural and agricultural resources and increasing the vibrancy and livability of the receiving zone.

Demolition Delay Ordinances

A demolition delay ordinance requires that when an application is filed to demolish certain categories of structures, a fixed period of time must elapse before the issuance of the permit by the building official. This requirement most commonly applies to proposed demolition of historic structures; in such cases, the code will require the local historic commission's endorsement on the application. This gives the commission the power to delay endorsement for a stated period of time to pursue alternatives, such as moving the structure or finding a buyer with an interest in restoration or adaptive reuse.

This same procedure can be used for purposes other than historic preservation. Many communities are experiencing a trend of existing small dwellings being torn down and the lots being redeveloped with larger homes. If the existing structures could be saved, they could be a good source of relatively affordable housing stock. While demolition delays are, by legal precedent, on firmer ground with historic preservation, a few communities have identified all housing as a resource and applied this kind of law, but it is a strategy that is open to legal challenge.

Final Note: The Challenges of Implementation

For the past seventy-five years, zoning has been the country's most powerful land-use control tool—for better or for worse—and has been a major determinant of economic growth, the housing market, spatial development patterns, and community preservation. It is usually not a quick and easy process to craft and implement zoning changes by means of a vote of the local legislative body. Achieving revisions to zoning of any substance and scope requires technical and political acumen; this is particularly true for tools that might be considered advanced or complex. A number of the methods in the tool kit suggested in this chapter will clearly present such challenges.

If you are a public official, citizen-planner, community activist, or even a newcomer to professional practice, there are some helpful suggestions to keep in mind when considering a particular zoning initiative for your city, county, or town. First, talk early on to experienced professional zoning experts, public or private, to determine the opportunities and constraints presented by the initiative that you are considering. Use their guidance in proceeding, or even in not moving forward for the moment.

Next, obtain similar zoning laws and provisions from other places and be prepared to learn from—but not necessarily borrow wholesale from—these sources. Talk extensively to local officials and board members within your jurisdiction to assess the political impediments and support for the proposed measure, and to identify the hurdles to be jumped on the way to success. When drafting the actual law or amendment, if you have the luxury of some resources with which to hire some short-term professional legal or planning assistance, then do it. If not, then you and your colleagues should draft the language as best you can, drawing on relevant models, and shape it as specifically as you can to the needs of your community. Gather volunteer supporters to conduct a campaign leading up to the local legislative vote, preparing the strongest supporting public information you can and disseminating it as widely as possible. Above all, do not become discouraged when the political path becomes muddy; keep slogging forward because the public benefit you envision will be its own worthwhile reward.

References

Arendt, Randall. 1994. *Rural by Design*. Chicago: APA Press.

Babcock, Richard. 1966. *The Zoning Game*. Madison: University of Wisconsin Press.

Babcock, Richard, and Charles Siemens. 1985. *The Zoning Game Revisited*. Cambridge, MA: Lincoln Institute of Land Policy.

Duany, Andres, Elizabeth Plater-Zyberk, and Jeff Speck. 2000. *Suburban Nation: The Rise of Sprawl and the Decline of the American Dream*. New York: North Point Press.

Freilich, Robert H., and Michael M. Shultz. 1995. *Model Subdivision Regulations*. Chicago: American Planning Association.

Haar, Charles, and Jerold Kayden, eds. 1986. *Zoning and the American Dream*. Chicago: Planners' Press.

Jacobs, Jane. 1963. *The Death and Life of Great American Cities*. New York: Vintage Books.

Kunstler, James. 1993. *The Geography of Nowhere*. New York: Touchstone Books.

Kunstler, James. 1996. *Home from Nowhere: Remaking Our Everyday World for the 21st Century*. New York: Simon & Schuster.

Lacy, Jeffrey R. 2002. *Growth Management Tools: A Summary for Planning Boards in Massachusetts*. Metropolitan District Commission, Division of Watershed Management, Quabbin Reservoir Section.

Mandelker, Daniel. 2003. *Land Use Law*. New York: LexisNexis Matthew Bender.

Mandelker, Daniel, and John Payne. 2001. *Planning and Control of Land Development: Cases and Materials*. New York: LexisNexis Matthew Bender.

Meck, Stuart. 2002. *Growing Smart Legislative Guidebook: Model Statutes for Planning and the Management of Change, 2002 Edition*. Chicago: APA Planners Press. Available from http://www.planning.org/guidebook/.

Metropolitan Area Planning Council. 2000. *The Conservation Subdivision Design Project: Guide to Developing a Local Bylaw*. Funded by the Planning for Growth Program of the Massachusetts Executive Office of Environmental Affairs. Boston.

Toll, Seymour. 1969. *Zoned American*. New York, Grossman.

Wickersham, Jay. 2001. "Jane Jacobs's Critique of Zoning: From *Euclid* to Portland and Beyond." *Boston College Environmental Affairs Law Review*, 28 (4): 547.

Ziegler, Edward, ed. 2004. *Rathkopf's The Law of Zoning and Planning*. Eagan, MN: Clark Boardman Callaghan/West/Thomson.

Web Resources

American Planning Association: *http://www.planning.org*. Many resources on smart growth, zoning, conferences, and publications.

Citizen Planner Training Collaborative: *http://www.umass.edu/masscptc/*. Educational opportunities, sample zoning bylaws.

Cape Cod Commission: *http://www.vsa.cape.com/~cccom/home.htm*. Regional planning and regulatory agency. Excellent model bylaws.

Mashpee Commons: *http://www.mashpeecommons.com/mashcomlp/about.htm*. Information about Mashpee Commons and excellent list of resources on new urbanism.

Municipal Code Corporation: *http://www.municode.com/*. Source of municipal regulations (including zoning ordinances) on-line.

Smart Growth Network: *http://www.smartgrowth.org/index.html*. Good references to sources of information on most aspects of community preservation.

Sustainable Communities Network: *http://www.sustainable.org/*. Source of references and case studies.

0.4 0.2 0   0.4   0.8   1.2   1.6 Miles

Photo: Mark Lindhult

Current and Future Land Use

GIS Applied

Jane Pfister, John Hultgren, Christian Jacqz, and Richard Taupier

W E ALL HAVE maps in our heads. Mental maps are the way we organize and envision our communities. But most people have a hard time imagining a landscape that hasn't yet happened. Decisions affecting the landscape are made piecemeal by both private and public entities, and changes happen incrementally and imperceptibly over time. Because of the private nature of development, most decisions are made with little connection to a shared vision of place. Geographic Information System (GIS) maps are becoming one way to address this problem. With GIS maps, the current situation on the ground can be viewed and evaluated and proposed changes can be modeled to show their effects. GIS maps can be powerful marketing tools and can facilitate public discussions.

Such public discussions, however, too often assume that all participants in these conversations are familiar with GIS and understand the ways the system works. This knowledge may not be in place. Thus, this chapter is intended to assist citizen-planners in becoming familiar with the rudiments of GIS mapping and with some of the ways that this technology can become a resource to citizens as they work with planners to envision the future of their communities and regions. This chapter begins with a definition of GIS and a bit of its history, then moves to a brief description of its four elements, and finally turns to a detailed Massachusetts case study to illustrate the diverse ways in which GIS is being used in planning.

What Is GIS?

In technical terms, GIS is a computer-based system that aids in the collection, storage, analysis, and display of spatial information. Such a system combines the capability to represent geographic features, both natural (such as rivers) and built (such as roads), with relational databases and tools for statistical analysis. A geographic information system enables planners to link various types of information, perform analyses, and communicate the results using maps. Data from a municipality's numerous departments, such as planning, transportation, and economic development, can be brought together, and then trends and interactions can be analyzed and visualized. GIS is well suited for identifying and analyzing factors that contribute to land-use patterns and identifying potential solutions. Better decisions can be the result.

Such systems are relatively new. Their development began in the mid 1960s, but during the first decade their uses were primarily exploratory, with large governmental organizations committing significant resources to developing this new technology. The systems have matured over recent decades and now are able to take advantage of the faster processing capabilities and greater data storage capacities of desktop computers.

The cost of GIS hardware and software is currently only a fraction of what it was twenty years ago. Today's typical GIS can be run on a desktop computer, often under the Windows operating system. As a result, many moderately sized municipalities, public and nonprofit organizations, and even small businesses can afford to purchase GIS. The range of data input technologies has grown as well, and organizations are finding effective ways to share data and maps to illustrate proposed plans or to show land-use conflicts, issues, and opportunities. Now virtually any moderately sized organization involved in land-use planning and regulation can be an effective consumer of GIS data and products and an effective user of GIS technology.

Because GIS has become so common, citizen-planners are likely to encounter it in many contexts. To be informed users of GIS, citizen-planners will need to be familiar with each of the four major "elements" of a GIS: (1) hardware, (2) software, (3) data, and (4) people.

Hardware: The hardware most often used for GIS is a single desktop computer or a network of desktop machines linked to a server on which data is stored. The cost of such a system typically ranges from about $2,000 to $3,000, depending on the computer's processing speed and RAM, screen size, amount of storage space, and whether a graphic accelerator has been added to increase output to the screen. For stand-alone systems some sort of backup data storage system is crucial so that system crashes don't result in the loss of project files or thousands of dollars of data.

Other, more specialized hardware equipment is also sometimes used in order to enhance data input and output capabilities. Global Positioning Satellite (GPS) units, for example, are sometimes used to gather new information from the field or to add greater accuracy to existing spatial data sets. Videography combined with GPS mounted on vehicles is also sometimes used to document road conditions or enable better pavement management. Similar systems mounted on small planes allow for rapid observations of damages from natural disasters, conditions of vegetative cover, or oil spills that may compromise coastal environments. Hardware equipment used for output often includes large-scale plotters or mid-size plotters, with the latter useful for routine applications (large images can be shown using computer screen projectors or sent off as PDF files that can be opened on virtually any computer and viewed at a wide range of magnification scales).

Software: Contemporary GIS software offers an impressive array of functions for relatively little expense. Organizations should expect to pay around $1,000 for a full-featured GIS package such as ArcView, MapInfo, or GeoMedia, and any of these common GIS software packages will provide nearly all of the GIS capabilities that most small-to-mid-size organizations will require. If additional capabilities are needed for more specialized projects, many GIS programs allow for the purchase of add-on software.

Data: Data creation remains the most expensive and time-consuming of the four major elements of a GIS, especially whenever the needed data has not previously been entered into a database and must be collected and entered by hand. Increasingly, however, prepackaged GIS-ready data is accessible from state and federal agencies (we later describe some of those prepackaged data sets[1]), and many agencies make available to the public millions of dollars worth of data. Digital photos are commonly obtainable as are large-scale data sets that show road networks and water features. It is now possible to build what are called base maps on which data sets of more local interest (zoning and parcel data, local infrastructure, or detailed land-use information) can easily be displayed.

People: Although at first glance it might appear odd to refer to people as "an element," in point of fact the individuals who administer a GIS operation and keep data current are crucial to the success of GIS. Even with all the advances in GIS software and data, these systems continue to be run

---

1. All states now make most of their GIS data publicly available, often over the Internet. Thus all states have made possible many applications of GIS to planning activities simply by virtue of the fact that they have made available data sets that would be well beyond the ability of local organizations to fund.

by specialists. Despite their importance, the people who staff any GIS operation remain the element that is most often overlooked and underappreciated. Municipal GIS offices have occasionally fallen apart when a key staff person left or the position was not funded in the next year's budget, and organizations that address system and data startup costs but fail to consider the annual costs of operation often flounder in achieving their GIS goals. The hardware, software, and data, much like bones, nerves, and muscles, cannot function without intelligence. Borrowing part of the time of a staff person as a way to build a functional GIS is also rarely successful because the software and data are sufficiently complex that the staff person needs a high degree of familiarity with them to make usage viable.

The four elements of GIS have now been briefly described, but what makes a good map? Good maps have some common elements including a title, north arrow, date and author, legend or key defining the map's symbols, scale, citation of data sources, and an inset or "locus" map locating the map within its larger geographic context. Scale shows the relationship of map distances to actual distances on the earth's surface. Scale can be expressed in three basic ways; as a ratio or representative fraction, a word statement, or a graphic scale. Most references to scale in this chapter are ratios or representative fractions which indicate how many units on the ground are equal to one unit on the map. For example, 1/25,000 means 25,000 inches (or other unit) on the ground is equal to one inch (or other unit) on the map. This relationship is very important to GIS data too because it indicates the relative geographic accuracy of the data itself. Maps are often known as large or small scale. A large-scale map shows greater detail because the representative fraction is a larger fraction, and consequently a smaller area of land is shown with greater detail or geographic accuracy.

These elements together result in complex, readily updatable maps of a sort not envisioned until the advent of GIS. With GIS maps it becomes possible to show relationships between past and present, to picture land uses of different sorts, or to model impacts of various community decisions. Maps become available for public discussions.

Examples of the Role of GIS in Planning

Many very simple land-use studies become feasible to do once a municipality has GIS capability—whether it invests in its own, works with its regional planning agency, or collaborates with a local college or private firm. It has become quite easy to create maps that show the relationships between zoning and actual land use, the loss of wetlands and agricultural lands, the spread of residential development, the need for additional industrial land, or the location of brownfields and other sites where pollution could quickly affect natural resources and people in vulnerable conditions.

Additionally, other types of planning become possible when GIS and new digital data sets are available. Watershed data can be used to display the full range of inputs to surface and groundwater resources and to study how the concentrations of different land uses could protect against threats from non-point source pollution. With such information, municipalities are able to see their role in a broader watershed ecosystem and understand how they affect and are affected by the upstream and downstream activities of their neighboring communities. Towns are able to consider the economic landscapes by using various types of employment, income, and purchasing data to map where people live, work, and shop (Plate 1).

With the availability of GIS, residents can become more active partners in these planning processes, ensuring that information used in analyses is complete and accurate. They can become advocates for the multiple perspectives that need to be balanced in a final plan. Citizens can build coalitions around issues and help persuade others to support a position or alter a proposed plan. In New Jersey, the community-based organization Hopeworks 'N Camden created a GIS map of dead streetlights in one neighborhood so that their group and local citizens could advocate more effectively for important infrastructure upkeep (Plate 2). The result has been a safer neighborhood (http://www.hopeworks .org). New uses of GIS technology, such as interactive town meetings, in which illustrations of competing plans can occur and real-time voting for alternatives can take place, are beginning to democratize planning and create the kind of participatory process for which many have long hoped.

Perhaps most important, citizens can access the same information used by experts, since virtually all public agencies in the United States have put their GIS data in the public domain. Although maps themselves have occasionally been used to obfuscate rather than clarify, more often the availability of maps has provided opportunities for local citizens to use their local knowledge to identify errors or see things on a map that are inaccurately shown or misleading. Thus, GIS maps can serve as a reality check on just how well local, regional, and state planners understand local conditions and the problems that they are attempting to resolve.

It has long been hoped that GIS software eventually would be in the hands of so many citizens that they would be able to take the same data sets used by the experts and create their own maps, thereby checking the validity of the analytical outputs of the expert-generated GIS maps. Such detailed use of GIS has yet to happen to a significant degree and so most often, even while the same data is readily available to citizens and experts alike, the vast majority of citizens must still view the data on maps created by others. In most cases that is adequate, but in adversarial situations the only way to verify the validity of GIS output can be to hire your own expert.

Data Sources and the Role of States

The sources of GIS data need to be well understood. In this regard, it is important to grasp the key role that states and other regional entities have played in generating base maps as well as other kinds of data essential to community planning. Individual states have devoted years, and in some cases decades, to creating databases that enable cities and towns to carry out detailed land-use planning. Without these databases (as well as those generated by the federal government) the GIS uses by municipalities described in this chapter would not be possible.

The way each state has drawn on the capabilities of GIS has been shaped by the challenges faced by that state. Individual states direct their efforts in different ways depending on the salience of different issues. Consider the densely populated state of Massachusetts. The Commonwealth has a long history of using GIS for planning activities at the local, regional, and state levels, with the range of uses continuing to grow. Initial interest in the 1980s focused on assessing conditions for locating hazardous waste treatment facilities. This emphasis was quickly followed with mapping of state-owned open space in order to monitor land-use changes. For over three decades, the loss of farmland, forests, and natural areas has continued to be a significant issue in Massachusetts, and GIS technology has been used to track, analyze, and illustrate how the landscape of the Commonwealth is being changed.

These land-use analyses were made possible by the state's commitment to creating many data sets at scales large enough to make the sets useful for both regional and municipal-level studies. Generally, data sets at scales from 1/25,000 to 1/100,000 are considered regional-scale data sets in that they show some detail but not so much as to make them too unwieldy to be used. Points and lines in data sets at 1/25,000 are accurate within 40 feet. Local-scale data sets for a densely populated area such as Massachusetts are generally at scales of 1/12,000 or 1/5,000, and some even at 1/1,200, wherein 1 inch would equal 100 feet on a map printed at scale. One of the many strengths of modern GIS software is that it can combine data at many different scales.

In Massachusetts, the greatest breakthrough in allowing more effective use of GIS for local-level planning came in the 1990s when the state decided to move ahead with a statewide program for creating what are called digital orthophotos at a scale of 1/5,000. Orthophotos are high-resolution geo-referenced images that have been corrected to remove distortions; they have been used to create a highly accurate base map for the entire state that has been used to improve other state-wide data sets such as roads, wetlands, and surface water features at that same scale and that allow for locational accuracies of within 10 feet (see Plates 3 and 4, following p. 98). Image base maps at that scale were also becoming highly suitable for the display of parcel boundaries and public rights-of-way. And, since state Department of Revenue regulations required the current accurate parcel maps, many towns took advantage of GIS technology to develop digital parcel maps that would allow the display of parcel data together with all the other digital data sets becoming available at the state level.

Also in the decade of the '90s, Massachusetts took other steps that encouraged use of GIS. Massachusetts mandated that GIS maps be included in the Open Space Plans created by any city or town. The ongoing updates through GIS of open lands protected by the state and federal governments, municipalities, land trusts, and other nonprofits enabled towns to begin to have a better sense of which lands were already under protection and which new lands should be considered for protection if open space goals were to be met.

Massachusetts also funded the mapping of statewide land use for 1971, 1985, and 1999. This land-use data could then be used to show the locations of changes with relative ease. State, regional, and local land-use planners could quickly see areas where rapid growth has become a threat to natural resources such as water, agricultural lands, and wildlife habitat. Moreover, planners could track how rapidly undeveloped land is being developed and how different zoning approaches are encouraging development to be quicker or slower, more sprawling or more compact.

Perhaps the greatest resource for local land-use planning provided by the state—and one that shows the remarkable capabilities of GIS—was individual buildout analyses for each and every city and town in Massachusetts. These buildout analyses are an important part of the story of how citizens and city planners, given the tools they need and want, can contribute to discussions about the future of their cities.

Community Planning Tools

What Is a Buildout Analysis?

A daunting planning task most communities face is to understand where things stand with regard to past, present, and future land use. In other words, how is land currently being used (e.g., where are the different types of housing, shops, and business located)? What will happen if existing land-use rules, zoning, and practices stay in place (e.g., how many new homes can be added, where will the industrial plants for companies be allowed)? This is where a buildout analysis using GIS and bringing together otherwise unwieldy amounts of data can come into play.

The simplest description of a buildout analysis is that it is a process by which a community can estimate the amount of additional development allowable under current zoning and other rules, the limitations to development created by those rules, and the likely impacts of currently allowable development on the community's natural and fiscal resources and infrastructure. Buildout analyses are often focused on residential land use, as this category of land use is expanding most rapidly and occupies the greatest total land area. Buildouts can, however, also be oriented to commercial and industrial land uses or a combination of all three. More specialized buildout models, which may be more aptly titled impact models, can be used to estimate the impacts of a significant development, such as a major new manufacturing facility, with many new employees who will need homes and increased infrastructure, and who will introduce a large contingent of new children into the local school systems.

Buildout models differ in terms of the inputs they require, the outputs they produce, and the analyses they use. Regardless of the specifics, however, on the input side buildout models typically require current land-use data, zoning, population growth projections, data on environmental constraints such as wetlands, steep slopes, and critical wildlife habitat, data on protected areas such as parks and watershed protection lands, conservation easements, agricultural preservation restrictions, and nonprofit conservation areas such as those owned by the Nature Conservancy or local land trusts that cannot be developed as a result of deeded restrictions.

The typical buildout model looks first at those lands that are already developed and are unlikely to be able to absorb additional residential units. Assumptions are made that none of the new growth will occur in these previously developed areas or that only a specific percentage of new growth will be accommodated by infill development (i.e., building on scattered lots).

In the typical buildout model, protected areas (such as wetlands) are also subtracted from the inventory of developable land. A map might be created that shows the combination of current land uses as well as those lands that are available for development. Once protected areas have been identified, the buildout analysis can then move in either of two directions. The most likely direction is to begin to consider the environmental constraints of water, wetlands, floodplains, and steep slopes, which are then treated as either partial or absolute constraints.[2]

A zoning overlay is then applied so that minimum lot sizes can be calculated for all areas and the maximum number of new lots can be estimated based on current zoning regulations. Population data can be used, in combination

---

2. Absolute constraints are those areas where no development could occur under normal conditions. But even an area with very steep slopes could see some development in dispersed flat areas if builders are willing to spend the additional resources to provide access. Generally areas of absolute constraint are also subtracted from lands that are currently available for development. Partial constraints can be addressed in a couple of ways. Wetlands, floodplains, and moderate slopes can be viewed as constraints that require larger building lots or as constraints that reduce the land available for development by a fixed or variable percentage. The modelers may assume that building lots with partial constraints will have to be twice as large as zoned or that only 50% of the land that falls under a partial constraint can be developed. The result is generally the same, but the process differs. After partial constraints have been included in the model, a map or calculation of net usable land area (NULA) is created.

with household size, to project how many new houses and how much additional land will be consumed in five, ten, or twenty years given a specified rate of population growth. The model can estimate how many years will pass before all the available land will be consumed by new residential units if the current zoning laws remain unchanged.

As noted above, many useful outputs can be produced through these sophisticated buildout models. Outputs can include calculations of how many additional residents could live in a town under current zoning regulations and typical household size. Estimates can be made of the size of total population at buildout, the total number of new houses that could be built, or the increased demand for a resource such as drinking water that will result if all available land is developed. Of course, the accuracy of the estimates depends on the input data. Many planners prefer buildout models in which parcel data as well as zoning information is included as input data for exactly this reason; infill potential can be more accurately assessed when estimates of new houses are based on availability of actual lots, remaining road frontage, and the potential for subdivisions. Town officials often report that without the more detailed data provided by parcel information, their experience has been that development potential is seriously overestimated.

Buildout analyses need not be limited to individual communities; if data sets exist, buildouts can also be carried out for counties or other larger political regions. Often, however, difficulties are encountered in attempting to carry out a buildout analysis for larger regions. In many locations, zoning regulations, for example, can vary substantially in neighboring communities and incorporating diverse zoning regimes into a single buildout model can be difficult. It can often be more useful to link existing individual buildout analyses (maps and statistical summaries) completed for contiguous communities. Similarities in data inputs and process must, however, be sufficient so as not to create widely divergent results from one area to the next. In the Massachusetts statewide buildout program, particular attention was paid to using uniform inputs and a standard analytical process so that the individual results could be aggregated across regional planning jurisdictions, watersheds, or even the entire state.

Valuable as buildout models are, it is important to remember that they remain estimates of the likely effects on land use of continued population growth under specified land-use conditions. Still, as estimates—even if the model outputs may be off by 5 percent or more—the results of buildout studies are useful for planning purposes. As discussed previously, the data sets created to enable the Massachusetts buildout process have become highly useful inputs into subsequent planning efforts. The maps created by the buildouts have become the subject of serious consideration by citizens and local and regional officials. These maps and data sets remain easily accessible on-line, and citizen-planners and planning officials would be well advised to be thoroughly acquainted with the content and potential uses of the data.

Specifics of the Massachusetts Buildout Process

The state was fortunate in having 1/5,000 scale orthophoto images for use during the data input process and also as image base maps on which the results of the modeling efforts could be displayed. Moreover, because the land-use data for much of the state was four to five years old when the buildout process began, the orthophotos became the means by which those older data sets could be updated to more accurately illustrate actual land use for the year in which the buildout study was being conducted.

The state developed a standard protocol for community buildouts, resulting in five GIS maps being produced for each community to illustrate current conditions and the projected buildout scenario. In addition, the process by which the maps were created was made explicit to communities so that they could be confident of the results. The full guidelines for the buildout studies can still be viewed on-line at http://www.mass.gov/mgis/buildout.htm.

The five maps included two sorts: two that illustrated existing conditions without any forecasting, and three that resulted from analyses of current conditions. The first map was simply the most recent orthophoto images of the area, joined and then clipped to the town boundary (see Plate 5). This map served as a reliable reference because the image reflected conditions at a specific date, unmodified by choices about how features should be represented or even what features should be shown, choices that must be made for vector maps. A second map simply illustrated current zoning (see Plate 6, which, with Plates 7–9, appears following p. 98).

The three additional maps were constructed based on a number of the assumptions outlined above. The first was entitled Zoning and Absolute Development Constraints (see Plate 7). This map showed land already developed, land protected as open space, and areas that were unlikely ever to be developed due to absolute constraints. The various categories of land were color-coded to make the map easily readable. Land that was potentially available for development was left in white.

The second constructed map was entitled Developable Lands and Partial Constraints (see Plate 8). It was essentially the inverse of the first map and illustrated details about those lands available to be developed. Hatched areas showed environmental constraints that could limit development. Statistical summaries printed on the same map sheets described, based on zoning, how many new residential units could be built on the available land. Even land without existing road frontage was shown as developable as long as no regulation prevented the creation of subdivisions and new access roads. In calculating the number of potential housing units, allowances were made for needed roads and other infrastructure that would also consume land so that the resulting estimates would not be overstated.

The third constructed map was entitled Composite Development (see Plate 9). This simplified map showed lands available for future growth as well as available areas with partial constraints. Zoning was also shown on this final map so that viewers could see what type of development could occur in each area.

Using Buildouts to Plan

Once the maps were created, the Massachusetts Executive Office of Environmental Affairs presented the results of the buildout studies in public forums throughout the state. These forums ranged from individual town meetings with local officials, to small regional "summits," to "super-summits" involving dozens of towns. Some were done for planning regions that roughly corresponded to county boundaries.

At these events, each community received its individual, customized buildout information. A loose-leaf binder was prepared and given to each community containing a hard-copy buildout report for the town complete with color maps and statistical summaries of the information generated from the analysis. In some cases statistics for regional planning or watershed regions were also included. In all cases CDs containing the reports and maps were included to ensure ease of reproduction and public accessibility.

The immediate response to the findings of the buildout analyses was often surprise. In many communities, the initial reaction was disbelief at the number of additional housing units that the report indicated the community could potentially absorb given its current zoning regulations. Communities also reacted with consternation on learning how little time was left before complete "buildout" would be reached at their current rate of population growth and land consumption. The maps and statistical projections generated new and extended conversations about the types of growth encouraged or discouraged under current approaches to zoning. Many participants were alarmed to discover that their communities were quite vulnerable to sprawl and that unmanaged growth threatened serious change to the community character.

At times local officials became caught up in debating the specifics of the growth projection model. They sometimes discounted the overall value of the buildout model if they were able to point to even a few local spots where the projections did not seem to be accurate. In some towns the reaction was one of overt skepticism because of mistrust of any approach initiated by the state.

In most cases, the public forums generated increased awareness of threats from growth and unmanaged development. Many communities became motivated to be more proactive about these issues and began to work on creating or updating master plans, open space plans, and economic development plans. Communities began to consider changes to zoning to better shape growth to be more consistent with local interests.

Completing a Community Development Plan

When in 1999 Massachusetts undertook town-by-town buildout analysis, state planners hoped this effort would serve as a major catalyst for local governments to engage in better land-use planning and to develop useful follow-up studies. In 2002 all Massachusetts towns were given the opportunity to apply for $30,000 to complete a community development plan (CDP). Nearly two-thirds of the towns did so. The planning process offered flexibility. Although each town was required to fulfill certain study requirements in the areas of housing, natural resources, transportation, and economic growth, each community also had the opportunity to negotiate a scope of services that would address those issues in ways that were specific to itself. Some towns wished to focus on infill potential to meet affordable housing needs, for example, whereas other towns wanted to examine the potential effects of village center zoning that would concentrate commercial activity and mixed uses to build compact and vibrant areas and limit sprawl. And while some towns did adopt the standardized approach, many other communities identified specific issues to which greater attention would be paid.

Because forums and a public survey were required parts of the community development planning process, local residents also had substantial opportunities to speak up. The participation rate varied by community, but in many towns participation was surprisingly large. In all communities, residents had multiple opportunities to be heard throughout the process and to comment on the final draft plan.

The community development plans that were created relied heavily on the data produced for the buildout analyses. Adding additional information allowed towns to envision, debate, and select development scenarios that included natural resource protection, equitable housing availability, economic growth, and transportation infrastructure.

As the CDPs were being completed, many communities chose to go beyond the requirements and use the momentum from the buildouts and the CDPs to go forward with master plans, infrastructure studies, and economic development plans. Some examples include:

- Amherst funded a GIS-based study to consider alternative scenarios for a "Village Center" in the area of Atkins Corner.
- Gloucester and Milford completed new master plans that went much further than the CDPs and gave them greater legal authority to implement those plans in the face of private proposals that might run counter to community preferences.
- Brimfield and Holland included new open space plans within their CDPs that would qualify them for state and federal funding to protect important land.

A final important element in the success of the Massachusetts approach was the substantive involvement of the regional planning agencies (RPAs). These intermediary organizations became significant players contributing to the completion of the buildout studies as well as to the creation of the community development plans. The benefits of involving regional planning entities were considerable. The method by which RPAs have been funded over time within the state allowed them to build up staff resources and expertise and become effective intermediaries between the towns and the state. Their knowledge of the communities within their regions and their effective working relationships ensured interaction with local officials and residents. Moreover, once the studies were completed, the RPAs continued to hold the reports and make them available together with the data sets developed during the planning processes. Changes in the local community leadership or GIS staffing would not disrupt the availability of the information.

As a result of the processes described in this chapter, state officials have gained deeper insight into the needs of local communities. Such insights continue to serve the state well as the Commonwealth works to create community-sensitive regulatory tools as well as develop more effective ways of interacting with municipalities. The basis has been established for the state and communities to share what works as well as to consider together what does not, and then take steps to address needed changes.

THE MASSACHUSETTS case study illustrates in detail how GIS can provide information in the service of decision-making. As has been seen, GIS allows for data to be brought together that are taken from different sources, that address different features of an area, and that aggregate characteristics in multiple ways. GIS allows for data to be considered from a variety of perspectives without requiring decision-makers to hand-draw a new map each time they move deeper into a problem analysis. Thus, GIS allows for flexible use of data; cities, counties, and states are all benefiting from that increased flexibility. For planning purposes, GIS has enormous potential, and throughout this chapter we have pointed to that potential. For this potential to be realized, however, citizen-planners must become conversant enough with the technology to ask questions about its use. We hope that this chapter will serve as a first step in the direction of providing citizens with the information they need to become full partners in the use of GIS in their communities.

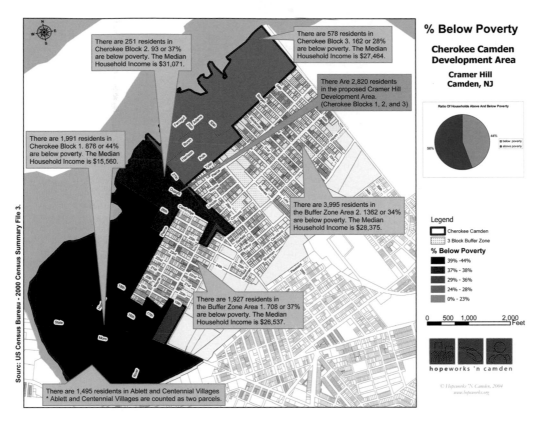

Plate 1. Mapping poverty to create change in Cramer Hill, Camden, N.J.
Source: Hopeworks 'N Camden, Inc.

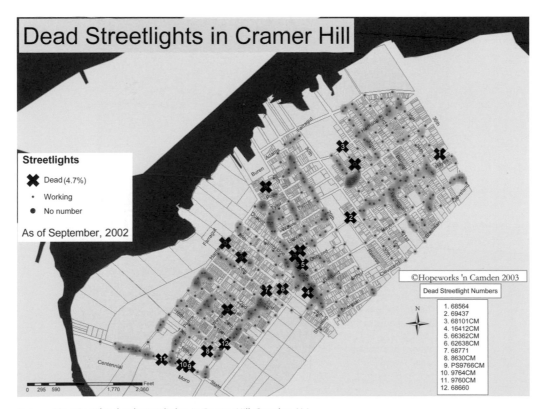

Plate 2. Mapping the dead streetlights in Cramer Hill, Camden, N.J.
Source: Hopeworks 'N Camden, Inc.

Plate 3. Orthophotography and compiled wetland boundaries, 1995.
Source: Mass EOEA.

Plate 4. Orthophotography (2001) and wetland boundaries (1995), same site.
Source: Mass EOEA.

The Massachusetts Department of Environmental Protection (DEP) used 1995 imagery to accurately delineate wetland areas, shown here by lighter blue outlines. Overlaying the wetland boundaries with 2001 color imagery makes very clear where development had occurred within those wetland areas, as highlighted here by red outlines. This innovative use of GIS gave DEP a new tool to find where there had been encroachments and, in cases where wetland alterations had not been properly permitted, to support the imposition of fines and remediation.

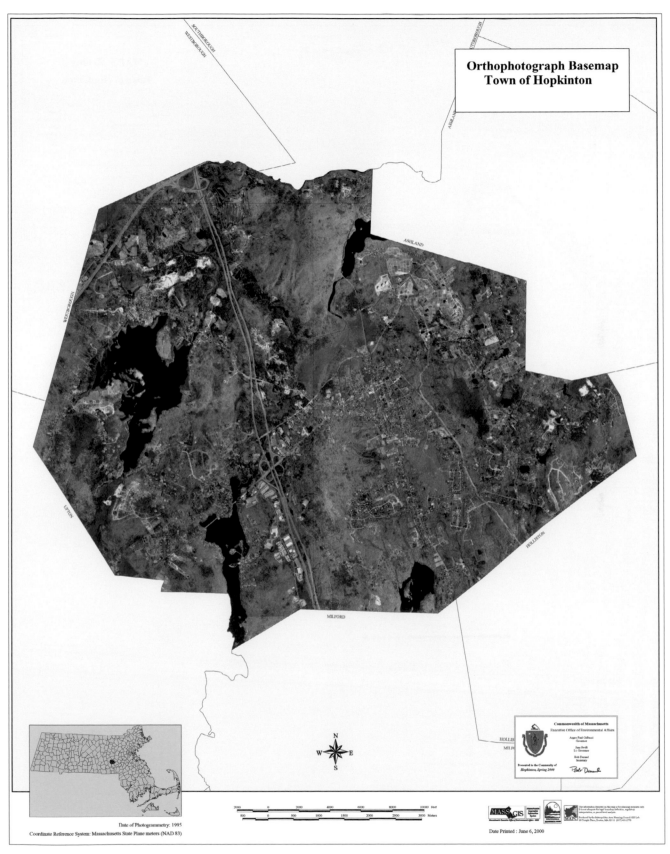

Plate 5. Orthophotograph basemap, Town of Hopkinton.
Source: Mass EOEA.

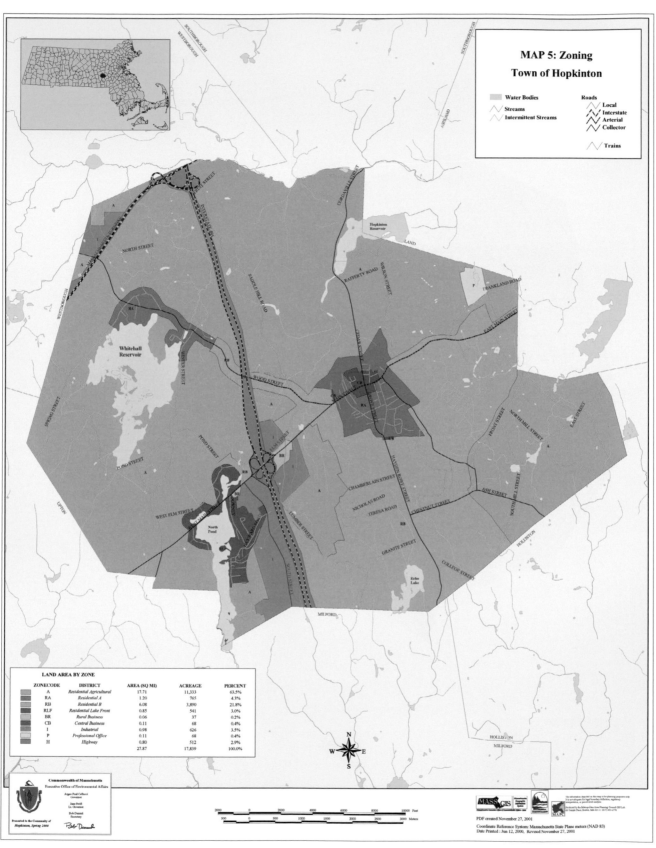

PDF created November 27, 2001

Coordinate Reference System: Massachusetts State Plane meters (NAD 83)
Date Printed : Jun 12, 2000 , Revised November 27, 2001

Plate 6. Zoning, Town of Hopkinton.
Source: Mass EOEA.

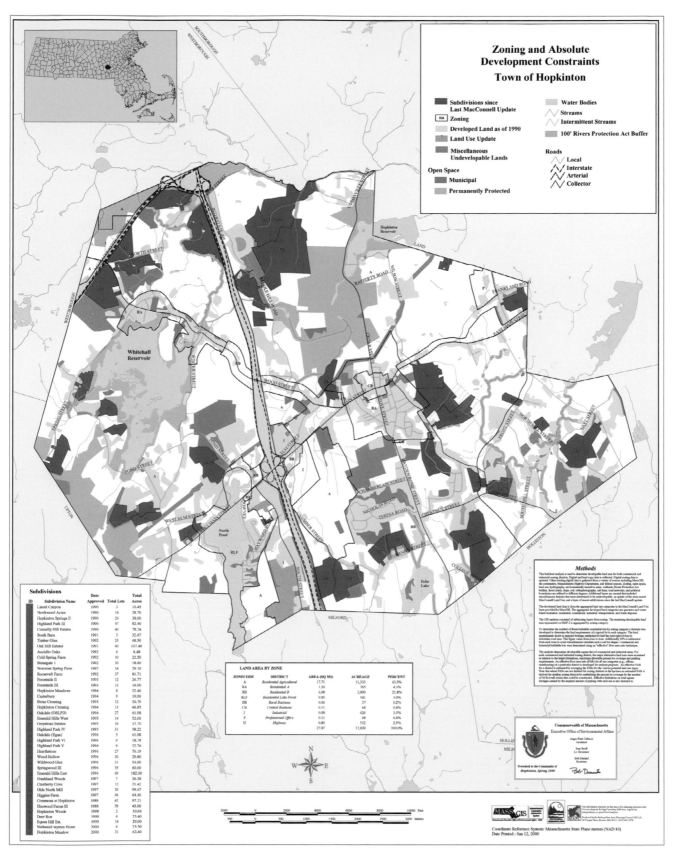

Plate 7. Zoning and absolute development constraints, Town of Hopkinton.

Source: Mass EOEA.

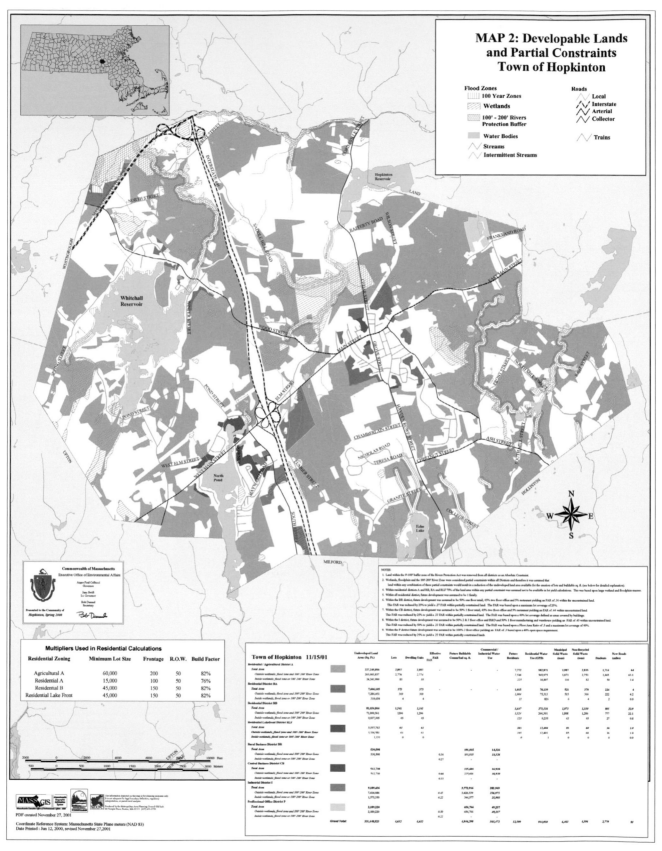

Plate 8. Developable lands and partial constraints, Town of Hopkinton.
Source: Mass EOEA.

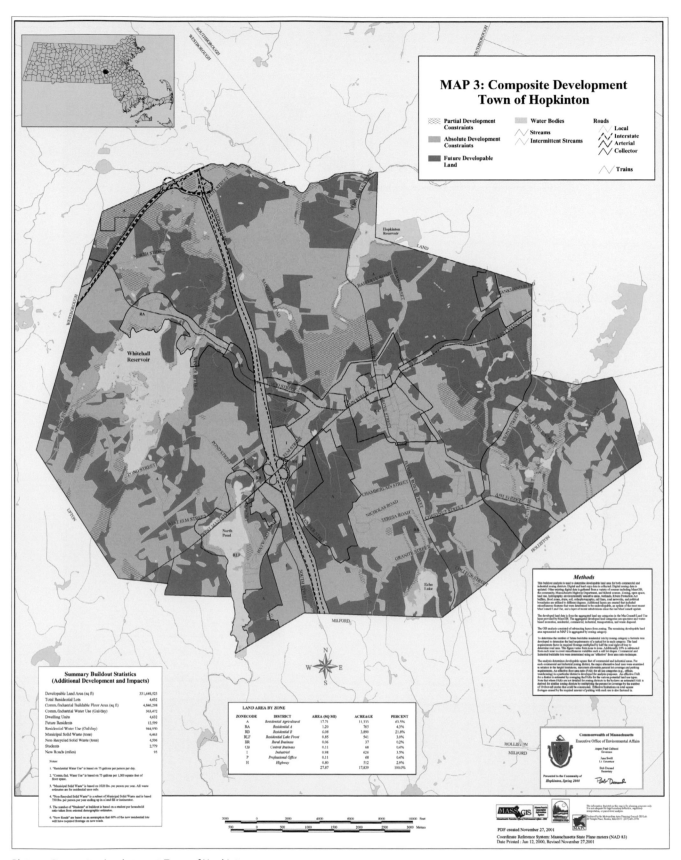

MAP 3: Composite Development
Town of Hopkinton

Partial Development Constraints	Water Bodies	Roads	
			Local
Absolute Development Constraints	Streams		Interstate
	Intermittent Streams		Arterial
Future Developable Land			Collector
			Trains

Summary Buildout Statistics
(Additional Development and Impacts)

Developable Land Area (sq ft)	331,648,523
Total Residential Lots	4,632
Comm./Industrial Buildable Floor Area (sq ft)	4,846,298
Comm./Industrial Water Use (Gal/day)	363,472
Dwelling Units	4,632
Future Residents	12,599
Residential Water Use (Gal/day)	944,950
Municipal Solid Waste (tons)	6,463
Non-Recycled Solid Waste (tons)	4,506
Students	2,779
New Roads (miles)	93

Notes:

1. "Residential Water Use" is based on 75 gallons per person per day.

2. "Comm./Ind. Water Use" is based on 75 gallons per 1,000 square feet of floor space.

3. "Municipal Solid Waste" is based on 1020 lbs. per person per year. All waste estimates are for residential uses only.

4. "Non-Recycled Solid Waste" is a subset of Municipal Solid Waste and is based 730 lbs. per person per year ending up in a land fill or incinerator.

5. The number of "Students" at buildout is based on a student per household ratio taken from external demographic estimates.

6. "New Roads" are based on an assumption that 60% of the new residential lots will have required frontage on new roads.

LAND AREA BY ZONE

ZONECODE	DISTRICT	AREA (SQ MI)	ACREAGE	PERCENT
A	Residential Agricultural	17.71	11,333	63.5%
RA	Residential A	1.20	765	4.3%
RB	Residential B	6.08	3,890	21.8%
RLF	Residential Lake Front	0.85	541	3.0%
BR	Rural Business	0.06	37	0.2%
CB	Central Business	0.11	68	0.4%
I	Industrial	0.98	626	3.5%
P	Professional Office	0.11	68	0.4%
H	Highway	0.80	512	2.9%
		27.87	17,839	100.0%

Methods

This buildout analysis is used to determine developable land areas for both commercial and industrial zoning districts. Digital and hard copy data is collected. Digital zoning data is updated. Other existing digital data is gathered from a variety of sources including MassGIS, the community, Massachusetts Highway Department, and federal sources. Zoning, open space, land use, hydrography, environmentally sensitive areas, wetlands, Rivers Protection Act buffers, flood zones, slope, soil, orthophotography, rail lines, road networks, and political boundaries are utilized to define the various land uses. Additional layers are created that included miscellaneous features that were determined to be undevelopable, an update of the most recent MassCouncil Land Use, and a layer of recent subdivisions since the last MassCouncil update.

The developed land data is from the aggregated land use categories in the MassCouncil Land Use layer provided by MassGIS. The aggregated developed land categories are open-space and water-based recreation, residential, commercial, industrial, transportation, and waste disposal.

The GIS analysis consisted of subtracting layers from zoning. The remaining developable land area represented on MAP 2 is aggregated by zoning category.

To determine the number of future buildable residential lots by zoning category a formula was developed to determine the land requirements of a typical lot in each category. The land requirements factor is required frontage multiplied by half the road right-of-way to determine road area. This figure varies from zone to zone. Additionally 10% is subtracted from each zone to cover miscellaneous variables such a odd lot shapes. Commercial and Industrial buildable lots were determined using an "effective" floor area ratio technique.

The analysis determines developable square feet of commercial and industrial areas. For each commercial and industrial zoning district, the major alternative land uses were examined in relation to the height limitations, minimum allowable percent lot coverage and parking requirements. An effective floor area ratio (FAR) for all ten categories (e.g., offices, warehousing) in a particular district is developed for analysis purposes. An effective FAR for a district is estimated by averaging the FARs for the various potential land use types. Areas that where FARs are not detailed for zoning districts in the by-laws an estimated FAR is derived for similar zoning districts by multiplying the percent lot coverage by the number of 10-foot-tall stories that could be constructed. Effective limitations on total square footages caused by the required amount of parking with ten is also factored in.

Commonwealth of Massachusetts
Executive Office of Environmental Affairs

Argeo Paul Cellucci
Governor

Jane Swift
Lt. Governor

Bob Durand
Secretary

Presented to the Community of
Hopkinton, Spring 2000

Plate 9. Composite development, Town of Hopkinton.
Source: Mass EOEA.

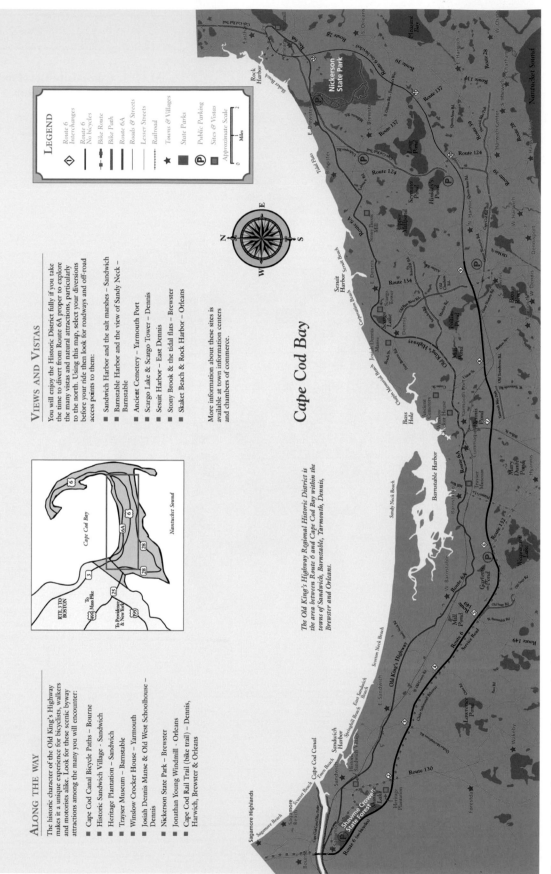

ALONG THE WAY

The historic character of the Old King's Highway makes it a unique experience for bicyclists, walkers and motorists alike. Look for these scenic byway attractions among the many you will encounter:

- Cape Cod Canal Bicycle Paths – Bourne
- Historic Sandwich Village – Sandwich
- Heritage Plantation – Sandwich
- Trayser Museum – Barnstable
- Winslow Crocker House – Yarmouth
- Josiah Dennis Manse & Old West Schoolhouse – Dennis
- Nickerson State Park – Brewster
- Jonathan Young Windmill – Orleans
- Cape Cod Rail Trail (bike trail) – Dennis, Harwich, Brewster & Orleans

VIEWS AND VISTAS

You will enjoy the Historic District fully if you take the time to divert from Route 6A proper to explore the many vistas and natural attractions, particularly to the north. Using this map, select your diversions before your ride then look for roadways and off-road access points among them:

- Sandwich Harbor and the salt marshes – Sandwich
- Barnstable Harbor and the view of Sandy Neck – Barnstable
- Ancient Cemetery – Yarmouth Port
- Scargo Lake & Scargo Tower – Dennis
- Sesuit Harbor – East Dennis
- Stony Brook & the tidal flats – Brewster
- Skaket Beach & Rock Harbor – Orleans

More information about these sites is available at town information centers and chambers of commerce.

The Old King's Highway Regional Historic District is the area between Route 6 and Cape Cod Bay within the towns of Sandwich, Barnstable, Yarmouth, Dennis, Brewster and Orleans.

LEGEND

- ◇ Route 6 Interchanges
- Route 6 No bicycles
- Bike Route
- Route 6A
- Roads & Streets
- Lesser Streets
- Railroad
- ★ Towns & Villages
- State Parks
- Ⓟ Public Parking
- Sites & Vistas

Approximate Scale

Cape Cod Bay

Nantucket Sound

Plate 10. MPO planning process: Planning a bicyle route

Preserving Natural Resources

Courtesy of Karen Mendrala and the City of Holyoke Planning Department

8

Biodiversity Conservation and Ecosystem Protection

Sharon McGregor and Jack Ahern

Historically, biodiversity and ecosystem protection were afterthoughts in local planning (Peck 1998). This is changing with increased public awareness that diverse animal and plant populations and healthy ecosystems are integral to protecting human health and quality of life. This new recognition coincides with and may derive from the evolution of environmental protection from discrete environmental elements (water, land, air, individual species) to a systems approach (ecosystem management, watershed planning, landscape ecological planning).

The axiom "think globally—act locally" is relevant to protecting biodiversity. With the right information and tools, a community can draft and implement plans for an ecological network that will sustain a diversity of animals and plants, and preserve water, wetlands, forests, and other natural resources essential for meeting human needs and maintaining a healthy environment.

The chapter begins with a definition of biodiversity and summary of the four primary categories of threats to it: habitat loss, invasive species, over-consumption and waste production, and global climate change. Next is a discussion about what saving biodiversity means, and why we should save it, with an emphasis on the relationship of biodiversity preservation to human well-being. This is followed by a step-by-step planning approach for local biodiversity protection, including preventing habitat loss and restoring species and habitats. The chapter finishes with case studies: a biodiversity assessment and conservation plan completed for multiple communities in a Massachusetts watershed, and an urban biodiversity protection program in Chicago.

What Is Biodiversity?

Biological diversity, or simply *biodiversity*, is the total variety of living things. Biodiversity can be measured by the total number of species present (species richness) (Heywood and Watson 1995). Expansion of urban and suburban areas is often the driving process responsible for a reduction in species richness. As habitat area is reduced, the smaller fragments that remain support fewer, different, and often non-native species.

Biodiversity is often subdivided into two fundamental categories of plant and animal species: generalists and specialists. The implications of the two categories and their respective habitat requirements for biodiversity planning are profound. Generalists are adaptable to a wide range of conditions, are not particularly sensitive to human disturbance and presence, and use multiple habitats to complete their life cycle. In the northeastern United States, animal generalists include deer, squirrels, and raccoons. Generalists enjoy ample habitat in fragmented urban and suburban environments. In contrast, specialists require specific habitat conditions that can be satisfied only in large intact areas of native vegetation, like forests, wetlands, or grasslands. Specialists are generally sensitive to human presence and disturbance. Animal specialists in the northeastern United States include the fisher, mink, several owl species, and Neotropical songbirds (songbirds like warblers and vireos that nest in the north and winter in the tropics). When landscapes are transformed by urban or suburban development, habitat for specialists decreases or disappears, while generalist habitat may increase. A main challenge for biodiversity planning is therefore to protect and manage habitat for specialist species and to provide connectivity between habitat patches (Bennett 1999, Forman et al. 1996).

It is easy to overlook biodiversity at the local level, since we usually think of nature as existing only where people don't live. Though much of the American landscape is now developed with buildings, roads, and parking lots, a great amount of biodiversity remains. There are thousands of species of native animals, plants, and fungi in each of the fifty states, and thousands more if you count the ones that can't be seen with the naked eye, such as microbes.

To some, this biodiversity represents a natural asset to be respected and protected—a legacy for future generations. To others, biodiversity is a luxury that can be compromised to meet social needs, like creating new places for people to live and work. Regardless of whether you view nature as intrinsically important or a resource for people to use, biodiversity is inextricably related with the environment that sustains us (Wilson 1988). Like the "canary in the coal mine," changes in local biodiversity can provide early warning of environmental changes that may have direct human consequences, including loss of water quality, destabilization of soils, loss in forest productivity, or change in quality-of-life values that are difficult to quantify: loss of recreational

Biodiversity at Different Levels

Biodiversity can be viewed at different interconnected levels —from invisible gene pools to huge physical landscapes of mountains or water. Simplistically, there are four major levels of diversity: genetic, species, natural community, and landscape. All levels are like a puzzle, where if one piece is missing the picture is no longer complete.

Genetic diversity refers to the variety of genes within individuals of a species. Variations in genes are responsible for minor variations in individual plants or animals: such traits as size, color, and some behavioral characteristics, to name a few. Genetic diversity provides for a healthy gene pool, and allows species to adapt to constantly changing conditions.

Species diversity refers to all the different types of species —from bacteria and single-celled organisms, fungi (mushrooms) and plants, to insects and other invertebrates, reptiles, amphibians, birds, and mammals. Species diversity is the level most people think of when they think about biodiversity. Biologists cluster species with like characteristics into genera, families, orders, and classes.

Natural community diversity is the variety of groups, or assemblages, of species living together. Massachusetts has described 105 different natural communities, including terrestrial (land-based), palustrine (wetland), and estuarine (located at the mouth of rivers in the coastal zone, where freshwater meets saltwater). (See specific examples of *natural communities* in "Key Terms for Understanding Biodiversity" sidebar.)

Landscape diversity is the range of ecosystems on the landscape, distinguished by land forms, vegetation types, soil, and climate.

Figure 8.1. Development of roads, buildings, or utilities can permanently alter topography, hydrology, and soils and remove vegetation.
Photo: Frances H. Clark.

opportunity, less frequent personal association with the plants and animals of a region, or loss of a community's rural identity and character.

To restate: Biodiversity is the variety of living things. "It includes the variety of living organisms, the genetic differences among them, the natural communities and ecosystems in which they occur, and the ecological and evolutionary processes that keep them functioning, yet ever changing and adapting" (Noss and Cooperrider 1994).

Thus, the variety of genes that give an individual animal or plant its "look" or behavior, different from that of another individual, even of the same species, is biodiversity. Biodiversity is the variety of natural communities—from vernal pool to oak-hickory forest to desert community—or the variety of ecosystems—from rocky intertidal zone to river floodplain to montaine forest (Figure 8.1). Biodiversity

is the variety of ecological processes, including the water cycle, photosynthesis, and nutrient cycling through which species interact with each other and with the environment. Biodiversity is also the variety of evolutionary processes, including the development of diverse physical features and behaviors among species for interacting with each other and the environment.

In summary, biodiversity is the variety of living things and their connections to each other and to the physical environment. The term is generally used to refer to native species in their proper places and balance. Biodiversity is not just rare species; it includes all forms of life. Biodiversity is not restricted to tropical rainforests—it is in every town and backyard! Humans are part of community biodiversity. We are connected to biodiversity by the water we drink, the foods we eat, and the air we breathe. We are also connected to biodiversity by our actions in daily living, actions that impact the existence and health of animals and plants. Humans are an integral part of the web of life.

Biodiversity is highly dynamic and difficult to measure. The total number of species in any habitat, natural community, or ecosystem change, due to both natural and human causes. The most basic measure of biodiversity is to count the number of species that occur in a single habitat. Another way to measure, examine changes in, and get a sense of the health of local biodiversity is to look at the populations of individual species. Fewer individuals (i.e., fewer than normally observed) of a locally indigenous species may indicate a problem. For example, a few decades ago, eagle and hawk numbers plummeted in the United States. The pesticide DDT had accumulated in the fish these birds were eating, causing a thinning of eggshells and reduced hatching success. Once the cause was identified and use of the pesticide was controlled, eagles and hawks made a comeback.

Changes in biodiversity can also be observed at the larger natural community level where species may change over time, due to natural or human-caused disturbance (World Conservation Union 2001). While the species may change, the roles served (each species has one or more roles, or niches, it fills) may or may not change. Roles or niches are an important aspect of biodiversity: They can stay the same, but different organisms—undesirable organisms when they are exotic invasive species—can fill them over time.

For example, a woody field can support a complex web of interacting species. There may be hawks and snakes that are predators, and rabbits and field mice that are prey and grazers of vegetation. Deer graze or browse vegetation, and a variety of trees, shrubs, grasses, and other plants perform photosynthesis. An assortment of mushrooms, worms, and microorganisms are engaged in decomposition. If the site is disturbed—for example, by new construction—some of these species will be eliminated. In the aftermath of the disturbance, other species may return, or different species may colonize. The hawks, as specialists, will only return if nesting sites (perhaps tall dead trees left from the disturbance) are available, and if field grasses remain to provide habitat for the rabbits and mice. The generalists, such as the deer, are likely to adapt to the new environment. New species such as coyote, gray squirrels, and Oriental bittersweet (a non-native species) may gain advantage and displace the species that dominated previously (Drake et al. 1989).

Ecological and Evolutionary Processes

Biodiversity is the variety of living things, natural communities, and ecosystems. It is also the variety of ecological and evolutionary processes that sustain living things and keep them ever changing and adapting.

A few of the *ecological processes* are:

The *water cycle*—the precipitation of water as rain or snow, the consumption or absorption of this water by animals and plants, percolation to groundwater, and evaporation or transpiration (the latter by plants) back into the air.

Photosynthesis—the process by which plants capture the energy of sunlight to manufacture a simple sugar and produce oxygen as a by-product.

Nutrient cycling—the production and use of nitrogen and other nutrients by plants and animals, and the decomposition of dead organic matter by microorganisms, fungi, and insects.

Movement—of organisms and material through the landscape; for example, animal movements, seed dispersal, and movement of sediment and organic matter in streams.

Natural disturbances—such as fire, floods, ice storms, insect outbreaks, and shoreline erosion and deposition. Note that these disturbances are beneficial in that they help to perpetuate biodiversity over the long term.

Examples of *evolutionary processes* are:

Birds' development of different beak shapes and sizes, according to what they eat (for example, finches have thick bills for cracking seeds).

Moths' development of coloration to match the background color of their habitat (for example, tree bark).

The flat body form of flounder, with eyes on top and mouth on the bottom, an adaptation for feeding on the ocean floor and keeping watch for predators.

Threats to Biodiversity

Biodiversity now faces several categories of threats, most of them caused by humans. Biodiversity has evolved in concert with natural disturbances, such as storms and floods, and usually rebounds after natural events, although the types of species may change. In contrast, humans create changes on the land that have extensive and more permanent effects on local biodiversity and that, in total, impact the health of the natural communities and ecosystems. Diminished health can be observed as a reduction in biodiversity (total numbers of species or populations within species), changes from predominantly native to non-native species, or diseases in certain animals or plants.

We have seen some fairly noticeable changes in the American landscape in recent years. There are an ever increasing number of housing developments and shopping malls, where once there were forests and farms. People report more sightings of wildlife in urban areas as natural habitats shrink. Deer and coyotes have been seen in cities, even Central Park in New York City, and bears have surprised residents in suburban towns. These species are being displaced from their preferred habitats and are attempting to reclaim former territories—areas that were once free of human encroachment.

At the same time, many species have experienced population declines with the rise in development. For example, there are fewer wild cats (bobcat, mountain lion, Canada lynx), box turtles (eastern and Florida box turtles), and snakes and lady-slippers than there used to be. Recent bird surveys have shown a decrease in the numbers of whip-poor-will, hooded merganser, and Arctic tern. Neotropical songbirds are becoming threatened as their habitats are altered locally, along migratory paths, in breeding areas of northern states and Canada, and in their Latin American wintering grounds. As noted above, the key threats to biodiversity are habitat loss in its various forms, invasive species, over-consumption and waste production, and global climate change.

Habitat Loss

The biggest threat to biodiversity is habitat loss: destruction, alteration, or fragmentation of areas of natural vegetation by development; and degradation of these areas by pollution, sedimentation, or disruption of natural processes (Gibbs 2001, Heywood and Watson 1995, Wilson 1988). Surprisingly, the rate of habitat loss does not correlate with the rate of human population growth. For example, since World War II, Massachusetts has seen a 100 percent increase in development, with the attendant destruction of habitat, but only a 10 percent increase in population!

The development increase has been accompanied by a change in development type and density. Historically, more people lived in towns and village centers. In the second half of the twentieth century, the auto transformed historical settlement patterns and encouraged low-density, auto-dependent development, often labeled as sprawl. Again, population growth contributed very little to this increase in housing development; reductions in average household size fueled the construction of additional housing units.

Where habitat is destroyed, some species migrate to new habitat if it exists in reasonable proximity and has capacity for additional species or individuals of an existing species, and if there are routes, or corridors, through which the animals can disperse to the new habitat (Bennett 1999, Forman et al. 1996). However, migrating species often face stiff competition against the established residents and perish (MacArthur and Wilson 1967). Sometimes local species try to return to the area that has been developed, but they are unsuccessful in reestablishing themselves because their food and breeding sites have been eliminated. Other species may have filled their former niches, preventing their return. Even if species survive the destruction of their habitat, the connections to other necessary species are often lost (for example, certain flowering plants may have lost their insect pollinators), and long-term survival becomes precarious (Figure 8.2).

Where development has not completely replaced open space, it has often altered, fragmented, or degraded it. For example, development that alters a wetland, though it does not destroy the wetland, may result in a net loss in function of the wetland habitat. Destroyed or altered, the habitat is effectively lost.[1]

---

1. Many people falsely believe that any wet area is a functioning wetland. Without proper protection and mitigation, a wetland becomes a "wet land"—a mere remnant of the former functioning wetland, having lost one or more functions (groundwater recharge, flood control, storm damage prevention, pollution attenuation, fish and wildlife habitat, etc.).

Fragmentation of habitat is less visible than outright destruction, but remains a serious problem for biodiversity, especially for specialist species. Fragmentation occurs when new construction of roads or buildings reduces intact areas of native vegetation to small isolated remnants. An example is building a new house in the middle of forty acres of forest. While it may look as if the new house has not changed much of the landscape, for the specialist species the impact can be substantial. The same elements that cause the fragmentation (roads, buildings, pavement, golf courses, agriculture) often represent barriers to species movement between remnant habitat fragments (Forman et al. 1996). Smaller, isolated populations of species in habitat fragments are more vulnerable to stresses, including disease, food shortages, and predators, and often suffer from inbreeding due to a reduced gene pool. While species can survive the initial effects of fragmentation, long-term survival depends on their ability to disperse to suitable habitats in the region.

Many animals require multiple, connected habitats to complete their life cycles. A species may feed and breed in wetlands and overwinter in upland areas. For example, several Massachusetts salamanders breed in vernal pools but spend most of the year in the surrounding uplands—in the winter, underground. Other species, such as fox, spend most of their lives in the forests or meadows of uplands, but use ponds, streams, and other wetlands as feeding areas and water sources. Fox, and many other species, also require connected land to migrate in search of new food sources, and for their offspring to disperse to new territories. Fragmentation not only inhibits animal feeding, breeding, migration, and dispersal, but also makes it easier for predators to catch prey.

Habitat degradation includes pollution and sedimentation, and disruption of natural processes. Pollution from toxic chemicals in the air or water, sewage discharges from septic systems or poorly maintained wastewater treatment plants, and runoff from roads, parking lots, lawns, and farmland can undermine the quality of aquatic and land-based habitat. Sedimentation occurs when soil is eroded from development sites and is carried by stormwater to wetlands or other "downstream" habitats. The excess sediment loads can smother plants and animals. Disruption of natural processes includes loss of natural hydrological fluctuations in rivers and streams from dams or depletion of groundwater, and the suppression of fire and floods.

Key Terms for Understanding Biodiversity

Can you see how the following are "nested" components of biodiversity, meaning each one fits into the next?

Species: similar and closely related individual organisms that are capable of breeding under natural conditions, and that usually do not interbreed with other species. Each of the following is an example of a separate species: great blue heron; California condor; pronghorn antelope; raccoon; paper birch; jack-in-the-pulpit; monarch butterfly; spotted salamander; Chinook salmon.

Habitat: the physical area in which a species is found and which meets its ecological needs (i.e., for feeding, photosynthesizing, gathering nutrients, breeding, nesting, shelter, resting, overwintering, migrating). Some species spend their entire life cycle in a very small area: a daring jumping spider's habitat might be a single oak tree and the ground surrounding the tree. Others require a large area: a common snapping turtle's habitat includes its pond or river, where it spends most of its life, and sandy upland near or distant from the pond for laying its eggs. Still others have different habitat requirements according to season: cat-tail marsh is the spring and summer home for Red-winged blackbirds, and Baja California is critical habitat for gray whales from December through March.

Population: a reproductive group of individual organisms of the same species occurring in the same place and time. Some examples are: elk sharing the same forest system; brook trout in a stream; northern bluet damselflies inhabiting a swamp; and mourning doves living in your neighborhood.

Natural community: a group of plants, animals, fungi, and microorganisms that live together in the same place. You might think of natural communities as analogous to humans' towns. They are described by the dominant species and physical features. Examples of natural communities of the United States are barrier beach; vernal pool; coastal plain pond; pitch pine and scrub oak barrens; floodplain forest; red maple swamp; sandplain grassland; oak-hickory forest; pine-cypress forest; mangrove forest; cypress savanna; palmetto prairie; Palo Verde–cactus shrub land; spruce-fir forest; redwood forest; tall grass prairie; and Great Lakes pine forest. Natural communities can be large or small; from a few square yards to thousands of acres. Often there are small natural communities within larger natural communities (for example, vernal pools in an oak-hickory forest). Because many natural communities share species, habitats, or physical characteristics, the community boundaries are often blurred. Some natural communities are fairly common and occur in many places across the state, while others are found in only a small number of locations. Many states have natural communities that are unique to their location, found nowhere else in the world!

Ecosystem: a living community of plants, animals, fungi, and microorganisms, plus their nonliving environment of soil, rocks, air, and water. Ecosystems can be large or small. Examples are the intertidal zone (the area between high and low tide) at your favorite beach; Stellwagen Bank, which is a large underwater plateau located north of Provincetown, Cape Cod, Massachusetts; the Everglades of Florida; Bryce Canyon in Utah; Mount McKinley in Alaska; and the Sonoran Desert in Arizona.

Watershed: the geographic land area where surface and groundwater flow to a common point; for example, to a river or lake. The United States has 2,149 major watersheds, defined by major rivers. Watersheds contain natural communities and ecosystems, and natural communities and ecosystems can, and often do, cross watershed boundaries.

Ecoregion: landscape units that contain similar environmental conditions, including landforms, climate, soils, water resources, and predominant vegetation. You might think of ecoregions as the natural equivalent of "counties," each containing smaller "towns" that are the natural communities. The United States has 81 described ecoregions. Ecoregions encompass one or more watersheds.

Plant and animal species are often described according to their relationship to the ecosystem in which they reside. Important terms for understanding the status of a species include:

Native: naturally occurring in a natural community as a result of natural processes of dispersal and range expansion.

Non-native (or alien): not naturally occurring in a natural community as a result of natural processes and range expansion. A non-native species may be introduced intentionally (i.e., brought into a natural community for some ornamental, agricultural, or hunting purpose), introduced unintentionally (i.e., "hitchhiked" via a plant, animal, car, truck, boat, plane, or train coming into the state), or colonize on its own with the help of some "unnatural" process. The giant kudzu of the southeastern United States and Oriental bittersweet in New England are examples of intentionally introduced non-native species. The hemlock woolly adelgid (an aphid that is killing native eastern hemlock trees) is an exam-

ple of a species that was introduced unintentionally. The eastern coyote, which populated New England only recently, colonized the state from the south, west, and north. Highly adaptable to suburban and even urban locations, the eastern coyote was attracted to the northeast by the abundant food sources (including garbage and house cats!). The absence of the eastern timber wolf, whose niche the coyote partially fills, is also considered a factor.

Endangered: in danger of extinction throughout all or a significant portion of its range, or in danger of extirpation. Federally listed endangered species in the United States include the Southwestern Willow flycatcher, whooping crane, black-footed ferret, green pitcher plant, and Hine's emerald dragonfly. State-listed endangered species include the short-eared owl of Massachusetts, Karner blue butterfly of Minnesota, and prairie shooting star of the prairie states.

Threatened: likely to become endangered within the foreseeable future throughout all or a significant portion of its range, or declining and rare and likely to become endangered in the foreseeable future. Federally listed threatened species in the United States include the American brook lamprey, loggerhead sea turtle, and white sedge. State listed threatened species include barrens bluet damselfly in Massachusetts, prairie milkweed of Minnesota, and the California trinity bristle snail.

Special Concern (some states): has suffered a decline that could threaten the species if allowed to continue unchecked; or occurs in small numbers or with restricted distribution or specialized habitat requirements such that it could become threatened. Species of Special Concern in Massachusetts include the gray seal, bur oak, and New England medicinal leech.

Extinct: no surviving individuals or populations anywhere. Extinct species include the passenger pigeon, Labrador duck, and eastern elk.

Extirpated: locally extinct, though continues to live elsewhere. Species extirpated from New England include the eastern timber wolf and regal fritillary butterfly (Massachusetts).

Returned: disappeared or eliminated from the local area for a number of years, but has returned. The northern raven, wild turkey, moose, and American beaver are examples of species that have returned to former habitat in many states.

Filled empty niche: a non-native species that has stepped into a niche formerly occupied by another, similar species. The eastern coyote is an example of this type of species that has partially filled the niche of the missing eastern timber wolf.

Urban and suburban residents have witnessed the devastating effects of pollution. Many rivers were so polluted by sewage thirty years ago that people could not swim or even touch the water without risk of sickness! Today, due to intensive efforts to clean up wastewater and stormwater discharges along rivers, people can safely use most rivers to row and sail. The goal, within the not-too-distant future, is to make all rivers fishable and swimmable again.

Habitat loss in its various forms also results from motorized recreation. Especially in coastal areas, impacts from all-terrain vehicles (ATVs) and off-road vehicles (ORVs) are being seen in pine barren, grassland, and barrier beach natural communities. Impacts include the destruction of nests, uprooting or trampling of vegetation, creation of barriers to wildlife movement (baby turtles and shore birds become trapped in tire ruts, and fall victim to oncoming vehicles or predators), and disruption of breeding and feeding. Jet skis threaten the biodiversity of lakes, ponds, and near-shore estuaries, by churning up shallow areas and disturbing wildlife.

Invasive Species

Second to habitat loss as a threat to biodiversity are invasive species, the introduction or natural spread of non-native, or alien, species. Alien plant species migrate on their own (by wind, water, or animal dispersal) or are intentionally planted by homeowners or landscapers, and can become established in new habitats. Some exotic alien species (for example, tulips) do not become established, spread, or otherwise integrate well into the existing biodiversity. These alien species, therefore, are not a problem. But others do spread, and displace, destroy, or out-compete native species. These problem alien species are called "invasives."

Invasive plant species have particular characteristics that enable them to out-compete natives. They generally have

Figure 8.2. Ledum Bog, a rare undisturbed kettlehole bog, has not changed since Henry David Thoreau described it over 150 years ago.
Photo: Frances H. Clark.

Preserving Natural Resources

highly viable and prolific seeds, and can tolerate a wide range of conditions, especially disturbed locations. Most important, they left their pests and diseases in their previous habitats, freeing them from the ecological controls that keep native species populations in check. For example, some trees such as the Norway maple are invasive in locations where they are not native (New England). Not surprising, therefore, some of our native species such as black cherry are considered invasive in other parts of the world (for example, northern Europe).

Common roadside flowers and weeds, such as dandelions, daisies, and stinging nettles, are invasive species. Kudzu is a rapidly spreading vine that has taken over vast areas of the American south. Purple loosestrife—a plant brought from Europe in the late 1800s—is now the dominant plant in many wetlands and riparian corridors, crowding out native plants such as cattails that provide food for birds and invertebrates. House sparrows, introduced from Europe, are displacing native bird species such as black-capped chickadees and eastern and western bluebirds, by invading the nest sites of these species. Green crabs, introduced in ballast water from ships originating in Europe, are now all along the Atlantic coast, threatening to out-compete native crabs, such as the Atlantic rock crab. Even house cats and dogs can become alien, invasive species. Free-roaming house cats kill tens of thousands of native birds, chipmunks, and snakes yearly. Feral or unleashed dogs run down deer, grouse, and other mammals and birds.

Invasive species can threaten entire ecosystems. For example, the hemlock woolly adelgid, an Asian scale insect the size of a period on this page, was accidentally introduced to the United States in 1920. It is infecting and killing many eastern hemlock trees. This infestation is ecologically significant, because the eastern hemlock provides food, cover, and nesting sites for wild turkey, red squirrel, porcupines, warblers, and many other species of songbirds. Because these are specialist species, when the hemlock is gone the animals cannot remain.

Some would consider the native white-tailed deer in the eastern United States an invasive species. The loss of predators such as wolves has allowed deer numbers to explode—overgrazing landscapes, preventing forest regeneration, and threatening wildflowers. Deer in excessive numbers also threaten humans, as hosts to deer ticks that carry Lyme disease, and as causes of automobile accidents.

Figure 8.3. Russian Olive is poised to invade one of the last field habitats for nesting birds in Massachusetts's Sudbury-Assabet-Concord (SuAsCo) watershed.
Photo: Frances H. Clark.

People can unintentionally aid the expansion of native invasive species, as has happened with the mallard duck. By feeding mallards, we have helped their populations to increase, at the expense of black ducks because mallards compete with black ducks for food and nesting sites.

The issue of invasives can best be understood and appreciated in the context of biodiversity. Since invasives thrive and multiply, they may create an impression of environmental health and vigor—a kind of lush green world. However, this vigor is achieved at the expense of biological diversity. As native and indigenous plant species are replaced with invasive exotics, they reduce habitat area and value, and native animal species are "muscled out." As native flora are replaced with invasive exotics, part of a community's unique character is lost. A kind of landscape homogenization occurs, with a few dominant wide-ranging species defining the visual and ecological character of broad areas, erasing subtle regional and local variations (Figure 8.3).

Over-Consumption and Waste Production

While habitat loss (in its various forms) and invasive species are the two principal direct threats to biodiversity, humans' patterns of over-consumption (of water, energy, and consumer products, as well as land) and waste production (of solid waste, organic waste, inorganic waste in the form of nitrogen and phosphorous, and toxic chemicals) are indirect causes of decreasing biodiversity. Current human demands are using natural resources more quickly than they can be renewed, and are discharging wastes more quickly than they can be absorbed. Over-consumption and waste generation can lead to ecosystem collapse. The depletion of groundfish stocks off the coast of New England and the northwestern United States are examples of ecosystem collapse from over-consumption of a resource.

Scientists and economists have conceived the "ecological footprint" as a way to measure the effects of consumption and waste generation on biodiversity and on the environment in general. An ecological footprint is the total ecosystem—or land—area needed to support a defined population, including their homes and areas used for food production and waste disposal, wherever that land is located on the earth. It recognizes that we survive on ecological goods and services from nature from all over the world. The present ecological footprint of a typical U.S. resident is ten to twelve acres. The ecological footprint of a typical person in a developing country, such as Bangladesh or India, is one-quarter to one acre. If everyone lived like the average U.S. resident, we would need at least three planet Earths to live sustainably! (Wackernagel and Rees 1996).

Global Climate Change

Warming of the earth's climate, caused by the buildup of carbon dioxide and other "greenhouse" gases in the atmosphere, is expected to have a profound effect on biodiversity, including the distribution and survival of species. For example, warmer average annual temperatures in New England could cause the die-off of the region's beloved and characteristic sugar maple trees: a dominant forest canopy species, and one intimately linked with the region's economy through tourism and the maple sugar industry. Global climate change is also associated with increased unpredictability in the weather, and with severe storms, both of which are hard on humans and other species.

As global temperature increases, rising sea levels may destroy coastal wetlands. Unless open spaces inland of the present coastline are protected, there will be no place for the species in these wetlands to migrate. Similarly, unless we protect a network of connected lands from south to north, warmer climate species will be unable to colonize new habitat to the north. Only birds will have a chance to relocate, provided we protect a diversity of lands that support their habitat needs.

What Does It Mean to Save Biodiversity? And Why Save It?

If the biota, in the course of eons, has built something we like but do not understand, then who but a fool would discard seemingly useless parts? To keep every cog and wheel is the first precaution of intelligent tinkering. (Leopold 1953)

Saving biodiversity means saving all the parts. The goal of biological conservation is to save genetic variability, species, natural communities, ecosystems, and ecological processes, so that a healthy environment can be sustained over time for animals, plants, and humans. It is important that we preserve various successional stages of natural communities because different species live in particular successional stages—from pioneer grasslands and old fields, to second-growth and old-growth forests. If biodiversity planning is successful, it may prevent the endangerment of species in the future. Once a species becomes endangered, where its numbers are so low that it is in danger of becoming extinct, it is far more difficult to restore that species to healthy population levels.

Biodiversity conservation involves reactive management or restoration strategies undertaken once a problem or issue has been identified. Examples include managing for a particular native species by removing competitive invasive species, or restoring a natural community that has been excavated by replanting the damaged area. Biodiversity conservation also involves proactive strategies, undertaken before a problem arises (for example, purchasing lands for conservation). Plans that integrate both are likely to be successful because certain sensitive species and habitats are best protected before they are threatened, while others are resilient and can be restored.

Saving biodiversity does not mean increasing biodiversity over what would normally occur in a given healthy natural community or ecosystem. For example, healthy meadows naturally have fewer species than some forest communities, and no purpose would be served by trying to increase the number of species in a meadow.

Saving biodiversity also does not mean keeping a natural community or ecosystem static or unchanged. Natural disturbances and ecological processes, such as storm damage and natural succession, actually help to support biodiversity. There are important exceptions: natural changes that are undesirable. For example, sometimes conservationists want to prevent the natural succession of a grassland community to a shrub or forest community. This is certainly true in southern New England and Long Island, where sandplains are now an endangered natural community, as well as in the prairies of the Great Plains where cedar trees are viewed as weeds. Here ecologists use controlled fire to manage succession, in order to preserve grassland and sandplain habitats.

Therefore, the goal of biodiversity planning is neither increasing biodiversity in a healthy natural community, nor keeping biodiversity static. Rather, the goal is to protect and restore the native species already present in a natural community or ecosystem, while, in most cases, allowing natural processes and disturbances over time.

We need to work toward this goal because biodiversity affects our lives, and our communities, mostly in positive ways. It sustains us, physically (preserving biodiversity makes for a healthy environment and healthy people), emotionally (preserving biodiversity increases our mental well-being), and practically (our use of nature). The loss of biodiversity affects our lives, and our communities, in mostly negative ways. Loss of biodiversity impacts us physically (loss of species and natural communities results in lower environmental quality, including the air that we breathe and water we drink), emotionally (loss of nature creates feelings of encroachment or spiritual loss), and practically (loss of nature can mean loss of favorite walking, swimming, birding, hunting, or fishing spots). Note that the practical effect of loss of biodiversity is often economic, such as the loss of fishing jobs and fishing-related businesses associated with the decline of our offshore groundfish species (Kellert and Wilson 1993).

Why is a particular ant, fish, clam, or grass species important, and why is a particular population of a species in your community important, especially if it is "in the way" of human activity? The spotted owl in the Northwest and the salt marsh harvest mouse in California have restricted timber harvesting and stopped a housing development, respectively. Why are these two relatively small species and the specific habitats in which they reside important in the big picture?

Seemingly "useless" parts are linked to other species for mutual survival, and to overall environmental health. They help to maintain the integrity, or healthy function, of the ecosystem in which they and the other species (including humans) are a part. For example, if the frogs and salamanders that depend on vernal pools are displaced by habitat destruction, an important food source for other species is lost. The species they prey upon can become nuisances. Without hawks, owls, and snakes, our communities would be overrun with rodents. Without gulls, which are scavengers, decaying animals would be more prevalent on our beaches and roadsides, causing potential human disease problems.

Saving the biodiversity where we live is extremely important because we have already lost more than 500 species and many natural communities and ecosystems across the 50 states. There are 539 documented losses, and undoubtedly an additional number of unidentified species were also lost. This incremental encroachment on species and their habitats is like unraveling the web of life that links and sustains biodiversity and ecosystems. The losses may start out localized, but as the unraveling continues, whole species and ecosystems can be destroyed. The United States has lost many species to global extinction, such as the sea mink and passenger pigeon. Many more species, including the Canada lynx and bog turtle, have been extirpated from certain states but survive elsewhere. We may never know the many smaller, but still important, species that have disappeared in various states (Barbour et al. 1998).

Approximately one-half of the United States' original wetlands—habitat for much of the country's biodiversity during all or part of life-cycles—have been physically lost since European settlement. This fact is a clarion call for saving remaining wetlands and the plant and animal species they support. The number of wetlands that have been altered by agriculture, coastal filling, and development, or degraded from pollution, adds significantly to a reduction of wetland functions in terms of the water supply, pollution attenuation, flood prevention, wildlife habitat, and other human needs and values. The extent of functional losses, in contrast to physical losses, has not been quantified.

Several natural communities have experienced a decrease in number and size due to development and pollution. Coastal plain pond communities, barrens communities, riverine communities, Colorado Desert wild buckwheat sand dune communities, prairie pothole wetland communities, pocosin wetland communities, and vernal pool communities are among those noted by the fish and wildlife agencies and the Nature Conservancy as imperiled and requiring conservation attention. While threats persist, a few species have been successfully restored, such as the grizzly bear and bald eagle.

Protecting Biodiversity and Ecosystems at the Local level

The goals of biodiversity protection programs are to restore rare species to healthy status and prevent common species from becoming rare. We know that restoration of endangered, threatened, or special-concern species can be a slow and costly process, and the outcome is often uncertain because we may not know how to restore a species and its natural community or ecosystem to their original condition. As a result, it is prudent to act proactively to prevent species from becoming rare in the first place.

A number of federal, state, and local laws protect biodiversity. However, many of these laws focus on specific issues or species, such as the Federal and State Clean Water Acts (cleaning up water resources) and Federal and State Endangered Species Acts (protecting listed rare species). On the horizon are attempts to create county, city, and town rare species lists, as a means for municipalities to measure local declines in species. Few existing laws protect common species, though there are some state and local efforts to do so. See "Web Sources" at the end of this chapter for federal biodiversity agencies and nonprofit organizations.

Saving "the Ark" of biodiversity in the United States will require a comprehensive strategy, with municipalities playing an important role. The strategy for biodiversity conservation has four primary components:

- Building a constituency for biodiversity and ecosystems through diverse education programs;
- Land protection through fee simple acquisition, conservation restriction, and creative development;
- Ecological restoration that restores whole ecosystems;
- Decision-making incorporating biodiversity and ecosystem considerations.

Local communities are the front line in biodiversity conservation. Cities and towns are central to conservation strat-

The United States has lost 539 species to global extinction since European settlement, including:

Atlantic gray whale (1750)

Porter's goldenrod (1800s)

Great auk (1844)

Lost sunflower (1851)

Labrador duck (1878)

Eastern elk (1880)

Sea mink (1890)

American thismia (plant) (1913)

Carolina parakeet (1914)

Passenger pigeon (1914)

Round combshell (freshwater mussel) (1925)

Santa Cruz Island monkeyflower (1932)

Las Vegas leopard frog (1942)

West Indian monk seal (1952)

Deepwater Cisco fish (1955)

Sources: Bruce A. Stein, Lynn S. Kutner, and Jonathan S. Adams, eds. 2000. *Precious Heritage: The Status of Biodiversity in the United States* (The Nature Conservancy and Association for Biodiversity Information. Oxford University Press). J. D. Williams and R. M. Nowak. 1986. "Vanishing Species in Our Own Backyard: Extinct Fish and Wildlife of the United States and Canada," in Les Kaufman and Kenneth Mallory, eds., *The Last Extinction* (Cambridge: MIT Press).

egies, including rallying the public constituency in support of biodiversity and ecosystem protection, protecting locally important biodiverse lands that link to each other and to the lands of statewide importance, restoration of damaged or degraded ecosystems, and land-use planning and decision-making that first protects biodiversity and ecosystems as the foundation for a healthy community. Here we present the fundamental steps for planning local protection of biodiversity.

Communities should map locally and regionally important habitats and biodiversity resources so that these areas can be prioritized for protection. The process outlined in this section will guide communities in the use of Geographic Information System (GIS) mapping (see chapter 7 for more on GIS) to identify "Important Habitat Areas" and the use of this data layer to develop a Biodiversity and Ecosystem Protection Plan for inclusion/consideration in municipal land use, open space, and master plans.

Step 1: Build a GIS library of habitat data.

A community may have existing habitat information, including:

- national and state wetlands maps: e.g., National Wetlands Inventory, vernal pools;
- state biodiversity maps, or biomaps;
- maps of federal and state-listed rare, threatened, and endangered species habitat;
- surficial and bedrock geology maps;
- soils maps;
- topographic maps;
- land-use/land-cover maps.

Obtain these maps from your local planning board or conservation commission. If they cannot be obtained locally, many states and federal agencies have the information available—again, see chapter 7.

Step 2: Analyze habitat information.

The maps and data collected in Step 1 should be analyzed for important habitat features, and to derive four component geographic "layers" as the foundation for your community's "Important Habitat Areas Map": 1) rare species habitat and rare natural communities; 2) large blocks of habitat; 3) corridors and connectors; and 4) wetlands, water bodies, and riparian corridors; each of these layers is further described below (Forman 1995). Note that these layers will overlap partially to significantly. These areas, together

with lands overlying and/or providing recharge to surface and ground drinking water sources, should be the "green" in a community's land-use or master plan. Biodiversity and ecosystems are key elements of a community's green spaces and are necessary to protect and manage for an environmentally healthy community.

(1) *Rare species habitat, rare natural communities, unusual species assemblages, and other biodiversity lands:* Rare species habitat maps should be available from your state natural heritage or fisheries and wildlife agency for all towns where rare species habitats exist. Though these maps are often produced for regulatory purposes, they provide valuable information for habitat planning. Rare natural communities, like rare species habitat, should be a priority for protection. Most rare natural communities have not been mapped by state fisheries and wildlife agencies. Natural communities that are not rare but unusual also merit consideration. Municipalities may be interested in identifying natural communities that are rare or unique within their boundaries, even if they are not rare across the state. For example, an unusual rock formation may provide habitat areas that are unique to the town or city, even if such formations are not rare in the state. Local knowledge and expertise may be particularly useful in locating these rare or unusual natural communities.

Biodiversity maps, such as the *BioMap* produced by the state of Massachusetts, may be available from the state natural heritage or fisheries and wildlife agency. Such a compilation of statewide biodiversity information can be an important tool for local land conservation. Massachusetts's *BioMap* is a blueprint based on biodiversity "hotspots" in the state—the most important intact terrestrial and wetland ecosystems that support the state's diversity of life. The *BioMap* identifies core areas important for rare species and exemplary natural communities, plus associated lands that buffer and protect the core areas and support non-rare species as well. Freshwater aquatic habitats were recently assessed in Massachusetts and complement the terrestrial map. This *Living Waters* assessment can also be obtained from the Massachusetts fish and wildlife agency. See http://www.mass.gov/dfwele/dfw/nhesp/nhbiomap.htm.

Local or regional biodiversity assessments are also available for some locations, while other biodiversity information may be available from "Biodiversity Days" inventories (expert-assisted citizen exploration and documentation of local species), or local experts. The Massachusetts Biodiversity Days Web Page, http://maps.massgis.state.ma.us/biodiversity/, contains city and town Biodiversity Days data.

(2) *Large blocks of habitat:* Large blocks of undeveloped habitat (e.g., forest, grassland, shrubland, emergent wetland) or large blocks of undeveloped land with varied habitats tend to serve as buffers against the adverse impacts of development. Specialist forest wildlife species are sensitive to "edge effects" and require substantial amount of "core area" at least 300 meters from the edges. Other species are "area sensitive" and require habitats of a certain size before they will be used. These large blocks are a first bulwark against the negative outcomes of fragmentation described above. Large patches are also important in supporting the movement of individuals among local populations, enabling subpopulations to recover after disturbance or local extinction.

(3) *Corridors and connectors:* Large areas of habitat are not by themselves enough to retain the ecological integrity of a region without corridors and connectors linking them with other large and small habitat areas. These links can be especially important where the remaining habitat areas are small and scattered. *Corridors* are linear areas that facilitate movement of mobile species between habitat blocks while *connectors* are small habitat areas that link larger areas while also providing intermediate habitat for less mobile species (e.g., redback salamanders, small mammals, plants). Ecological integrity and population viability for sensitive species and populations are enhanced by these links, which permit gene exchange.

(4) *Wetlands, water bodies, and riparian corridors:* Many terrestrial species must have access to water. Conversely, many wetland wildlife species require adjacent uplands.

Figure 8.4. Streams and associated wetlands provide important wildlife corridors, especially through developed land.
Photo: Frances H. Clark.

Preserving Natural Resources

Massachusetts's SuAsCo Biodiversity Protection and Stewardship Plan

Courtesy of Frances Clark, Carex Associates, Lincoln, MA.

In 1998, the Sudbury, Assabet and Concord Watershed Community Council (SWC) organized a Rivers Vision Forum and formed a Habitat Task Force, whose work paralleled the work of the forum's other task forces on water quality and quantity protection, open space protection, recreation planning, and outreach. The Habitat Task Force focused specifically on habitat values for wildlife and plants. The resulting Biodiversity Protection and Stewardship Plan builds upon the existing open space and greenways planning by emphasizing biodiversity—native plants and animals, their habitats, and their ongoing interactions—across the watershed. The plan assesses what species need in order to survive in the watershed, given the constraints of development. The plan focuses on regionally significant, rather than state-wide or locally significant species and habitats, which differentiates it from municipal open space plans and the Commonwealth's Natural Heritage and Endangered Species Program's *Atlas, BioMap,* and *Living Waters* assessment. However, these other sources were particularly helpful in determining the plan's priorities.

The plan uses two interrelated components to determine the Biodiversity Sites: Natural Communities and Focal Species. Natural Communities are distinct assemblages of biodiversity, including micro-organisms, lichens, fungi, plants, and animals. The plan includes good examples of all the natural community types found in the watershed within Biodiversity Sites or other protected conservation land. A Focal Species approach was used to indicate which animals and plants are important to protect. Regional naturalists chose the Focal Species using their best professional judgment. The occurrence of Focal Species helped to determine sites for protection and stewardship actions and the necessity for linkages and buffers.

The Natural Communities and Focal Species were used to identify the biodiversity sites that are regionally significant. Each site is outlined on USGS maps. These sites serve as strategic points for cooperative conservation projects by municipalities, land trusts, and state agencies, so that each can use their limited resources for the best effect.

The plan that resulted from this process provides clear goals and objectives and sets specific tasks that can be accomplished. It also offers a means for measuring success by continuing to inventory the condition of Biodiversity Sites and the presence of the Focal Species over the long term. Note that this case study is also described in chapter 9, with more detail on its relation to watershed planning.

Additional information on this program can be obtained via the Web at: http://www.suasco.org/.

Protection of rivers, streams, lakes, ponds, wetlands, and associated riparian and upland breeding, overwintering, or feeding areas is an important element of habitat protection (Figure 8.4).

Step 3: Field-check existing data, perform field surveys to gather new data, and receive public input on the existing and new information.

In this process, maximize the use of local experts, both professional and amateur naturalists, to perform field work. Public input should be received via an advisory committee and public forums. Members of the public may be familiar with the habitats and biodiversity where they live and could help finetune the data based on years of observations. All this data should be entered into the biodiversity GIS system.

Note, however, that federal- or state-listed rare species habitat locations should be reported to the state fish and wildlife agency and not made public.

Step 4: Use the information developed in Steps 1–3 to complete a Draft Biodiversity and Ecosystem Protection Plan for additional public input.

The plan should have two parts: a *map* of areas important for habitat reasons, and a *narrative* that includes descriptions of each habitat area. The map should identify areas of greater and lesser importance (Figure 8.5). The narrative should describe how importance was determined, so that the basis for decisions and priorities will be explicit and retrievable. The narrative should also provide detailed descriptions of the mapped areas, including natural community

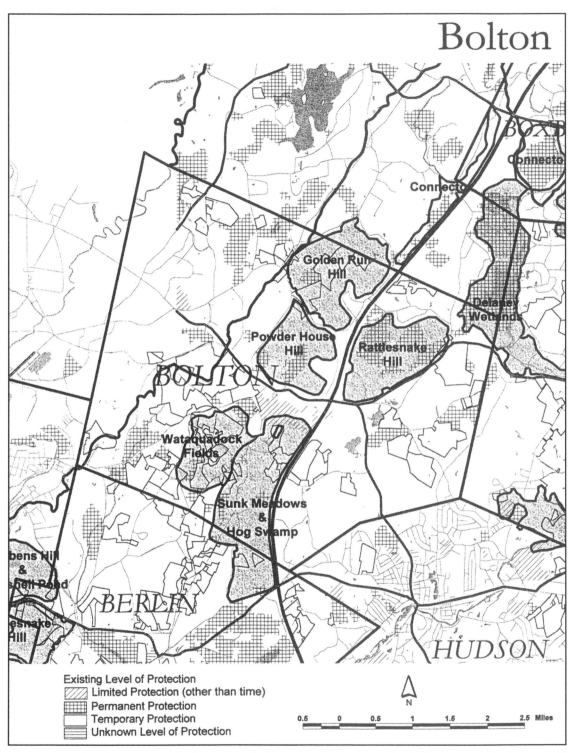

Figure 8.5. Sample draft map showing lands important for habitat reasons, and current levels of protection. A final map should identify areas of greater and less importance and have a companion description of the habitats.

Source: SuAsCo Biodiversity Protection and Stewardship Plan, written by Frances H. Clark. Map by Bill Giezentanner.

Chicago Wilderness Biodiversity Recovery Plan

Courtesy of the Chicago Wilderness Program.

A 1995 survey of DuPage County, Illinois, forest preserves revealed that 80 percent of the county's natural areas had declined to poor health. This alarming news resulted in development of a coalition of 88 regional organizations determined to build the Chicago region into the world's first urban bioreserve. The coalition includes local governments, state and federal agencies, centers for research and education, and conservation organizations. Their initial action was to identify existing wilderness in the region, and they found that the Chicago Wilderness Program currently includes 200,000 acres of protected conservation land in Illinois, northwestern Indiana, and southeastern Wisconsin. To further protect the biodiversity living on this land and link it into corridors, their next step was to develop the Chicago Wilderness Biodiversity Recovery Plan. Completed in 2000, the plan states as its overall vision: "To establish a broad policy of beneficial coexistence in which the region's natural heritage is preserved, improved, and expanded even as the metropolis grows."

The plan is intended to complement the major efforts of several regional planning commissions. It identifies 49 natural community types, including 25 that are rare or uncommon at the global level. Approximately 1,500 native plant species occur in the region, making the Chicago metropolitan area one of the more botanically rich metropolitan areas in the United States.

The plan is also built on the recognition that natural communities and species are the basis of the region's environmental health. Natural communities provide ecological services including maintaining water quality, flood control, assisting crop pollination, and pest control. Biodiversity is also appreciated for its contribution to the quality of life for the citizens of the region and to the region's long-term economic vitality.

The Biodiversity Recovery Plan identifies eight primary goals:

1. Foster a sustainable relationship between society and nature in the region.
2. Enrich the quality of the lives of the region's citizens.
3. Involve the citizens, organizations, and agencies of the region in efforts to conserve biodiversity.
4. Develop citizen awareness and understanding of local biodiversity to ensure support and participation.
5. Improve the scientific basis of ecological management.
6. Protect globally and regionally important natural communities.
7. Restore natural communities to ecological health.
8. Manage natural communities to sustain native biodiversity.

The plan is implemented through the efforts of the members of the coalition's 88 organizations, local, state, and federal elected and appointed officials, private landowners, and recognized leaders in the region, and also citizens who engaged in the planning process through a successful public participation program. It includes a number of specific recommendations aimed to operationalize and realize the broad goals:

1. Manage more land to protect biodiversity.
2. Preserve more land for biodiversity.
3. Protect high-quality streams and lakes through watershed planning and mitigation of harmful activities to conserve aquatic biodiversity.
4. Continue and expand research and monitoring.
5. Apply public and private resources more extensively to inform the region's citizens about their natural heritage and what must be done to protect it.
6. Adopt local and regional development policies that reflect the need to restore and maintain biodiversity.

The plan is designed to act at the landscape, ecosystem, and individual species levels of biodiversity. The foundation for its vision already exists in the region's protected areas, in environmental regulations, in the investments already made to improve sensitive aquatic systems, and in the public and private institutions whose missions include a concern for the region's natural environment. The plan is significant for its broad geographical area of concern, plus the fact that it involves a large and growing metropolitan region, and that it provides a model for coalition-building and public-private collaboration.

Additional information can be obtained at www.chicago wilderness.org, and www.chicagowilderness.org/pubprod/brp/index.cfm.

types, species present, threats to the species and habitat, management needs, and locations for further assessment. (Again, location information for rare species should be kept confidential and reported to the state fish and wildlife agency.)

Step 5: Incorporate the public comments in a Final Biodiversity and Ecosystem Protection Plan for implementation.

The final biodiversity plan should reflect the public values and goals, as well as local knowledge, expressed in the hearings and written comments on the draft plan.

Implementation begins with securing local approval of the plan (i.e., city council/town meeting and municipal board approval). With local approval, tools can be developed and applied to protect the important habitat areas. Funding sources include local property tax surcharges or real estate transfer taxes, state grant programs for land protection and aquifer protection, and land trust funds. Less-than-fee protection options include purchase of conservation restrictions and local bylaws such as a wildlife corridor bylaw, a bylaw to minimize lawn area and maximize natural vegetation, a wetland and wildlife habitat bylaw, and voluntary habitat management agreements. Models of these bylaws can be obtained from environmental nonprofit organizations and regional planning agencies. Implementation of the plan should also include management of public access consistent with biodiversity and ecosystem protection goals, and engaging volunteers to help prevent and control invasive species on protected lands. Consult with state wildlife management agencies and environmental nonprofit organizations for guidance on preventing and controlling invasive species. Municipalities should also review their own policies, such as committing to use of native species and reducing fertilizers and other chemicals on public lands, and in general be sure that the local policies go as far as possible in protecting and restoring biodiversity.

THE MYRIAD of animal and plant species is the metaphorical canary in the coal mine that provides early warning of environmental problems. Changes in biodiversity can signal changes that are not yet apparent, for example groundwater contamination that can take decades to be felt. If humans are to have clean air to breathe, clean water to drink, and a healthy landscape, we *must* protect biological diversity. Only by protecting biodiversity can we be assured of having a truly healthy environment for people and wildlife.

Like politics, all biodiversity conservation is local. Biodiversity conservation is an essential component of local environmental planning and management. In the United States, cities and towns (and, in many states, county jurisdictions) are where land-use and conservation decisions are made. Consequently, local governments and local citizenry—linked one to another—are defining the landscape within which we, our children, and all future generations will live. In choosing to protect biological diversity—or not—local governments and citizens are also defining the health of this landscape, and the health of the humans and wild things the landscape supports. The role of local officials and citizens in the biodiversity conservation task is, therefore, critical.

This chapter is a guide for protecting your corner of nature. We wish you success, and the enjoyment of this living world.

References

Barbour, Henry, Tim Simmons, Patricia Swain, and Henry Woolsey. 1998. *Our Irreplaceable Heritage.* Massachusetts Division of Fisheries and Wildlife's Natural Heritage and Endangered Species Program and The Nature Conservancy.

Bennett, A. F. 1999. *Linkages in the Landscape: The Role of Corridors and Connectivity in Wildlife Conservation.* Gland, Switzerland, and Cambridge, UK: IUCN.

Drake, J. A., et al., eds. 1989. *Biological Invasions: A Global Perspective.* New York: John Wiley and Sons.

Forman, Richard T. T. 1995. Landscape Mosaics: The Ecology of Landscapes and Regions. New York: Cambridge University Press.

Forman, Richard T. T., Wenche E. Dramstad, and James D. Olson. 1996. *Landscape Ecology Principles in Landscape Architecture and Land-Use Planning.* Washington, DC: Island Press.

Gibbs, W. W. 2001. "On the Termination of Species." *Scientific American* 285: 40–49.

Heywood, V. H., and R. T. Watson, eds. 1995. *The Global Biodiversity Assessment.* United Nations Environment Programme. Cambridge, UK: Cambridge University Press.

Kellert, Stephen R., and Edward O. Wilson. 1993. *The Biophilia Hypothesis.* Washington, DC: Island Press.

Leopold, Aldo. 1953. *Round River.* New York: Oxford University Press.

MacArthur, R. H., and E. O. Wilson. 1967. *The Theory of Island Biogeography.* Princeton: Princeton University Press.

Noss, Reed F., and Allen Cooperrider. 1994. *Saving Nature's Legacy.* Washington, DC: Island Press.

Peck, S. 1998. *Planning for Biodiversity: Issues and Examples.* Washington, DC: Island Press.

Wackernagel, Mathis, and William Rees. 1996. *Our Ecological Footprint.* Gabriola Island, British Columbia: New Society Publishers.

Wilson, E. O. 1988. The Current State of Biological Diversity. In *Biodiversity*, ed. E. O. Wilson and F. M. Peter, pp. 3–18. Washington DC: National Academy Press.

World Conservation Union–IUCN, Species Survival Commission. 2001. *The SSC Red List Programme Webpage,* [Internet. on-line]. [18 November, 2002]. Available from World Wide Web: http://www.redlist.org/info/ programme.html.

Web Resources

Massachusetts Biodiversity Web Page: http://maps.massgis.state.ma.us/biodiversity/

Massachusetts Natural Heritage and Endangered Species Program: http://www.mass.gov/dfwele/dfw/nhesp/nhbiomap.htm

National Biological Information Infrastructure: http://www.nbii.gov/geographic/us/federal.htm

National Wildlife Federation (NWF): www.nwf.org

The Nature Conservancy: www.nature.org

United States Environmental Protection Agency (USEPA): http://www.epa.gov/

United States Fish and Wildlife Service (USFWS): http://www.fws.gov/

USGS Biological Resources Discipline (BRD): http://biology.usgs.gov/

USGS Biological Resources Discipline, National Wetlands Information Center: http://www.nwrc.usgs.gov/

USDA Natural Resources Conservation Service: http://www.nrcs.usda.gov/

World Wildlife Fund: www.worldwildlife.org

Photo: Steve Smith

9

Watershed Planning
Securing Our Water Future

Mark P. Smith, Brian Howes, and Joan Kimball

W ATER IS the lifeblood of our communities and our environment. It is a fundamental part of our lives, yet it is taken so much for granted that we often don't recognize its importance and its fragility. We turn on the tap in our homes and water flows. Generally, the water is safe to drink, tastes fine, and it is always there. Many people don't even know where the water comes from—other than from the tap. Water seems to be always available for drinking, for washing, for business, for agriculture, and for our industry. It is indispensable, yet is rarely considered in our daily lives. This chapter briefly describes the natural water cycle which supports these uses and then discusses four issues communities should address to protect their water resources: water quantity, water quality, stream barriers, and managing water supplies.

One of the purposes of this chapter is to show the interconnectedness of the natural system and human needs. Fully addressing these interconnections requires careful planning and thinking by communities and by individuals. All our actions are cumulative and affect far more than may be first apparent. The broader community and its municipal officials will in large part ultimately determine the amount of water needed and how wastewater is handled. Community planning is essential.

The Natural Water Cycle

The natural water cycle of precipitation soaking into the ground, running over the land into rivers and streams, flowing downhill to larger and larger water bodies, and evaporating again is the circulation system that sustains the water in our environment and keeps our waters clean. The water cycle fills our lakes and ponds, keeps our rivers and streams flowing, supports our forests and fields, our wetlands, and the natural biodiversity of our communities. Water flows ultimately to the ocean, where, in our estuaries, it mixes with ocean water to create the fertile nurseries and feeding grounds that play a critical role for our ocean ecosystems. Figure 9.1 pictures this process.

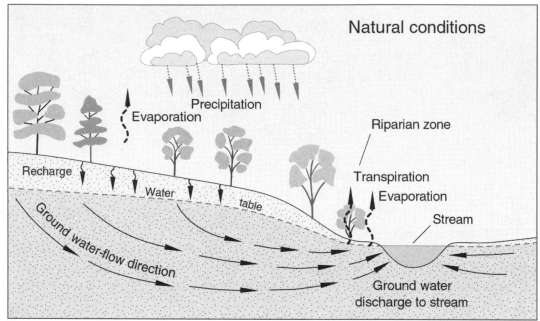

Not to scale   USGS

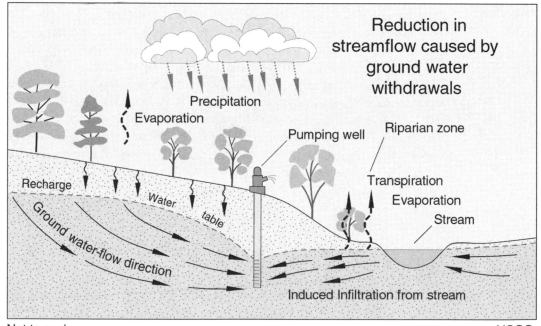

Not to scale   USGS

Figure 9.1. Water cycle.

Source: G. E. Granato and P. M. Barlow, 2005, *Effects of alternative instream-flow criteria and water-supply demands on ground-water development options in the Big River Area*. Rhode Island: U.S. Geological Survey Scientific Investigations Report 2004-5301, 110 p. Available at http://water.usgs. gov/pubs/sir/2004/5301/. By permission.

Natural Variability of Water

The natural variability of water through the different seasons of the year provides the rhythm of our environment and support for the natural world of plants and animals. Fauna and flora in their natural communities have evolved to depend on the seasonal rainfall and naturally fluctuating stream flows. High water levels in spring provide the necessary conditions for the breeding of many species including fish and amphibians. Some native river fish species cannot survive without these natural cycles of high water levels. If the natural water cycle is altered, these river species are gradually replaced with more tolerant species typical of ponds and lakes. Rivers also need high flows in spring and fall to allow fish to migrate to breeding areas and to maintain floodplain forests, and they need occasional very high "scouring" flows to keep rivers clean of silt and sediments.

The high spring flows typical in New England are due in large part to the thawing of the winter's snow. Melting snow pack provides the critical recharge of our groundwater. This groundwater is a key source of water that fills our rivers and streams and keeps our lakes and ponds full, especially during the times between rainfall events and when warm temperatures and water uptake by plants leads to low water levels and dry soils.

Rivers and streams also need the low flows that occur during the warmer months of the year and during drought conditions. These low flow conditions are important to allow the germination of certain plant species and to provide isolated pools and backwaters that serve as breeding areas free from larger predators. Streams are naturally low during these months because evaporation due to the warm temperatures and use of water by trees and other plants captures rain before it reaches water bodies such as rivers and streams, or lakes or reservoirs. During this time of year most of the stream flow comes from the groundwater—groundwater that was recharged in the spring by melting snow and spring rains.

This natural cycle sustains the water we use in our daily lives, replenishing our groundwater wells, filling our reservoirs. To protect a river or stream requires protecting all these flows—the high flows, the low flows, and the timing of when these flows occur.

Water Quality

Our environment is also attuned to thrive on the quality of water found in natural conditions. When in its natural state, such as a forest or grassland, the ground over and through which water flows after it falls as precipitation or melts from snow acts as a natural filter. As water flows down rivers and over riffles and rapids, life-sustaining oxygen is added to it. This clean, cool, oxygen-rich water is ideal for a wide range of fish, amphibians, and other water-dependent animals and plants. It also provides us with clean, safe, and good-tasting water that generally requires minimum treatment to protect the health of our residents. Without the natural water cycle and its ability to absorb many nutrients and pollutants, the cost of treating water to drinkable standards would be much more expensive.

Water is a renewable but finite resource. The clean and plentiful water we need for our communities and our environment depends on the ability of the natural water cycle to remain intact. The cycling of water through the environment makes it a *renewable* resource. But the amount of water flowing through each phase of this cycle in any year is limited, and thus water is a *finite* resource—one that is limited in quantity and that can be degraded in quality.

Changing the Water Cycle

Development, Water Quantity, and Stream Flow

As communities develop they change the natural water cycle by changing the quantity of water in different parts of the cycle. Development can reduce the amount of water available as groundwater and stream flow and, in some cases, impair water quality. By building new roads, houses, shopping malls, or industrial complexes, we prevent water from entering the ground, thereby increasing stormwater runoff and decreasing groundwater recharge. This results in higher storm peaks and increased flooding and less flow in streams between storms and in the dry summer months. In addition, when we withdraw water to supply new developments and provide for the increased population, we use water normally available for stream flow and wildlife.

Water withdrawals can reduce stream flows and even dry up rivers and streams, lower water levels in ponds and lakes, and dry up wetlands. These impacts are caused either by direct withdrawal of surface water, or by withdrawing the groundwater that serves as the base flow of these water bodies.

Water withdrawals affect the natural water cycle especially in summer, the time when water levels are naturally low, and also the time when our water demands are highest, primarily for outdoor use such as lawn watering. These seasonal demands can double or triple water use just when there is less water available in the natural cycle. These conditions are even more extreme during droughts. While we cannot predict when droughts will occur, we can be certain that they will occur. Communities that have adequate storage capacity are in a better position to meet peak demands and survive droughts while protecting natural water resources. Reservoirs and other storage facilities can be filled during high flow winter months and the water saved for use in low flow periods.

Finally, across many states there are numerous water supplies that were built long before current environmental protection laws were put into place, and withdrawals from some of these are causing significant impacts to the environment. In some cases, fixing such problems may only require managing existing sources differently, such as providing adequate releases from reservoirs and pumping from wells further away from rivers during low stream flow periods. In other cases, it is possible to reduce the need for water by reducing leaks, encouraging water conservation, changing industrial processes, or developing new bylaws that discourage excessive lawn watering and encourage groundwater recharge. As less water is withdrawn from the natural water cycle, more is available to support healthy aquatic communities.

Because rivers have naturally variable flows and because maintaining this flow variation is important, our goal should always be to use the smallest amount necessary and to keep flows as close to their natural condition as possible.

Wastewater and Stream Flow

Communities also change the quantity of water in the water cycle by what they do with their wastewater (also called sewage). Communities discharging wastewater usually discharge it far downstream or into the ocean, short-circuiting the natural water cycle and changing the flow regimes in our rivers and streams. Sewer systems can also exacerbate

Planning on a Watershed Basis

Securing the water future of our communities and our environment will require that communities plan their futures in a manner that sustains our water resources. A sustainable future depends upon identifying and protecting the natural areas, sometimes called the "green infrastructure," needed to protect water resources for human and ecosystem use. It will also require changing development practices so that they do not short-circuit the water cycle, providing opportunity for the water to be naturally filtered, and recharging natural storage areas in aquifers, lakes, ponds, and wetlands.

So how can communities build a sustainable future for themselves and the environment? Both a long-term plan and immediate action are needed. Water supply and water resource issues require long-range planning and vision. Communities should consider what will be needed in 20, 50, or 100 years. However, we cannot wait to act to secure what we will need for the future and protect the water cycle that will sustain us and our environment.

A key to understanding the water cycle is to recognize it as a dynamic system with interconnected parts. Planning and subsequent actions must be undertaken on a watershed basis. Watersheds are the natural geographic areas within which all water drains to a single water body. Our natural world is divided into watersheds—with rivers and streams forming the link between upstream and downstream communities.

Solutions to water quantity and quality problems must be based on this watershed context. What one community does affects water in other communities and other parts of the watershed. A sustainable water future will require complementary actions by all communities within a watershed based on a common understanding of the functioning and limits of a watershed and its resources.

stream flow problems when pipes are old and poorly maintained. Significant amounts of clean groundwater infiltrate these sewer pipes through cracks and are sent directly to the wastewater plant. Many homes have their roof drains, sump pumps, or storm drains flow directly into the sewer system, causing relatively clean stormwater to flow into our sewer pipes. In many communities the combination of infiltration of groundwater into sewer pipes and the inflow of stormwater (known together as infiltration and inflow or I&I) accounts for half of all the wastewater reaching our treatment plants!

Ironically, we create similar problems with storm drain systems that move stormwater away from streets, buildings, and parking lots. By building storm drains that discharge directly into rivers and streams to prevent flooding, we bypass the chance for precipitation to recharge the groundwater and increase the opportunities for flash flooding. Some communities have required new developments to retain stormwater on site so that it percolates into groundwater, thereby decreasing the impacts of stormwater on streams.

The Clean Water Act and Continuing Threats to Quality

In the mid-twentieth century, rivers were full of sewage, contaminants, and industrial waste; the Cuyahoga River in Ohio actually caught fire because of the presence of oil-slicked waters. Our nation responded to these health and environmental problems by passing the Clean Water Act in 1972. The purpose of the act is to "restore and maintain the chemical, physical and biological integrity of our nation's waters." One of its major tenets requires states to determine if water bodies are meeting state water quality standards, and it requires industry, wastewater plants, and other direct discharges to be regulated. Great strides have been made in addressing pollution sources through federal and state permits which control how much pollution can be put into our water bodies. However, many of our water bodies continue to fall short of water quality standards.

Wastewater

During the thirty years since the passage of the Clean Water Act, wastewater treatment plants have been built, industrial discharges have been controlled, and our rivers have become cleaner. Attention still must be given to ensure that we adequately control direct discharges to our waterways, that their permits are written with sound limitations to protect the rivers, and that the permits are enforced. Industrial dischargers and wastewater plants that discharge to surface waters are required to use only receiving waters that have adequate stream flow to dilute wastewater and to prevent short- and long-term negative impacts. When rivers lack the capacity to assimilate the wastewater they are receiving, problems such as fish kills, collapse of aquatic systems, threats to human health, aesthetic problems, odors, and loss of recreational opportunities, as well as loss of potential sources of water supply, occur and can result in adverse impacts to agriculture, industry, and real estate.

As we improved the quality of our large discharges from wastewater treatment plants and industry (pollution from the ends of pipes is called point source pollution), experts began to notice that runoff (or non–point source pollution) also brings many sources of pollution to our water bodies. Every time it rains, the water washes over the landscape and carries whatever is in its path into our rivers, streams, lakes, and ponds. From developed areas it brings metals, oils, grease, toxics, and pathogens. From working landscapes and lawns it brings pesticides and fertilizers. Also, atmospheric deposition of metals, nutrients, and other substances carried in the air often far from the source of the pollution contributes to water quality degradation. By adding contaminants and short-circuiting the natural cycle that cleans water, we are degrading the quality of our waters. Rather than serving as a natural filter, the ground in more developed areas becomes a source of pollution.

Increasing development results in new impervious surfaces—roads, parking lots, rooftops, and even highly manicured lawns—that prevent rain from recharging into the ground. Movement of water over and through the ground is a way to naturally "clean" the water of sediment, nutrients, and other pollutants it may contain. Studies have shown that as we increase the amount of impervious surface, our rivers change shape and behavior. By creating buffers, rain gardens, swales, and retention basins, we can slow stormwater runoff and significantly increase groundwater recharge. Porous paving materials can also be used to minimize the impacts of roads and parking lots.

Finally, many of our older communities were built before modern understanding of pollution issues. In particular,

The Water System Legacy

Perhaps the most visible example of long-range water supply planning is the legacy of some the water systems we inherited from earlier generations. The largest example in Massachusetts is the system that serves the metropolitan Boston area. This system, managed by the Massachusetts Water Resources Authority (MWRA) and the Department of Conservation and Recreation (DCR), provides 2.5 million residents of over 40 cities and towns with clean, safe water.

During the first half of the twentieth century leaders in the Boston area realized that even in this water-rich region, Boston was desperate for water. As a result, over time, two major reservoirs were built in rural areas in the central part of the state: the Wachusett and Quabbin reservoirs. Building the Quabbin Reservoir was not cost-free at the time, and it was a divisive solution, especially for people in western Massachusetts. To get good drinking water for the eastern metropolitan area, four inhabited towns were evacuated and flooded, requiring people to be relocated. Citizens in central and western Massachusetts became determined to find alternatives to transferring water across the state for the Boston metropolitan water district.

In 1977 local leaders came together to form the Water Supply Citizens Advisory Committee (WSCAC) to ensure that other western rivers were not "taken" for eastern metropolitan areas. Wisely the WSCAC focused on the need for water conservation and leak detection in the communities receiving water from the MWRA system. Water conserved becomes a source in itself. WSCAC now serves as an advisory group on water conservation and watershed issues.

Today these reservoirs can provide about 300 million gallons a day of remarkably clean, safe water. Ongoing watershed protection activities around and upstream of the reservoirs have protected this important resource. In addition the communities that benefit from this system have been encouraged to protect the local water sources they have, providing over 30 million gallons a day in additional water.

This system remains viable and secure because of major investments in water conservation and leak detection over the last decade. The MWRA has reduced the average water use from 330 to 250 million, saving almost 80 million gallons a day, or almost 25 percent. These investments in conservation and infrastructure have allowed the system to recover from being over-extended in the 1980s, and have ensured its viability, and the viability of the communities that depend on this water, for years to come.

many urban areas have combined sewer systems (CSOs) that were built to handle both sewage and stormwater. During large rainstorms these systems may overflow directly into waterways, spilling millions of gallons of untreated sewage. Solving the CSO problem will require support from all levels of government.

Stream Barriers

Rivers and streams are changed not only by the water withdrawals and sewer systems of our communities, but also by physical barriers that prevent movement of water and species up and down rivers and streams. These barriers—dams, culverts, and bridges—change the hydrology of rivers and block the natural movement of fish and other aquatic species throughout the main stem and tributaries. Many dams were built for agricultural and industrial purposes that no longer exist. Many states are assessing dams and removing unused or unnecessary dams to restore aquatic habitat, fish passage, and water quality and ecosystem health. For those dams that are in active use or are providing other public benefits, they are adding fish ladders, bypass channels, and rock ramps to allow as much fish passage as possible. Culverts and bridges are also being designed using "fish friendly" designs that allow the passage of fish and other wildlife.

Dams and structures also affect water quality in rivers and streams by restricting flows and altering natural flow regimes. In addition to presenting obstructions to fish passage, the ponding of water behind dams allows sediment to accumulate—sediment which is often contaminated. These sediments can be a continual source of contamination as they become disturbed and resuspended. Depending upon the levels of contamination, sediments may need to be stabilized, isolated, or removed. Rivers naturally move sediments through watershed systems, and disruption of this sediment transport can have detrimental affects on water quality. One way to restore the natural sediment regime and protect future flows is to remove the dam or obstruction.

Protecting Water Quality and Supply

Protecting the quality of our drinking water is a top concern of every community and every water supplier. Key to each protection effort is the need to protect the watersheds around our reservoirs and the zones of contribution around our groundwater wells. These areas can be protected through land acquisition and zoning tools to ensure that potential contamination sources are minimized or eliminated. There are only a limited number of areas that can provide safe, clean water in adequate quantity for human use and do so with minimal impacts to the water cycle and the environment. These areas should be identified and protected, whether or not the water from these sources is needed immediately. Waiting to protect them may mean they are lost to development or contamination.

While public water supply is a critical water use, there are other uses that can have potentially large impacts on water resources. Power plants, cranberry bogs, and manufacturing facilities can be large water users. Many industries have been willing to develop water-use plans to both minimize costs and protect water supplies and the environment. Some industries can develop closed-loop systems that reuse the same water, while others may be able to install alternative technologies; some of the most creative solutions have come from several different industries that have designed joint systems to share and reuse water.

Ensuring Our Water Future

Understanding the issues that confront us is only the first step. Developing a long-range plan and taking steps to implement it are key to ensuring that states have both sustainable communities and environmental resources. Communities need to plan systems where their water supply, wastewater disposal, and stormwater management systems work together in a way that minimizes impacts to natural water resources. We can build and operate these holistic

systems so as to protect the water cycle–a cycle that is the life-blood of our environment.

In order to protect both the natural ecosystem and our future water supplies, communities need to look into the future and see the alternatives in terms of water resources and in terms of community growth. One tool that allows communities to understand growth projections is a buildout analysis that depicts the maximum development allowed under current zoning. These analyses offer a chance to see what a community will look like if it develops as currently allowed and what it will look like under alternative zoning scenarios. Buildouts provide a good starting place for planning because the potential water needs for alternative zoning strategies can be compared to each other and to existing water supplies (see chapter 7 for more on buildout analysis and GIS).

Without planning and foresight, development may occur on land critical to protecting rivers and streams or that might have supported sustainable water supply. For example, during the 1990s, Massachusetts was developing 44 undeveloped acres each day, or 16,000 acres per year. To the extent that these are located in areas that could serve as future water supply, we make a sustainable water future that much harder to achieve.

There are three key steps to implementing a long-range vision that will meet the water needs of our communities and our environment:

1. Preserve what we have;
2. Identify and protect what we need;
3. Balance our water budget.

Preserve What We Have

Communities must work to preserve local sources, so they can continue to preserve adequate habitat for native biodiversity and provide high-quality, safe drinking water. Key aspects of these efforts are:

- determining the amount of water needed in the natural environment as well as for reasonable demands of the human community;
- managing water withdrawals that meets the needs of humans and the natural environment;
- protecting the land around our water supply sources and other natural water resources; and

- implementing zoning controls such as water overlay districts, to avoid locating incompatible uses near our water resources.

Preserving what we have also means using water more efficiently and preserving the investments we have made in our water systems. Most communities can save 20–30 percent of the water they use by making real investments in water conservation efforts. By investing in efficient household fixtures and appliances and in leak detection and repair efforts, communities can mine their own system for new water.

Summertime water demands and drought conditions can present particular challenges. Water suppliers often struggle to meet peak demands just when the streams and aquifers are naturally lowest and least able to provide water. Excessive peak demands can also jeopardize a community's ability to fight fires and cause water pressure problems. Water conservation and drought management are crucial for saving water for both future human consumption and the ecosystem.

Much of the summertime water use is expended primarily on lawns and landscapes. Many communities are taking a close look at lawn watering. Some people use rain barrels and cisterns to collect rainwater for lawns, reduce lawn areas, plant native species that do not require watering, and plant drought-resistant varieties of grass with the expectation that it will grow dormant during droughts. Through education, local bylaws, water bans, and innovation, communities, landscapers, homeowners, and businesses can dramatically reduce the amount of water going to lawns.

Communities also need to be prepared for droughts, with plans for ways to temporarily reduce water demands so that we can get through droughts with minimal impacts to the environment. These plans should tie water-use restrictions to water levels in our streams, in the groundwater, and in our reservoirs so that temporary restrictions can be used strategically to maximize their benefit.

Identify and Protect What We Need

Now is the time to find our remaining environmentally sound water sources before they are lost to development or contamination. Just as water supply areas should be a key part of the larger mosaic of protected open space, so should

SuAsCo

The SuAsCo watershed is composed of the three smaller watersheds of the Sudbury, Assabet, and Concord Rivers. The three rivers total 266 miles in length and drain a watershed of 377 square miles; 365,000 people live within the watershed, and 29 miles of these rivers were designated as federally recognized wild and scenic waterways. The watershed lies along the outer belt of the Boston metropolitan area, where many communities are experiencing rapid growth. The SuAsCo watershed is home to numerous smaller treatment facilities operated by municipal governments.

The Assabet River suffers from severe eutrophication caused primarily by excess phosphorus and nitrogen discharged from seven wastewater treatment plants, from bottom sediments, and from stormwater. The situation is exacerbated by the existence of dams that create pond-like, rather than river, environments. The connection between low flow conditions and wastewater discharges is perhaps best shown in parts of the Assabet River where wastewater constitutes about 85 percent of the flow during summer months.

Six communities along the river have decided to form the Assabet River Consortium, with assistance from the Organization for the Assabet River, to coordinate their efforts to develop wastewater management plans that reverse impacts to the river and protect stream flow and other resources.

As the SuAsCo is facing a water quality problem, the watershed team has worked with the Department of Environmental Protection to undertake a Total Maximum Daily Load (TMDL) for nutrients for the three rivers. This TMDL will evaluate both point and non-point sources of nutrients to develop a comprehensive control strategy. In conjunction with this effort the team is seeking to undertake a hydrologic study of the watershed to determine how flows, particularly low flows, are exacerbating the problem. Note that this case study is also described in chapter 8, with more detail on its relation to biodiversity planning.

Local Efforts

Water suppliers, river advocates, neighborhood groups, and individuals have made big differences in their communities. In several communities, river advocates have joined with water suppliers to educate the community about ways that landowners can implement pilot projects, demonstrating that landowners can save water both for rivers and for future water supply needs. Through education and pilot projects, landowners learn to:

- Minimize lawn size; plant drought-resistant grass species; mow lawns at highest possible height to create healthy roots and reduce die-offs; reduce fertilizers;
- Plant native species that do not require watering;
- Collect and reuse water for landscaping needs (rain barrels and/or cisterns);
- Reduce leaks and use low flow toilets, showerheads, washing machines;
- Implement techniques for water conservation.

Communities have implemented these steps:

- Replace and retrofit pipes to reduce infiltration of groundwater into sewage pipes;
- More effective water bans when flow in rivers reaches critical low levels;
- Reevaluate wastewater treatment plants that take water out of the watershed, and find ways to keep water local;
- Structure water rates to reflect the actual usage of water;
- Stormwater bylaws that require new developments to keep stormwater "on site";
- Bylaws that prohibit new underground sprinklers;
- Bylaws that regulate the size of new lawns;
- Leak detection in water system pipes;
- Rebate programs for low flow toilets, washing machines. and other appliances;
- Drought management plans;
- Protection for water supply zones;
- Bylaws that regulate leaking underground storage tanks;
- Removing dams and other stream barriers.

areas that are still intact, functioning natural systems. Many of our most biologically diverse and ecologically important areas are located in and around natural water bodies. Communities should identify and protect areas that are suitable for future water supplies as well as the important landscapes we protect for ecological reasons. These areas can also serve as valuable open space for passive recreation and provide areas where our residents can explore and enjoy the natural world.

Balance Our Water Budget

Securing the future of our water supply will be a failure if it is at the expense of our environment and the natural biodiversity of the state. Balancing the water budget requires that public and other water supply withdrawals and diversions do not exceed the capacity of the source and its continued ability to sustain healthy aquatic and other water-dependent ecosystems.

We need to ensure that our communities and our water and wastewater systems can be operated so as to minimize impacts to local water resources such as rivers, streams, lakes, ponds, and wetlands. We also need to be able to restore those areas where our worst impacts already occur.

Measures that we can take to balance our water budget include:

- keeping our water local by using it close to its source;
- utilizing smaller, decentralized wastewater treatment plants that discharge water back to the ground;
- utilizing stormwater systems that capture the runoff from roofs, driveways, and parking lots and recharge it into the ground rather than piping it to the nearest stream; and
- finding ways to reduce impervious surfaces that prevent rain from recharging our groundwater. Cluster developments, porous pavement, and other green development techniques can help control impacts from impervious surfaces.

Managing Multiple Sources

Local water supplies are primary sources of water for many communities. Interconnections between local systems and neighboring ones are an important way to provide system redundancy. If part of the system fails, through contamination, structural failure, or other reason, the interconnection can still allow safe water to enter the system. Back-up and redundancy often come from connections to larger regional water supply systems. In particular, water systems in older industrial towns were originally built for big industrial uses that no longer exist, and may have capacity to back up smaller nearby water systems. These interconnections for supplemental supplies should be within the same watersheds to help protect our natural water cycle. Such interconnections will be an important component in giving communities the flexibility to meet reasonable peak demands and to survive droughts without major impacts to the environment.

Interconnections may also include access to desalination plants that turn saltwater into freshwater—though the high cost of the water from these systems will likely limit their use so that they will help us to meet only a small part of our overall need. Decisions about desalination projects must take into account the saltwater-freshwater balance so important to aquatic resources in estuaries. While these systems may be able to supplement local supplies, the danger is that they will fuel growth that exceeds the carrying capacity of our lands and watersheds. Communities need to address growth management issues at the same time they are securing their water future.

Ultimately any water withdrawal has an effect on the natural water cycle, but depending on the timing, location, and magnitude, some withdrawals can be less damaging to our natural resources. Water suppliers may be better able to protect the environment if they have more sources from which to choose. Wetland impacts may be minimized if towns have several wells so they can meet their needs by rotating their use, rather than pumping all the wells all the time. Turning a well off gives the groundwater a chance to rebound and minimize impacts to wetland, rivers, streams, and ponds. Maintaining this environmental benefit is important to ensure these wells are not converted to full-time use.

The potential for a new groundwater source to have an impact on surface water resources, such as rivers, streams, lakes, ponds, and wetlands, is often related to the proximity to these resources. Locating wells farther from these water bodies can reduce impacts. Reducing or stopping the use of the well during critical low stream flow or spawning periods can minimize environmental impacts. Even so, any withdrawal can cause groundwater levels to drop unless the resulting wastewater is returned to the watershed.

Ipswich River

The Ipswich River runs almost 40 miles from its headwaters in northeastern Massachusetts to Massachusetts Bay, draining a watershed of about 155 square miles that includes all or parts of 17 communities. The overarching issue of concern is that parts of its headwaters run dry on a regular basis during peak water demand summer months. The severity of this situation has led the Ipswich River to be named the third most endangered river by American Rivers, a national environmental group.

The communities within the watershed rely primarily on local groundwater sources for their public water supplies. Three communities divert water directly from the river during winter months to fill reservoirs, though these communities are outside of the watershed. Though many of the communities within the watershed are at least partially sewered, there are no municipal wastewater discharges to the river. The sewers carry water out of the watershed for discharge to Massachusetts Bay.

The U.S. Geological Survey, in conjunction with the Massachusetts Department of Environmental Management, has undertaken two studies to identify the cause and impacts of the problems facing the Ipswich. The first is a comprehensive groundwater model of the watershed to model the impacts of water withdrawals, wastewater disposal, precipitation, and other factors on the stream flow and groundwater levels. This study has demonstrated that the no-flow and low flow conditions are primarily the result of numerous water withdrawals and a regional wastewater system that conveys water out of the watershed.

The second study is a habitat study to determine how these low flow events affect the ecological health of the river. This study provides the basis for determining the range of flows required to restore a viable natural habitat to the river. Both studies were undertaken with substantial public input. The Ipswich River Watershed Association has worked to establish an Ipswich River Management Council that is working on a watershed-based plan to restore the river. The plan will focus on water conservation, decentralized wastewater facilities, stormwater recharge, and new supplies to supplement water sources.

Managing Our Wastewater Systems

Communities can also work to balance their water budget by reducing the negative effects of sewer systems on stream flow, by keeping water local. This can be accomplished by encouraging properly functioning septic systems or on-site cluster wastewater treatment plants suitable for a single neighborhood, which allows clean wastewater to return to the ground. If building a sewer is the only option, communities should ensure that wastewater is treated and discharged as close to its original source as possible. Also, upgrading old pipes, fixing leaks, and disconnecting roof drains and sump pumps from the sewer system are an easy way to keep this water local rather than having it go into the municipal system that carries this water away from where it falls as precipitation.

PRESERVING WHAT we have, identifying and protecting what we need, and balancing our water budget will allow us to reclaim and protect a water cycle that maintains a healthy ecosystem. This effort will require new partnerships—such as river advocates and water suppliers, landscapers and anglers, town officials and water users, industry and residents. It will require changes in goals and expectations and regions, municipalities, water and wastewater providers, and residents all working together.

Web Resources

American Rivers: www.amrivers.org. A nonprofit organization dedicated to protecting and restoring America's rivers.

American Water Works Association: www.awwa.org. International nonprofit scientific and educational society dedicated to the improvement of drinking water quality and supply.

Center for Watershed Protection: www.cwp.org. A nonprofit organization that provides local government, activists, and watershed organizations with technical tools for protecting streams, lakes, and rivers.

Green Infrastructure: www.greeninfrastructure.net.

The Nature Conservancy: www.nature.org/. A global non-governmental organization dedicated to the preservation of the plants, animals, and natural communities that represent the diversity of life on Earth by protecting the lands and waters they need to survive. This site offers information on conservation planning and biodiversity protection. See also their Sustainable Waters Program, which has resources and tools related to water quantity and stream flow protection issues, at www.freshwaters.org.

Rivers Network: www.rivernetwork.org. A national nonprofit organization that offers information and resources on river and watershed protection.

Trust for Public land: www.tpl.org. A national (U.S.)nonprofit organization that conserves land for people to enjoy as parks, gardens, natural areas, and open space.

U.S. Environmental Protection Agency: www.epa.gov. Contains a wide range of information on environmental protection, watershed protection, and community planning.

U.S. Geological Survey: www.usgs.gov. Contains many studies and reports related to water resources and water resources management.

Water Environment Federation: www.wef.org. WEF is a not-for-profit technical and educational organization with members from varied disciplines who work toward the WEF vision of preservation and enhancement of the global water environment. The WEF network includes water quality professionals from 76 member associations in 30 countries.

Photo: Nedim Kemer

10

Natural Land
Preserving and Funding Open Space

Robert L. Ryan and Arthur P. Bergeron, Esq.

COMMUNITIES ACROSS the country face the challenge of preserving and maintaining open space from the threat of encroaching development. For those local residents and government officials interested in protecting open space, it is essential to integrate its preservation with broader community goals, and to think of open space preservation as a "development" option like other forms of real estate development. Open space provides multiple benefits for a community including maintaining environmental quality and biodiversity, protecting drinking water supplies, preserving historic and cultural resources, providing recreational opportunities, preserving community character, and creating economic opportunities.

Open space preservation is often undertaken both by municipalities and by local, regional, and national land trusts, and the tools described in this chapter are relevant to governments, non-governmental land trusts, and citizen groups.

This chapter outlines the multiple benefits of open space protection, describes constituency-building techniques to mobilize those who share these interests, and then illustrates creative land acquisition and protection options that communities can use to leverage limited open space funding. It also shows residents and officials the basic tools to calculate the potential profit from traditional development, and devise land planning strategies that make open space preservation a reasonable alternative. Preservation techniques that will be discussed include management agreements, conservation easements, limited development, and overlay zoning to protect specific resources that are important to a community, such as scenic hillsides, viewsheds, wetlands, and other habitat areas. Case studies from rural, suburban, and urban communities are used to illustrate the strategies described in this chapter.

Multiple Roles of Open Space

Open space helps to create livable communities. Crowded cities, such as New York City, are much healthier places to live because of the presence of nearby parks, such as Central Park.

Suburban communities also benefit from an abundance of parks, playgrounds, and preserved natural areas. Likewise, the rural character of many small towns and villages is created by the surrounding countryside that charms local residents and tourists alike.

Unfortunately, open space is a valuable and threatened commodity in many communities. In the state of Massachusetts alone, it is estimated that approximately 44 acres of open space are developed every day, or a total of 25 square miles per year (Steel 1999). The statistics at the national level are even more staggering: the National Resource Inventory conducted by the USDA Natural Resources Conservation Service (1997) estimates that between 1992 and 1997 close to 16 million acres of land were developed. Farmland is by far the most threatened open space resource. Of the total 16 million acres of new development in that five-year period, nearly 9 million acres was farmland, an area equal to the combined size of Massachusetts, Connecticut, and Rhode Island. Local residents and government officials concerned about the demise of open space in their communities need to better understand the multiple roles of open space in order to develop the necessary local support to fund preservation efforts.

While the term "open space" is often used in planning and conservation circles, it has a rather generic meaning. As some planners have suggested, the term "green space" does a better job describing urban land which is not occupied by buildings and transportation systems (i.e., roads, streets, parking lots) and is primarily vegetated. For the purpose of this chapter, open space will be viewed broadly to include municipally owned open spaces, such as parks, playgrounds, nature preserves, and trails, as well as other types of public and private open space, such as school yards, cemeteries, farmland, forests, undeveloped lots, and even utility and transportation corridors.

In heavily built-up urban areas, the only remaining open land is usually found along streams and rivers, utility right-of-ways, and abandoned industrial areas. Many cities and towns have capitalized on these overlooked resources to revitalize their communities. For example, the City of Los Angeles is converting an abandoned railyard into much-needed parkland for inner city residents as part of an effort to create a new park and trail system along the much-maligned Los Angeles River (Sorvig 2002). Cities as diverse as Chattanooga; New York; Portland, Maine; and Louisville have also created parks along their formerly industrial waterfronts. Local leaders and government officials concerned about open space protection need to look creatively and opportunistically at the array of open space in their communities in order to preserve, protect, and enhance these resources.

Multiple Benefits of Open Space

A broad-based constituency of supporters is needed to gain public approval for open space preservation, both for funding acquisition and for revising planning policies and regulations. By understanding the multiple benefits of open space, conservationists are in a better position to "make the case" to preserve it and to recruit allies who might be concerned about a particular benefit, such as recreation opportunities. The benefits of preserving open space include protecting environmental quality and biodiversity, nurturing human health and well-being, preserving and enhancing community character and sense of place, and creating economic opportunities.

Protecting Environmental Quality and Biodiversity

The benefits of preserving open space cover the spectrum of the environment, including air, land, water, and plants and animals. Undeveloped land is critical to maintaining clean water in streams, rivers, and other water bodies. In fact, studies have shown that as the percentage of developed land increases in a watershed, especially when over 25 percent of the area is buildings and pavement, there is sharp decline in water quality and aquatic life (MacBroom 1998). Not only is clean water essential for wildlife and fish, it is also critical for municipal drinking water supplies. For example, the City of New York has preserved thousands of acres of undeveloped land surrounding its reservoirs in rural upstate New York, because open space protection is more cost effective than building a multi-billion dollar water filtration plant (Daily and Ellison 2002).

Urban open space is also home to many species of plants and animals, including many endangered species. Protecting the range of biodiversity on the planet is a concern not only for distant, tropical rainforests, but also right in one's own backyard. Many endangered species in the United States are actually found within metropolitan regions. For

Eastern Promenade Trail, Portland, Maine
Degraded Industrial Waterfront to Urban Park

This urban case study illustrates the success of an opportunistic strategy for creating usable open space from abandoned rail corridors and vacant industrial land. The urban waterfront in Portland, Maine, like those of many American cities, was devoted to industrial uses, including railyards which capitalize on the transportation needs of a working port city. Unfortunately, this created a situation where the city's residents were cut off from the recreational opportunities afforded by valuable waterfront land (Figure 10.1). To change this and support a renaissance in Portland, public-private partnerships undertook the acquisition and transformation of an abandoned rail line and industrial area into a waterfront park and trail system.

Portland is the largest city in Maine and its commercial and population center. The City of Portland has a series of waterfront trails in its Back Bay area, but access to the ocean waterfront along Casco Bay from the downtown and urban neighborhoods was severely limited by industrial development and rail corridors. A local nonprofit group, Portland Trails, has been working with the city to promote the development of a 30-mile greenway network of pedestrian and bike trails (Portland Trails 2002; Trust for Public Land 2002). This trail system has its roots in the city's Shoreway Access Plan, which was commissioned in 1988 in response to the rapid waterfront development that threatened to further isolate the public from its waterfront (Smith 2002).

Figure 10.1. *Before:* Industrial land along Portland's waterfront prior to park development separates the city from its waterfront.
Photo: Trust for Public Land.

The Canadian National Railway Company owned 30 acres of waterfront property in downtown Portland including an abandoned railyard and railroad line. The company was interested in divesting itself of this valuable excess property. A city-wide moratorium on waterfront development in 1987 along with the slow economy of the early 1990s made the company willing to negotiate a sale (Smith 2002). However, the Maine Department of Transportation, which according to state statute had the right of first refusal to purchase abandoned rail lines, was slow in its negotiations with the company. A group of private residents working with Portland Trails along with city officials saw this as a unique opportunity to provide public access to the city's waterfront as well as to revitalize an abandoned industrial area. In addition, this parcel provided a key linkage to waterfront trail efforts being developed south of this site. Unfortunately, the fair market value of the property, estimated at $1,248,000, needed to be raised quickly (Trust for Public Land 2002). A national nonprofit group, the Trust for Public Land, was instrumental in assisting Portland Trails and the city in protecting this parcel. The National Park Service Rivers and Trails Program also provided grants and technical assistance to Portland Trails for this project.

The Trust for Public Land worked as an intermediary to negotiate and broker this creative land acquisition deal. In 1993, the trust purchased the 30-acre parcel from the Canadian National Railway Company and worked with several government partners and a private company to convey this land into public ownership. The Maine Department of Transportation used $800,000 in federal highway funds to purchase the majority of the property, 25 acres of rail line and trestle bridge along Portland's waterfront. This purchase was one of the first uses of 1991 Intermodal Surface Transportation Efficiency Act (ISTEA) funds for open space acquisition and trail development (Trust for Public Land 2002). The Eastern Promenade project qualified under four of the ten criteria for ISTEA funding, including providing pedestrian and bicycle access, acquiring scenic easements, and preserving abandoned rail corridors (Smith 2002).

A small one-acre parcel of the railroad land was sold to a local company to give them access to the waterfront. The City of Portland purchased the remainder of the waterfront land, a 5-acre parcel with the abandoned railyard, for $318,000. The city worked with a local ship-building company, Bath Iron Works, to develop a parking facility for use both by workers at their nearby facility and by users of the planned waterfront trail.

Figure 10.2. *After:* Eastern Promenade Trail, Portland, Maine. Successful park development transforms abandoned rail corridor.
Photo: Amanda Walker.

The City of Portland developed the abandoned rail corridor into a 1.7 mile multi-use trail with spectacular views of Casco Bay (Figure 10.2). In addition, the Maine Narrow Gauge Railroad operates a railroad along the corridor for tourists (Portland Trails 2002). This incredibly popular urban park is used by bicyclists, walkers, skaters, and joggers and is estimated to receive over 2,000 visitors per day (Rooks 2001). One of the park's founders, Nathan Smith, describes it as "the jewel in the crown of two miles of priceless waterfront access" (Cohen 2000, p. 2). The City of Portland, Portland Trails, and neighboring communities have worked to create further connections from the Eastern Promenade to other existing trails and parks and to enhance public access to the region's rich waterfront and riverfront resources (Greater Portland Council of Governments 1997).

The Eastern Promenade exemplifies the importance of identifying open space opportunities in less than ideal settings, such as abandoned industrial land, and having a regional open space vision that can be developed incrementally. Public-private partnerships between local and state governments and nonprofit groups were key to the success of this project, as was the ability to find an intermediary party, in this case the land trust, which was flexible and creative in its approach to land protection.

example, the Chicago Wilderness Project estimates that the highest concentration of endangered species in the entire state of Illinois occurs within the Chicago metropolitan region (Chicago Regional Biodiversity Council 1996). Urban waterways are also homes to biodiversity—the rivers and harbors surrounding New York City are home to over 250 species of fish (Botkin and Keller 1995). (See chapter 8 for more on biodiversity.)

Open space plays an important role in moderating the climate in urban areas. Street trees and other vegetation cool urban areas, which because of the high percentage of buildings and paving are much warmer than surrounding rural areas (Botkin and Keller 1995). Urban trees also remove dust and pollutants from the air. For example, research in Tucson, Arizona, estimates that "planting 500,000 desert-adapted trees over five years could be worth more than $236 million to the city" in the form of savings on air-conditioning and other costs (McPherson quoted in Lawson 1992, p. 42). In the city of Stuttgart, Germany, corridors of forest land have been preserved to provide a natural airflow through the dense urban environment, bringing clean air from the surrounding rural areas and diluting urban air pollution, as well as moderating the climate (Spirn 1984).

Nurturing Human Health and Well-being

Protected open spaces are essential for human health and well-being. From the founding of the first urban parks, planners and landscape architects have recognized the recreational benefits of open space as a place for physical activity and restoration in crowded urban neighborhoods. The need to provide places for people to recreate is just as important today, especially as the sedentary lifestyle of many Americans including children has led to record-levels of obesity and other health-related problems (Wilson 2002; Trails and Greenways Clearinghouse, undated; U.S. Department of Health and Human Services 1996). Parks and trails provide opportunities for people to improve their physical health. Unfortunately, many newer communities have not created the large, connected park and greenway systems that are part of many older cities (Wilson 2002).

Preserving open space for recreation purposes can garner widespread support from those groups who might be most likely to benefit, including walkers, bicyclists, skiers, boaters, and other sporting groups. Passive recreation, such as viewing land from a distance also has many supporters including birdwatchers (e.g., Audubon Society), dog owners, wildflower clubs, and nature-lovers.

Preserving areas of nature, open space, and trees and other vegetation can have psychological as well as physical health benefits for local residents. There is a growing body of research which points to the power of nature to restore people from the stress of modern life, including mental fatigue (Kaplan, Kaplan, and Ryan 1998; Frumkin 2001). The positive benefits of nature have been found in a range of settings and populations, including hospital patients' recovery from surgery, office workers' productivity and job satisfaction, children's ability to concentrate and do well in school, especially those with Attention Deficit Disorder, and even prisoners' health and behavior (Frumkin 2001; Ulrich 1984; Taylor et al. 2001; and Moore 1981). Urban trees can also have a positive impact on building community in inner-city neighborhoods (Kuo et al. 1998). Many residents do not need these scientific studies to persuade them—people appreciate nearby green spaces as places to enjoy after a hectic day at work.

Enhancing Community Character and Sense of Place

Protecting open space is often about protecting what makes a community special and unique. The hillsides surrounding San Francisco's Golden Gate, the Lakeshore in Chicago, and the Hudson River Palisades of New York City are all preserved open spaces that give these American cities their character. At the small-town or village scale, a forested hillside or surrounding farmland helps create a unique sense of place. Furthermore, preserving open space helps to create distinct edges that stop the blurring of community boundaries that is characteristic of urban sprawl. Defining what is unique about one's community and identifying places that are special to local residents is an important part of the overall planning process (Hester 1990).

Historic and cultural resources are often found within valuable open space. Historic farms, cemeteries, battlefields, town squares, and gardens are all important pieces of a community's character. Preserving these cultural resources requires preserving the open space that surrounds them. Local and state historical groups have been very active players in the fight for preserving open space and fighting urban sprawl (e.g., Massachusetts Historical Commission 2000) and are an important part of building a coalition for preserving open space.

Creating Economic Opportunities

While quality-of-life issues such as community character can be difficult to define, they are nonetheless important factors in individual and corporate economic decisions. In other words, open space sells. Homebuyers are willing to pay a premium for homes adjacent to parks, nature preserves, golf courses, lakes, rivers, and beaches. Communities are rated high as places to move or retire to based on many factors, including the percentage of parks and other open space amenities. Corporations consider quality-of-life issues for their employees when evaluating where to expand their businesses. Public investment in parks and open space has been found to provide a strong economic generator for municipal coffers in the form of increased property values for private land adjacent to parks and open space and economic investment by the private sector (Garvin 1996).

Preserved open space in the form of farms, forests, and other natural resources also benefits the economy directly by the money that is generated from working the land itself. In many states, agriculture is a multibillion-dollar part of the economy. Scenic, historic, and cultural resources are also economically important for tourism revenue that depends on attracting people to the countryside, forests, mountains, beaches, and other tourist destinations.

Finally, communities need to balance the need for new housing and the desire to preserve open space. On the one hand, preserving open space makes economic sense for many communities because it puts less of a burden on municipal services than do other types of development, particularly residential development. New residential development often costs more in municipal services (e.g., schools, police, fire protection) than it generates in tax revenue, and thus can be a net drain on local revenues. Open space including farmland requires much less in municipal services than it generates in taxes and is a net gain for many communities. In fact, a study of seven Massachusetts towns found that tax rates were much lower in rural areas with abundant open space than in more developed areas (Trust for Public Land 1999). On the other hand, protecting too much open space can impact the ability of communities to provide housing, especially affordable housing. An equitable approach to planning requires that towns accommodate the demand for new housing while preserving valuable open space.

Citizens and government officials concerned with preserving open space need to be able to articulate the argument for preserving nature from a variety of vantage points including economics, aesthetics, environmental, public health, social and cultural, and even community character. The next section will introduce some tools and techniques for maximizing open space preservation with limited economic resources.

Protection Planning Strategies

Communities need to take various types of approaches to preserve open space. In rural communities with abundant open space resources, a proactive approach is more appropriate. Open space needs to be protected before development occurs. Tools such as agricultural zoning and overlay districts (described below) can protect the largest area of land for the least cost to a municipality. In suburban or urban communities with little undeveloped land, a more opportunistic approach makes sense. Converting abandoned rail lines into rail trails is one example of an opportunistic open space planning strategy. Another example is converting abandoned industrial riverfront land into parks. In such opportunistic planning, municipalities are likely to purchase land outright for parks or develop a public-private partnership with willing land owners. Some communities have even resorted to eminent domain to obtain valuable parkland.

Regardless of the type of community, the goal of open space protection should be to build a linked open space system rather than isolated parks and open spaces. Connected open space systems are referred to as greenways. According to Charles Little in his book *Greenways for America* (1990, 1), "A greenway is a linear open space established along either a natural corridor, such as a riverfront, stream valley, or ridgeline, or overland along a railroad right-of-way converted to recreational use, a canal, scenic road, or other route. It is any natural or landscaped course for pedestrian or bicycle passage. [It is] an open space connector linking parks, nature reserves, cultural features, or historic sites with each other and with populated areas." Greenways provide a way to connect people to parks and open space along pedestrian and biking corridors that are free from automobile traffic (Flink and Searns 1993).

Station Road Farm, Amherst, Massachusetts

Saving Agricultural Character with Minimal Funds

In this case study, creative land acquisition strategies were used to craft a conservation proposal to protect a 101-acre horse farm in Amherst, Massachusetts. A developer approached the existing owner with an offer to purchase the land for approximately $1.2 million dollars with a plan to develop ten residential lots. This proposal relied on extending the existing town sewer, which would have encouraged more development of nearby farmland (Figure 10.3). The town's planning objectives for the area are to steer development to existing village centers and preserve the rural character of this outlying area. In the end, the town protected this farm and the agricultural character of the area using only $75,000 in local government funds (Amherst Conservation Commission 1999; Newcombe 1999).

Amherst, a college town in the scenic Connecticut River Valley, has seen a steady increase in development and population due to its high quality of life and stable economy. The town has actively protected farmland and conservation land through purchase of development rights and other strategies, including an agricultural overlay zone that requires clustering of new residential development to help preserve the town's remaining farmland.

The horse farm, known as the Station Road Farm property, is located in South Amherst amid a large block of active farmland (Figure 10.4). This farm contains many important open space benefits which helped build the broad-based support for its preservation, including conservation, aquifer protection, biologic diversity, historical interest, recreation, and scenic value.

Figure 10.3. Large lot development such as this new home near the Station Road Farm was the major development threat.
Photo: Robert L. Ryan.

Figure 10.4. The working horse farm is preserved as permanent conservation land which is leased back to a farmer.

The farm is within the aquifer recharge area for one of the town's drinking water supplies, and development could negatively impact water quality. Biologically, the farm ranks very high because it provides an open grassland habitat, a rarity in forested New England, and is estimated to contain 112 species of birds. The stream that bisects the farm drains the adjacent 1,000-acre Lawrence Swamp.

The land is adjacent to several town-owned conservation areas, as well as near privately owned farms that are permanently protected under the state's agricultural preservation program. In addition to two active equestrian operations which provide recreation benefits, the farm is adjacent to two important regional trails, the Norwottuck Trail, administered by the Commonwealth of Massachusetts and the 42-mile Robert Frost Trail. The farm was the site of the town's poor farm during the 1800s. From an aesthetic standpoint, the farm is important for the scenic views it provides of the adjacent farmland and forested hills from the town common of the historic village of South Amherst (Figure

10.5). The importance of farmland to the rural character of South Amherst had a major impact on local support for preservation of this farm.

The land protection proposal for Station Road Farm crafted by Pete Westover of the Amherst Conservation Commission is a brilliant example of public-private partnerships, creative funding, and conservation entrepreneurship (Figure 10.6). The private landowner was willing to work with the town to conserve the farm as long as the town could equal the developer's offer for his land. In order to raise the $1.2 million purchase price, the 101-acre farm was divided into two parcels. The town agreed to purchase the lower 81.5 acres with the equestrian operations for $875,000. The farm owner was willing to receive payment over a three-year period in order to minimize his tax liability. The town raised the purchase price by using $75,000 of town funds (the majority of which had been earmarked for purchase of development rights for farmland and aquifer protection), $100,000 in private donations from local residents and land trusts, $265,000 in state

Figure 10.5. Scenic farm views preserved from development.
Photo: Robert L. Ryan.

Figure 10.6. Limited development such as this large home was used to partially fund protection of the farm in the background.
Photo: Robert L. Ryan.

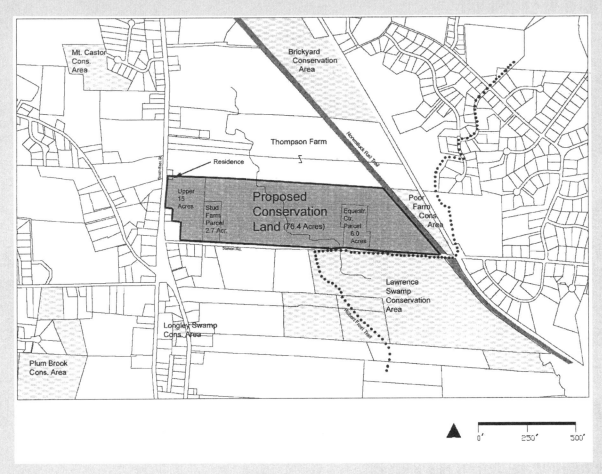

Figure 10.7. Plan of Station Road Farm, Amherst, Massachusetts.

funding from a self-help grant program aimed at conservation land, and $435,000 from resale of the equestrian barns and complex on a 8.7 acre parcel to private interests. The new private owners rented the remaining 76-acre pastureland from the town (Figure 10.7). This strategy ensured that the farm could remain an active working farm, but the town would have control over future management practices that might affect the local aquifer and drinking water supply.

The upper 15.85 acres of the farm including the historic farmhouse were valued at approximately $375,000. These were preserved by two local land trusts, a nearby college, and the town. Hampshire College was looking for a home for a college administrator and agreed to purchase the farmhouse with a 1.8 acre lot. Two local land trusts, the Kestral Trust and Valley Land Fund, acted quickly and purchased an option on the remaining 14-acre hayfield in order to give the town and nearby college a chance

to raise the money to protect this parcel. The college agreed to assist the town in raising $375,000 from a private foundation either to purchase the development rights to the hayfield or to purchase it for town conservation land.

This case study presents several important lessons in creative land preservation. The first is the importance of a key individual who is knowledgeable about land acquisition strategies and funding tools, and who can lead the fight for preserving land. The second lesson is that even costly open space land can be protected with very limited expenditure of public funds. The third lesson is to work with willing private landowners to meet their financial and personal goals for their land. And the final lesson is, in order to build a groundswell of public support for preserving open space, the particular piece of land must be valued from many different perspectives and must contribute to the creation of a larger open space network.

Greenways are very efficient from a land protection viewpoint, because they protect linear corridors of open space, such as river valleys, which are often the only remaining open space in many developed areas. Stream corridors, in particular, often have the highest ecological value and are in many cases unsuitable for development. While some greenways focus on providing recreational amenities, others corridors are protected solely for their environmental value and do not provide public access. By linking together larger protected natural areas, greenways preserve the valuable natural corridors that ecologists have determined are essential for protecting biodiversity (Smith and Hellmund 1993). Since many historic and cultural resources also occur along river corridors, greenways can incorporate multiple benefits including recreation and environmental protection, as well as historic and cultural preservation (Fabos and Ahern 1995). See Ahern (1995) for a more detailed description of planning approaches for greenways.

Planning Tools and Techniques

Communities can use a wide array of tools and strategies to preserve valuable open space. These tools will be discussed with regard to their effectiveness at land protection and their cost to local governments.

Planning and Zoning Regulations

(1) Comprehensive planning: The most cost-effective but often most under-utilized tools for open space protection are comprehensive planning and local zoning. Comprehensive or community master planning should identify valuable open space where development would cause irreparable harm to significant natural resources including floodplains, wetlands, streams, shorelines, aquifers and other drinking water supplies, and wildlife habitats. Other landscapes which might also pose a hazard if developed include steep hillsides, unstable soils, and coastal areas subject to hurricane damage, flooding, or erosion. In addition, the comprehensive planning process should identify productive natural resources such as prime agricultural and forest land that provide economic value to the community (Kaiser et al. 1995). Unfortunately, while many comprehensive plans identify valuable open space resources, these resources are inadequately protected when the plan is implemented

through local zoning. In addition, in many states comprehensive plans are not legally enforceable documents, but rather guides for community planning.

(2) Zoning: Municipal zoning can be used in many creative ways to protect open space including land-use zones, overlay zoning, and land-use bylaws and regulations. Depending upon state-enabling legislation, municipal governments have the power to zone land to restrict it for particular uses, such as residential, commercial, and industrial use. The legal basis for zoning is to protect the public health, safety, and welfare. The courts have upheld communities' rights to include protecting a community's historic character, if properly defined in local ordinances, and if private landowners' rights to use their property have not been taken away without just compensation.

Some examples of zoning for open space include agricultural, forest, and coastal or floodplain zoning. Agricultural zoning and property tax relief are considered the two most cost effective policies for protecting large areas of farmland (Daniels and Bowers 1997). Agricultural zoning restricts the use of the land to farming and allows only minimal residential development. For example, agricultural zoning in rapidly growing Lancaster County, Pennsylvania, allows one building lot per 25 acres, with a 2-acre maximum coverage (Daniels and Bowers 1997). Productive open space land can also be zoned for other natural resource uses. In Hanover, New Hampshire, productive forestland on steep hillsides has been zoned for forestry with a minimum lot size of one residential unit per 40 acres; ranchland in Santa Barbara County, California, has a 100-acre minimum lot size.

One of the most popular ways to protect open space is through large-lot zoning, in which homes must be built on one or more acres of land. While this may be appropriate in areas where this is the traditional density, it also causes significant problems. Large lots can turn out to be "too big to mow, too small to plow"—in other words, despite best intentions they can increase the fragmentation of functional open space. We generally don't encourage this type of zoning.

In addition to zoning land for open space, municipalities can use overlay districts to limit development in areas that are unsuitable for building. "Overlay district" is a planning term for additional regulations that are superimposed on parcels that already have an existing zone, such as residential use. Overlay districts often cover specific landscapes.

For example, floodplain overlays restrict development in areas that are subject to flooding. Hillside ordinances are another example. The City of San Diego, for example, limits development on slopes greater than 25 percent. Overlay districts are also often used to protect historic and scenic resources. Some municipalities prohibit development on important ridgetops or mountain ranges. For example, San Luis Obispo, California, prohibits development over a particular elevation on the scenic hills surrounding this picturesque town. Overlay zones can also be used for protecting farmland. Amherst, Massachusetts, has a prime farmland overlay district that requires new residential development to be clustered on a section of a parcel, leaving the remaining prime farmland permanently protected.

Zoning for open space is not, however, without its limitations. One of the limitations of local zoning for protecting open space is that it is not permanent, but can be changed by the local government when development pressure increases. As well as frequently lacking political support, environmental zoning is often criticized for being too weak or ill-conceived. For example, in many localities agricultural zoning has not been effective because the minimum lot size is often too small (e.g., 5–10 acres) to sustain viable farming operations. (See chapter 6 in this book for more information about zoning.)

(3) Cluster development: Local governments can require or provide incentives for residential development to be clustered on the least environmentally sensitive part of a property, while the remaining land is left as permanently protected open space. In recent years, this planning tool has been renamed conservation subdivision by some planners (Arendt 1996). In this new version, proponents of cluster development have tried to address the criticism that such developments often result in fragmented and unusable open space. By planning a municipal or regional open space network prior to development, communities can identify the important open spaces that they would like to protect as part of cluster developments. Developers are more likely to build cluster developments if they receive incentives such as a density bonus or a streamlined permitting process, or if cluster developments are "as-of-right" and do not require a special permitting process. An initiative to make cluster zoning the standard in parts of Massachusetts is detailed in chapter 2. While cluster development done carefully can be quite helpful, it cannot fix bad underlying zoning. For example, clustering does not solve the problem of agricultural protection, as putting new residents near farms still often spells the coming end of farming, because suburban homes and farms do not intermix well. And unless the protected open space resulting from clustering is linked with other protected open spaces, small, privatized, and fragmented open space may be the town's only result from this zoning approach.

(4) Natural resource ordinances and subdivision regulations: Many municipalities have passed planning ordinances that protect certain landscape features regardless of the type of land use that is allowed. For example, Ann Arbor, Michigan, has a tree ordinance that requires developers to replace any trees which are removed during construction. In San Marino, California, homeowners and developers are prohibited from cutting down historic live oak trees, which give this community part of its character. Local governments can also create stricter wetland and stream protection ordinances that go beyond federal or state standards. For example, Amherst, Massachusetts, protects a larger area around isolated ephemeral forest wetlands called vernal pools than do state regulations. Other communities have used these types of ordinances to protect cultural features as well, such as prohibiting historic stone walls from being removed. But such ordinances, though important for protecting features that give a community its character, do not necessarily protect large areas of open space.

(5) Subdivision regulations: In many municipalities, local governments have the power to exact fees or open space donations from developers as part of approving new subdivisions (Flink and Searns 1993). The idea behind these regulations is that land developers should provide parks and open space for the people who will be living in these new neighborhoods, rather than transferring this burden to the local government. In some communities open space fees are used to purchase parkland, while in others they are used to protect other types of open space such as farmland or forests. The community's comprehensive plan and open space plan are vital for ensuring that a community receives parkland that helps build a viable open space network. For example, San Diego has identified its canyons or stream valleys as land that should be donated to the city when development occurs.

Land Acquisition Strategies

Up to this point, the open space planning tools that have been discussed require minimal cost to local government, yet can provide extensive open space protection.[1] However, with many regulatory approaches the land remains in private ownership and is not open for public recreation. Also, many communities lack the political will to implement these regulatory approaches. To address this many towns turn to the acquisition of land in one form or another. The most common methods are the following:

(1) Purchase: Purchasing open space land provides permanent protection, as well as public access for recreation and other use. Fee simple purchase is the most costly option for protecting open space, and only a limited amount of land can be protected in this manner. Furthermore, the purchase of conservation land by local governments and nonprofit groups removes it from the tax rolls and, in the short term, can increase property taxes for remaining landowners (Trust for Public Land 1999). This approach makes the most sense for the lands that are highest priority for conservation, particularly in highly developed areas where open space is scarce.

(2) Land donations and bargain sales: Many communities have benefited from land donations by civic-minded residents and businesses. Landowners' desire to see their land protected for future generations is a strong motivation for donations to land trusts (Ochterski 1996). These donations provide tax benefits to the donors, as well as benefiting the community. Some landowners are willing to sell their land for a reduced price, or bargain sale, to a local government or nonprofit group in exchange for the tax benefits. Land donations can be facilitated by developing a working relationship with local landowners, understanding their particular motivations for wanting to donate their land, and meeting these needs through creative financial planning, such as living wills.

(3) Limited development: Local governments and nonprofit groups such as land trusts have the ability to develop land to less than its highest potential as allowed under current zoning. For example, a valuable piece of forest land can

be purchased by a town or land trust for protected open space. A few house lots could be developed on the least environmentally sensitive section of the land and sold on the private market to recoup some of the expense of purchasing the property. When combined with other goals of local government, such as providing affordable housing, limited development can be an innovative strategy for protecting open space with limited funds.

(4) Purchase of development rights (PDR) programs: A landowner has many separate property rights, including the right to develop the land as allowed under current zoning and the right of trespass (i.e., determining who can use the land). Each of these rights can be sold separately. PDR programs involve the sale of the development rights to a government entity or nonprofit group. The private landowner retains title to the land, but can no longer develop it for more intensive use as specified by the particular program. For example, fourteen states have agricultural preservation programs which purchase the development rights to farmland, as do many local governments. The farmer continues to farm the land and can sell it or pass it on to heirs, but it cannot be developed for residential, commercial, or more intensive use. In Massachusetts alone, approximately 40,000 acres of farmland have been protected through this type of program (Massachusetts Executive Office of Environmental Affairs 2000), and nationally purchase of development rights programs had protected 345,746 acres by 1997 (Daniels and Bowers 1997). While PDR programs are good at protecting land in perpetuity and keeping it in private ownership, development rights can be expensive to purchase, which limits the amount of land that can be protected. In addition, purchase of development rights does not allow public access to private land. A related but more complex version of this is transfer of development rights programs, which are discussed in chapter 6.

(5) Easements: Private landowners have the rights to sell or donate specific rights on their land through legal mechanisms called easements. Easements can be granted in perpetuity and remain in force for all subsequent landowners. Easements can be granted to individuals, nonprofit groups such as land trusts, and government agencies. There are several types of easements that are important for open space protection. Some (right of public access easements) allow the public to access sections of a parcel for recreation. Conservation easements permanently restrict the development

---

1. Tax structures, such as taxing farmland and open space on its use value rather than its developed value, are another important strategy for open space protection, but are applicable more on the state level than locally.

and future use of the land to something like its current use. A joint-use easement is a cooperative arrangement between utilities and municipal or nonprofit groups to allow the public recreational access to existing paths of utilities.

(7) Land leases: One short-term strategy for developing an open space network is to lease land from private and institutional landowners. While leases are not usually a long-term solution for protecting privately owned land, they can slow development until funds can be raised for more permanent protection. In some cases, local governments have negotiated long-term leases from the state government and federal government for public open space.

(8) Land trade: Another strategy for creatively developing an open space network is to exchange land with more development potential which may be owned by the local government for land with higher value for conservation. This technique is particularly suited for building larger blocks of contiguous open space and parkland. Care must be taken that the land which is traded is of equal monetary value.[2]

Valuing Your Open Space for Development and Preservation

Prior to using the land acquisition strategies outlined above, it is important for communities that are interested in preserving open space to understand the actual value of a piece of land for development. By learning to think like a developer, local communities are better prepared to develop creative solutions for preserving open space with limited resources. General principles of how developers think are presented in chapter 4, while here we focus on the economics of land development.

The permanent protection of land as open space is a development option, just like building homes or a new commercial area. By not actively imposing development restrictions on the land, a community has made the tacit decision that other development options are preferable, either because members of the community support increased development or because permanent protection does not seem "worth it." When a community has determined

that the land is "not worth saving," it usually means that land preservation costs too much. But how much is too much? To answer this question, communities need to understand how developers value land.

For the purposes of this section, we will presume that the land in question is farmland, that it is zoned for the development of single-family homes, and that there is a market demand for new homes. The basic structure of this analysis applies, however, whether the site is a "brownfield" with an old factory on it that is zoned for industrial uses, or whether it is a cornfield that is zoned for agriculture. To preserve the land, a community needs to know the competition.

Suppose that the parcel one wants to save is currently a farm field, a large rectangular 43-acre parcel with 800 feet of frontage on an existing road. The field extends back from the road about 2,365 feet to a stream. Assume that the land is zoned for single-family homes on one-acre lots, and that each lot is required to have 200 feet of road frontage. Assume further that each house lot has a current market value of $100,000.

The typical residential developer expects to make at least 25 percent profit on each successful subdivision. This may seem like a sizable profit, but from the developer's perspective, this level is needed because (1) many subdivisions take years to complete, so there is value to the length of time that the initial investment is tied up; and (2) real estate development is a risky business, and many subdivisions fail, so the developer has to make up for the losses from other projects.

The developer will analyze the development of this parcel in two parts. First, he or she will immediately try to subdivide areas from the main parcel that already have existing road frontage. Given the road frontage requirement of 200 feet, this will yield three house lots (using three acres) along the existing road, while leaving the remaining 200 feet of the original 800 foot frontage to provide access for a new subdivision road. At $100,000 per house lot, this means that the developer can make $300,000 without doing anything, while still leaving 40 acres to be developed.

The standard assumption when planning subdivisions is that roads, utilities, and other related work, together with the vagaries of lot layout, will consume about 20 percent of the land in every subdivision. Therefore, the rule of thumb for determining the number of lots that can be created for a subdivision is to take 80 percent of the size of land being

2. Portions of this section are based on Flink and Searns 1993, pp. 101–119, who derived their work from *Tools and Strategies: Protecting and Shaping Growth* (Regional Plan Association, 1990). Other sources include American Farmland Trust 1998; and Daniels and Browers 1997.

Table 10.1. Calculating Costs for Preservation Instead of Development

Line name and calculation		
a	Total acreage	43
b	Zoning	1 house per acre
c	Sale price of land per lot	$100,000
	Land developed as of right, based on road frontage	
d	Possible lots*	3
dc=e	Gross revenue	$300,000
bd=f	Acreage used	3
	Land subdivided and road added	
a-f=g	Remaining acreage	40
g20%=h	Roads, etc. = 20% of land	8
g-h=i	Land available for house lots	32
i/b=j	Acreage divided by zoning = possible units	32
jc=k	Gross revenue	$3,200,000
	Total revenue	
e	Revenue from 3 lots (frontage lots)	$300,000
k	Revenue from subdivided lots	$3,200,000
e+k=l	Total gross revenue	$3,500,000
	Costs	
	Road frontage (32 lots/0.5 x 200 ft.)	3,200
	Estimated cost per foot for roads, sewer, water	$200
m	Costs for roads, sewer, water	$640,000
n	Services (lawyers, etc.)**	$360,000
m+n=o	Estimated costs	$1,000,000
	Profit calculation	
l	Total gross revenue	$3,500,000
p	Est. profit goal	25%
kp=q	Gross profits	$875,000
	Developer ability to pay for land	
k	Total gross revenue	$3,500,000
q	Gross profits	$(875,000)
k-q=r	Remaining profit available to cover costs	$2,625,000
o	Estimated costs	$(1,000,000)
r-o=s	$$ available to pay for land	$1,625,000
	RECAP: Project costs	
s	Land	$1,625,000
o	Development costs	$1,000,000
q	Profits to developer	$875,000
s+o+q	Total project value	$3,500,000

*Possible lots based on frontage: 800 feet of road frontage /200 foot required per lot = 3 lots + 200 feet for road to new subdivision

**Services cost calculated as 50% of hard costs (roads, sewers) = $320,000 + $40,000 cushion for unexpected expenses

purchased, then divide by the residential lot size allowed by the current zoning. In this example, the 40 acres x .8 (80%) divided by 1 acre per lot would equal 32 lots. At $100,000 per lot, the lots will yield $3,200,000 to add to the $300,000 the developer made on the three lots subdivided at the beginning of the project, for a total revenue of $3,500,000. Assuming that the developer wants to make at least 25 percent from his investment, the project will need to cost less than $2,625,000 including the cost of the land to produce the profit that will make this development worthwhile.

Of course, from the total revenue, the developer's costs need to be subtracted. The biggest cost is road construction. Each of the 32 new house lots will require 200 feet of new road frontage, for a total of 6,400 feet. Since homes will be built on both sides of the new roads, the total road length that the developer will need to build will be 3,200 feet. Currently in Massachusetts, the cost of building a new road including the pipes for sewer and water is about $200 per foot. Therefore, the road costs on this project will equal at least $640,000. The developer will also have other costs, like lawyers, engineers, insurance, and the interest on the loan to cover all the project costs. Assuming that these other costs will equal another $360,000, the developer's cost for developing the land total about $1,000,000, and the profit is adequate as long as the cost of purchasing the land is less than $1,625,000. The cost of the land plus its development costs would be a total cost of $2,625,000, which would yield 25 percent profit on revenues of $3,500,000 from the sale of the house lots.

The community can use this new information to help strategize ways to save this farm field. First, the community could raise the $1,625,000 to purchase the farm using some of the strategies outlined in this chapter; or second, the community could reduce the developer's revenue or increase his costs, thereby reducing the amount of money that the developer will have to purchase the land. For instance, the community may have existing local land use controls or environmental laws limiting development near streams, thereby reducing the number of lots that can be built. Suppose that local ordinances reduce the proposed subdivision by four lots. This would reduce the developer's revenue by $400,000, making the total revenue only $3,100,000, and lowering the amount that he can spend and still make a 25 percent profit to $2,325,000. Of course, reducing the number of lots reduces the required road frontage by 800 feet

and the required road length by 400 feet, thereby reducing his development costs by $80,000. Thus the new road would cost $560,000 and the entire development costs will be $920,000, giving the developer $1,405,000 to spend on the land.

There is no end to the different ways in which a community can approach this or any other land preservation problem, whether the result is saving all or part of a piece of land. The best approach to each unique situation is to figure out the effect of proposed preservation strategies, zoning ordinances, or other bylaws on the development potential of land for other purposes. These skills require the services of experts such as lawyers, accountants, and even developers to help create realistic projections. Some of the larger land trusts can assist communities by approaching owners with land preservation options, because they have the staff with expertise in calculating the development potential of a piece of land.

Conclusion

Preserving open space requires developing a constituency of supporters from across the community to garner the necessary financial and political support. The key to successful land protection efforts is to promote the multiple benefits of open space such as environmental protection, recreation, and economic redevelopment. While preserving particular important parcels is good, for the long run it is essential that a community develop a larger vision for an open space network that will preserve the community's character while still allowing intelligent development to occur. The examples described in this chapter both had a long-range vision. In the case of Amherst, it was the desire to protect agricultural land and rural character. In Portland, the vision was to create a network of parks and trails to provide public access and revitalization to its scenic waterfront.

As part of long-range open space planning, communities should develop benchmarks or indicators of progress toward land preservation. Gathering baseline information about the size and percentage of protected open space in one's community is one way to begin this process. Indicators to assess progress in open space protection include increases in acreage of protected lands, miles of new trails, and public access to recreation resources such as rivers and lakes (see the Appendix). By developing a database of open space protection, communities can highlight their achievements to potential funding agencies. Additionally, celebrating milestones in land preservation (e.g., the first hundred acres of preserved farmland or the first ten miles of bike trails in town) can help garner publicity and support for further preservation efforts. There are a myriad of challenges to preserving land—celebrating your community's progress on the way is an important part of community building. Developing a legacy of protected open space is the centerpiece of community preservation for future generations.

References

Ahern, Jack. 1995. Greenways as a Planning Strategy. *Landscape and Urban Planning*, 33: 13–155.

American Farmland Trust. 1998. *Fact Sheet: The Farmland Protection Tool Box*. Washington, DC: Farmland Information Center, American Farmland Trust.

Amherst Conservation Commission. 1999. Self-Help Application for Station Road Farm, Amherst, Massachusetts. Report Submitted to the Commonwealth of Massachusetts, Executive Office of Environmental Affairs, Division of Conservation Services.

Arendt, Randall G. 1996. *Conservation Design for Subdivisions: A Practical Guide to Creating Open Space Networks*. Washington, DC: Island Press.

Botkin, Daniel, and Edward Keller. 1995. *Environmental Science: Earth as a Living Planet*. New York: Wiley.

Chicago Regional Biodiversity Council. 1996. *Chicago Wilderness: An Atlas of Biodiversity*. Chicago: Chicago Regional Biodiversity Council.

Cohen, Ted. 2000. Jewel in the Crown: A Path Connecting the Eastern Promenade and Baxter Boulevard Becomes a Reality. *Portland Press Herald* (June 4, 2002). Accessed on-line (Sept. 16, 2002), http://outdoors.mainetoday.com/biking/trail060400.shtml.

Daily, Gretchen C., and Katherine Ellison. 2002. *The New Economy of Nature: The Quest to Make Conservation Profitable*. Washington, DC: Island Press.

Daniels, Tom, and Deborah Browers. 1997. *Holding Our Ground: Protecting America's Farms and Farmland*. Washington, DC: Island Press.

Fabos, Julius Gy, and Jack Ahern, eds. 1995. *Greenways: The Beginning of an International Movement*. Amsterdam: Elsevier.

Flink, Charles A., and Robert M. Searns. 1993. *Greenways: A Guide to Planning, Design, and Development*. Washington, DC: Island Press.

Frumkin, Howard. 2001. Beyond Toxicity: Human Health and the Natural Environment. *American Journal of Preventative Medicine*, 20 (3): 234–240.

Garvin, Alexander. 1996. *The American City: What Works and What Doesn't*. New York: McGraw-Hill.

Greater Portland Council of Governments. 1997. *Cumberland County Regional Trails Plan*. Report Prepared by Regional Trails Plan Advisory Committee, Greater Portland Council of Governments, Portland, ME.

Gustanski, Julie Ann. 2000. Protecting the Land: Conservation Easements, Voluntary Actions, and Private Land. In Julie Ann Gustanski and Roderick H. Squires, eds., *Protecting the Land: Conservation Easements Past, Present, and Future*. Washington, DC: Island Press. Pp. 9–25.

Hester, Randolph T., Jr. 1990. *Community Design Primer*. Mendocino, CA: Ridge Times Press.

Kaiser, Edward J., David R. Godschalk, and F. Stuart Chapin, Jr. 1995. *Urban Land Use Planning*. 4th ed. Urbana: University of Illinois Press.

Kaplan, Rachel, Stephen Kaplan, and Robert L. Ryan. 1998. *With People in Mind: Design and Management of Everyday Nature*. Washington, DC: Island Press.

Kuo, Francis E., William C. Sullivan, Rebecca L. Coley, and L. Brunson. 1998. Fertile Ground for Community: Inner-city Neighborhood Common Spaces. *American Journal of Community Psychology*, 26 (6): 823–851.

Land Trust Alliance. 2000. *National Land Trust Census 2000*. http://www.lta.org.

Lawson, Simpson. 1992. Landscape Research Is Making Advances in an Array of Topics. But Are the Results Being Used? *Landscape Architecture*, 82 (3), 38–48.

Little, Charles. 1990. *Greenways for America*. Baltimore: Johns Hopkins University Press.

Massachusetts Executive Office of Environmental Affairs. 2000. *The State of the Environment*. Boston.

Massachusetts Historical Commission. 2000. *Preservation through Bylaws and Ordinances: Tools and Techniques for Preservation Used by Communities in Massachusetts*. Boston.

Moore, Edward O. 1981. A Prison Environment's Effect on Health Service Demands. *Journal of Environmental Systems*, 11: 17–34.

Newcombe, Nancy. 1999. Buying the Farm: Station Road Land Deal Up for a Vote at Town Meeting. *Amherst Bulletin*, 32 (16): 1, 6. (April 23, 1999).

Ochterski, James A. 1996. Why Land Is Protected: Motivations Underlying Real Estate Donations to Land Conservancies. Master's thesis, : University of Michigan.

Portland Trails. 2002. Eastern Promenade Trail. Portland Trails website. Accessed on-line (Sept. 16, 2002), http://www.trails.org/map_files_eastern_prom_page_description.html.

Pruetz, Rick. 1997. *Saved by Development: Preserving Environmental Areas, Farmland, and Historic Landmarks with Transfer of Development Rights.* Burbank, CA: Arje Press.

Rooks, Douglas. 2001. Portland Has So Many Transportation Projects It's Hard to Keep Up. *Maine Trail Magazine* (July): 5. Accessed on-line (Sept. 16, 2002), http://ww.mbtaonline.org/trails/july01_p5.htm.

Smith, Daniel S., and Paul C. Hellmund, eds. 1993. *The Ecology of Greenways.* Minneapolis: University of Minnesota Press.

Smith, Nathan. 2002. Personal communication, Oct. 24,.

Sorvig, Kim. 2002. Abstract and Concrete: In Los Angeles, a Park Creates an Abstraction of an Abused River. *Landscape Architecture,* 92 (5): 34–40.

Spirn, Ann Whiston. 1984. *The Granite Garden: Urban Nature and Human Design.* New York: Basic Books.

Steel, Jennifer. 1999. *Losing Ground: An Analysis of Recent Rates and Patterns of Development and Their Effect on Open Space in Massachusetts.* 2nd edition. Lincoln, MA: Massachusetts Audubon Society.

Taylor, Andrea F., Francis E. Kuo, and William C. Sullivan, 2001. Coping with ADD: The Surprising Connection to Green Play Settings. *Environment and Behavior,* 33 (1): 54–77.

Trails and Greenways Clearinghouse (undated). Health and Wellness Benefits. Washington, DC: Rails to Trails Conservancy and Conservation Fund.

Trust for Public Land. 1999. *Community Choices: Thinking Through Land Conservation, Development, and Property Taxes in Massachusetts.* Boston: New England Regional Office.

Trust for Public Land. 2002. Eastern Promenade Fact Sheet. accessed on-line (Sept. 16, 2002), http://www.tpl.org/tier3_cd.cfm?content_item_id=7820andfolder_id=259.

Ulrich, Roger S. 1984. View through a Window May Influence Recovery from Surgery. *Science,* 224: 420–421.

Wilson, Alex. 2002. Sprawl and Health: Are Modern Land-use Patterns Making us Sick? *Environmental Building News,* 11 (4): 1, 10–13, (newsletter) BuildingGreen Inc., www.BuildingGreen.com.

Enhancing Community Strengths

Photo: Nedim Kemer

11

Transportation
Linking Land Use and Mobility

Jeff Levine

Engineers have traditionally conducted transportation planning. However, like many types of specialty planning, transportation planning is difficult to separate from other planning. Land use, environmental protection, economic development, and even housing issues interrelate with planning for the movement of goods and services.

Yet at the same time, transportation planning is so technical that it is very difficult to incorporate these other disciplines. The challenge in transportation planning is to remember these links while still simplifying the complex web of interrelationship enough to make good recommendations to the powers that be. The challenge to the community is to make sure that transportation planners get it right.

Context

Transportation is most closely linked with land use, the environment and public health, the economy, public safety, public finance, and social equity. Looking at each of these in turn helps create a context for transportation planning:

Transportation and Land Use

Transportation and land use are like the snake eating its own tail. Land use creates the need for transportation, but it is also often created by the development of transportation infrastructure. This connection became most evident after the creation of ring highways around major metropolitan centers. Roadways that were designed to help people avoid driving through the dense land use of the urban center ended up becoming relatively densely developed themselves, this time with a focus on the ring road itself rather than on downtown. That development resulted in new traffic congestion in the ring road, leading sometimes to the development of a second ring road, which in turn brought new office parks and housing, and so forth.

At some point transportation planners noticed a pattern. Whenever they built new roads, people started driving more and longer, and the new roads filled up much faster than projections had indicated. The big investments in new highways did not solve congestion; they just moved people and jobs to the new highways and created more driving. Some chose to ignore this. Others chose to use it as a rationale for not improving transportation infrastructure at all. "Why build new roads?" they ask. "They just fill up with more cars." While that argument is not made as often with transit or pedestrian improvements, it could be just as valid for them. The solution is not to ignore the issue or to use it as a reason to throw up your hands, but to be aware of the relationship and make your transportation improvements where you want your development to occur, keeping them away from places you don't want to develop.

However, the mechanisms that approve and fund transportation projects often ignore this relationship. Under federal programs for transportation funding you must first demonstrate that current land-use trends or existing travel patterns justify the need for a new road, transit line, or other improvement. In other words, the federal government will fund only transportation improvements that serve the current land-use patterns, not ones that will change those patterns.

This is a major challenge to transportation planners who believe roads and rails should be built where it makes sense for people to live, rather than where current patterns show people will live. For example, the current trend may be for a metropolitan area to continue to grow in the direction of a wetland that contributes to the water quality of the region, on which the economy of the area depends. Existing transportation funds would be more likely to pay for a new road into the wetland than one that avoids it and may therefore encourage growth in areas that are less sensitive.

This is as true for transit as it is for highways. The federal "New Starts" program, which is designed to pay for new transit systems in cities that don't have good transit, requires that you demonstrate that the growth that would occur *without the new transit line* justifies creation of the transit line, entirely ignoring the land-use impacts of constructing the new line.

This problem is most likely not due to any conscious policy of the federal government. That's good news because it is really a perspective that should change. Until it does,

transportation planners have to make land-use projections that justify transportation decisions.

Transportation and the Environment

Traveling produces pollution, whether by automobile, train, boat, or even foot. However, some transportation pollutes more than others (see Figure 11.1). While pollution from walking is primarily limited to the environmental costs of additional human exertion and the occasional stinky shoe, driving alone in a poorly tuned vehicle produces high levels of air pollutants, releases oil that creates water pollution, and creates noise pollution that affects nearby homes.

The goal of good transportation planning is not to eliminate the environmental impacts, but to reduce them as much as possible. What does "as much as possible" mean? Different people would have different definitions. I define "as much as possible" as finding a balance between the competing goals of providing mobility, such as economic development, personal fulfillment, exercise, and pleasure.

Transportation impacts the environment in universal ways, in localized ways, and in unusual ways.

Universal ways include the emissions produced by vehicles. Automobiles produce nitrogen oxides, carbon dioxide, carbon monoxide, and other chemicals when they combust gasoline. Even the newer, cleaner automobiles produce significant emissions, although not nearly as much as older vehicles. Some of these emissions, like carbon monoxide, cause direct harm to humans who breathe them. Others, most notably nitrogen oxides and carbon dioxide, don't immediately harm people but are strongly suspected in long-term impacts to people and the environment. The carbon dioxides emitted by cars are a considerable contributor to the increases in greenhouse gases in our atmosphere. Most scientists agree these greenhouse gases are creating global warming, which will likely lead to significant loss of farmland across temperate areas like the United States, melting of icecaps that will result in higher sea levels and flooding of many coastal cities, and other impacts such as increased storm activity due to changing wind patterns.

The reduction in emissions from automobiles is one of the great success stories of government regulation and engineering can-do. In the twenty years following government regulation of harmful emissions from cars, the number of miles traveled in cars roughly doubled. However, the

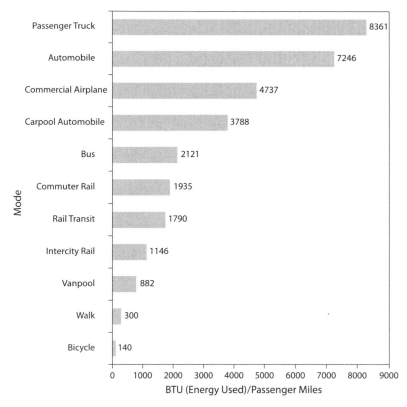

Figure 11.1. Comparing environmental impact of travel modes.
Source: Deborah Gordon, *Steering a New Course: Transportation, Energy and the Environment* (Washington, DC: Island Press, 1991), p. 35. Data is from 1987 but has probably not changed much since that time.

amount of emissions produced by vehicles did not increase nearly as much; in fact, emissions of certain pollutants like carbon monoxide went down considerably (see Figure 11.2). The challenge for the early twenty-first century is to reduce those levels further, while fighting the ever-increasing numbers of miles traveled by Americans.

Localized ways include noise pollution and runoff from roads and rails. Noise pollution from buses and automobiles is everywhere. Noise pollution from rail transit vehicles is limited to rail corridors but is usually more significant because rail vehicles produce more noise.

When the Interstates were constructed, neighborhoods near them suddenly became aware of how much of an impact noise could have. For example, in Somerville, Massachusetts, I-93 produced background noise levels as loud as a loud vacuum cleaner, with frequent noise "spikes" even louder. The constant change in sound levels has a far worse effect than a constant loud hum, with serious public health

impacts (Lewis 1997, p. 235). Some people got used to the new noises, but many others did not. In response, some of the highways that travel through the densest neighborhoods have been fitted with sound barriers that help muffle the noise. But these barriers are expensive and require maintenance, and therefore have not been built in every location where they would be useful. Of particular concern are areas where multiple hazards occur, such as at truck loading areas, which create noise, air, and water pollution. These are often in poor inner-city areas, giving rise to environmental justice concerns.

Runoff from roads and rails are similarly expensive to manage. Well-designed systems can trap oil or other contaminants in catch basins, but these systems need to be cleaned and maintained regularly. Recently there has been some progress made with the design of organic systems that rely on swales or artificial wetlands to clean runoff. These systems can take up more land and be more expensive to

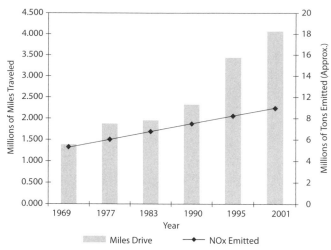

Figure 11.2. Miles traveled and emissions from cars compared.
Sources: National Personal Transportation Survey, 1969-1995, and National Household Travel Survey, 2001, both from the Environmental Protection Agency Office of Transportation and Air Quality. Note that methodology for determining number of miles driven changed between 1990 and 1995, so comparisons of figures before and after 1995 should be made cautiously.

construct initially, but have the benefits of being largely self-maintaining and more attractive than traditional engineered systems.

Unusual ways are not always predictable and are sometimes counter-intuitive. For example, by creating a new bike path near an environmentally sensitive area, planners may help create a constituency to protect that area permanently. If people can't see a place they are less likely to protect it. Of course, the benefits to this area must be balanced with the damage that may be done to it by hacking a new path through the woods, but they should not be ignored.

Transportation and the Economy

A good transportation system is essential to the economic health of a region. No matter what the reader might think of free trade, its arrival and expansion make it more likely that each region and country will focus on those industries that it does best. This specialization produces a strong need to move these goods and products quickly and efficiently, whether by truck, rail, or even fiberoptic cable. Highway expansions and efforts to permit double-decker train cars (known as "double-stacking") are both efforts to improve the economy of a region by improving access.

Moving people around in the region can have economic benefits as well, as shown by the economic growth that tends to accommodate new transit lines. For example, it is hard to imagine downtown Boston thriving without the Massachusetts Bay Transportation Authority (MBTA) rapid transit lines.

At the same time, it is important that the transportation system not encourage economic development that exceeds the ability of that area to handle new growth. Building a highway or commuter rail line will inevitably make that area more attractive for development, whether the communities can handle it or not. For example, the construction of Route 6 down the spine of Cape Cod led to significant growth in housing and industry. The increases were so large that many people fought the extension of the four-lane roadway to prevent additional growth in lower Cape Cod. Similarly, the extension of commuter rail service to southeastern Massachusetts in the 1990s accelerated development of former agricultural and forest lands into subdivisions, leading many to wonder what the environmental benefits of this rail line really were.

In addition, there are times when transportation improvements may actually hurt the economy by changing the character of an area in a way that makes it less attractive. Communities in Vermont have fought hard to have their state transportation department not widen their narrow, often covered bridges, the ones that contribute so much to local sense of place and the tourism that thrives on it. A similar story unfolded on Route 6A on Cape.

Transportation and Safety

Safety is one of the most traditional transportation planning goals. Many of the Interstate projects in the middle of the twentieth century were justified on safety grounds, and for good reason. Interstate highways are safer for long-distance travel than local roads (although when accidents occur on Interstates they are more often fatal). In addition, better roads offer safer emergency access for fire trucks, ambulances, and other public safety vehicles. It is often forgotten that a major justification for the Interstates was to ensure that military convoys could easily move around the country in case we were attacked. To this day, Interstate roads are designed with pavement that can withstand the movement of tanks!

Planning for the Old King's Highway

Route 6A on Cape Cod is one of the oldest roadways in the country and is often referred to by its original name of the "Old King's Highway" (OKH). The OKH winds along the northern shore of the Cape, past old houses and cranberry bogs and stone walls, with views of Cape Cod Bay occasionally wending their way into view.

Of course, as an old roadway, it is very narrow and does not meet modern highway standards. In fact, it is one of the narrowest state highways in the country, sometimes as narrow as 40 feet. The narrowness of the road has led to accidents and made it difficult to accommodate bicycles and pedestrians, since it often doesn't even have a sidewalk.

The Massachusetts Highway Department (MHD), which owns the roadway, has been concerned for some time about safety on the road. MHD has also been concerned that the road is not consistent with statewide pedestrian and bicycle accommodation policies. Since the department owns the highway, it is responsible for paying for upkeep and repairs, which gives MHD a lot of power over what happens to the road.

However, the OKH is also unique in another way: it is the focus of one of the largest historic districts in the country. Everything near the road is subject to the review of a regional historic commission. Everything, that is, except the road, since courts have found that MHD is exempt from their review. That has frustrated historic preservationists, who believe that the OKH should be preserved.

Like any road, it occasionally needs repairs or reconstruction. Each time that happens, the debate over the OKH heats up. (See, for example, "The Old King's Highway Resists Updating," *Boston Globe*, Nov. 1, 1992, p. 44.) It's an interesting case of what happens when different transportation planning considerations, all valid, clash with one another. In this case, safety and finance are on one side and community and land-use concerns are on another. And the resolution is an example of how sides must compromise in such a dispute.

Twice in the 1990s MHD proposed widening parts of the OKH to provide better sidewalks and straighter, wider travel lanes. Both times local preservationists cried foul, saying that MHD should repair the roadway without making significant changes to its layout. It is one thing to have statewide policies, they said, but another to apply them without looking at special situations.

The first time this conflict came up, MHD backed down and simply didn't improve the road at all. The second time, the OKH Regional District Commission challenged MHD in court, saying the department should have to come before the commission to get approval for its plans. After all, the whole historic district was named after the road!

Meanwhile, the Cape Cod MPO conducted a study of some of the issues involved. Rather than agreeing that the road should be widened to accommodate bicycles, the MPO decided that this was an unusual case where bicycles should be encouraged to use alternative roads. They studied alternatives and published a map of where to bike along the OKH corridor (see Plate 10).

The courts sided with MHD. However, the issue got so much publicity that residents of other parts of the Cape became concerned that MHD was jeopardizing the health of the whole area by harming what makes the Cape a unique place. This issue has economic impact, as Cape tourism is largely about seeing the historic character of the area. State legislators from Cape Cod put forward legislation that required MHD projects on historic roads on the Cape to hold extra public hearings (detailed in "Public Gets New Input on Road Work," *Cape Cod Times*, Dec. 23, 2002). It's not the solution most preservationists would prefer, but at least it allows a chance for additional public feedback.

In many ways safety is more important than ever before. When the typical American drives about 20,000 miles a year, it is inevitable that we would worry about how safe we are while driving those miles. Many people therefore invest in sports utility vehicles (SUVs) or light trucks that are often larger and are therefore seen as safer. The proliferation of SUVs has made it more difficult for people to choose small, fuel-efficient cars, which may seem less safe when surrounded by big vehicles. The requirements for air bags and state safety inspections, while having valid safety reasons, have made cars less affordable to the poor and reduced lower-income mobility. In addition, safety has become a factor in planning for bicycle and pedestrian facilities. Police presence is often required to keep a facility safe. Safety factors and liability concerns are also a problem in trying to plan "rail-with-trail" facilities in which bicyclists use paths that parallel the corridors of active trains. In this era of Homeland Security, planning more secure transportation facilities has become a high priority and has changed many other aspects of planning.

Transportation and Finance

Finally, there is the issue of money. If we had all the money in the world, everyone would be putting their Interstates underground like Boston's Big Dig. But we don't. Trying to find money for transportation projects inevitably affects their nature, because all money comes with strings attached.

Those that control the money have a lot of say over what is built. The federal government controls most of the money, so the president actually has a lot of say over what gets built in your neighborhood. For example, the federal government has made a priority of bus service for rapid transit (known as "Bus Rapid Transit" or BRT) rather than building new rail lines. The argument is that a BRT line is cheaper, more flexible, and more efficient than a new rail line. Others argue that it is the permanence, speed, and quality of travel that attract people to rail rapid transit and that BRT cannot satisfy those needs. For now, the federal government is winning this argument, because it controls the money for building new rapid transit lines.

In recent years private developers, who see the benefits of transportation improvements near their land, have been coming to the table with money to help build transportation systems if a system meets their needs. This is not a new

Bus Rapid Transit

It's not very often that a new method of public transportation is invented, but that is what the federal government and other supporters claim has happened in the past 20 years with the introduction of "Bus Rapid Transit," or BRT. However, many other transportation planners dismiss BRT as a gimmick designed to prevent the construction of new, efficient, light rail transit systems where they are needed.

BRT is conceived of as a combination of buses and rail rapid transit. Special buses that are more comfortable and cleaner than traditional buses run on their own dedicated roadways with stops that are farther apart than the traditional one- or two-block distance between stops. In theory it is almost like a rail transit system on rubber tires, but with much lower infrastructure cost. However, in order to provide more flexibility and lower costs, BRT service is not always on dedicated busways (or bus lanes). Instead, while BRT travels on its own busways when possible and to avoid the worst congestion, it often travels on the same roads as cars, slowing when they slow down. For example, Seattle has a bus tunnel with several stations that runs beneath downtown, but the buses have to travel in mixed traffic once they leave the tunnel and fan out around the city. This provides more flexibility and lower costs but leaves BRT open to critics who believe it is essentially a fancy name for a bus.

The idea of BRT was imported from Brazil, Australia, and Canada, where some BRT systems have existed for several years. Pittsburgh had one of the first BRT systems in the United States: in the 1980s the first significant U.S. busway was built between Pittsburgh's western suburbs and downtown, allowing buses to get downtown without traveling on congested roads. It was such a hit that Pittsburgh has moved forward with other busways. It has also built a small light rail transit line. Other BRT systems in the United States (or systems that resemble BRT) exist in Minneapolis/Saint Paul, Seattle, Orlando, and Dade County. Boston just opened part of a BRT system as a replacement for a former heavy rail line, to much criticism from transit advocates.

BRT systems are being discussed all over the country. Like them or not, they appear to be around to stay, since the federal government has made a priority of providing scarce transit funding to BRT systems unless it can be clearly demonstrated why a rail system is needed.

idea: many of the transportation improvements before the 1950s were entirely funded by private developers seeking to add value to their land. Private parties seeking to attract pioneers to land out west, for example, built the intercontinental railroads. But since the growth of the federal role in transportation in the 1950s, private contributions have been limited to some roadway improvements required as part of their permitting. However, in the past ten years private developers have decided that they can again play a more active role. A private developer in East Cambridge is offering $50 million to relocate and rebuild a rapid transit station in order to place it closer to the developer's land, and, incidentally, enable an expansion of that rail line further north. This relocation and rebuilding had previously been proposed by the MBTA, but they put the project on hold when they couldn't find the money to complete it. The private developer, by paying for the transit station, completes a project with significant public benefit but also unlocks the potential of its land for dense urban redevelopment. This sort of public-private partnership is likely to become more common in the near future.

Transportation and Social Equity

One of the main complaints about the construction of the Interstates is that the planners and engineers chose majority low-income and minority communities to bear the heaviest burden of construction and operation. It has been noted that, if you wanted to guess where an Interstate would be built in a city, you could draw a line through the African American neighborhoods and you would often be right.[1]

Such racial and class insensitivity may not have been intentional. Typically the relocation costs and property acquisition costs were far lower in lower-income areas than they would have been in more upscale neighborhoods. However, the effect was the same whether it was intentional or not.

More recently, there have been criticisms that decisions to suspend or cut back on transit service have similarly been concentrated in lower-income or minority neighborhoods. When Boston's MBTA decided to relocate the Orange Line from lower-income and minority Washington Street to an

alignment further west, it promised to replace the Washington Street elevated with comparable service. That rapid transit line was replaced 15 years later with a Bus Rapid Transit line. MBTA planners said the new service was better than the old, because it was cleaner and provided a direct ride to the airport and other important destinations. Local activists decried the replacement service as inadequate and are still fighting for a light rail line along Washington Street.

The federal government has begun to take issues of social equity seriously. Metropolitan Planning Organizations are now required to factor issues of "environmental justice" into their planning. The federal government, in response to the Washington Street controversy, went as far as requiring the Boston area to redo parts of its Regional Transportation Plan to demonstrate sensitivity to environmental justice. The Washington Street neighborhood, however, still awaits the return of their light rail.

Participation and Process Case Study: Transportation Planning

Decisions on which roads to widen, what new roads to build, and what new transit services to provide are very complicated. There are many different types of transportation planning activities that involve chances for the community to get involved. The goal of this section is to give you some tips as to the types of review and meetings that occur, and your best strategies for getting listened to at them. Many of your opportunities will occur as part of three main types of planning processes: the Metropolitan Planning Organization process; the National Environmental Policy Act processes or their state equivalent; and local government zoning/development review. There are others, such as the capital planning processes for cities, port authorities, and regional transit agencies. And in some parts of the country there is a regional planning process with its own rules, as on Cape Cod or at Lake Tahoe. These processes often follow the model of one of the above systems, though, so we will concentrate on those three.

Metropolitan Planning Organization (MPO) Process

The Metropolitan Planning Organization process, which was set up by the federal government in 1990, gives a lot

---

1. Alan Altshuler, *The City Planning Process: A Political Analysis* (Ithaca: Cornell University Press, 1965), outlining the history of locating I-94 in Saint Paul, MN, does not quite go this far but clearly sees some prejudice in the decision-making.

of power to a little-known committee, not out of any desire to avoid the public, but to make sure that no one agency controls all transportation planning. Each region generally has its own MPO. For example, in Massachusetts there is a Boston area MPO, a Central Massachusetts MPO, a Cape Cod MPO, and ten other MPOs that each controls transportation planning and funding in its area. In Massachusetts, each MPO area matches the borders of a Regional Planning Agency (RPA), and the MPO is generally staffed by the RPA. However, the RPA does not control the MPO. Each MPO generally has representatives from the state, the RPA, and local municipalities.

Each MPO structures its transportation planning around two main documents: a Regional Transportation Plan (RTP) and a Transportation Improvement Program (TIP) (see Figure 11.3). The RTP is a long-term document that outlines policies for the region in the next 20 years, and identifies projects that the MPO believes should take place in that time frame. The RTP is updated every three years, and must be "fiscally constrained." In other words each MPO gets a bucket of money to spend for the next 20 years and can't spend more than that on projects in the RTP.

The TIP is simply a list of projects from the RTP that the MPO really wants to pay to construct in the near future. It usually is limited to the next three to five years, although the most important part of the document is the upcoming year's spending plan. For a project to get into the TIP, it must be in the RTP, and it must also have a completed design. Funding in the TIP is divided into categories. Some of these funds are earmarked for projects that provide congestion mitigation and air quality improvements. These so called CMAQ funds can be used for things like bus shuttles or bicycle paths. Other funds are allocated for projects that improve the quality of life for people near a transportation project. These "enhancement" funds can be used for streetscape beautification, or even the moving of a historic lighthouse which is a tourist attraction.

Generally the design process for projects also has its own public hearings. In Massachusetts, hearings are held twice during the design of a project, once fairly early on (at the "25% design stage") and once toward the end (at the "75% design stage").

There are almost too many chances to provide comments during the MPO process, since there are so many documents to read and so many comment periods. Comments

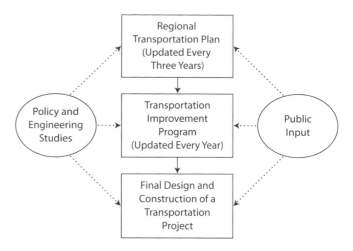

Figure 11.3. MPO planning process.

are taken seriously, though, provided you are commenting on something that the document in question really can change. It can be time-consuming to be involved in the MPO process, but well worth it, and the availability of the Internet has made it much easier. Most MPOs really want public reaction, and often get far too few pertinent comments when they put documents out for feedback!

NEPA and State Environmental Review

Most large transportation projects have to be reviewed under the federal National Environmental Policy Act process, and many smaller ones need to be reviewed by state versions of the process. In Massachusetts, that process is Massachusetts Environmental Policy Act (MEPA) review. These processes are designed to evaluate the impacts of the proposed projects on the environment. However, the term "environment" is used broadly, and therefore includes not only traditional "environmental" impacts like air and water quality and wildlife habitats, but also things like traffic generation, historic preservation, and quality-of-life issues.

The NEPA and MEPA processes are not strict regulatory processes. They do not result in the issuance of a permit or a final sign-off. Instead, MEPA and NEPA issue a "certificate" instead of a permit, and that certificate is used to guide other permitting processes. The certificate can condition those approvals upon mitigation that minimizes impact to the environment, but it is up to the agency that actually issues the permit to enforce those conditions.

The NEPA, MEPA, and other state processes are all generally similar (see Figure 11.4). When a project is initiated, the proponent—generally a public agency in the case of a transportation project—submits an initial report, variously referred to as an Environmental Assessment, an Environmental Notification Form, or the like, to the appropriate national or state Environmental Protection Agency office. That form serves as formal notification that the proponent wants to do the project, and allows the proponent to seek a waiver from the full process if it believes such is warranted. Comments are taken on that form, and NEPA or the state EPA then decides if a waiver should be granted (if one is sought), and, if not, what specific environmental impacts the proponent should study in a more detailed stage of review. This decision is referred to as the "scope." Before issuing the scope, NEPA, the state EPA, or other state equivalents often hold a "scoping session" that may include a site visit open to the public, a presentation of the proposed project, and a chance for feedback from the public. Written feedback is also taken.

The next step is the creation of a Draft Environmental Impact Statement or Report, which is the proponent's first attempt to address the issues outlined in the scope. The draft report is then made available for public comments and, based on those comments, NEPA or the state EPA tells the proponent what additional work it needs to do to create a final draft.

The final draft is called the Final Environmental Impact Statement, or Final Environmental Impact Report. Comments are taken on this version as well, and, if the EPA office feels it is good enough, it issues a final "certificate" that says that the report is complete and that the proponent has agreed to make certain changes to the project to minimize its environmental impacts. That certificate is used by other agencies in deciding whether any permits or funding they may be considering for the project should be issued or granted.

Local Development Review

Local governments often can have direct impact on transportation, but only in response to developments proposed by the private sector. Local government generally does not have any power over other government bodies, such as state transportation authorities. However, private developers are taking a more active role in transportation planning, and therefore local permitting is becoming a place where local planning objectives can be implemented.

Most large projects have to get some local permits. As described above, sometimes a zoning change is needed to allow the project to move forward (such as a change from residential zoning to commercial zoning); sometimes the zoning requires that a project get a special permit and/or site plan approval in order to proceed; and sometimes a project may be able to proceed under zoning, but requires local review of its layout under subdivision or site plan review processes. These three processes vary from lots of local control (zoning changes) to some control (special permit review) to less control (subdivision review.) However, they all give the local government at least a chance to comment on the project and suggest that it include transportation improvements. How citizens can best be involved in these processes is described in chapter 1.

The developer will usually produce some sort of transportation study that outlines the impacts of the project. Any improvements a developer might make must, by law, be generally related to the impacts of the project. In other

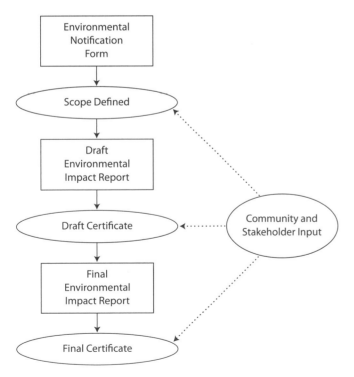

Figure 11.4. MEPA planning process.

words, the developers of a large new apartment building could reasonably be asked to provide a bus shelter in front of the building but could not be expected to build a new rapid transit station in another part of town.

Innovative Tools and Approaches

Transportation planning is changing in exciting ways. Many of the transportation planners and engineers coming out of school now have learned that transportation is interrelated with other planning goals, and that it isn't as simple as building new roads in response to projected growth and existing congestion. It is encouraging to hear engineers mention in public settings that you can't always build your way out of congestion, for example, or that you might want to focus your transportation infrastructure where you want growth to occur. Engineers are generally very smart, and they have become far more sympathetic to community concerns because they know that is the right thing to do and that it allows projects to actually get built, rather than end up in court.

Unfortunately, the tools transportation planners and engineers use have not kept up with the level of understanding in the field. Travel demand is still predicted by assuming everyone travels in the same way, and with the assumption that land use will not be affected by new infrastructure. Congestion is always assumed to be inherently bad, even when slowing traffic may actually make the area around a roadway more livable. Citizens with a comprehensive view of what their community needs can sometimes influence transportation planners to take these more holistic considerations into account as they undertake planning for a project or a town. They can also encourage transportation planners to consider some alternative and innovative tools and techniques that are now emerging as viable transportation options. Some of these include the following:

Transit-Oriented Development (TOD)

Planners now understand that development that is properly designed around a rapid transit station can result in higher ridership on the transit line, more people walking in the development, and less traffic. It is not enough, however, to build just any kind of projects near a station. The area surrounding the station must have the proper mix of uses

Level of Service

If you learn only one technical term in transportation engineering, you should learn about Level of Service (LOS). Not only is it easy to understand, it is also one of the most frequently used terms in transportation documents.

The idea behind LOS is to compare different levels of congestion to grades you might get in school, giving traffic engineers a way to compare conditions on different roads or at different times. Levels of Service can be used to look at roadways, intersections, or even just one part of an intersection. A LOS of A indicates a low level of congestion, just as it would indicate a good grade. LOS C means that there is some congestion but not enough to reach gridlock. A LOS of F is a failing grade for a roadway or intersection; cars may be getting through, but they have to wait for several light cycles or they are slowed to a crawl. There is one main difference between LOS and school grades—there is a LOS of E, between D and F!

One thing that is often misunderstood is that one intersection with an LOS F may be far worse than another with the same grade. It is like two students who get Fs—one may have just barely failed while the other one never even came to class. Being told that something is an LOS F should prompt the question: "How bad is it?"

While we might wish that all roads should be at an LOS of A or B all the time, the amount of asphalt that would take makes it probably an unrealistic goal in any but the most rural communities. In urban areas a reasonable LOS is C or D, and even an F may be appropriate at rush hour. What these levels reflect most is our expectations about what is reasonable, and what is reasonable has to include a trade-off between congestion and some of the less desirable outcomes of wider and bigger roads.

(some residential, some commercial, some retail); must have sidewalks and other pedestrian amenities like properly scaled lighting; must be attractive enough that people want to be out of their cars and linger; and must be responsive to the market demands of the specific location.[2]

TOD can be developed at virtually any type of transit node. Most frequently, it is designed at a rapid transit station, but it can also occur at a location where many bus lines come together, where a commuter rail station is located out in the suburbs, or at a ferry terminal. Even a Bus Rapid Transit station (see case study) can serve as a location for Transit-Oriented Development.

Traffic Calming

Engineers have figured out that people don't always obey speed limits (I told you they were smart!). Rather, if you design a road so that it looks safe to drive at 45 miles per hour, most people will drive 45 miles per hour on it, even if the speed limit is 30. In the past, engineers preferred to design roads for higher possible travel speeds in order to make travel as safe for vehicles as possible, and often still design for the m.p.h. they think speeders will achieve, rather than the expected legal speed.

However, designing roads this way has made them far less welcoming to pedestrians and bicycles. Communities have called for roads that are designed so that cars have to slow down as they travel through, so that drivers will actually slow down whether or not there is a police officer with a radar gun. Designing a road for a lower travel speed is generally referred to as "traffic calming," and centers on the idea of making a road appear a bit smaller or more complicated so that people naturally slow down.

Common traffic-calming techniques include curb extensions (sometimes called "bumpouts"); textured crosswalks; roundabouts; and raised crosswalks. Curb extensions are simply wider sidewalks at intersections, narrowing the pavement so cars have to turn more slowly, and shortening

the amount of distance a pedestrian has to cross the street. Textured crosswalks, such as brick, concrete, or asphalt that is colored and stamped with a pattern, all make pedestrians feel safer crossing a street and encourage drivers to slow down. Roundabouts are small rotaries, designed to allow automobiles to travel through intersections without stopping, but requiring that they slow down. Raised crosswalks are a combination of a speed bump and a crosswalk; the whole crosswalk is raised slightly to slow cars down. Sometimes the entire intersection may be raised as a "speed table."

One challenge in traffic calming is the need to design a road so that cars won't get into accidents. With careful planning, traffic calming techniques can meet the specific needs at a location without jeopardizing safety.

Another challenge is the fact that most local Departments of Public Works (DPW) don't like traffic-calming techniques. They cost money to maintain and make it harder to plow in the winter. It is not that DPWs are necessarily lazy; in austere times they simply don't have the money to take on new tasks such as fixing brick sidewalks or adding an extra snow plow so the crews can work more slowly around curb extensions. Similarly, fire chiefs may worry that they won't be able to get their trucks through a street fast enough in a crisis. Respecting the viewpoint of DPW will help come to a viable compromise. For example, using colored concrete in curb extensions rather than brick saves on maintenance costs while accomplishing the same goals; and some effective design techniques don't actually make the road any smaller.

Environmentally Sensitive Design

It has become increasingly popular to design transportation systems so that the pollution they produce is managed close to the source through well-designed systems that both prevent the spread of the pollution and create more pleasant surroundings. For example, every road or parking lot produces water runoff that is polluted with oil. A traditional way to handle this runoff is to direct it into stormwater drains and then allow it to flow to a treatment facility where additional chemicals are added to clean the water. Another way to handle this runoff is to send it into large underground containers (catch basins). Those basins filter out the oil and allow the water to flow back into the local watershed. The drawback is that catch basins must be cleaned periodically.

---

2. Transit-oriented development is slightly different from two other beasts: "transit-adjacent development," in which transit is near a development but does not meet the other goals of TOD; and "development-oriented transit," in which a developer or planner wants to add value to a site by bringing in transit to serve it. Credit goes to Allan Hodges of Parsons Brinkerhoff for the concept of transit-adjacent development and to Peter Calcaterra of the MBTA for the concept of development-oriented transit.

A third approach involves using natural ecosystems to clean the runoff. While more land-intensive, this approach creates a new ecosystem rather than an engineered system to handle the problem, and, once created, this ecosystem manages itself. In such a system the runoff would flow into a newly created wetland where the water would naturally filter. The oil left in the new wetland would gradually accumulate in special plantings that are not harmed by it. This can slow the rapid flow of stormwater through waste management systems and thereby prevent flooding and the need for expensive new treatment facilities.

Intermodal Centers

Imagine you want to get from your summer home on Cape Cod to a meeting in Boston. You could drive and put up with the traffic and parking problems, not to mention ignoring the environmental impacts of driving alone. Or you might want to drive from your home to a bus station and take a bus to Boston. This alternative is attractive if you can park at the bus station for a while. This is the basic idea behind an intermodal center.

An intermodal center is a place where you can easily change from one transportation mode to another. Intermodal centers may be served by buses and trains and be connected to nearby neighborhoods with bicycle and pedestrian trails. They may have parking lots to allow for park-and-ride commuting. Intermodal centers are being built all over the state and country. If properly designed and managed they make it easier to avoid driving alone and can have significant land-use and environmental benefits.

Public-Private Partnerships

I mentioned earlier that the private sector is becoming more involved in transportation planning. Government agencies are trying to make it easier for these partnerships to form and succeed. The federal government has created programs that provide attractive financing to private developers who want to construct public improvements. State agencies are seeking to sell unneeded land and even the air rights over roadways to private parties to help knit together neighborhoods torn apart by major roads or rail systems. These types of public-private partnerships are often linked with TODs.

Alternative Vehicle Fuels

Finally, people have been talking about alternative vehicle fuels (AVFs) since the oil crises of the 1970s, but for most of that time it has just been that: talk. Electric cars didn't have enough acceleration and needed time-consuming rechargings; compressed natural gas vehicles didn't have enough refueling stations and couldn't travel in tunnels; and other technologies were not advancing fast enough to attract real interest.

Recently, significant progress has been made on one type of AVF: the "hybrid" gas-electric vehicle. The hybrid has a gas engine and an electric engine. When the car is accelerating, it uses the gas engine. When it is cruising along at a good speed, it switches to the electric engine. And when it slows down, the brakes recharge the battery. Essentially, a hybrid uses more of the energy from gasoline than traditional gas engines, and therefore pollutes less, without needing to be fueled with a hard-to-find substance or sacrificing performance.

Hybrids are selling well in many urban areas and appear to be increasing in popularity. However, they are not as clean as most AVFs. Future research, currently focusing on hydrogen-powered fuel cells, may help reduce the environmental impacts of automobiles. At the same time, new buses are being built that run on compressed natural gas or cleaner diesel.

Getting Started

Much of the information you need to be informed about transportation planning is available on the Internet. Most decent-sized MPOs have Web sites and include links to much of the information you need to get involved. Start with http://www.pvpc.org/marpa/html/marpa_index.html in Massachusetts or http://www.ampo.org for the rest of the country if you don't know your local MPO. In Boston, you can reach the Boston MPO at http://www.ctps.org. You can also learn about your local regional planning council at http://www.narc.org. A few very useful books are also described here to get you started.

History of American Highways and Automobile Dependence

Divided Highways by Tom Lewis (New York: Viking Penguin, 1997) provides a great history of the Interstate system. *Rites of Way: The Politics of Transportation in Boston and the U.S. City* by Alan Lupo, Frank Colcord, and Edmund P. Fowler (Boston: Little, Brown, 1971) does a good job of describing what happened in Boston when people wanted to stop construction of an Interstate through their neighborhood. Jane Holtz Kay's *Asphalt Nation: How the Automobile Took Over the Nation and How We Can Take It Back* (New York: Crown, 1997) provides fuel to the fire for those who seek to reduce the influence of the automobile on our society.

Current Transportation Challenges and Opportunities

Suburban Gridlock by Robert Cervero (New Brunswick, NJ: Center for Urban Policy Research, 1986) is a good book for understanding transportation planning and needs in the suburbs. *Stuck in Traffic* by Anthony Downs (Washington: Brookings Institute, 1992) talks about the dilemma of planning for sound land use while facing an overwhelming backlog of traffic congestion. *Steering a New Course: Transportation, Energy, and the Environment* by Deborah Gordon (Washington, DC: Island Press, 1991) provides the best overview of alternative vehicle fuels I have seen, despite being a little dated and therefore a little behind the times with respect to the hybrid gas-electric vehicle. For more information on Bus Rapid Transit, start with the federal clearinghouse at http://www.fta.dot.gov/brt and another informational site called "BRT Central" at http://www .homestead.com/brtc/files. For the dissenting view on BRT, examine http://www.lightrailnow.org.

Alternative Modes

Any number of books on New Urbanism or Transit-Oriented Development can provide a good starting point for how to plan for pedestrian, bicycle, and transit accommodation. *Suburban Nation: The Rise of Sprawl and the Decline of the American Dream* by Andres Duany, Elizabeth Plater-Zyberk, and Jeff Speck (New York: North Point Press, 2000) is a good place to start, as is *Transit Villages in the 21st Century* by Michael Bernick and Robert Cervero (New York: McGraw-Hill Professional, 1996), if you can find it.

Finally, I wish I could point to a great book on the nuts and bolts of rapid transit that is easily understood by non-experts. I am sure that one is out there, but I have not yet found it. I recommend searching the Internet for the information you need.

Web Resources

Association of Metropolitan Planning Organizations: http://www.ampo.org

Boston MPO: http://www.ctps.org

BRT Central: http://www.homestead.com/brtc/files

Federal Highway Administration's National Household Travel Survey/National Personal Transportation Survey: http://www.fhwa.dot.gov/policy/ohpi/nhts/index.htm

Federal Transit Administration's BRT Clearinghouse: http://www.fta.dot.gov/brt

Light Rail Now: http://www.lightrailnow.org

Massachusetts Association of Regional Planning Agencies: http://www.pvpc.org/marpa/html/marpa_index.html

National Association of Regional Councils: http://www.narc.org

U.S. Environmental Protection Agency Office of Transportation and Air Quality: http://www.epa.gov/otaq

Photo: Jeffrey Blankenship

12

Housing and Community Preservation
A Home for All

Toni Coyne Hall and Linda Silka

Housing is central to all of our lives. As Michael Stone has written:

> Housing is more than physical shelter. The residential environment consists not only of the dwelling unit but the site and setting, neighbors and community, municipality and public services, habitability and accessibility, rights and responsibilities, costs and benefits. Yet housing is even more than the residential environment, for it is only in relation to those who inhabit and use it that housing has meaning and significance—not only physical and economic, but emotional, symbolic and expressive. We occupy our houses, and, for better and for worse, they become our homes. (1993, 14)

It is becoming increasingly difficult for American families to achieve even the most basic National Housing Goal (declared in 1949) of "a decent home and a suitable living environment" (42 U.S. Code Sec. 1441a). There is simply not enough housing available that is adequate, accessible, and affordable. The solution that communities often turn to when faced with a housing crisis is to build new housing. Certainly new housing is needed, but this single-minded focus on its construction is increasingly recognized as contributing to sprawl and also as failing to take advantage of the many opportunities to reclaim existing underused structures for housing.

As we shall see in this chapter, the great benefit of the community preservation approach is that it calls attention to the need to consider all elements together that shape a community's future—that is, transportation, open space, historic preservation, economic development, *and* housing. Each factor influences the others: new housing is a major consumer of open space, transportation needs are affected by decisions about where to locate new housing, adaptive reuse can create more housing, and decisions about which industries to recruit affect the need for housing in the future. In short, all these factors must be considered together if there is to be any hope of adequately addressing housing needs.

The intent of this chapter is to look at how communities can proceed in analyzing their housing stock while also taking into account transportation, open space, economic development, and opportunities for historic preservation. We will show how the creation and preservation of housing can become a key part of community preservation, compatible with the protection of open space and historic features, and enhancing of the quality of life in our communities. A further purpose of this chapter will be to demonstrate the importance of communities considering housing opportunities across the range of incomes. We will show that housing considerations need not degenerate into divisive debates. Instead, discussions of how to provide housing for all community members can be opportunities for community initiative, community involvement, and community control.

Two additional points will underlie our analysis. First, we want to emphasize that it is never too early for communities to begin considering the adequacy of their housing stock. The unfortunate fact is that communities often realize only too late that something is amiss with the range of housing available. For example, a community may find that housing prices have rapidly skyrocketed and suddenly young people who grew up there can no longer hope to raise their own families in that place. Or, in trying to recruit a new company, a community's leaders may discover that they can't "land" that prospective company because of insufficient housing or because the housing that is available is priced beyond what new workers can afford.

The second theme that links the various concerns raised in this chapter is that many stakeholders must contribute to solving the housing problems faced by our communities. Too often people assume that the housing crisis is somebody else's responsibility, perhaps that of federal, state, or city government, housing agencies, community development corporations, private developers, or individual homeowners. Most communities have discovered, however, that no single group has sufficient authority or sufficiently deep pockets to single-handedly fix the housing problems. Housing problems generally cannot be solved by one group or even in most cases by one community working in isolation. Only when groups work together and draw upon their many collective resources are communities able to put into place an array of attractive housing options that will maintain a city's vibrancy.

In keeping with the community preservation focus, the information provided here is focused at the community level rather than at the state or national policy levels. We begin by assuming that you and other community members are about to undertake a housing analysis and, although this chapter is not intended to serve as a full-blown "how to" manual, we take you through some of the steps, language clarifications, and innovations that many communities are adopting to improve the prospects of preserving their character and opportunities for future generations.

Analyzing Housing

If your community is like most, you will not have the resources to hire dedicated experts on housing. Except in the largest of urban areas, community volunteers and citizen-planners are often largely on their own in trying to understand the changes in the housing market and the likely impact that housing cost and availability will have on a community's future. In these circumstances, many communities start by first creating a snapshot inventory of their housing stock. Your community might begin by undertaking an inventory of current housing stock using information from the U.S. Census Web site (information that is available for every community in the United States), your city's planning department, or other sources. Such an inventory often includes data on the number of houses and apartments that exist in your community, what the median value of these properties is, the range of values represented, and the rental rates for apartments of various sizes. Your community will also likely find it beneficial to look at housing stock across time: has the number of housing units stayed the same, declined, or increased? Has the proportion of different types of units (e.g., rental units, single-family housing, multifamily housing, housing for restricted ages) remained the same?

A 1997 study, "A Profile of Housing in Massachusetts" (p. 5), points to other questions about housing that communities often find useful to consider. These questions include:

- How does production of multifamily housing by communities compare to demolition, conversions to owner-occupied homes, and abandonment?
- What percentage of new homeowners is in the low-income population?

- Who are the owners of rental housing today, and what are the characteristics of these owners relative to the units they own?
- In which nearby communities have increases in average rents and home prices most dramatically outpaced increases in income?
- What are the impacts of changes in a regional, state, or federal economy on homeowners with the most serious affordability problems, such as female-headed households, homeowners of color, and low-income, first-time buyers?
- How do changes in public policy and the economy impact low-income families' ability to obtain and maintain their hold on housing?

Another consideration which is relevant for some older communities is:

- How many housing units are in serious arrears on their property taxes, or have been foreclosed on by the city for nonpayment of taxes? Are they grouped together in a few "problem" locations?

It is also important to compare the existing housing stock with census projections of the likely population breakdown for the community. For this, the sorts of questions that are helpful include:

- How many elderly householders are there now, and how many are expected in ten or twenty years?
- What percent and number of households in your town have children at home and what percent do not? What is the average household size?

Even such first steps aimed at creating a housing inventory can reveal surprising features of your community's housing situation. In comparing housing against incomes you may find, for example, that the available housing is no longer affordable. Salaries may have stagnated at the very time that housing costs have greatly increased. Or, you might find that changes in housing prices are very real but are limited to one segment of the housing market (e.g., rental property has become very limited and thus the rental rates have undergone rapid increases). Or you may find that certain kinds of units have "gone off line"; for example, the many two-family houses owned by elderly couples that once provided affordable apartments are no longer on the

market because the owners are unable to manage the process of being a landlord. You might discover that zoning changes requiring increased lot sizes for new homes or calling for razed multifamily dwellings to be replaced by single-family homes have had the inadvertent effect of reducing housing stock in an already tight housing market. A high number of tax-delinquent properties suggests both problems and opportunities for redevelopment that can stabilize whole neighborhoods. A projected significant increase in households without children may suggest that large-lot single-family homes are not what will be needed in town in the future. In short, a variety of useful facts about your community's housing situation can emerge from the analysis of available public data. These facts can then serve as the background for discussions about what to preserve and what may be the gaps in the available housing stock.

Clarifying Terms, Making Progress

As your committee gathers information on the status of housing and turns to reporting this information to others in the community, one of the first things you will likely discover is the importance of being very clear about how the various terms will be used. As groups share their findings, many discover that they need to avoid confusions among common terms such as housing *need, preference,* and *demand* if they are to forestall misunderstandings. Consider the differences in these terms. *Need* is the most basic concept, and it calls attention to the basic levels of adequacy: that is, is basic, minimally adequate housing available in sufficient quantities? *Preference*, by contrast, is individualized and is often influenced by prevailing tastes. Preferences express a standard above that of basic adequacy (e.g., many people prefer to live in a 1-family house rather than 2–4-unit buildings; some people prefer Cape-style homes to ranches even though there is no compelling evidence that one of these types of housing is inherently better for meeting basic needs).

Demand is an economic concept, in which preferences are measured by the ability and willingness to pay; many preferences are not manifested in demand because of inability to pay, a lower priority in regard to other preferences, or because that item isn't on the market and thus the preference isn't expressed in ways that can be seen (e.g., people who would prefer a townhouse are not buying them because the market isn't building attached units). Entrepreneurs typically are more interested in demand than need or preference, and they therefore undertake market research to assess likely demand; policy-makers, on the other hand, are generally more interested in need, and they often focus on having needs assessments done to clarify level of need. Both policy-makers and entrepreneurs may have some interest in ascertaining preferences, and needs assessments and market research may use some of the same methods and sources, but the fundamental purpose of the two is different. As your committee communicates its findings about your community's housing situation you will want to point out what you found that is related to need, what to preferences, and what to demand.

Just as it is important to distinguish among need, preferences, and demands, it is also important to recognize that the term *affordable housing* is used in widely different ways and toward different ends. Communities are finding that they are able to achieve more fruitful discussions about housing when residents first devote some time to ensuring that they mutually understand how they are using terms such as "affordable housing" "below market housing," or "community housing" and agreeing on the terms to use.

So, what are some of the confusions of terminology that lead to contentiousness and how can these confusions be avoided? With regard to affordable housing, some use the term primarily as shorthand for public housing or the "projects." Others use "affordable housing" to refer to *any* housing other than that which is strictly market-rate. In still other cases, the term has been associated with a specific dollar amount (e.g., our city needs more housing that is under $300,000). In some states (Massachusetts, for example) the term has now taken on a very specific meaning associated with a particular law (in Massachusetts, Chapter 40B) that mandates the minimum percentage of a municipality's housing that must be affordable. And we cannot look to the federal government as the final arbiter of this issue of how to define affordable housing. Although the U.S. Department of Housing and Urban Development plays a very significant role in housing and annually publishes figures on the cost of housing in metropolitan areas (figures that are used for allowable Section 8 housing, the program which gives needy families vouchers for rent costs), these figures typically aggregate information from different segments of a metropolitan area that can have widely varying costs. The key thing is to be sure that everyone in your group is using the same terms to mean the same thing, preferably in ways that will make sense to your state agencies.

Many communities are discovering that what they are confronting is, in actuality, an affordability *gap*. That is to say, it is not the sheer cost of housing that is problematic. Instead, it is the fact that the average family income in a community is insufficient to enable a family to afford the cost of an average house or rental unit there. The affordability gap approach can remove some of the emotional quality from discussions.

Your housing committee should be prepared for the depth of feeling that emerges when different ways of addressing problems of housing affordability are proposed. This contentiousness often reflects the importance that people place on housing. Many homeowners have much of their net worth tied up in their housing, and maintaining or even increasing the value of that housing is of paramount importance. On the other hand, those same residents often have children or grandchildren who would like to be able to live nearby and who may face the prospect of being priced out of the local market if dramatic escalations in housing costs continue. Once conflict overwhelms discussions, it becomes difficult for communities to find their way to the creative solutions that other communities are discovering to address housing shortages or the fact that housing costs are outstripping available incomes. Opening up new ways of thinking about affordability can help communities see that the challenge of affordability can be approached in different ways, such as through zoning changes, adaptive reuse, and an emphasis on infill and clustering. Below we suggest some of the ways that communities are now thinking about housing in the context of other issues.

Situating Housing Analyses within Community Preservation Concerns

Once your community has a strong sense of what is available in the current housing stock and you have clarified how various terms will be used, you should carry out a more in-depth analysis of housing taking into account your community's plans for economic development, open space, transportation, infrastructure, and other aspects of community preservation. As we illustrate below, a full understanding of present and future housing pressures and costs will be achieved only by treating housing as deeply tied to and influenced by other issues. Throughout the remainder of the chapter we situate housing analysis within these different community preservation topics. The intent is to suggest that there is no single ideal place to start in order to understand what housing decisions will do to a community or what the impact on housing will be of various nonhousing decisions.

Housing from the Perspective of Economic Development

As community leaders envision the kind of an economy their region can aspire to, they need to consider the housing stock as an integral part of that planning. Too often communities pursue their economic goals in the absence of an understanding of the limitations imposed by available housing, or they develop housing goals without being fully cognizant of how particular policy decisions about housing (e.g., increasing lot size minimums) can impact the long-term prospects for a diverse and sustainable economy. Even when community leaders *have* considered housing and economic development together, they have sometimes blithely assumed that large companies can be readily attracted that will raise the local wage structure, thereby increasing housing's affordability, or that the affordability gap can be closed by simply expanding the supply of housing.

Such assumptions overlook the extent to which economic development and housing costs are tied together in complex ways. Each—high housing costs or economic booms—can impact the other. New businesses coming to an area can increase the number of housing units that are needed. High housing costs can eventually cause new businesses to shy away from areas that are increasingly expensive. New and expanding businesses can change the overall pattern of wages, and these changes, in turn, can affect what people can afford to pay for housing.

Many regions of the United States have just experienced a period of "red hot" price increases in housing. This period of rapid increases may be leveling off. We may be in for a breather, but one where our anxieties now focus on the security of our jobs rather than on housing prices becoming out of reach. Indeed, the changing economic climate is a reminder of just how closely tied together jobs and housing are, and unless housing is affordable given the incomes in

the area, housing will continue to be a problem. A community in its entirety must begin to recognize that the lack of affordable housing is more than just a concern of low- and moderate-income individuals. In reality, our inability to address the current housing needs of all residents will undermine our efforts to sustain both social and economic development in our region.

So, how might a community begin to think about how housing needs impact the economy and how housing needs are impacted *by* economic development? An instructive example comes from the approach to understanding the relationship taken in Greater Boston. In *A New Paradigm for Housing in Greater Boston* (Center for Urban and Regional Policy), the authors first note the extent to which economic boom in Greater Boston has generated a demand for new housing:

> Greater Boston's economic renaissance, begun nearly two decades ago, has endowed the region with an extraordinary labor market where unemployment remains below 3 percent and family incomes are rising faster than in almost any other metropolitan area in the nation. The market has been so strong that it has attracted professional workers to the region from other parts of the country and a new wave of immigrants from abroad. But prosperity brings its own challenges. None is more acute than the region's severe housing crisis. Vacancy rates are now so low that home prices and rents are being bid up substantially faster than most household incomes. Between 1995 and 1999, the median price of a Greater Boston home shot up a nominal 35 percent while incomes rose by a healthy, but more modest, 25 percent. As a result, many long-time residents in the region, in addition to many newcomers, are facing a severe affordability gap between their incomes and what they must pay to rent housing or purchase a home. Prices and rents are rising so quickly that not only are the poor in trouble, but an increasing number of working and lower middle income families worry that prosperity may price them out of the Boston housing market. (Executive Summary, p. i)

These housing researchers found that once vacancy rates go below a certain level, a premium on housing stock arises such that the rates of increase in housing costs will outpace increases in income. The authors of *A New Paradigm* (p. ii) argued that when vacancy rates are very low—below 1 percent for homes and below 3 percent for rental units—"any increase in family income will be met by an even faster in-crease in housing prices and rents." The researchers went on to note: "Prices and rents could rise as much as 40 per-cent faster than family incomes, if vacancies remain at the current rate. This will mean that tens of thousands more families will be forced to pay an ever higher share of their incomes for basic shelter or leave the region altogether."

Sprawl is another outcome of low vacancy rates and high housing prices. Families will "drive to qualify," and move further and further from their work sites. This impacts sus-tainability, as people drive more miles and use more gas, and also impacts family and community time, as precious free time is eaten up in the commute. The "drive to qualify" is a significant source of regional sprawl as distant exur-ban areas provide lower-cost single-family housing. The implications for any community is that the community's housing committee needs to be in regular communication with those groups who are overseeing economic develop-ment planning or the planning of any other activity likely to impact housing demand. When housing becomes scarce or unaffordable, the people who leave because they are un-able to afford housing may well represent the community's future leaders.

Housing and Zoning

The need for housing will also be impacted by decisions made about community goals that, on the surface, may seem far afield from housing. Preexisting community deci-sions on industrial development zoning, for example, can have a tremendous impact on housing. Zoning essentially mandates how much of a community's acreage is available for commercial development as compared to housing and other uses. With community buildout analysis (see chap-ter 7 of this book), it is possible to examine likely future development through the lens of these existing zoning laws; the pressures on housing and needs for water and schools can be estimated using standard guides of how industrial development adding a particular number of jobs translates into added pressures on infrastructure. In central Massa-chusetts, this process of analyzing housing need that would result from buildout demonstrated that the industrial de-velopment allowable under current zoning would lead to a daunting upsurge in housing demand. Again, by approach-ing the analysis of housing in what might at first seem an

Local Housing Models and Opportunities

Communities throughout the country are using creative approaches to achieve their housing goals. Here we focus on some Massachusetts communities' initiatives. Details of each of these can be found on the community home page or through the Community Preservation Web site.

- Homeownership without speculation: community land trusts, limited-equity coops and condos: Cape Ann Community Land Trust; Magnolia Cooperative Housing.
- Community housing through historic preservation: Crocker and Cutlery project in Montague; Obed Baker House in Westwood.
- Approaching the 40B 10 percent affordable housing re-quirements through community initiatives: Westwood and Lincoln.
- Expanding low-income housing through acquisition rather than new construction: Watertown and Westwood scattered-site public housing.
- Zoning flexibility to allow accessory apartments, thereby providing housing opportunities for lower-income house-holds while assisting "house-rich but cash-poor seniors," often within the envelopes of existing homes: Westwood.
- Purchasing deed restrictions or purchasing land-with-lease-back, to preserve small, relatively affordable single-family homes and provide financial help to lower-income home-owners: the ECHO Program.
- Using housing to help revitalize older town centers and downtowns: infill and upper stories on commercial build-ings: Middleborough.
- Innovative site planning for new construction: maximizing open space preservation, minimizing infrastructure costs: Wildlands Trust schematic site plans.

indirect way suggested by community preservation, a community can develop a fuller picture of upcoming housing needs that can be estimated based on different strategies for industrial development.

Once communities begin examining zoning, other possibilities for using zoning, in addition to industrial zoning, as a tool to address housing problems become apparent. Zoning is being used, for example, as a proactive tool to achieve greater housing affordability. Some communities are reconsidering recent decisions about zoning that disallow mixed uses, such as apartments over retail or condominiums in office buildings or parks. Other communities have looked at the inadvertent consequences on housing of imposing ever-larger size limits on lots. Remember that, given limited land, larger lots equal fewer housing units in a town. And in some cities (Chicago, for example), zoning has been used to create areas where if potential homeowners agree to have only one car they are eligible for special mortgage rates for housing units that are built with fewer parking spaces and near public transportation.

This section has shown that housing can be impacted by seemingly unrelated factors such as industrial zoning; the next few sections show how housing is interlinked with other community features such as infrastructure, sprawl, green space, and density. A community might start with a concern with any of these community preservation issues and find that housing decisions emerge as a central factor in the discussions.

Housing and Infrastructure

A community's housing analysis needs to be tied to an examination of the impact on infrastructure of particular housing decisions. Just as housing, zoning, and economic development are far from independent, so too housing and infrastructure are interlinked, sometimes in obvious ways but frequently in subtle ways as well.

Many analysts have documented that housing is increasingly being built on ever larger lots that are located without regard to and often at some distance from existing public transportation. When new housing is built on land that was previously undeveloped, then greater need is created for roads and sewers and a variety of other kinds of infrastructure. As communities are discovering, these infrastructure costs are not one-time expenses. Communities frequently

end up with significant long-term costs related to the additional maintenance burdens imposed by a growing number of miles of roads and sewers. Communities have begun to consider the costs of adding new housing at their edges as compared to the costs of "infill" development where houses are built on empty lots in established neighborhoods or where new housing is created in underused buildings that are located on existing streets and sewer lines.

Community leaders are beginning to pay closer attention to the links between housing decisions and the infrastructure costs that will need to be shouldered by taxpayers. Your committee might consider whether the housing being proposed is sufficiently near existing public transportation and whether planned housing will require new infrastructure. Some communities are even going a step further and looking at possibilities for increasing housing stock that is close to public transportation, again as a possible way to reduce the cost of the housing and reduce the burden to taxpayers of added infrastructure costs. Similarly, it makes sense to direct new housing development to areas with room in existing schools, rather than to outlying areas that will require new elementary school construction. Although the decisions will vary as a function of the particular community and of the range of housing that is needed, the fact that communities are linking housing to other aspects of community life is proving beneficial for many communities. This is seen most fully, as we shall see next, in looking at housing in the context of sprawl and its impact on a community's character.

Housing and Sprawl

The appetite among Americans for new homes with spacious lawns seems inexhaustible, and efforts to meet these demands are rapidly absorbing whatever green space still exists in many localities. Many communities have thus turned their attention to the pressing question of how to avoid sprawl. If the character of communities and regions is to be preserved, communities are finding that they must pay attention to identifying innovative ways to expand housing without exacerbating the problems of sprawl.

Once your committee starts looking at the relationship between housing, sprawl, and community preservation, you will find the relationship is a complicated one, but one that needs to be understood if you are to make progress in preserving community character while also meeting housing needs. Too often the working assumption within communities has been that they must choose either to stagnate or to sprawl: either a community will keep adding housing which will result in sprawl or it will avoid sprawl but will not grow.

So, if a community adds more housing, must sprawl be the inevitable result? Careful evaluation of existing communities has shown that sprawl is not the result of the number of houses, or even the size of lots; rather, it flows out of decisions about land/housing/location configurations. It is indeed the case that if communities mandate through their zoning that new houses must be built on ever-larger plots of land, the effect will be sprawl. Yet, as planners such as those associated with the New Urbanism movement have shown, openness and green space need not be sacrificed in order to gain new housing. Communities can alter the placement of houses on green space, clustering of housing is possible, and housing can be built on infill lots and in old mill space. Many possibilities can be considered for breaking the equation that new housing equals increased sprawl.

Housing and Green Space

As noted above, community choices are often framed as if they were part of a zero-sum game: that is, if those who favor preserving green space win, then those who favor the creation of more housing inevitably lose. In other words, if a community decides to set aside land as dedicated open space, then inevitably less land will be available for housing, and this scarcity will push up housing costs. And, indeed, it is the case that if nothing else is done when significant amounts of land are removed from development, that which remains will be scarcer and hence more costly.

There are ways around this, however. First, the amount of land preserved by communities is often not a significant percent of the available land, and often is land that would not have been easy to build on in the first place—such as wetlands and steep slopes. Thus, often land preservation has little effect on the land market. When land preservation starts to become significant enough to impact the general price of land, other steps are appropriate. Density, discussed in the next section, can be increased elsewhere in town, and housing can be clustered to preserve valuable open spaces that are contiguous with other town-owned or otherwise

preserved land. These issues are more fully discussed in chapter 10.

Density in Housing

When housing is considered as a community preservation issue, almost inevitably the issue of density emerges. For residential buildings, density means the number of dwelling units per acre that can be built under existing zoning, and is often abbreviated as du/ac. Building higher-density housing is the clearest way to reduce sprawl, yet the claim is often made that communities have little choice but to encourage low-density housing. Developers claim that Americans abhor dense housing and always prefer large houses with large lawns and thus communities that offer this type of housing. Claims that these preferences are entirely fixed often loom large in the deliberations of communities about whether any way can be found to deal with housing shortages other than by sacrificing green space. Yet such preferences, if absolute, place communities concerned with reining in sprawl in a difficult position. To meet such preferences, either sprawl is accepted as an inevitability or Americans must forgo their dreams and accept the fact that living in smaller, more crowded spaces has become an unfortunate necessity.

Increasingly, communities are recognizing that these preferences are not as rigid as has often been assumed. Researchers are trying to understand why some kinds of high-density housing are well received and have positive economic consequences for community. For example, high density such as that found in neighborhoods in Manhattan or Boston's Back Bay is highly preferred—as their rents and sales prices show!

David Dixon has pointed out that the most costly areas in Boston are also the most densely populated. In his essay "Fear and Loathing of Density," Dixon calls for a revitalization of older urban areas as an economic development strategy, and he reviews the experiences of Cambridge, Chicago, and Cleveland to reinforce his assertion that population density can bring about economic prosperity. In Cambridge, increases in density have spawned an increase in local business activity and have provided needed revenues for a transit system. In Chicago, development initiatives surrounding the Cabrini-Green housing complex prompted the city to change direction regarding density. Until recently, the city

Enhancing Community Strengths

sought to maintain density levels at or below 30 units per acre. Current policy allows 30 to 60 units per acre, with a mix of structures ranging from single-family homes to multifamily apartment buildings. Cleveland has begun developing housing with densities as high as 50 units per acre, in an attempt to revitalize community activities.

Dixon also debunks several myths surrounding density. Dense urban developments do not reduce property values, he contends; rather, development increases property values regardless of how it is done. He also suggests that density itself does not cause gentrification, and that gentrification is more of a by-product of a shortage of mixed-income and affordable housing developments. Dixon also points out that it is not density that increases traffic volume; this phenomenon is more attributable to urban sprawl and a concurrent lack of public transportation infrastructure. "The problem is not density, but how we shape density. The last 15 years have produced terrific examples of higher-density housing and commercial development that enrich neighborhoods in cities across America. We need to focus on learning from these examples and use them to build a new understanding —and perception—of density" (Dixon, 37).

Experiences with higher-density housing are not limited to the United States. Many immigrants new to the United States, for example, are very familiar with mixed-use zoning and high-density housing from their home countries. They are aware of some of the benefits and liabilities of living in neighborhoods where one can live, work, shop, and walk. They are used to intergenerational housing that is situated within densely organized neighborhoods. Community planners associated with the school of "New Urbanists" have drawn attention to the many positive features of high-density, mixed-usage neighborhoods; immigrant leaders new to the United States can bring lived experience to the New Urbanism analysis of how to reconfigure housing beyond the commonplace suburban model.

A key point to be made is that in some stages of the housing life cycle, the single-family house with a lawn is often the desired norm for Americans. Two-parent households with time to spend on lawn maintenance and children to use the yard may well prefer this style of housing. But this is actually a small slice of the population. Single-parent households with limited time for home maintenance, families without children, and the elderly often prefer the relative simplicity of smaller-lot single-family houses, or townhouses, condo-

miniums, or high-quality apartment living. Thus, higher-density housing may be what is most desired.

We have found it helpful in the past to describe increasing density not as "high" density, but as "traditional" density— the sort of density of pre–World War II neighborhoods or traditional small towns. This perspective suggests that very low density suburban settings are a historic aberration, and that a return to traditional density is simply getting back to the type of housing that was normal for American communities prior to these last few decades. Achieving just this level of density in new construction could significantly improve the sustainability and the affordability of housing in many U.S. communities.

Because the word "density" is so fraught with emotion, it can also be very helpful to show people what different densities look like rather than just use terms or numbers. Take an existing older section of your or a nearby town that has withstood the test of time, and ask your planning staff to calculate the number of dwellings per acre for that neighborhood. Then take a few pictures of the neighborhood, and show them to people as you talk about increasing the zoning density in unbuilt parts of town. This will go far toward alleviating the fears that the term "high density" may create.

Challenges Ripe for Inventive Solutions

Much in this chapter has suggested that creative problem solving is especially critical at this point in time because solutions that were once deemed workable can no longer be counted on to meet the new housing challenges. One of the striking features of the field of housing is that many intriguing new ideas are emerging that can help your community and others think through new dilemmas. In the next few subsections we briefly point out some of the innovative work that is now being directed at devising new definitions, new policies, and new solutions.

Shelter Poverty

Some of that innovative thinking has focused on devising new concepts that better capture the nuances in housing need. Consider, for example, Michael Stone's innovative concept of *shelter poverty*. With regard to the question of "what standard of affordability?" most housing policies automatically use 30 percent of income as the standard. Thus, housing is assumed to be affordable if no more than 30 percent of a family's income must be applied toward housing costs. Although this 30 percent standard remains the most familiar and widely used indicator as to what constitutes affordability, such a standard masks deep differences across income levels in income available for housing. In an innovative solution to this problem, Stone has developed a more realistic sliding scale of affordability that he has termed the "shelter poverty" standard, a standard that challenges the conventional percent-of-income approach. The shelter poverty standard reveals that, in general, larger, lower-income families realistically can afford less than 30 percent of income, while smaller, higher-income families can afford somewhat more than 30 percent (see Stone, Werby, and Friedman 2000).

Adaptive Reuse

Another idea that has come of age is that of adaptive reuse, what some have characterized as looking for housing where it might least be expected. As noted earlier, one of the important steps many communities have taken is to recognize that housing problems are not always solved through building new housing (particularly because building more new housing may worsen other features communities want to preserve). Chapter 15 on adaptive reuse outlines many such possibilities and points to the significance of communities having in place methods for evaluating the suitability of previously overlooked structures (e.g., abandoned mills) that could be turned into housing. Models for adaptive reuse are proliferating, with some emphasizing subsidized housing, some mixed uses, some market-rate housing. Communities have sometimes even been able to turn the environmental contamination that may plague old buildings into a way to capture targeted financing (such as financing for brownfields redevelopment) for conversion and rehabilitation.

Adaptive reuse is not without its challenges, and communities need to be aware of some of those challenges. As discussed in chapter 14 on brownfields, for example, the potential problems can include contamination of buildings and lands. That chapter considers these issues in detail and points out how such obstacles can be overcome. Adaptive reuse and historic preservation should be considered as one element in a housing committee's list of possibilities to investigate.

Preserving Affordable Housing into the Future

Once communities have finally created affordable housing, they then struggle with the issue of how those units will be kept affordable and whether fair and equitable ways can be found for the owners of affordable housing to be kept from selling their houses at market rate. Innovative strategizing has gone into addressing issues such as these that focus on how hard-won housing successes can be maintained. Some communities have found ways to design income eligibility rules that maintain themselves over time. Others have shown how to design "riders" to subsidized mortgages that mandate how much of an increase in the value of a house will be allowable at the time of resale. In other words, communities are devising solutions to new and emergent dilemmas. The Fannie Mae Foundation Web site is just one of many sites that includes useful ideas about how communities are identifying problems and then working their ways toward innovative solutions.

Providing for Innovative Housing Projects

A key approach to improving housing affordability and adequacy is to rethink zoning so that it encourages alternatives to single-family houses on large lots. Co-housing, for instance, is the result of a process in which a group of potential residents get together to design their own new neighborhood, typically with smaller, attached townhouse units, a large common house that serves multiple functions, and a significant amount of open space. Zoning that makes this easily permitted will make it more likely to be built. The town of Amherst, Massachusetts, for instance, recently passed a new zoning bylaw designed for co-housing projects, which can be viewed on the town's Web site. Similarly, well-designed cluster or conservation subdivision bylaws that permit this style of building as of right (rather than by a more complicated special permit process) will encourage this development process. Most directly, simply decreasing the minimum lot size required to build on in-town locations that are well served by existing infrastructure and services is likely to have very positive benefits in multiple areas of community preservation.

Residential/Commercial Mixed-Use Downtown Building Revitalization in Montague

Turner's Falls is one of the five villages in the Town of Montague, population about 8,500, which is located in rural Franklin County in western Massachusetts. Turner's Falls is the main commercial area for Montague. The major through street has town offices and several mixed-use structures with small retail/offices on the ground level and upper-story residences. The commercial center is active, serving residents who can walk to services and workers from some of the remaining manufacturing plants on the outskirts of the downtown. Over the past several years private and public resources have rehabilitated some of the structures, and major improvements to the street and sidewalk have significantly enhanced the appearance of the area.

Two historically significant buildings in the downtown were on the verge of demolition or at least further neglect unless preservation action was undertaken. The advantage the Town of Montague had over other similar efforts is that a number of stakeholders worked together to envision and obtain financing for the purchase and rehabilitation of these structures.

In 1997 the Crocker Building (see Figure 12.1)—a building that served as one of the gateway buildings to the downtown—suffered a major fire that gutted the structure and resulted in the death of one tenant. With the town condemning the building, the future use of this brick row house was in doubt. Diagonally across from the Crocker Building is the Colle Opera House. Since

Figure 12.1. Renovated Crocker Bank Building, Turner's Falls, Massachusetts.
Photo: Elisabeth Hamin.

Figure 12.2. Renovated affordable housing, Turner's Falls, Massachusetts.
Photo: Elisabeth Hamin.

the 1980s the town has considered a variety of development techniques to restore this building. Attached to the Colle Opera House is a series of brick row houses that contained 60 one-bedroom units (see Figure 12.2). In need of major repairs, only half of these could be occupied. Those that were occupied lacked central heat, and continued difficulty with criminal activities further made these units unsafe for both residents and businesses.

A strategy to immediately stabilize and rehabilitate these structures was sought. The town approached Rural Development Inc., an arm of the Franklin County Regional Housing and Redevelopment Authority, and Historic Massachusetts, Inc. (HMI) to determine how these structures could best be preserved. HMI agreed to take title to the property and obtained funding from the Massachusetts Historic Commission to secure the funding until a development team and financing could be organized and secured. A limited dividend organization was formed with the assistance of Rural Development Inc. This entity sought funding from over five partners to secure necessary financing to rehabilitate the two buildings. Loans and grants forming the basis of a complicated financing structure came from organizations including the Massachusetts Department of Housing and Community Development, Massachusetts Housing Investment Corporation, the Property Casualty Initiative, Massachusetts Historic Preservation Project, Massachusetts Housing Partnership, and the Community Economic Development Corporation. These resources (close to $6 million) plus low-income and historic tax credits ensured that the rehabilitated residential units—a total of 48—provided long-term affordable housing.

What Does It Cost to Build or Rehabilitate Housing?

One might simply assume that if vacant land or empty buildings are available, a little money or a little effort can turn these resources into housing. Things are a bit more complicated than that. To create more housing we need to think about some of the following:

- If we build housing, how much will the land and building cost and what do those costs per unit translate into in terms of rental rates or housing prices?
- If we rehab existing buildings, how much will the rehab cost be (including things like lead removal and historic rehab costs) and what do these costs per unit translate into in terms of rental rates or housing price?
- What options are available if the land or building is a brownfield (a site that is potentially contaminated) and how do we figure out those open-ended costs?
- If we have the choice to build either a house or an apartment building on the same plot of land, what rate of profit would we clear making one choice versus the other?
- Given the local median income, how much could we spend in developing housing and still have people be able to afford the fair market rent?
- What funding resources are available to reduce the cost of rehabbing housing or building new housing the costs of which cannot be fully covered by the potential renters?
- Given the cost of building, what level of income would families need to afford the housing being built by various groups?

For example, the Coalition for a Better Acre (CBA) has discovered that costs (including financing) for rehabbing houses means that CBA cannot afford—without special subsidies or project-based Section 8 vouchers—to build such housing for families with income at 30 percent of the median or less (for example, income less than $23,000 a year, based on Lowell's $72,300 median family income). In other words, even community development corporations may not be able to afford at present to build housing for those who are at the lowest income levels.

Finding the Funding to Bring Creative Ideas into Being

Once a community has reached the point of developing creative housing plans, locating funding to bring these plans to life may still be a struggle. The community might, for example, have a goal of underwriting housing for elders, or municipal employees, or young families. Important as such goals are, the plans to achieve them can be difficult to put in place because of the lack of funding. The federal government was previously more of a partner in the creation of affordable housing than is the case at present. Communities are finding that they must also look to state initiatives; a state may have various programs (in Massachusetts, for example, the Community Preservation Act provides some funding for affordable housing). The best approach is simply to contact your state's agency responsible for housing and see what assistance they can provide.

Locating Additional Information

Communities can find many free resources on the Web that provide suggestions on community approaches to housing problems. Relevant Web sites are listed at the end of this chapter. A few examples are highlighted here. The Fannie Mae Foundation's Web site is an excellent place to go if one wants to learn about community innovations in housing. Timely articles are included on the approaches being taken by different communities, and the KnowledgePlex search tool that is a part of this Web site allows users to locate recent articles on community solutions to housing dilemmas. Another useful Web site—regardless of whether one is in Massachusetts—is the EOEA community preservation Web site. This Web site illustrates a problem-solving approach that includes all of the elements of community preservation, and the site has information about a variety of tools useful for community planners who want to integrate housing, economic development, preserving open space, and limiting the need for new infrastructure. For those communities that are struggling with making more low-income housing available, much useful information can be found at the CHAPA Web site. Here viewers can learn, for example, how to compare available housing against various measures of the cost of living in their area. The Web site for U.S. Housing and Urban Development is also replete with resources and tools, and includes examples of how communities are addressing particular housing problems.

In addition to useful Web sites, reports have also been developed by communities that illustrate how cities are situating housing problems within the context of community preservation. Community leaders in Lowell, Massachusetts, developed a 90-page question and answer guide entitled "Meeting Lowell's Housing Needs: A Comprehensive Look" (available at http://www.uml.edu/centers/CFWC/pastprojectscfwc.htm#housingreport). In order to download and view this report, scroll down to the housing report abstract and select the download report option. "Meeting Lowell's Housing Needs" was designed to gather together hard-to-find data about past and present rents, housing costs, expiring use, plans for economic development, zoning changes, and income profiles, so that community groups could address housing problems with relevant information. Lowell is an old industrial community with extreme economic cycles where recently housing costs have been rapidly escalating, gentrification has become a danger, and there is a large and growing immigrant community. The report includes a historic view, examining the cyclical nature of housing problems and job problems in the region, and embeds housing in an analysis of economic development plans. The Lowell report also includes detailed information about all of the different groups (e.g., HUD, state housing authorities, community development corporation) that have often been assumed to have the resources to solve housing problems, and the report lists which tools they have to address housing and which tools they don't have (but are often assumed to have). All of the report's information, considered together, can be used to lay out an action plan that fully considers the opportunities and challenges of improving a community's housing situation.

THE ESSENCE of the community preservation approach is to recognize the futility of taking on housing as an isolated issue. Instead, economic development planning should include a focus on housing. Housing and transportation should be considered together. A focus on open space should consider how to mitigate the impact of preserving open space on the cost of housing. Although groups often realize that they need to take an integrated approach, it can still be challenging to figure out where to start. This chapter has shown some of the ways communities can begin. An integrated approach of the sort described here, achieved through building alliances, can serve communities well in their goals of preserving the past and developing a viable future.

References

Center for Family, Work, and Community, University of Massachusetts–Lowell. 2002. "Meeting Lowell's Housing Needs: A Comprehensive Look." Full report is available at: http://www.uml.edu/centers/CFWC/pastprojectscfwc.htm#housingreport.

Center for Urban and Regional Policy, Northeastern University. 2000. "A New Paradigm for Housing in Greater Boston." Full report is available online at: http://www.curp.neu.edu/sitearchive//roundtable.asp?id=1286.

Dixon, David. 2001. "Fear and Loathing of Density." *Architecture-Boston*, Fall.

Stone, Michael. 1993. *Shelter Poverty: New Ideas on Housing Affordability*. Philadelphia: Temple University Press.

Stone, Michael, Elaine Werby, and Donna Haig Friedman. 2000. "Situation Critical Report 2000: Meeting the Housing Needs of Lower-Income Massachusetts Residents." Full report is available online at: http://www.chapa.org/RecentReports.htm.

University of Massachusetts Donahue Institute. 1997. "A Profile of Housing in Massachusetts." Available at http://www.donahue.umassp.edu.

Web Resources

Massachusetts

Citizens Housing and Planning Association: www.chapa.org
Federal Home Loan Bank of Boston: www.fhlbboston.com
Historic Massachusetts: www.historicmass.org
Massachusetts Association of Community Development Corporations: www.macdc.org
Massachusetts Community Economic Development Assistance Corporation: www.cedac.org
Massachusetts Department of Housing and Community Development: www.state.ma.us/dhed
Massachusetts Housing (Massachusetts Housing Finance Agency): www.masshousing.com
Massachusetts Housing Investment Corporation: www.mhic.com
Massachusetts Housing Partnership Fund: www.mhpfund.com
Situation Critical: Meeting the Housing Needs of Lower-Income Massachusetts Residents: www.mccormack.umb.edu/csp/csp_housing.htm

Town of Amherst Zoning Bylaws: http://www.town.amherst.ma.us/ departments/Planning/. See especially Section 4.5

WeOwn Network/ARCH: www.weown.net

Women's Institute for Housing and Economic Development: www. wihed.org

National

Affordable Housing and Smart Growth: Making the Connection: www.neighborhoodcoalition.org/H%20and%20SG.pdf

British Columbia Ministry of Social Development and Economic Security, Toward More Inclusive Neighbourhoods: www.sdes.gov.bc.ca/housing/neighbour

Community Builders, Inc: www.tcbinc.org

Enterprise Foundation: www.enterprisefoundation.org

Family Housing Fund: www.fhfund.org

Fannie Mae Foundation: http://www.fanniemaefoundation.org/

GCA Strategies, building community support: www.gcstrategies.com

Housing Trust Fund Project: www.communitychange.org

Institute for Community Economics: www.iceclt.org

Local Initiatives Support Corporation: www.liscnet.org

National Congress for Community Economic Development: www.ncced.org

National Housing Conference: www.nhc.org

National Housing Institute/Shelterforce: www.nhi.org

National Housing Trust: www.nhtinc.org

National Low-Income Housing Coalition: www.nlihc.org

Neighborhood Reinvestment Corporation: www.nw.org

NIMBY Report: www.nlihc.org/nimby

Smart Growth for Neighborhoods: Affordable Housing and Regional Vision: www.smartgrowthamerica.org/nnhousing.pdf

U.S. Department of Housing and Urban Development: www.hud.gov

Photo: Chris Curtis

The New Economy
Thriving amidst Change

Zenia Kotval and John R. Mullin

C OMMUNITIES INCREASINGLY see their economic development goal as one of attracting job-generating industrial development and face the need to develop a plan that will achieve this goal. Communities need to know a great deal to succeed at what has become a formidable task, and many have few resources to hire experienced planners to assist them. This chapter is intended to provide information to communities and others that may be embarking on just such planning. The consulting we have undertaken around the country has shown us firsthand the rapid changes that are taking place in the economy and how communities will need to be resourceful and creative if they are going to succeed at self-preservation while at the same time attracting new jobs.

The "New Economy" of the twenty-first century is different from the industrial economies of previous decades. Competition, consumer demand, and resource restructuring are all transforming the way business operates in today's highly competitive market. Emerging technologies, global markets, the changing role of government, and the redirection of public resources are just some of the forces affecting the way industry is transforming the nature of work. These emerging trends are increasingly influencing the way communities engage in industrial development. It is thus essential that anyone involved in local economic development have a firm grasp of how and where the marketplace is moving.

The first half of the chapter spells out the major trends that are dramatically changing the nature of the issues that communities need to be aware of. The second half takes readers through a step-by-step approach that communities can follow in this changed environment to develop an effective comprehensive economic development strategy.

Major Trends in Community Economic Development

As we shall see, many past truisms no longer hold, or at the very least must be modified in significant respects if communities are to succeed in the twenty-first century in their community economic development efforts. Increasingly, communities are discovering that they must adapt to the marketplace; they need to become more proactive in controlling how and where they stimulate development; they must show greater concern for providing the necessary ingredients for industry to succeed; and, their planning processes must increasingly reflect world events and the speed of change. The first half of this chapter outlines eight emerging trends concerning industrial development that we have noted over the past decades in our consulting practice and academic research and that are driving these changes in what communities need to do. The trends described here are not exhaustive nor will they be reflected in all parts of the country.

(1) Land is not enough. In community after community, local promotional efforts have followed the optimistic but misguided practice of signaling interest in promoting development and attracting businesses by doing little more than placing a prominent sign at the edge of town proclaiming something like "Maplewood Means Business: Industrial Land Available." And communities then wait and wait and wait. The land considered available for sale for industrial purposes may well consist of little more than the corner lot of the late farmer James's farm that is being sold by his heirs. Often such land lacks even the most basic infrastructure improvements: it has no water or sewer services, no easy access to highways, and no protective covenants. And such towns, as they wait, often puzzle over why the next great company is not being attracted to this land. Unfortunately, simply having land available is rarely enough in today's intensely competitive environment.

If a community is interested in attracting first-rate industrial development, then a group of basic requirements must be met. Far too often communities remain unaware of these requirements and thus fail to include them in their economic development planning. The typical industrial park needs 50 to 100 acres of land and should be within 15 minutes of a major highway and 30 minutes of an airport. In addition, the site must be environmentally clean, have water, sewer, and telecommunications infrastructure, and should be buffered from residential neighborhoods. Of the previously listed attributes, the absence of water and sewer systems represents perhaps the greatest barrier to success. Without such systems, a community is unlikely to succeed in attracting industrial development. Indeed, we know of one community offering industrial land without such

services where, ironically, the sign saying "We Mean Business" fell down long before any business tenant could be attracted.

(2) Taxes are (not that) important. When we first broke into economic development in the late 1960s, the planner's economic development toolkit was far less sophisticated than it is today. The common wisdom at that time was that low taxes were both necessary and sufficient to attract industrial firms. Although some truth remains to this rule of thumb, today most firms look beyond taxes to a series of other factors. Firms often place great emphasis, for example, on infrastructure improvements (i.e., upgraded water and sewer systems), the quality of schools, proximity to an airport, and the availability of a trained workforce. Amenities count when a community wishes to attract high-quality companies. Examples of the importance companies place on such amenities are by no means hard to find. Consider, for example, the case of the Pfizer Corporation. The Pfizer Corporation selected New London, Connecticut, as the site for its 2,000-employee research and development firm. Virtually all the many locations that Pfizer examined were able to offer the company tax/cost reduction packages. No sites other than New London, however, were able to offer the high quality-of-life factors desired by Pfizer employees. In fact, today, well after Pfizer's project is operational, Pfizer continues to recommend certain communities in the region for employee relocation largely because of their good schools and related lifestyle amenities. A second example illustrating the importance many companies place on quality-of-life factors concerns the decision of Cisco Industries Systems to locate in Boxboro, Massachusetts. Other cities and towns were willing to offer Cisco a much better financial package than the town of Boxboro could offer. And yet, again for quality-of-life reasons, the company selected this small town.

These examples should not be taken to suggest that taxes will never be important. Taxes continue to be a factor in many site decisions. Increasingly, however, other factors are equally, if not more, important. Failure to attend to them will leave communities poorly positioned to work out effective development plans.

(3) Communities should devote their educational efforts to creating a strong K-12 educational infrastructure rather than focusing on generic workforce education. We know of no company that is fully satisfied with the federal, state, local,

nonprofit, or private sector programs available for workforce education. Although the efforts of the Private Industry Councils and Regional Employment Boards are to be applauded, the fact remains that worker training is often an "on-the-job" phenomena. More than ever, we hear from the private sector the mantra: "Just get us a worker with the basic skills and we will do the rest." We know of one company, for example, that has taken this approach to the ultimate: Taco Industries in Cranston, Rhode Island, brings in the Community College of Rhode Island to its plant floor and offers its workers a series of semester-long courses ranging from English as a Second Language to Basic Management to Geometry. This program has been remarkably successful.

Communities sometimes assume that in order to be competitive they should invest their dollars in workforce development training. Such a focus is unlikely to attract new industry, industry that often wishes to customize the training its workers will need. Instead communities need to be able to ensure prospective companies that the quality of basic K-12 education is strong and will continue to be so.

(4) At the local level community colleges can sometimes be more important than major universities. Major universities tend to be oriented to pure research, abstract analysis, and peer reviews, and often pay limited attention to meeting the technical job skill requirements of local industry. Community colleges are sometimes better able to adapt to local circumstances quickly and inexpensively and should be considered in community economic development planning. For example, Central Vermont Community College, located near Barre, the center of America's granite industry, was able to develop courses that assisted workers in this industry. In Leominster, Massachusetts, a pioneer plastics city, Mt. Wachusetts Community College developed courses for improving the skills of plastics workers. In Springfield, Massachusetts, the efforts of Springfield Technology Community College to create a fully wired industrial incubator were so successful that the college received the Economic Development Administration U.S. Department of Commerce's 2001 Excellence in Urban or Suburban Economic Development Award, as well as the International Economic Development Council's 2002 Excellence in Economic Development Award.

(5) "Be Wired or Be Gone." The telecommunications revolution is creating regional winners and losers, with rural and isolated small towns increasingly on the losing end.

To date, many parts of the nation are not fiber-optically wired or lack broadband capabilities. Unfortunately, until connectivity is achieved, businesses in these communities will remain at a competitive disadvantage. The importance of connectivity is thrown into sharp relief by decisions where companies have chosen old mill sites that are wired over new sites that are not. We are also familiar with companies that have left regions because, as these companies grew, they needed modern telecommunications systems that were simply unavailable in the region where they were located. These trends, troubling as they might be, indicate that richer communities will gain and the poorer ones will continue to suffer.

(6) Zoning issues are becoming increasingly complex. Communities that have taken the first steps toward developing strong master plans and contemporary zoning by-laws or ordinances are often better prepared than others to attract industrial development. However, from an economic development perspective, there are several trends in master planning or zoning practices that communities should know can work against effective economic development. First, too many communities are failing to select the best possible parcels for industrial, office, or service use. We jokingly use the formula GL = IL to refer to the approach of too many communities whereby they equate Industrial Land with Garbage (or worthless) Land. Too often, communities first designate lands for residential use, then for commercial use, then for open space/agriculture, and only lastly for industry. We know of one relatively prosperous community that once zoned more than 700 acres for industrial use. Yet, after a careful examination of the parcels, we determined that fewer than 10 percent of them were actually developable. The key point here is quite simple: communities that are serious about recruiting industry must be able to find land that meets the needs of industry. Second, in addition to the failure to select appropriate sites for industry, too many communities add further barriers by allowing for industry only under special permit or exception provisions. Only if the owners can meet certain infrastructure, traffic, fiscal, and environmental considerations and also considerations of community character protection is the company allowed to build.

Special permits or exceptions should be used with great caution. Such restrictive provisions can clearly be needed in special circumstances, yet they can become an obstacle to economic development when they become a condition of building in all instances. Moreover, given that industry leaders often want to build rapidly, they frequently avoid those communities that have set up politically difficult or time-consuming processes. Third, company leaders often want some guarantees concerning the sorts of neighboring uses allowable. The "tinkering" with established industrial zoning must be done with great care. Developers often want to ensure the quality of their investment. Thus, attempts to change zoning once companies have invested are generally viewed negatively by those companies. For example, we worked in one community that housed one of New England's best-planned industrial/office parks. Last year, despite our recommendation, the planner recommended changing a key parcel to retail. That parcel now houses a 110,000-square-foot Stop and Shop Supermarket whose retail function does not mesh well with the existing industrial uses. Because of cases like this, we increasingly see developers placing restrictive covenants on their deeds and insisting that nearby properties also be subject to such restrictions. In summary, our work has indicated the benefits of fixed zoning combined with strong performance measures and the use of covenants. Such procedures hold the potential for all parties to win.

(7) Sustainable development is becoming increasingly important. We are now beginning to see some small-scale examples of sound, sustainable economic development practices. Often these are occurring without a great deal of fanfare and with limited attention to the potential they represent. Firms are beginning to pick up on these practices because they are beginning to see that through such practices they may be able to save money, speed up processes, and at the same time act as good neighbors. A focus on sustainable development is most likely to be seen in areas where there are industrial clusters or locations where it can easily happen. If sustainable development takes time or is difficult to introduce, then it is likely not to be pursued. Of all of the trends we have noted, this is perhaps the least obvious at present. Nonetheless, we expect more in the future.

(8) Finally, Economic Development and Industrial Corporations (EDIC) are increasingly important. In the past communities too often have completed their planning and zoning and have then simply sat back and waited for development to occur. Yet when development did take place, communities were often disappointed in the result.

The company that came to town failed to live up to the community's expectations. Instead of attracting a high-end quality mall, the town might only attract a low-end, cheaply built strip mall facility. Or, instead of a major manufacturer providing good high-paying jobs, a warehouse might come to town.

To avoid such outcomes many communities have begun creating Economic Development and Industrial Corporations or EDICs. Such corporations typically purchase or control key parcels and then aggressively pursue the "right type" of company for the town. Through the efforts of an EDIC, the ambitious goals of a master plan and zoning can more easily be met. Such an approach has often worked quite well. Consider Gloucester, Massachusetts, for example. The city is home to one of the East Coast's largest fishing fleets. For this reason, it has in the past attracted extensive "flash freezing" and warehousing facilities. Such companies typically pay low wages. The goal of Gloucester's mayor was to attract a more diversified base that would build on Greater Boston's high technology base and provide higher-wage jobs. Unfortunately, though, each time an industrial parcel came up for sale, the existing fishing firms that provided only low-wage jobs were able to quickly purchase the land. To overcome the problem of municipalities being unable to move quickly, the mayor helped to organize an EDIC. Once that was in place, when a 100-acre parcel came up for sale, the EDIC immediately purchased it. Today, this parcel in Gloucester is home to a fully diversified high technology office park.

As this example suggests, it is rare when there is a direct match between the availability of land and the right type of company. An extended period of time is often needed to bring the two together. Clearly, an EDIC can help in this regard. Because speed of change in our industrial base is increasing, such an approach is becoming all the more important. In our 30 years as economic development planners, we have seen Greater Boston shed industries (i.e., textiles, shoes, defense equipment), gain new ones (electronics, computer manufacturing) only to shed them and, more recently, embrace software, biotechnology, and genetic research. All of this in a relatively brief three decades! At the same time, with the rise of the European Union and NAFTA, competition is clearly global. We, as economic development planners, will have to accept more "value heavy/weight light" manufacturing and an increase in the service-based economy. Our communities will have to be vigilant in terms of ensuring that they are prepared for the next wave.

Not all of the eight trends described above will be found in all parts of the country, and not all of them will occur simultaneously. However, it is increasingly clear that the industrial future will require communities to be vigilant, flexible, and prepared. The changes that are taking place are likely to be chaotic, nerve racking, and, at the same time, quite exciting. Communities will need to plan or they are likely to find that in the future they will be "planned upon." In addition, local economic development practitioners will no longer be able look to the federal government for resources. Communities will increasingly need to forge new partnerships with the private sector and pay closer attention to the needs of the business community. There will be an increasing need to focus on "quality"—quality jobs, quality infrastructure, quality labor force, and quality living environment rather than on traditional bricks-and-mortar development.

The first step toward coping with the new economy will entail communities becoming aware of and knowledgeable about emerging trends that will impact the way that business will be done in the region in the coming years. We recommend communities undertake a comprehensive economic development strategy. Throughout the remainder of this chapter we outline in detail the steps that a community can take to design such a strategy that is attentive to all of the trends we have described.

A Comprehensive Economic Development Strategy

A comprehensive economic development strategy (CEDS) describes the problems, needs, potentials, and resources of the area; presents the community's visions and goals; sets the strategic direction for the action plan; establishes priorities and projects for implementation; and outlines standards for annual evaluation and update of the process.

Preparing a CEDS document can take much of a community's time and energy. From the very outset the organizing and staffing needs should be understood. A critical part of organizing the approach is the establishment of a CEDS committee. This committee ideally includes people from the public, private, and nonprofit sectors. We suggest inviting the political leaders, representatives from economic

development and business organizations, representatives of the employment and training sectors, and other health, education, social service, professional, and special interest groups.

Once such a committee is formed, its first order of business should be: defining the working relationships with other local, regional, and state institutions; ensuring that adequate staff resources are available; and adopting a committee work program that defines tasks, sets responsibilities, and establishes timelines and uses subcommittees when necessary to accomplish the work program. There are four strategic components of the CEDS to answer these four questions:

- where do we stand now?
- what does the region want to achieve?
- how do we get there?
- how are we doing toward achieving the goals?

Analysis of the Region and the Community (Where Do We Stand Now?)

The economic planning and development process begins with an analysis of trends across the region. It is essential that communities be able to identify those companies that are currently being formed, expanding, leaving, or downsizing. We believe that a regional as opposed to community focus is key because the United States has become a nation of commuters. Local companies can no longer promise local jobs for local folks. It is also critical that communities interview a cross-section of companies (e.g, large, medium, small, manufacturing, service, locally owned, nationally owned) now in their area to determine their long-term prospects within the region. Such a regional analysis should include summaries of:

- The state of the regional economy (strengths and weaknesses);
- External trends and forces (opportunities and threats);
- Partners for economic development; and
- Resources for economic development.

Once the trend assessment has been completed, we generally urge communities to assess their current economic assets. These will include the workforce, land use and zoning, infrastructure, business climate, and entrepreneurial atmosphere. In terms of the workforce, it is important to identify ages, skills, stability, and availability.

Such an infrastructure audit should include an examination of the distribution systems and their capacity. The audit must also include an examination of sewer and waste disposal, water supply, highways, gas, electricity, and telecommunications capabilities. Several issues need to be addressed here. The first relates to the condition of the utility systems. In terms of water, will there be a sufficient supply as the community grows? In terms of highways, is there capacity such that there will be no change in the level of service? In many states, if there is a decline in the level of service along a highway, it must be corrected by the community or the developer. In terms of gas and electricity, is there enough capacity to ensure a steady supply? Finally, in terms of telecommunications, if communities do not have the latest technologies then, simply stated, those communities will not be able to compete.

Furthermore, one needs to examine the relationship between a region's larger and smaller firms. Local economies that are dominated by one industry remain precarious. We often urge communities to ensure that their industries are integrated as extensively as possible. Finally, the inventory must examine the region's entrepreneurial climate. The importance of this is that companies formed by local residents tend to stay local. They tend to buy local, finance local, and support local causes. We urge communities to look at the types of companies being formed, the patents and licenses being granted for the community, and the buying practices of the larger companies. By so doing, a community will have a snapshot of the local economic climate.

A Vision Statement (What Does the Region Want to Achieve?)

A vision statement is a positive and practical future image of the area in ten to twenty years. Such a statement should convey a sense of meaning and purpose, a sense of values and cultural heritage, a sense of place and community character, a sense of leadership and civic participation, and, above all, a sense of hope and enthusiasm.

Increasingly, communities are developing visions of what they want to be like as they grow, prosper, and change. Community vision statements have become popular, we believe, for four reasons. First, given the speed and pace of change, citizens want to have the sense of security within their own communities that is provided by a vision statement. Second, residents are investing more and more of their private capital into their own homes and are strongly interested in protecting and enhancing their properties. Third, the sense of direction provided to businesses by their vision statements has trickled into the public sector and is leading to more communities adopting this approach. Indeed, business has long practiced visioning as a means of creating clarity of purpose. Finally, a publicly approved and "bought in" vision of the future provides elected officials, board members, and residents a roadmap of where a community is and what it desires to become.

How does a community begin to prepare a vision for itself and then turn this vision into a statement that reflects its values and direction? There is no single approach. At the very least, the vision needs to be based on current trends that place the community in a global, national, state, and regional context. Many communities carry out a series of studies or investigations to gather the relevant information. A first study might gather concise facts about factors that are influencing the community. A second study might survey local values. Ideally, such a survey will be professionally prepared and broadly disseminated. It should be drafted, tested, reviewed, and sent to every household. We have had great success in obtaining the assistance of local colleges and regional planning agencies in writing these survey instruments. Community leaders should expect that the findings will be challenged. Over the past five years, we have noted at least five instances where the findings ran counter to popular perceptions and the results therefore generated extensive and heated debate! A third study might include a visual character survey. This survey, using photographs and, frequently, models, is designed to determine how residents feel about how the physical form of the community is emerging.

Once these studies have been completed and digested by the committee, we urge the community to call a town-wide charette or workshop to prepare the town's vision. Workshops of this sort have been most effective when up to one hundred people come to the session. An excellent facilitator will be needed to make the session a success. The purpose of the charette is to identify the community's strengths, weaknesses, opportunities, and threats, to identify the community's core values, and to draft the statement. The

Economic Development Excerpt from the Billerica, Massachusetts, Master Plan Document

The Town of Billerica is a regional employment center within a suburban community. Commerce and industry account for nearly 24 percent of the assessed value of the community. In pursuit of a balance between economic vitality and the quality of life, the following goals with associated objectives and expected results were developed:

Goal 1: The Town of Billerica should continue to attract new business to maintain a stable tax base. The diversity of the businesses is key to surviving fluctuations in the economy. Targeted new businesses should be in keeping with the character of the Town.

Objective A: The Town should develop a list of the businesses that are located in Town including information regarding type of business, type of employees, expansion potential, site requirements, etc.

Expected Results: A comprehensive list of local businesses would be developed. This list will assist the Town in learning about the existing market and be a valuable resource when the Town and/or realtors want to attract businesses to locate in Billerica.

Objective B: The Town should develop a list of the type of businesses that it would like to attract.

Expected Results: The Town will develop a list of the types of businesses that it would like to attract.

Goal 2: The Town of Billerica must work with the existing business community to maintain the Town's economic vitality. Established businesses should be encouraged to grow in Billerica, creating jobs and capital investment for the local community and for the region. Strong public-private partnerships are essential to economic stability.

Objective A: The Town should schedule company tours with local businesses.

Expected Results: The Town will schedule tours regularly with local businesses, i.e., one or two per month.

Objective B: The Town should explore the possibility of tax incentives for expanding local businesses.

Expected Results: If appropriate, the Town will provide tax incentives for expanding local businesses.

Objective C: The Town should explore the possibility of a small business loan pool to assist small businesses that create or retain jobs as they expand.

Expected Results: If appropriate, the Town will create a small business loan pool to assist small businesses that create or retain jobs as they expand.

Goal 3: The Town of Billerica's economic development policy should seek to create and retain good jobs for Billerica residents, and to promote job opportunities in local businesses to the residents.

Objective A: The Town should work through the School Department to prepare students for the requirements of local jobs.

Expected Results: The Town and the School Department will, together with local businesses, prepare students for work in the local workforce.

Objective B: The Town should work through the School Department to promote job opportunities in local businesses to residents.

Expected Results: A working relationship between the Town, the School Department, and local businesses will be developed to promote local job opportunities to residents.

Objective C: The Town should ensure that there are a variety of housing types available to future workers of all levels.

Expected Results: A variety of housing types will be developed and available in Billerica.

Goal 4: Recognizing that the retail shops help to define the character of the community, the Town of Billerica should encourage the growth of small shops within existing retail space, rather than focusing on the large users. Shops, and the goods and services they render, should be in keeping with the character of the Town.

Objective A: The Town should schedule company tours with local retail shops to determine if there is anything that the Town can do to help the businesses succeed.

Expected Results: The Town will schedule tours regularly with local retail shops, i.e., one or two per month.

Objective B: The Town should work with the local Chamber of Commerce and the State to develop a list of the retail businesses that are already located in Town including information regarding type of business, type of employees, expansion potential, site requirements, etc.

Expected Results: The Town will have a better understanding of its retail businesses and what they need to grow and be successful.

Objective C: The Town should explore the possibility of a small business loan pool to assist small retail businesses that create or retain jobs as they expand.

Expected Results: If appropriate, the Town will create a small business loan pool to assist small retail businesses that create or retain jobs as they expand.

participants should have summaries of the findings from the values survey and the visual character study but not the whole study—too much information tends to cause people to focus on details when the intent is to create something that is more holistic.

The above approach is but one of many. It is, however, one that works. Once the initial statement is delivered to the CEDS committee, that statement should be further discussed and refined—fully respecting the point that it truly reflects the perspectives of the community. The committee typically then votes on the vision and presents it to the elected leaders of the community, where it will begin to become incorporated into the civic culture.

Goals, Objectives, and Strategic Actions (How Does the Community Get There?)

Once the community establishes its vision, this vision needs to be translated into short- and long-term goals, and objectives that will lead to the achievement of the goals. Goals are broad statements while objectives need to be measurable steps.

Strategic actions are carefully selected approaches that propose responsibility for implementation. Strategic actions to promote economic development usually fall under five major categories:

The first is Locality Development. This set of actions focuses on local processes intended to make the community more attractive to businesses. Typical strategies might involve the community buying and holding prime land for specific types of development; pre-clearing industrial sites; building speculative buildings; creating flexible and performance-based zoning; and streamlining the permitting process.

The second set of action steps focuses on Business Development. Strategies here are aimed at making it easy for business to develop and prosper. Most of these strategies are typically geared toward small businesses. These might include Business Assistance Centers that specialize in business planning, identifying financial programs, group marketing, promotion programs, and some product development expertise. Incubators are another form of business development where several small businesses can co-locate in one space, share common office facilities, and share resources at relatively low cost.

The third area of action steps often focus on Human Resource Development. Typically, strategies are aimed at employment and training such as creating "first source agreements" with businesses which give local people first preference for jobs in exchange for local government help in some other way (a tax break for example). Customized training or developing skill banks also falls within this group.

The fourth type of action steps consist of creating Financial Resources and Incentives. More and more communities are exploring the possibility of creating innovative tax incentives as a way to promote desired commercial and economic development. These incentive tools include negotiated tax agreements and multi-year tax abatements. Tax abatement financing is attractive since it is virtually the only finance tool available at the sole discretion of local government. Tax abatements might be given to businesses to offset property, sale, or inventory taxes. For a neighborhood or group of parcels where redevelopment is especially desired, communities may want to establish tax increment financing.

Another local financing strategy now being used by some communities creates a local revolving loan fund or capital bank, often undertaken by forming a strong partnership that brings together public funds (such as government grants), private funds (such as commercial banks and private corporations), and nonprofits (such as foundations). The passage and subsequent utilization of the Community Reinvestment Act) requires banks to be players in "community development" within the communities in which they are located. They can contribute funds directly (make loans) or indirectly (make grants or loans to community development corporations or revolving loan programs that focus on community development) within their jurisdiction.

The fifth group of action steps that can result from a community's vision relates to Business Retention and Attraction. There are six basic elements in the implementation of a Business Retention and Attraction Program:

- Presenting a package of good basic information about the community and what it offers business: Community Information.
- Meeting with and maintaining regular contact with entities such as state economic development agencies (this is where some businesses seek data when they are considering moving or seeking assistance): Sales Representation.
- Working with existing businesses in the community to

Tax Increment Financing

Tax increment financing is a technique used to disperse the cost of development to those government agencies that will benefit from the increased tax base that a TIF project will generate. First a TIF area needs to be defined by the TIF authority. The assessed property valuation of this area is frozen for a specific period of time (usually ranging from ten to twenty-five years). This frozen value is referred to as the "tax increment base value," and it remains the same for the life of the project. The TIF authority then uses its powers of land assembly, sale, site clearance, infrastructure developments, etc. to improve the district and make it more attractive to business and developers.

Once the land has been secured by the TIF authority, it is usually sold to a real estate developer, who is responsible for attracting business to the district. As private investment begins to accumulate, the assessed valuation and corresponding property taxes generated by the district increase. However, this increase is not channeled to the taxing body (the Town). Instead, this revenue is earmarked for the TIF authority and is used to finance any debt that the authority accumulated when making improvements to the district. The difference between the "tax increment base value" and the assessed value after development is known as the "tax increment".

There are two basic ways for the TIF authority to raise the initial monies needed to finance the infrastructure improvements. First, the authority can pay for improvements as they go, using the tax increment from the previous year. This method can be quite slow as development may occur only gradually. However, the authority does not need to issue bonds, thus reducing the risk of the project. The second financing method, which is more common, is the issuance of bonds (either general obligation bonds or revenue bonds). These bonds give the authority an immediate means of financing a TIF project. The issuance of bonds entails a higher risk. If development fails to occur or does not reach expected levels, it will be difficult to pay off the bond issues. Thus there is a trade-off between the higher risk of using bonds and the increased speed of development.

assure them that they are wanted, and assisting them to stay and grow: Business Visitation.

- Establishing both a single point of contact and a welcoming committee for businesses interested in moving to the community: Ambassadors.
- Being ready to act quickly and without confusion—for businesses time is money, delay is costly and a waste of money: Quick Action.
- Sustaining the program over time. Progress is often incremental, and like interest it compounds if the principal is not withdrawn: Maintenance of Effort.

Finally, there is one other aspect of a community's industrial plan that requires additional careful thought: Who will oversee the implementation of the plan? We raise this issue because, too frequently, the answer is no one! We urge communities to look to forming an industrial development committee or commission with the charge of overseeing the economic base of the community.

Evaluation (How Is the Community Doing?)

We end with the question of how communities can track whether their efforts at economic development have been successful. In order for communities to evaluate and measure the success of their efforts, they will need to define indicators and performance measures for success, and design a process to evaluate progress and outcomes against stated goals. An *indicator* is a measure or a set of measures that describes a complex social, economic, or physical reality. A list of suggested indicators is included in the book's appendix. A *measure* is one data point that acts as a gauge to tell us how well or poorly we are doing with respect to an indicator. Measures use quantifiable data, preferably collected over time, to identify trends and assess whether conditions are improving, staying steady, or deteriorating. Measures used will change over time to reflect relevance, availability of new data, and developments in society.

Criteria used to select measures include:

- Relevance and impact: Is the indicator associated with one or more issues which people care about and which have meaningful policy impacts?
- Validity and availability: Are the measures objective, statistically defensible, and credible? Is the data verifiable and easily and affordably reproducible for future reports?

- Simplicity: Are the measures appealing and understandable to the general public and to policy-makers?
- Ability to aggregate information: Does the measure contribute to the understanding of the important or broader issue expressed by the indicator? For practical reasons, indicators that aggregate information on broader issues are preferred.
- Ability to reflect trends: In order to understand and determine long-term impacts, can the data reflect trends over time? Is data in time series available?

Economic development is perhaps the most difficult to accomplish of all of the planning elements facing a community. It is fraught with concern over health and safety, often requires financial outlays for the community, is increasingly risky because of rapid shifts in world economic trends, and frequently takes years of effort before any positive return on investment can be realized. Still, despite these problems, there is a need to have a balanced economy and expand our tax base. It is worth the struggle. In sum, by creating a climate of action; moving quickly on short-term–low-cost actions; creating committees to study and develop policies and regulations that are carefully and slowly put together; and developing a funding plan that is based on the community's ability to pay, we are convinced a community's plan can be an effective, long-term guide to improving the quality of life for local residents.

References

Blakely, Edward, and Ted Bradshaw. 2002. *Planning Local Economic Development, Theory and Practice.* 3rd ed. Thousand Oaks, CA: Sage Publications.

Fitzgerald, Joan, and Nancey Green Leigh. 2002. *Economic Revitalization: Cases and Strategies for City and Suburb.* Thousand Oaks, CA: Sage Publications.

Kotval, Zenia, John Mullin, and Kenneth Payne. 1996. *Business Attraction and Retention: Local Economic Development Efforts.* Washington, DC: ICMA Press.

McLean, M. C., and Kenneth Vortek. 1992. *Understanding your Economy.* 2nd ed. Chicago: APA Press.

Web Resources

Creating a Comprehensive Economic Development Strategy. Published by EDA, and available at http://www.eda.gov/xp/EDAPublic/Research/PlanForEcoDev.xml.

Economic Development Administration (EDA), U.S. Department of Commerce: http://www.osec.doc.gov/eda/

Economic Development Division of the American Planning Association: www.edd-apa.org

Economic Development Institute: www.occe.ou.edu/edi

International Economic Development Council: www.iedconline.org

University of Michigan, Institute of Labor and Industrial Relations. Community Organizing and Economic Development resources online: http://www.ilir.umich.edu/noframes/urban/ed5.htm

V

Keeping the Best

Massachusetts

Brownfields Success Stories

Massachusetts Department of Environmental Protection

Kendall Square Redevelopment Project • 2006 Phoenix Award Winner

November 2006

MassDEP • One Winter Street • Boston • Massachusetts 02108 • 617-292-5500

Courtesy of Mira Development, LLC

14

Brownfields Redevelopment
Reconnecting Economy, Ecology, and Equity

Veronica Eady

BROWNFIELDS ARE all around us. They pepper nearly every neighborhood in the United States. They could be the vacant lot on the edge of town. They are the abandoned textile mill near the railroad tracks. They could be the decaying gas station, the old Boys and Girls Club, they may even be the charred remains of a home a block from the elementary school. In fact, a parcel of property need only pose the mere *perception* of contamination in order to be placed in the category of rejected, unappealing, and often unsafe land we call brownfields.[1]

Though policy-makers and residents alike have for decades decried the burden blighted properties place on the aesthetic, economic, and emotional character of communities, a growing body of stakeholder groups is acknowledging the valuable assets these properties represent. As our population expands, our demand for public services, such as schools, grocery stores, and libraries also expands. Developable land, in turn, has become scarce. Recycling a brownfield site can help save money by reusing land with existing infrastructure. It can preserve historic buildings and build social capacity by giving residents an opportunity to reenvision, reinvent, and restore the places they hold most dear, their neighborhoods.

This chapter explores the threats and opportunities posed by brownfields, while placing brownfields in a context, both historically and prospectively. Reusing brownfields can bring many benefits, including environmental cleanup, jobs, and community cohesion. It can also bring challenges, including identifying the level of cleanup that will satisfy the community without economically overburdening new development, and preventing gentrification from the reuse. This chapter identifies tools for brownfields recycling, as well as pitfalls those tools may

---

1. Prior to the passage of The Small Business Liability Relief and Brownfields Revitalization Act in 2002, the U.S. Environmental Protection Agency defined brownfields as "abandoned, idled, or underused industrial and commercial facilities or properties where expansion or redevelopment is complicated by real or perceived contamination." See, e.g., L. Hernández, T. Estrada, and C. Garzón, *Building upon Our Strengths: A Community Guide to Brownfields Redevelopment in the San Francisco Bay Area* (San Francisco: Urban Habitat Program, 1999).

present. And finally, the chapter suggests methods for communities to measure progress in their own restoration efforts.

Classifying a Property as a "Brownfield"

The term "brownfield" received its legal definition, embedded in federal legislation, in 2002, with the passage of the Small Business Liability Relief and Brownfields Revitalization Act (Public Law 107–118, January 11, 2002). That statute defines a brownfield as "real property, the expansion, redevelopment, or reuse of which may be complicated by the presence or potential presence of a hazardous substance, pollutant, or contaminant." Often, the slightest perception that contamination may exist on a site has been enough to dissuade developers, potential buyers, and banks from making a deal. Although brownfield sites generally do not have complex or severe contamination problems, the lack of a legal framework for potentially contaminated sites has kept the wary at arm's length in a desperate effort to avoid being sucked into the liability vortex known as Superfund.

Brownfields have contamination that is something short of "Superfund" sites, those extremely contaminated sites governed by the Comprehensive Environmental Response, Compensation, and Liability Act, also known as the Superfund Law.[2] The 1980 Superfund Law, basically, created a mechanism by which the U.S. Environmental Protection Agency (EPA) could directly clean up the nation's most egregiously contaminated sites and could sue potentially responsible parties for cost recovery. EPA could tap the Superfund, a trust fund derived from taxes on the petroleum and chemical industries,[3] for the remediation of these sites. Superfund has been severely criticized for its broad liability scheme, providing without proof of fault that any "potentially" responsible party is strictly liable for the entire cleanup of the site. A bank that foreclosed on a Superfund property, for example, would become a potentially responsible party that could be held liable. A company responsible for a tiny fraction of co-mingled contamination could be held liable for the entire cleanup. Girded with the power of Superfund, the EPA could sue any single party remotely connected to the contamination for full reimbursement. This led to ancillary litigation between the potentially responsible parties. Many critics have come to believe that the Superfund has become nothing more than a tool to line the pockets of skillful environmental lawyers.

With no federal legislation carving out exceptions from the Superfund law for brownfields sites, developers, banks, and potential buyers have had very good reason to avoid working with any site having perceived contamination. The brownfields movement was an outgrowth of frustration and confusion surrounding Superfund.

EPA created a brownfields program in the absence of a legislative mandate. In the mid-1990s, EPA began funding site assessments and job training for technicians at brownfield sites. The agency also created several pilot programs to jumpstart brownfield reuse in communities across the country. In addition, many states established cooperative approaches called "Voluntary Cleanup Programs" to foster private sector participation in the cleanup of brownfields. Voluntary Cleanup Programs allow private parties to clean up a contaminated property under a state-approved work plan. Most states require the private party to cover state oversights costs, but the private party receives a release from liability upon completion of the cleanup provided there were no unforeseen circumstances such as previously undiscovered contamination appearing later on at the site. Nevertheless, it was states such as Pennsylvania and Massachusetts that trail-blazed the brownfields movement with innovative legislation (Hirschorn 2000) which prompted inventories and aggressive marketing of brownfield sites while providing assessment and remediation funding, environmental insurance subsidies, and tax credits.[4]

Threats and Opportunities

The scholar Robert D. Bullard of Clark Atlanta University defines sprawl as "random unplanned growth characterized by inadequate accessibility to essential land uses such as housing, jobs, and public services that include schools, parks, green space, and public transportation."[5] Bullard

---

2. 42 U.S.C. §§ 9601 *et seq.* (1980).

3. The Superfund tax no longer exists.

4. See, e.g., Chapter 206 of the Acts of 1998, An Act Relative to Environmental Cleanup and Promoting the Redevelopment of Contaminated Property (otherwise known as the Massachusetts Brownfields Act), August 5, 1998.

5. R. Bullard, G. Johnson, and A. Torres, "Race, Equity, and Smart Growth: Why People of Color Must Speak for Themselves" (2001), available at: http:// www.ejrc.cau.edu/raceequitysmartgrowth.htm.

suggests that "uneven development between central cites and suburbs, combined with the systematic avoidance of inner-city areas by many businesses, has heightened social and economic inequalities."[6] Despite these tensions between urban and suburban development characterized as sprawl, brownfields exist in both urban and suburban as well as in rural communities.

Still, a disproportionate number of brownfield sites are located in America's inner cities. In New England, for example, industrial processes date back to the early settlers of the seventeenth century. Communities like Woburn, Massachusetts, were heirs to the toxic legacy of tanners long before the W. R. Grace Company, made famous by the book and film *A Civil Action*, was a glimmer in Woburn's eye. The contamination in our inner cities and other industrialized areas is very old. In order to reuse a brownfield site, a developer would first have to trace the ownership and land-use history, then identify the contamination and remediate it with the risk of unchecked legal and financial liability. When faced with a choice between tackling a site with centuries of contamination or developing pristine open space, many developers and businesses seeking to expand make the easy choice to take the open space, where often state highway departments are happy to build new off-ramps to spur other economic growth. And while contemporary economic engines, such as the high technology and biotechnology industries, increasingly set up office parks on "greenfields" on the outskirts of towns, inner cities are struggling to find economic, aesthetic, and transportation projects that will pump new life into them.

But a brownfield can scar a suburban or rural neighborhood as easily as it can an inner city. Residents who have struggled to have brownfield sites cleaned up or simply secured by a fence know what a nuisance they pose. This type of property—abandoned, desolate, even spooky—is what members of the legal profession might term an "attractive nuisance." It may attract child-explorers looking for an adventure. It can attract drug users or traffickers looking for privacy. It may attract homeless people looking for a secluded place to sleep or store their belongings. Regardless of who might enter the site or for what purpose, a brownfield can be a serious danger, exposing unsuspecting people to toxic chemicals remaining at the site or to crime.

Brownfields can also pose dangers not associated with entering a property. They can threaten underground sources of drinking water through seepage of chemicals or metals or migration into groundwater. Where there is soil contamination, brownfields can impact vegetables that neighbors may grow in nearby private or community gardens. In some cases, brownfields can even threaten indoor air quality in neighboring buildings. This happens when the chemicals contaminating a brownfield site volatize or, in other words, become part of the air. Volatile organic compounds (VOCs) have been known to emanate from soil or groundwater and seep into basements of nearby homes and buildings. At one particularly thorny site in Massachusetts called Modern Electroplating, this type of off-gassing threatened office workers and a day care center in the building next door before the contamination was discovered.

As America's appetite for growth increases, as we gobble up farmland and other open spaces, brownfields also provide an opportunity to avoid sprawl and to direct growth to areas where infrastructure such as roads and railways already exists.

A company relocating to Woburn would not need to strike a deal with the highway department for a new off-ramp. The company would not need to lay gas or water connections or electrical or telephone lines. Woburn can provide existing rail and highway connections as well as utilities, offsetting some of the advantages of building a new operation on undeveloped land. Because industrial development often occurred on waterways to provide manufacturers with access to shipping ports, cities like Woburn also provide easy access to America's rivers, already channeled and dredged and ready for economic activity.

Brownfields are an opportunity for stakeholders to work together to envision new uses for these old industrial sites that were not so long ago considered ideal for economic activity, leveraging new vitality for neighborhoods, vitality that may include new or refurbished public transportation amenities, new housing or parks, or new stores and other services.

Rural Brownfield Sites

Ironically, a wrinkle for certain brownfield sites continues to be a lack of appropriate incentives to clean them up,

---

6. R. Bullard, "Residential Segregation and Urban Quality of Life," in *Environmental Justice: Issues, Policies, and Solutions,* ed. B. Bryant (Los Angeles: CAAS Publications, 1994), p. 81.

despite legislative incentives discussed below. Inner-city brownfields may easily lend themselves to redevelopment through incentives such as tax credits or other abatement of back taxes on the property. A rural brownfield site, on the other hand, may not be as susceptible to the attraction of conventional economic incentives. Significantly less dense than our inner cities, rural areas may lack the tighter fabric of proponents for brownfields redevelopment. That is, in an inner-city area, a brownfield site may prompt the formation of a coalition of stakeholders rallying for a successful result. The coalition might include city and county officials, community development corporations, a chamber of commerce, neighboring residents, or neighboring businesses that see the potential community-wide benefit of reactivating a brownfield site. By contrast, in a rural area, a site may have no close neighbors. There may be a largely decentralized local governmental body. There may be no closely unified group of stakeholders to raise money or persuade elected officials and prospective developers to take an interest in the site. A rural brownfield site may be surrounded by abundant open space that may seem like the obvious choice for development rather than going through what could be a comparatively cumbersome process of assessment, remediation, and redevelopment.[7] Rural areas may lack transportation for workers at the future use of the site to travel to and from work. This scenario is all too familiar in states like Pennsylvania that, apart from its major cities, has large swaths of open space and populations that are small and diffuse.

A town like Ellwood City, Pennsylvania, for example, may not respond to economic incentives designed to encourage the redevelopment of brownfields. Ellwood City is about 50 miles northwest of Pittsburgh. With a population of around 8,600, it has no form of public transportation, scant if any taxicab service, no appreciable highly skilled or educated labor force, and a few heavy industry operations related mainly to the steel industry. Ellwood City may benefit from the assistance of its borough and county governments as well as its elected officials and chamber of commerce. Nevertheless, a new Wal-Mart may choose to build on the ample open space that rings Ellwood City rather than attempt to use a brownfield site that carries with it uncertain liability

issues. Ellwood City is a classic example of how sprawl happens. Moreover, with Ellwood City's slow but steady decline in population over the past 20 years, it is difficult to imagine much of a demand for new schools, housing, or even office spaces.

Indeed, rural communities face special challenges that should be addressed holistically and regionally. The problem of limited resources, both financial and human, must be addressed in a manner that is tailored to the unique characteristics of rural areas. Communities like Ellwood City can learn from the experiences of similarly situated communities much more easily than they can learn from those of an inner city, even if that city is nearby Pittsburgh.

Environmental Justice and Concomitant Job Growth

"Environmental justice" embraces the notion that no community, regardless or race or income, should bear a disproportionate environmental burden or have more than an equitable share of noxious land uses in the neighborhood. Statistics show that low-income and non-white or "minority" neighborhoods in the United States bear a distinctly disproportionate environmental burden. Moreover, these populations have the highest unemployment rates. Brownfields, located overwhelmingly in the nation's inner cities and other economically depressed areas in close proximity to significant low-income and non-white populations, are an opportunity to promote environmental justice through both reducing the pollution load on overburdened communities and creating new jobs.

Minority Worker Training Programs

In response to environmental justice concerns, to promote equity, and to leverage the promise of brownfields redevelopment, the federal government launched the Minority Worker Training Program in the mid 1990s. This vigorous, career-oriented program funded by EPA and the National Institute of Environmental Health Sciences (NIEHS)[8] is carried out mainly by urban community-based nonprofit organizations offering comprehensive training to young

---

7. See "Reclaiming Rural America's Brownfields: A National Report on Rural Brownfields Redevelopment," National Association of Development Organizations Research Foundation, December 1999.

8. NIEHS is a federal agency under the Department of Health and Human Services.

minority adults. The curriculum provides intensive training in construction trades, lead, asbestos, and hazardous waste handling, health and safety, and life skills, leading program graduates on a direct path to apprenticeships and technical jobs associated with brownfield cleanups. Through the Minority Worker Training Program, in fact, over 2,600 (as of March 2004) minority young adults have been trained in worker health and safety for construction and environmental cleanup. The program boasts a job placement rate of 64 percent overall.[9]

Employing the Local Community

With proper planning, brownfields reclamation also has a keen potential to promote environmental justice by generating permanent "end use" jobs, in addition to construction and remediation jobs, which are usually temporary—to employ people living near brownfield sites and revitalize the local economy through the spending power of the employed.

The unprecedented growth of certain new industries has drawn many planners, developers, and local officials to hope that community revitalization can be piggybacked on continued rapid growth of these businesses The high tech industry, for example, has significant potential for job growth, and is generally perceived as an environmentally sound alternative to the various types of manufacturing that may have contributed to many of today's brownfield sites.[10] Nevertheless, there are important questions to be considered with respect to job growth and any new business reusing a brownfield site. Will the jobs provided by these operations actually benefit those living in the existing community? Or will the new business relocate current employees to the new location rather than hire local residents and perhaps also drive up the cost of living for those who already live in that community? These are critical questions that require communities and developers to give thought to the prevailing skill and education levels of the local community.

In the Roxbury neighborhood of Boston, many planners and developers have held out hopes that the biotechnology industry that has built a boutique enclave in nearby Cambridge will move to Roxbury and bring this long-struggling community, which has an unemployment rate that outpaces that of the City of Boston by orders of magnitude, out of the economic doldrums. Residents, on the other hand, question whether the promised office and high-skilled jobs will be awarded to members of the community.

From an environmental justice perspective, communities and developers alike must assess early in the process whether the jobs created by brownfields reuse match the local workforce. With proper planning and thought, brownfields redevelopment is an outstanding opportunity for economic revitalization through employment of the local community.

Unintended Consequences of Brownfields Redevelopment

Just as sprawl may result when communities fail to embrace brownfields revitalization, gentrification can sometimes result when communities *do* embrace it. Gentrification is "the middle-class resettlement of older inner-city neighborhoods long occupied by working class or underclass communities. Gentrification can happen as revitalization of a community increases property values and creates living conditions (in particular high paying property taxes) that residents and original businesses cannot afford."[11] No scholar or practitioner has yet been able to come up with a surefire formula for avoiding gentrification. Often gentrification will creep into a community simply because of housing shortages, as has happened in recent years in neighborhoods long marked by prevailing society as undesirable, for example, Harlem in New York City or Roxbury in Boston. During the economic growth of the 1990s, families that would never have previously considered living in these neighborhoods suddenly discovered the lovely historic buildings and the beautiful vistas. In Harlem, Starbucks, the Disney Store, and other upscale businesses opened their doors for business. Even former President Bill Clinton decided to place his office in the center of Harlem. Outwardly, Harlem had "arrived." But

9. NIEHS/EPA Brownfields Minority Worker Training Program, September 1, 2000–August 31, 2001, National Institute of Environmental Health Sciences, Division of Extramural Research and Training, Worker Education and Training Program, Research Triangle Park, NC.

10. While the high technology industry may seem cleaner and safer than traditional manufacturing operations, some argue that high technology manufacturers place a toxic burden on neighborhoods and workers. See, e.g., Southwest Organizing Project, http://www.swop.net/intel_info.htm.

11. M. Singer, *Righting the Wrong: A Model Plan for Environmental Justice in Brownfields Redevelopment* (Washington, DC: International City/County Management Association, 2001).

the residents who had called Harlem home for generations were entirely unthrilled by rising housing prices and competition for both housing and jobs, even while they may have been glad for quick access to some of these businesses without having to leave their neighborhood.

Besides being ever-cognizant of whether the jobs being created will benefit the residents of the existing community, communities faced with brownfields redevelopment opportunities must also ask whether the businesses opening their doors will serve existing residents or whether they are intended to serve "outsiders" or new residents. Local governments must work hard to ensure that housing remains affordable for long-term residents. This seems like a tall order. But when all stakeholder groups, including community residents, sit at the table from the very beginning stages of redevelopment, the results can be phenomenal.

Clearwater, Florida, has created a model for public participation in brownfields redevelopment. The City of Clearwater Environmental Justice Action Agenda, signed in September 2000, was the product of visioning, discussions, and meetings that in the end allowed the city to adopt a community-driven approach derived from close partnerships with community development corporations and local government to ensure that brownfield projects address the needs of the existing community first.[12] In pricey cities like New York and Boston, it makes sense that community planning should address critical issues of housing costs at the outset before inviting glamorous new businesses to open their doors for operation.

A developer should never envision his project as one that will make Roxbury, largely a low-income and non-white neighborhood, like Back Bay, a tony, largely white community. An apple can never, ever be an avocado, no matter how much genetic engineering is applied. The same holds true for our neighborhoods. We must remember that every neighborhood in America has its own character, which should reflect the needs and interests of its residents.

New Brownfields on Top of Old: The Success or Failure of Institutional Controls

A healthy skepticism about brownfield reuse can sometimes be rooted in a suspicion that reusing a brownfield site will

12. Ibid.

lead to a brownfield site of the future. This suspicion is understandable considering how the remediation framework operates. One tool for brownfields redevelopment is something called an "institutional control." Massachusetts' framework includes its state version of institutional control, the Activity Use Limitation (AUL). Like other institutional controls, an AUL is a deed restriction that dictates limitations on the use of the property. With the aid of an AUL, a brownfield needs to be cleaned only to the level that will accommodate its intended end use. A parking lot may receive a low level of remediation, leaving the pollution in place and "capping" it so that it does not migrate to other sites or to the surface. An AUL would be attached to the deed on that parking lot, limiting the use of that property to parking. An AUL "runs with the land," meaning that even if the land is sold the AUL still applies to the property. By using an AUL or other institutional control, a developer or landowner may keep the pollution in place or site some other polluting operation at the site that will not violate the AUL. This scenario, of course, supports the skeptic's argument that the brownfields movement promotes the re-creation of new brownfield sites layered on top of the old.

One response to this claim is that many brownfields statutes require very clear community benefits such as jobs, notice to interested parties, and opportunity for public comment before a project becomes eligible for economic incentives. Residents engaging in community efforts to reuse brownfield sites should be sure to take full advantage of every opportunity for public input. A parking lot with pollution in place will not likely generate many jobs. Of course, this does not guarantee that a parking lot will not be built and pollution left in place. We know that parking lots *are* built on brownfield sites.

Another response would be to place sustainable land uses on a brownfield site. So-called sustainable land uses are not without their negative connotations. A tire recycler using the latest technologies that strictly limit and prevent pollution to the local neighborhood is still a tire recycler. A community is naturally going to imagine noxious odors, to name one of many possible objections. Yet, a tire recycler can be a net environmental benefit to a community, lightening the load of illegally disposed-of tires in streams or on empty lots with perceived contamination—brownfields! While calls for maximum cleanup are understandable, there are also cost-benefit concerns. Any reasonable business person is concerned about the cost of removing severe contamination if a removal is not necessary under an AUL, and part of the overall goal is to make the cost of reusing urban land similar to the cost of greenfield development. Addressing this balance requires involvement from the broad community. Residents whose trust of businesses and government may have long ago eroded must be allowed at the table from the outset of a process to develop a clear vision for brownfields revitalization and what sustainability means for their community.

Perhaps the opposite of putting a parking lot on a brownfield site and leaving pollution in place is putting a school or housing on a brownfield site. This type of end use generally requires a very, very high level of cleanup, in order to avoid dangers such as volatizing of chemicals causing indoor air quality concerns, as discussed above with Modern Electroplating. All the same, both Los Angeles and New York have run into serious problems with locating schools on or near former brownfield sites. Planning for brownfield reuses that involve schools or children should be undertaken very carefully. Volatized chemicals from brownfield sites that are not properly remediated can silently produce deleterious health effects in our children. And in the end, the school may have to be closed, creating serious financial losses to the school districts, cities, and towns involved.

In response to similar problems in the Chicago area, Citizens for a Better Environment (CBE), a Milwaukee nonprofit organization, drafted rules intended to strengthen environmental regulations associated with schools and other public areas. CBE posits that regulatory changes are necessary to ensure that proposed schools, parks, and playgrounds undergo complete and careful remediation before becoming available for public use.[13]

The Brownfields Toolbox

Economic Incentives

Legislation provides a number of tools for communities working on brownfields issues. Brownfields statutes in many states offer tax credits and other economic incentives to attract prospective developers to brownfield sites.

Through federal legislation, EPA can now put forward up to $200 million per year for brownfields work. This funding includes cleanup grants of $200,000 that are available to community development corporations and other nonprofit organizations as well as cities and towns, a clear nod acknowledging the important role that community-based organizations play in revitalizing communities. Nonprofit organizations are also eligible through some state funding mechanisms (including EPA's state revolving loan program) to obtain grants and loans for site remediation. Massachusetts' innovative brownfields law provides for grants and loans as well as subsidized environmental liability insurance that can cover cost overruns and other unexpected circumstances.

There are other key federal and state agencies with funding possibilities, such as the Department of Housing and Urban Development (HUD). HUD's Community Development Block Grant program and even its Enterprise Zone designation program have figured prominently in brownfields initiatives. The Army Corps of Engineers, the National Oceanic and Atmospheric Administration (NOAA), and other water-missioned agencies and programs have been instrumental in facilitating brownfields reclamation, particularly where efforts are related to rivers, streams, and harbors. The now defunct Massachusetts Watershed Initiative funded the inventorying of brownfield sites in at least one watershed. The goal of that project was to facilitate community input into reuse decisions and to identify end uses that improve the watershed. The Massachusetts Executive Office of Environmental Affairs has also played a critical role in transforming brownfields to open space through its Self Help and Urban Self Help grant programs. Other states likely offer similar financial assistance tying the reuse of brownfields to the restoration of the environment, its waterways, and its open spaces.

Liability Incentives

We know now that brownfields are not as contaminated as severely as the nation's worst sites, Superfund sites. The challenge now is to relieve brownfields to some extent of the liability reputation associated with Superfund. Institutional controls, such as AULs, for better or worse, have forwarded the liability discourse a great deal. With careful consideration and crafting, an AUL can make moving within the brownfields remediation world much less daunting and

---

13. Citizens for a Better Environment, "Protecting Our Children from Contaminated Schools, Playgrounds and Parks," http://www.cbemw.org/brownfields.html.

much more attractive to developers who would not otherwise consider a project on a brownfield site.

Additionally, through federal and now a growing number of state statutes, so-called innocent parties—banks, purchasers, municipalities that may have exercised a tax foreclosure on a property—can be held harmless from liability so long as they did not cause or contribute to the contamination. These innocent parties generally receive blanket liability protections under the statute itself. Regulators are now even willing to enter covenants-not-to-sue with parties at fault. These covenants are legally binding agreements that responsible parties will be relieved from liability, including liability to third parties, at certain "appropriate" liability endpoints before the remediation is complete in its entirety, and of course once the property is entirely clean.[14] These agreements must meet certain notice and comment requirements, and they may be "re-opened" under special circumstances, such as the discovery of fraud.[15]

The Community Speaks

Among the most important tools captured in brownfields legislation are the requirements of community input and real community benefits. Since its inception, many critics have decried the brownfields movement as another vehicle to rob community residents of power and keep them at bay. During the early years of the brownfields movement, it indeed seemed that the input of residents was at best an afterthought. Developers, chambers of commerce, and government officials have now come to appreciate the power that communities can wield with respect to land-use choices. An unhappy group of residents can sway elected officials and decision-makers away from a project proposal. And now, due to brownfields legislation, there is a legal framework that in many cases requires meaningful community benefits such as jobs or open spaces or affordable housing before a developer can take advantage of economic and liability incentives like the covenant-not-to-sue program.

Some brownfields programs include explicit provisions for public involvement and plans that outline ongoing public outreach and distribution of information relating to a remediation. No longer is public outreach a meeting with a local board of health or a single conversation with a single religious leader. Developers and government officials alike are now required in a growing number of states to address ongoing concerns of communities. The Modern Electroplating example, above, actually involved a community panel that played a prominent role, through processes facilitated by the Boston Redevelopment Authority, in the selection both of a redevelopment proposal and of the developer. This example illustrates that there are opportunities even beyond the strictures of brownfields laws that government officials can exercise to provide additional avenues for meaningful public involvement.

Many states as well as the federal government through the EPA offer technical assistance grants to assist communities in making sense of highly technical brownfields remediation documents. For many communities, the bottom line is that residents most affected by the blighted and unsafe conditions of brownfield sites have most at stake and must be part of the decision-making process.[16]

Any brownfields project that incorporates a fully engaged community of residents will result in an outcome that is responsive to the needs of that community and consistent with the values of that community.

Legislative Pitfalls

Asbestos Remediation

Like any initiative, some brownfields laws and policies have discrete pitfalls. For example, questions linger with respect to how to handle asbestos within a building. Even if a developer does not intend to preserve a building on a brownfield site, if there is asbestos in the building materials—the roof, the vinyl tile floor, the coating, the pipes—brownfields funding may not cover the cost of removing the asbestos. And under the National Emission Standards for Hazardous Air Pollutants (NESHAP),[17] asbestos must be removed before any demolition or renovation can take place. Some very creative projects with strong community backing have run aground as a consequence of costs associated with expensive asbestos removals.

---

14. See, e.g., 940 Code of Massachusetts Regulations (CMR) 23.00: Brownfields Covenant Not to Sue Agreements.

15. See, e.g., 940 CMR 23.09.

16. For recommendations for responsive brownfields revitalization, see *Race, Poverty, and the Environment: A Journal for Social and Environmental Justice* 8, no. 1 (Winter 2001).

17. 40 Code of Federal Regulations (CFR), Part 61.

In older cities where generations of demolitions predate the asbestos handling practices of the NESHAP, there may be residual asbestos in soils. Brownfields money, generally, can be used to remediate asbestos in soils. Nonetheless, states such as Massachusetts should consider legislative fixes to correct the problems presented by asbestos in building materials.

Tax and Cost Recovery Liens

Tax delinquencies on properties can be a problem where municipalities are constitutionally required to recover back taxes. A similar problem has arisen with cost recovery liens. If an agency, such as a state department of environmental protection (DEP), spends any money on cleaning up a property, it often will place a lien on that property. At Modern Electroplating, for example, regulatory officials shut down the facility during ongoing electroplating operations. They then conducted emergency actions so that the facility would not pose an imminent public threat. The Attorney General's Office levied criminal charges on the owners of the operation. With a now insolvent and criminally liable owner, the state DEP had no immediate way of collecting on the lien. Government agencies under the watchful scrutiny of their inspectors general often have no recourse that would allow them to forgive a lien or keep it from encumbering the property. Therefore, the lien can present an obstacle to an otherwise viable brownfields redevelopment deal. Liens can in some cases be negotiated, reduced, or mitigated. In Massachusetts, there is even precedence for the DEP to mitigate the lien and offset some of the back taxes, exclusive of interest and penalties.

Some brownfields legislation has given cities and towns the legal authority to abate back taxes on encumbered properties. Nevertheless, there remains a need to adopt a comprehensive legislative approach that will allow DEPs and other agencies with lien authority clear avenues for releasing liens that will not violate the "public trust" doctrine requiring them to recover public monies expended on brownfield sites.

Measuring Brownfields Success

Scientific Indicators

There are a number of objective indicators a community can use to measure its progress with brownfield cleanups.

An obvious scientific indicator is a comparison of the number of acres of brownfield sites with the number of brownfield acres restored, by neighborhood and by land-use type.[18] This information is likely publicly available through readily accessible computer or paper records or through Geographic Information Systems (GIS).

Similarly, one could measure the improvement of air or water quality in close proximity to these contaminated sites. Public health and public safety figures may also lend insight into brownfields progress. By measuring the indoor air quality of buildings in close proximity to brownfield sites, both before and after the remediation, one could determine whether the incidence of respiratory disease or illness related to brownfields has improved. Even a simple health survey of workers or students near a brownfields site or community health center records might be helpful in measuring progress with brownfields.

One might even measure social capital. Are there new associations formed to promote or engage in the cleanup of brownfield sites? Are there stronger networks between residents and businesses? Any of these indicators might suggest that there is more than an episodic case of community planning around brownfields redevelopment, and instead momentum is actually building for a movement that can lead to a community-wide renaissance. Appendix A further discusses indicators.

It seems, though, that there should be some other long-term measurable goals. The most defensible response to the problem of creating new brownfield sites on old is to plan more sustainable land uses. Rather than planning for a parking lot on a former incinerator site, why not try to attract a manufacturer of housing that is resource-efficient? This would provide good, measurable indicators such as number of decent-paying jobs, new affordable housing units produced and located in the city, energy or water saved by the new housing as opposed to existing housing in the area.

There are various scientific-type indicators of success or measurable progress with brownfield sites because brownfields impact communities in so many ways—health, safety, employment, tax rolls, natural resources.

---

18. The Boston Foundation, "The Wisdom of Our Choices: Boston's Indicators of Progress, Change, and Sustainability" (2000). http://www.tbf.org/indicators/summary.

Simple Indicators

One need not be a scientist to measure the changes in one's community. Hints of change exist all around us. The legal announcements section of the local newspaper may include requests for proposals for brownfield projects. One might also check with the local redevelopment authority for these notices or notices of public hearings. When attending public meetings, notice whether the attendance is getting healthier or more sparse.

The local library is usually a repository for information regarding site brownfields remediations and other environmental regulatory processes. This is simple research anyone can do to measure how much brownfields activity is happening in a particular community.

A thoughtful walk through a neighborhood can offer huge insights into change. Heavy moving equipment, or groundwater monitoring wells protruding from sidewalks near brownfield sites are indicators that some sort of assessment or remediation is going on. These are things that often go unnoticed. But they are subtle (or not-so-subtle) indicators that change is afoot.

Other simple indicators might be more children playing outside, or new or refurbished parks or businesses. Is there less vagrancy in and around abandoned buildings? Or are, simply, some of the neighborhood's abandoned buildings disappearing? There are many, many simple signs of hope in every neighborhood. Sidewalks are widened, trees are planted, a state or local government agency has posted its promotional sign that it is funding a park overhaul.

For those who live in a colder climate, a good time to look for these simple signs is during the spring or summer months when the ground is no longer frozen. This is when much of the change takes place. A walk in the early spring followed by monthly walks throughout the summer and fall is a good way to observe regularly and record ongoing changes and the pace of those changes.

Conclusion

Over the past decade, brownfields redevelopment as a movement has evolved rather dramatically. More and more funding is available for sites. Statutes with economic incentives and clear liability provisions are in place at the federal level and in many states. Properties have been returned to productive uses, relieving blight and public health and safety nuisances in our neighborhoods. But perhaps most important, communities have secured a seat at the bargaining and visioning table. In 1995, the Waste and Facility Siting Committee of EPA's formal federal advisory committee on environmental justice, the National Environmental Justice Advisory Council (NEJAC), held a series of five public dialogues across the nation to gather community input on issues relating to EPA's brownfields initiatives. Those dialogues culminated in a publication, "Environmental Justice, Urban Revitalization, and Brownfields: The Search for Authentic Signs of Hope."[19] Of the many comments taken during those dialogues, perhaps the most resounding one related to community vision and comprehensive community-based planning.

Local communities across the nation have developed vibrant and coherent visions for healthy, sustainable futures that meet local needs and priorities. Brownfields and all community revitalization efforts must be based upon such visions.

The brownfields movement has inched closer to honoring this statement. The Clearwater experience is a stunning example of how government, in this case local government, can respect the input of residents and incorporate their needs into an action agenda; and there are more in the works. Communities need to have access to resource materials and networks of similarly situated communities and residents in order to support themselves and each other in the effort to reinvent themselves as environmentally safe places to live, attend school, and do business in the twenty-first century. The social capital realized from community involvement in brownfields and land-use decision-making is key to successful brownfields redevelopment that will yield long-term positive results.

One other critical component to a positive brownfields result is sustainability. It was unsustainable practices that left America with a legacy of polluted and dangerous brownfield properties. We must now make sustainable choices in order to leave a proud legacy for our children and grandchildren. As citizens of the earth, and now that we know well the negative consequences of toxics in our lifestyle, we should be making consumer choices and business choices that are prudent. The example mentioned above of a manufacturer

---

19. EPA publication number 500R-96-002 (1996).

of sustainable housing that uses fewer natural resources embodies what should be the future of brownfield sites. With cleaner choices for land uses, no longer will policy-makers have to grapple with the notion that environmental burdens are distributed disproportionately based on race and class. There will be no environmental burden.

A vibrant and sustainable brownfields movement is essential to slowing what has increasingly become the unfettered development of our open spaces and farms. Rural spaces are especially threatened because rural brownfield sites may need incentives that are more tailored to rural circumstances. On their face, many brownfields laws and policies seem to cater to inner-city sites without reflection on what incentives might be more appropriate for rural brownfield areas. Legislators and policy-makers must give special attention to the needs of rural communities. They should provide additional funding, education, and personnel to work on rural brownfield sites that are on the front battle lines of sprawl. Often ringed by abundant open spaces, the nation's rural brownfield sites struggle to compete with pristine places or farmland that does not carry the stigma of contamination.

By redeveloping brownfields with a cautious eye toward avoiding gentrification consequences, we can preserve the inherent character and history of our local communities, urban and rural alike.

The Indicators Project, a project of the City of Boston's Sustainable Boston initiative and the Boston Foundation, published a report in 2000 on Boston's indicators of progress, change, and sustainability. Its vision for the environment is a good vision for brownfields redevelopment: "A community that delivers safe water, air and land to residents, provides habitat for a diversity of species, and handles the impact of human activities within ecological limits and offers attractive places for the enjoyment of residents and visitors alike."[20]

This should be a central goal of brownfields revitalization in any community.

Web Resources

Hirschorn, J. "Where Do We Grow From Here? New Mission for Brownfields: Attacking Sprawl by Revitalizing Older Communities." National Governors' Association, 2000. Available at: http://www.nga.org/center/divisions/1,1188,C_ISSUE_BRIEF^D_306,00.html.

International City/County Management Association: http://www.icma.org/. The ICMA represents local governments and has various helpful toolkits and guidebooks.

National Association of Development Organizations: http://www.nado.org/. NADO provides training, information, and representation for regional development organizations in small metropolitan and rural America. The Web site has several helpful publications.

U.S. EPA: http://www.epa.gov/. The EPA has undertaken significant study of how to deal with brownfields, and provides funding for various local actions.

Web searches on brownfields with the name of your state will yield the names of state government agencies relevant to your location that may be able to provide funding and guidance for your local initiative.

---

20. Boston Foundation, "The Wisdom of Our Choices."

Photo: Samalid Hogan

15

Adaptive Reuse of Buildings
If It Is Already Built, Will They Come?

Robert Forrant

The Empire Grill was long and low-slung, with windows that ran its entire length, and since the building next door, a Rexall drugstore, had been condemned and razed, it was now possible to sit at the lunch counter and see straight down Empire Avenue all the way to the old textile mill and its adjacent shirt factory. Both had been abandoned now for the better part of two decades, though their dark, looming shapes at the foot of the avenue's gentle incline continued to draw the eye. Of course, nothing prevented a person from looking up Empire Avenue in the other direction, but Miles Roby, the proprietor of the restaurant—and its eventual owner, he hoped—had long noted that his customers rarely did.

No, their natural preference was to gaze down to where the street both literally and figuratively dead-ended at the mill and factory, the undeniable physical embodiment of the town's past. . . .

—RICHARD RUSSO, *Empire Falls*, 2001

NEW ENGLAND can lay claim to being the birthplace of American industry, as the many mill buildings that dot the landscape can attest. This industrial legacy is apparent whenever an industrial smokestack or a prominent mill clock comes into view. Most New England mill complexes were extremely sturdy four- and five-story brick structures with high ceilings, enormous windows to let in natural light, and few partitions so that large looms and other machinery could easily be moved. Many had considerable parking in their interior courtyards. Yet in an economy no longer dependent on large-scale manufacturing, numerous abandoned mills, just like novelist Richard Russo's mill in fictional Empire Falls, have become run-down eyesores and targets for vandalism and arson. And, like the characters in Russo's account of life in Empire Falls, thousands of New Englanders have been forced to come to grips with their own "mill histories"; in the decades immediately following World War II, textile mills, apparel factories, paper mills, and other large industrial structures emptied out.

These buildings often occupy prime real estate, usually a large "physical footprint" in or near the center of town. Such structures dominate the urban landscapes and present a tremendous challenge to development officers intent on recharging their community's economic base. Today's mill reuse efforts—the environmental cleanup and interior redesign of large structures built primarily for nineteenth- and early twentieth-century industry—prominently feature in urban social and economic development. This approach has also become an essential part of efforts directed at preserving and enhancing the ever-shrinking green spaces in our cities and suburbs. This chapter will provide examples of these mill redevelopment efforts and make suggestions for how communities can undertake this process. We begin with a bit of history.

The Rise and Decline of the Mill Town

When Samuel Slater built his first mill in Pawtucket, Rhode Island, on the banks of the Blackstone River he could not have imagined that such buildings would be part of development discussions over one hundred and fifty years later. The Blackstone River provided energy for numerous mills stretching from the Massachusetts border down to Providence. In Lowell, the Boston Associates built a canal and water-power infrastructure for the country's first textile district. Factories along the Merrimack River in Lawrence and Lowell and along the Connecticut River in Holyoke, Springfield, and Chicopee fueled the nation's nineteenth-century industrial revolution and provided work for thousands of immigrants.

Between 1920 and 1980, however, things changed: Holyoke, Lawrence, and other mill cities in the state and around New England suffered through loss of jobs and then population. Abandoned factory complexes became a familiar sight. Today even the most casual visitor to Lawrence's Essex Street or Holyoke's Main Street will encounter closed storefronts, decayed mills, and apartment blocks that in their glory days once provided work for and housed thousands of first- and second-generation immigrant workers. Compare this abandonment to the new development and vibrancy one sees in a drive along Interstate 495, one of Massachusetts's high tech corridors. What was once open space is now taken up by high tech manufacturing buildings and software office parks. What were once apple orchards, dairy farms, natural ponds, and woodlands have become the locations where today's leading-edge production takes place. In the new, so-called knowledge-based economy, the

cities that dominated the state's late nineteenth- and early twentieth-century economy did not share in the Commonwealth's high tech renaissance.

A cursory review of wage and employment growth in the 1990s in five of the region's cities confirms the unevenness of the development that is now taking place. An expanded base of computer hardware, semiconductor, and engineering companies in Beverly along and just off Route 128 boosted the town's average wages 69 percent. In 1990 Beverly and Lawrence had similar average wages, yet by 2000 a 31 percent gap existed. Lynn started the period with wages 17 percent higher than in Beverly; it finished with wages 3 percent lower. "Median household income fell during the longest economic expansion in U.S. history," the *Boston Globe* reported, "in most of the state's major cities, including New Bedford, Pittsfield, Springfield, and Worcester" (Flint and Dedman 2002; Rodriguez and Dedman 2002; Kirchoff and Dedman 2002, 1). These communities have a conspicuous feature in common, unfilled mill space.

This relocation of good work away from older cities and the "malling" of green space are by no means limited to New England; throughout the country such trends have contributed to what HUD has called the "doubly burdened cities," that is, communities that face a combination of high unemployment and significant population loss or high poverty rates (HUD 2000; HUD 1999). Despite the remarkable economic expansion of the 1990s and over twenty years of targeted public funding aimed at improving life in once-thriving older industrial cities, the gap between rich and poor in the United States grew over the 1990s. The bottom one-fifth—many residing in the nation's former steel mill cities, tire and rubber cities, and one-industry textile and apparel mill towns—saw their after-tax income slip 12 percent from 1977 to 1999, while the after-tax income of the wealthiest one percent grew an astonishing 120 percent during the same period.

Far too many smaller metropolitan areas (less than 100,000 people), cities like Holyoke and Lawrence, Massachusetts, face the "double trouble" of relatively high unemployment coupled with either high poverty rates, population loss, or both. HUD concluded that: (1) unacceptably high unemployment persists in one in six central cities; (2) there is steady population loss in one in five central cities; (3) there are persistently high poverty rates in one in three central cities; and (4) there has been a serious decline in the downtown retail and service sector in these cities (Siegel, Baran, and Teegarden 2001). The resource that these older urban cores *do* have, however, is underutilized mill buildings. Thus, mill reuse in older industrial cities is increasingly recognized as one way to resolve the issues associated with growth and social equity documented by HUD.

How then can abandoned mills become a part of a comprehensive approach to community development? Businesses can often be attracted to their cheaper-than-prevailing market-rate space; neighborhoods can be reinvigorated in the spaces surrounding these once-abandoned complexes; neighborhoods can become involved in reuse planning; and the ongoing dispersal of employment to green spaces can be avoided (Halpern 1995; Wiewel, Teitz, and Giloth 1993). Indeed, the mill reuse movement to be described below integrates the goals of four crucial development activities—urban planning, brownfields cleanup, historic preservation, and land protection—and as such can pack a powerful punch if done right. Many states, including Massachusetts, have gotten this message.

Understanding the Benefits of Reuse

How then can communities marshal arguments for reuse? How can reuse be linked to community preservation? Reuse is increasingly seen as recycling writ large; it is the reuse of urban spaces in old industrial communities for housing, office space, light industry, and high tech start-up companies, as well as for cultural activities. Economic development officers are increasingly pointing out the potential benefits of adaptive reuse of abandoned mill space. As just one example, in its 2001 *Economic Development Strategy for the Merrimack Valley,* the Merrimack Valley Planning Commission pointed out that tenants of refurbished mills are very often "young companies in fast-growth sectors." Renovated mill buildings provide "fashionable working environments," they argue, and they add, "Keeping a good supply of competitively priced mill space available gives the region a distinct competitive advantage in attracting new investment and retaining expanding industries with a unique product that draws attention to the region's industrial heritage" (2001, 11).

Throughout the country, a variety of additional arguments have been offered for reuse. The *Journal of Property Management,* for example, has argued: "Developers can save up to 40 percent on construction costs, preservationists want to see historic buildings skirt demolitions, and commercial tenants looking for large spaces in tight downtown markets have more options through reuse" (Wadsworth 1997, p. 26). For Thomas Wright, director of the New Jersey office of the Regional Plan Association, "Adaptive reuse brings back a tax base to downtowns that need it. It is one large, important piece of the puzzle" (Wadsworth 1997, 27). Ken Schroeder, a principal architect in a large Chicago design firm believes that abandoned factories and mills "work very well for open space office concepts" (Wadsworth 1997, 27). Many neighborhoods in the cities HUD described as "left out" of the 1990s economic boom are being physically transformed through mill reuse plans. According to Jerry Mitchell, a professor in the School of Public Affairs at Baruch College, the City University of New York: "The urban renewal projects of the 1960s and 1970s were largely financed by federal grants, led by city planning departments, and characterized by a broad-based development strategy involving the widespread removal of old buildings." Although Mitchell notes that large-scale development projects occasionally still occur, the "new downtown revitalization process is often self-financed by local businesses, initiated by innovative public-private partnerships, and typified by an attention to historic preservation, consumer marketing, small-business development, pedestrian access" (2001, 115–16). This approach to development has been referred to as "urban husbandry": public-private partnerships work in small-scale organizations to "reinvigorate and build on existing community assets in order to stimulate a place-based rejuvenation" (Gratz and Mintz, 1998, 61). By extension, it is hoped that the bulldozer will appear less and less in remaining environmentally pristine countrysides.

Revitalization and Reuse of Old Mills: Some Examples

The examples of reuse efforts below illustrate the wide variety of uses now being made of mill spaces; reuses include museums, restaurants, businesses, and condominium, rental, and subsidized housing. These examples also suggest the variety of partnerships that have been created to further these reuse efforts. The partnerships include local, state, and sometimes federal government, private developers, and universities and other major anchor organizations.

- The arts have become an important focus in adaptive reuse. Consider *Poughkeepsie, New York*. There the population dropped 33 percent since 1950 as mills and then downtown department stores and grocery stores closed. The city government and several private developers are breathing new life into a 13-acre abandoned industrial site hard along the Hudson River, and the Mid-Hudson Children's Museum opened in an empty building on the river front. Artist Peter Max purchased the empty Luckey Platt department store from the city for $1 and plans to turn it into a small museum and cultural center to showcase his work and that of other modern artists and also to serve as a space for art courses and public forums on topics like the creative process and the environment (Foderaro 2002).
- In *North Adams, Massachusetts,* the Sprague Electric mill complex became the Massachusetts Museum of Contemporary Art (Manning 2001); in *Salem* an aggressive effort by private developers is well under way to develop condominiums, a visitors' center, and mixed-use office space in several downtown commercial buildings that were unused or underused since the Burlington Mall and Liberty Tree Mall were built within a 30-minute car ride from the city (Borseti 2002).
- Many redevelopments have been multipurpose. In *Lowell, Massachusetts*, the renovation of a historical mill into 257 elderly apartments, at a cost of approximately $10.5 million, helped to revive the sagging fortunes of the downtown. The imposing mill building situated close to the Merrimack River is a designated national landmark. In the same city, the Boott Cotton Mills, the most intact surviving example of the earliest stages of Lowell's mill construction, was rebuilt starting in 1989, with generous state and federal assistance. Today it is home to a working textile history museum and an education center visited every year by a steady stream of tourists interested in the nation's history and by thousands of school children studying the U.S. industrial revolution. The Wannalancit Building, a third reclaimed mill building in Lowell, utilized a unique university–private sector partnership, and is now home to over twenty high tech start-up companies, regional offices of several state and federal economic development agencies, and several University of Massachusetts–Lowell research centers (www.doorsopenlowell.org/boott_mills.htm). In addition, city planners established an incentive program that helps with down payments on building purchases, provides grants for renovations, and offers assistance to artists looking for appropriate space. The city hopes to integrate artists into downtown life and believes the activity that artists produce will draw other people back to the city (McQuaid 2002).
- These mill redevelopments are by no means limited to the Northeast. Across the South, textile mills that were built when industrialists abandoned New England are also being reused. The Atherton Cotton Mill in *Charlotte, North Carolina*, part of a textile complex built in the 1890s, was transformed into mixed-use space that includes a brewery, three eateries, retail and office space, and live/work condominiums. In *Atlanta, Georgia*, the Fulton Bag and Cotton Mill, constructed in 1881, closed in 1977 and stood empty until a reuse plan commenced in the mid-1990s. Three buildings containing 237,000 square feet were renovated, creating 206 loft-style apartments, helping to solve the city's acute housing shortage (Groves 1999). In *Durham, North Carolina*, efforts have been made to reuse many of the cigarette industry's old mills and office buildings. There "imaginative developers, tax credits for historic preservation and the increased demand for interesting spaces within the city core" have preserved the city's industrial architecture as a vital part of downtown life. Apartments, retail space, and start-up software businesses will inhabit the space (Ariail 2000).
- Some redevelopment has focused specifically on business development. The *Merrimack Valley* Economic Development Council describes three successful projects, one in a former flax mill in *Andover*, in the Kunhardt Mill in *Lawrence*, and in a contaminated factory site in *North Andover*. The Kunhardt Mill is today home to a successful women's clothing manufacturer, and office space is used by the economic development council. At the North Andover site, a partnership between the City of Lawrence and site developers extended the city's Economic Target Area designation to the mill so that the Sweetheart Cup Company could receive needed investment tax credits to clean up the mill. Lawrence received a commitment that 35 percent of new jobs will be filled by Lawrence residents in a long-term plan that envisions the company employing 500 people. If not for the innovative partnership, Sweetheart would most likely have ceased operations in Massachusetts. The Merrimack Valley Planning Commission

What in the World Is a Wannalancit?

The following is a partial list of the companies, state and federal offices, and University of Massachusetts–Lowell research centers that occupy space in the Wannalancit Building: Alpha Imaging Technology, IBEX Processing Technology, Q-mation, Versient, Inc., Spry Technology, Triquent Semiconductor, Vascular Technology, Datawatch Technology, Lockheed Martin Environmental Services, the Small Business Administration's regional office, the Massachusetts Office of Business Development, the New England Trade Adjustment Assistance Center, and the university's Center for Family, Work, and Community, Center for Industrial Competitiveness, Center for Atmospheric Research, and Research Foundation. On land adjacent to the nearly full building the city, state, and university in a series of jointly funded efforts built a new hockey arena and entertainment complex, a minor league baseball stadium, and a new university recreation and fitness center.

notes that in the upper end of the river valley there is a concentration of mill buildings in Lawrence, Haverhill, Amesbury, and Methuen, many of which are beginning to fill back up. They add that renting in the Merrimack Valley in converted mill spaces is "significantly less expensive" than suburban options (MVPC 2001, 13). In several instances the mill spaces are part of cyber districts, with occupants able to quickly and reliably access the Internet.

- Many projects for adaptive reuse have emphasized the reclamation of contaminated property. In *Beverly, Massachusetts,* the mid-1990s renovation of the cavernous industrial building known to long-time residents as "The Shoe" is indicative of how reuse can help revitalize a local and regional economy. Built in the early years of the twentieth century, "The Shoe" was home to the United Shoe Machinery Corporation that, until it closed in the early 1970s, produced shoe-making equipment for global export. Before Woburn-based Cummings properties management began the reuse effort in 1996, less than 10 percent of the site's 34 acres of floor space was occupied. The building was also on the Massachusetts Department of Environmental Protection's list of contaminated sites. To make the project viable, the state and the city worked out tax and environmental cleanup agreements with Cummings. Soon after the renovations began, space started to be leased and the building quickly filled up (Mira 1997).

These examples indicate some of the processes by which the adaptive reuse of small or single complexes has taken place. Cities are increasingly investigating broader, large-scale strategies by which adaptive reuse is a cornerstone to redevelopment of entire communities. Providence, Rhode Island, Clinton, Massachusetts, and Holyoke, Massachusetts, represent three cities at different points in this broader, deeper approach to adaptive reuse. By considering these examples, we can begin to see in more depth the promise as well as the obstacles to adaptive reuse as a transformative economic development process that is consistent with community preservation.

The Providence, Rhode Island, Renaissance

In the early 1990s Providence made what was seen as an unlikely transition from a typical old New England manufacturing center—dominated by antiquated and environmentally contaminated textile mills—to become the leader in a new regional economy dominated by knowledge-based businesses and cultural activities. Providence, a city of 151,000, is located approximately 45 miles south of Boston. Providence experienced a period of sharp contraction after the Second World War as core industries fled to the non-union and lower wage southern United States and overseas. Providence faced a difficult renewal task as it wrestled with the panoply of problems associated with older industrial cities —abandoned, empty, and environmentally contaminated factory buildings, rapid employment loss, and population loss. According to one account: "By 1990, suburbanization and economic decline had closed all of the downtown's major retail stores; downtown had become a 9–5 workplace. Traditional revitalization strategies were no longer feasible in the new economic reality." Four years after this story appeared, the United States Conference of Mayors honored Providence with a City Livability Award. Today, Providence is an example of how flexible public and private investment in existing buildings can invigorate a community. Contemporary Providence is in the midst of a renaissance as it draws on its industrial heritage and historic mill space to boost high technology industry and simultaneously utilizes once-abandoned mill space to nurture a strong services-based and arts and entertainment-based economy.

In 1900, Providence's 2,000 manufacturing plants represented almost 50 percent of the state industrial sites (Kirk 1909; Gilkeson 1986). According to one contemporary account, "Providence manufactures everything from a carpet-tack to a locomotive" (Woodward and Sanderson 1986, 56). Forty textile mills employed the majority of Providence residents well into the twentieth century; as late as 1940, of the city's 34,000 manufacturing, 5,000 were in cotton mills, 1,400 in rayon mills, 6,500 in woolen mills, and 5,700 in related textile firms (Gilkeson 1986). However, from 1948 to 1987 Providence lost more than 36,000 manufacturing jobs—a staggering 60 percent of the manufacturing job base. Starting in the late 1960s the city took advantage of federal legislation and began to preserve much of its early architecture as part of an overall development strategy.

The 1968 passage of the National Historic Preservation Act led to the establishment of the Rhode Island Historical Preservation Commission. The commission prepared a blueprint for the restoration of several properties in Providence, and between 1976 and 1986 it administered federal tax

Real Estate Market Implications

"According to the base forecast, 21,200 new jobs will be created in the Merrimack Valley by 2010. At an average density of 330 to 500 square feet per worker, the employment forecasts for the Merrimack Valley indicate a potential demand for seven to ten million square feet of office and industrial space over the next ten years. If this were to be accommodated on green field sites, it would absorb 500 to 800 acres of industrial land. There is an amply supply of older buildings to be renovated that could accommodate much of this demand."

Merrimack Valley Planning Commission's *Economic Development Strategy for the Merrimack Valley*, 2001, 25.

benefits for the rehabilitation of historic, income-producing buildings to 144 projects valued at $108 million in the city (Woodward and Sanderson 1986). After a second wave of renovation and preservation in the early 1990s Providence began to market itself as the "Renaissance City." Accompanying the restorations, office buildings, apartments, hotels, the Rhode Island Convention Center, a shopping center, and a 16-screen movie theater were constructed in a designated Downcity District. A brisk walk around downtown Providence provides substantial evidence—to the eye, ear, and palate—that much of its growth was fueled by the arts, theater, cultural, restaurant, and entertainment industries. From the city's Empowerment Zone application: "The arts is about energy, passion, communication and making connections. We have embraced arts, culture, and design as an economic engine, but also as a reminder of the important role that beauty plays in all our lives and in the health of our neighborhoods."

The Downcity Arts Project took advantage of 1996 state legislation that authorized Providence to turn one square mile of its downtown into an Arts and Entertainment District. Artists and performers living in the district pay no state income tax on what they sell, and their customers pay no sales tax on artist-made products they purchase in the neighborhood. Thus, artists are encouraged to combine their homes, studios, and galleries in restored downtown buildings. To create living and work space, property owners in the district get additional tax breaks for converting vacant buildings into rental units. One project typifies this development strategy. The Smith Building, long-empty and located near City Hall, was renovated in 1998 into 36 loft apartments and studios with a community room and gallery at street level. Developers soon began work on three additional buildings on the same block.

Artists from Boston and New York relocated to the district to escape high rents. For example, Boston painter David Lowenstein opened a gallery in Providence in 1999, paying $1,500 a month for the space. He noted, "If you can even find the space, you won't get it for less that $5,000 a month in Boston." Artists have moved to the city from such places as Washington, DC, Santa Fe, and Baltimore (Malone 1999). Located within the Arts District are several renovated buildings from earlier periods of the city's architectural history; the restorations are part of a development strategy to integrate the city's history into its future growth.

The city's riverways, topography, and natural beauty were admired in the nineteenth- and early twentieth centuries; however, industrial misuse, neglect, and misguided development turned them into a late twentieth-century blight. The three rivers that curved through Providence were polluted because industrial waste was dumped into them unchecked for over fifty years. In some parts of the city the rivers were even paved over, while the downtown was cut off from direct access to Narragansett Bay on the Atlantic Ocean by a federal highway. Miles of downtown river walkways were built and the rivers cleaned up. Now river and canal tours on Italian-style gondolas are a tourist attraction, and in the spring, summer, and fall restaurants offer outdoor dining along the rivers. The Coalition for Community Development—a consortium of corporations and institutions with offices or interests downtown, including several banks and colleges—was active in securing private sector funds for the environmental cleanup, and several million public and private dollars were invested in the restoration of abandoned industrial sites. The "brownfield sites" had been stumbling blocks to neighborhood revitalization in certain areas of the city. The cost of the cleanup of the industrial pollutants left behind when heavy industry exited Providence easily exceeded the market value of the property. Thus, there is an important public sector role here because very often once the land and buildings have been cleaned up, private sector investment follows.

In 1998 the federal government designated Providence as one of fourteen national "Brownfield Showcase Communities." The designation makes the city eligible for federal grants and low-cost loans, state loans, and state tax incentive programs to stimulate cleanups. For example, in late 1999 the state legislature awarded the city $450,000 for the cleanup of an abandoned river-front mill property as part of a larger project to complete a river walkway and bikeway through the entire city. The same year Providence announced a plan to redevelop 355 acres of property along the waterfront, another abandoned industrial area of the city. To finance the project the city has secured state and federal funds to clean up the sites. It has also established a consortium among the city's hospitals and universities to contribute a portion of the needed capital and locate new buildings on the cleaned-up sites.

What can we conclude from the Providence example? First, the city's development leaders, realizing that traditional strategies were not going to stop the decline of the downtown, concluded that innovative plans were needed to attract "non-traditional" development targets. Second, because the task of revitalizing the downtown was such a large enterprise, a significant public-private partnership was needed. Here, the public sector proved vitally important in obtaining federal and state dollars to clean up older industrial sites that the private sector then agreed to help fill up. Third, residents recognized the value of historic buildings and convinced public officials that it would be far better to try to preserve many structures rather than subject them to the wrecking ball, and the ensuing renovations and restorations helped Providence market itself as the "Renaissance City." With restorations under way, the city could begin to link the arts, architecture, and entertainment into an attractive and forward-looking rebuilding approach.

Clinton, Massachusetts: Success on a More Limited Scale

Now let's look at a very different setting that will show us how a small mill city can creatively combine reuse with an overall redevelopment effort linked to the creation of jobs and elderly housing. Located in central Massachusetts, Clinton has two mills listed in the National Historic Register: the Bigelow Carpet Mill and the Bigelow Carpet Company Woolen Mills. The Bigelow Carpet Mill was designated a historical landmark in 1978 and soon thereafter became the home of the global plastics company, Nypro Plastics. In a recent effort to keep Nypro jobs in Clinton, the town, state, and company negotiated a deal to build a new research and development facility there. The town provided a fifteen-year graduated tax abatement for the building, and the state provided an additional 2 percent discount on taxes for the purchase of capital investment. The new R&D facility should add 100 workers and increase the probability of retaining the existing 900 manufacturing jobs. This is a good example of mill reuse that generates revenue for the town through real estate taxes and employment along with the multiplier effect for local restaurants, banks, and other services used by employees.

The Lancaster Mills, yet another old mill building in Clinton, closed in the 1930s. A group of local citizens bought the land and building and transferred ownership to Little-Ives Publishing of Boston, the parent company of Colonial Press, Inc. During the 1950s and 1960s Colonial Press, then the largest book printer on the eastern seaboard, employed almost 2,000 people in Clinton. After several consolidations and mergers, Colonial Press fell on hard times, finally going out of business in 1977. Thereafter several firms, including Ray-O-Vac, Weetabix, Eagle Traffic Company, Dunn and Company, and Legacy Publishing were tenants in the building. For sale in 2002, the building had no tenants in April 2006. A third complex of mill buildings, the Prescott Mills, was acquired by local businessmen and renovated in the 1980s for elderly housing. The complex is a for-profit business and provides tax revenue to the town of Clinton. Because the complex is for elderly housing the tax assessment has been negotiated at a lower rate.

Clinton has several vacant mills and hopes to work on some zoning changes that will protect the community and attract new businesses. These new businesses are expected to be offshoots—referred to as "biotech sprawl"—of the biotechnology investments taking place in nearby Worcester. Clinton developers anticipate anything from R&D facilities to office services required by the industry to settle in Clinton's available mill space. For a small city like Clinton, geographically tucked out of the way and unable to generate the kinds of visits and outside investment that Providence's high-profile renovation and reuse efforts generated, a strategy tied to resolving specific community problems, in this case housing and job creation, appears to be working. And once again we see the value of public-private partnerships to make the adaptive reuse approach work.

Holyoke, Massachusetts

Finally, let's look at another city posing yet different problems. Between 1920 and 1980 Holyoke lost one-third of its population and thousands of jobs as the owners of textile and paper mills made serial moves to the U.S. South and eventually overseas. Who lives in Holyoke these days? Among the city's roughly 44,000 residents, 60 percent are Latinos. Labor market, housing, and educational problems have slowly developed over decades. More than 59 percent of the Hispanic community now live below the poverty line—compared to about 14 percent of non-Hispanic whites—and close to 80 percent of Hispanic children live in poverty. Working people and the unemployed in Holyoke suffer during economic downturns and never catch back up

New Life in Old Mills

Holyoke and its neighbor East Hampton are making a concerted effort to revive old mill space in several mixed-use complexes. With spectacular views of the Connecticut River Valley through oversize windows, hundreds of thousands of square feet of space are slowly being opened in both cities for artists, law offices, start-up software firms, furniture makers, coffee shops and restaurants, and loft-style apartments. Paradise One, a gay and lesbian retirement community, is being planned for mill space in East Hampton. Eighty condominium units will be built. In Holyoke, in 2005 the poorest city in Massachusetts, a 700,000-square-foot building is undergoing renovations. It now houses "45 business, from an educational theatre company to a Hispanic-owned bilingual newspaper, a marketing firm, a children's furniture designer and several technology-related businesses" (Chamberlain 2006, 16). Nearby a smaller mill building is being turned into residential units. Developed Eric Shuher notes: "Holyoke is ready to transform itself. There is a natural progression underway, and getting market-rate housing downtown is critical" (quoted in Chamberlain 2006, 16).

during periods of prosperity. In 1970, almost 40 percent of residents worked in manufacturing; by 1990, 24 percent did so. In 2000, the figure was roughly 15 percent.

The large paper and textile mills that served as magnets for immigrant labor in the nineteenth and early twentieth centuries still dominate the built landscape and pose a tremendous challenge to the city's long-term development efforts. The city's master plan notes that Holyoke "was founded as an industrial community, and the large brick mill complexes downtown continue to define its identity—both visually and culturally" (Holyoke 1999, 3). These buildings contain approximately 60 percent of the available open industrial space in the city and thus represent a critical component of any development effort, particularly when the city is already largely "built out."

As far back as the early 1970s mayors and economic development officials believed Holyoke's future was linked to the use of affordable, subdivided space in mill buildings. Today portions of buildings house small woodworking, printing and publishing, and graphics arts businesses, and one fairly large building is home to the regional offices of several Massachusetts social services agencies. One 220,000-square-foot space now houses several start-up companies, a community meeting and performance space, and a restaurant. Plans are far along to turn one wing of the complex into a charter school for grades K-8, and overtures have been made to nearby University of Massachusetts–Amherst to locate some programs there. The complex is part of a larger vision for downtown revitalization that calls for the formation of a Canal Arts and Industry District. Already in the area are a state-funded Heritage Industrial Park, a Children's Museum, a restored carousel, and the Volleyball Hall of Fame. These efforts are linked to the city's ongoing efforts at historic preservation contained in a plan prepared in 1991.

WHAT ARE the lessons from these brief case studies? First, in Providence, Clinton, and Holyoke development officials launched a determined effort to rebuild their communities with the adaptive reuse of old industrial buildings as an integral part of their overall plan. By so doing, these quite different cities attracted state and federal funds to abate environmental contamination and turn architecturally attractive and centrally located spaces into private sector investment opportunities. Second, historic preservation, rather than blocking progress, helped attract public and private investment dollars, and particularly in Providence's case, led to creative marketing opportunities for its downtown arts district. Third, while all three communities were interested in generating employment opportunities for residents, it appears that while the cleanup and renovation of sites is never easy, it is a lot easier than growing employment opportunities.

Environmental Issues

In this section we take a closer look at the environmental concerns raised by adaptive reuse. As the many examples in this chapter show, adaptive reuse not only often raises a host of environmental issues; it can also offer opportunities to address lingering environmental problems standing in the way of economic development in old, industrial communities. Too often, though, traditional measures of economic development fail to take into account the ways adaptive reuse can add benefits that are tied to environmental cleanups.

Traditional evaluations of economic development programs are generally based on quantitative program goals. These evaluations typically focus on questions such as: *How many jobs were created? How much new investment entered the target area? How many start-up firms took advantage of an available tax credit program? How many residents attended a training program?* Such traditional measures often fail to take into account the adverse environmental consequences that can result from some economic development programs or that can be avoided in cleanup and reuse of abandoned mills. The historian Adam Rome cites a 1971 essay by the president of the Council of State Planning Agencies on land-use regulation that is useful here. "In the city fringe areas," the president wrote, "vegetation is stripped, topsoil is buried, steams are channeled into culverts, hills are leveled, valley and marshes are filled and whole new communities occupy areas which were formerly forested or farmed. The adverse impact of these phenomena on human and natural life and resources is what we call the environmental crisis" (Rome 2001, 226). The reuse of mill spaces at the very least can slow this encroachment down, and it is something that can be measured quantitatively.

By the late nineteenth century mill owners and their financial backers had created an environment described by the historian John Cumbler, "in which rivers and streams were polluted by wastes dumped from mills and tenements, fish were excluded from spawning grounds, and mill towns filled with smoke and foul odors" (Cumbler 2001, 5). At the time there emerged a confrontation over the environmental consequences of unchecked industrial growth. "Industry that brought wealth and prosperity, at least for many of the region's inhabitants," Cumbler concludes, "brought real costs in terms of added industrial wastes and pollution and reduced fish in the rivers." Then a debate emerged that sought to resolve whether the environment ought to be used as a sink—a waste dump—or as a resource for everyone to enjoy on into the future. Industrialists fought off challenges to their rights to utilize the environment as they saw fit, and at times they were "joined by industrial communities that like the manufacturers enjoyed the privilege of dumping their waste sewage into the nearest running water and were concerned to maintain industrial employment." New Englanders examined whether the state had any authority and power to "ameliorate and control the byproducts of urbanization and industrialization" (Cumbler, 6).

There is an emerging consensus that one legacy of our industrial history, mill buildings, ought to become part of the solution to a litany of development problems. The state and federal governments are partners in these undertakings with the Clean Water Act, the Clean Air Act, the Environmental Protection Agency, toxics use reduction regulations in Massachusetts, and support for community land preservation. Quality of life, social and economic development, and regard for the environment are indeed joined, and refurbished and vibrant mill buildings are a testament to this. Harking back to their early roles as symbols of progress, adaptively reused industrial buildings can still signify progress.

Integrating Mill Redevelopment into the Social Fabric of a City

Other challenges lay ahead for communities that chose to pursue adaptive reuse. A central challenge is that if mill redevelopment is to be successful, it must be integrated into the social fabric of the city. We need to be very clear that simple and cynical attraction strategies premised on low wages and cheap rental space cannot invigorate the economy for any sustained period of time. Instead, we must think creatively about which kinds of enterprises and community initiatives will provide for long-term economic and environmental sustainability if we are to avoid reproducing the "roller coaster economy" our mill cities have experienced in the last half of the twentieth century. To avoid this roller coaster phenomenon, important questions about any reuse project should be asked, including:

- What role can the mill space play in neighborhood revitalization?
- Can the new uses for the space provide for youth employment?
- How can the entire reuse project contribute to the stabilization of neighborhoods? For instance, are there going to be jobs in the space that people in the adjacent neighborhoods can fill?
- What of immigrant and ethnic-owned businesses? Can these firms be helped into the revitalized space to promote their businesses, strengthen civic pride, and translate into greater civic participation?

On a practical level, the urban planning and research organization Industrial Economics Incorporated recently joined with the U.S. Environmental Protection Agency to review eleven local government efforts across the country that explicitly linked economic development with brownfields cleanup and reuse efforts. Many of these projects involved reuse of mill buildings. The cities reported several benefits from their efforts, including the following:

- Individual economic benefits of job creation, wealth creation, and home ownership.
- Economic multiplier effects including growth in local retail businesses, growth in commercial real estate development, and growth in services such as daycare.
- A better business environment from upgrades of the communication and transportation infrastructure around reused brownfield areas.
- Growth in mixed-use development and a reduction in greenfield development.
- Accrual of benefits to existing residents, the elderly, children, and low-income and minority populations adjacent to the cleaned-up and reused sites.

To summarize, the renovation and conversion of old industrial and commercial space for use as housing, art studios and museum space, and new industries and research centers is an important tool when communities confront their "mill history." Public-private partnerships are often formed during the process, and in many cases neighborhood residents become engaged in defining what the project will look like. Just the environmental cleanup of structures that are often located next to residential neighborhoods represents an important public good. Once cleaned up, these sites offer a welcome alternative to the far too prevalent greenfields approach to regional development. The "suddenly new spaces" offer investment opportunities for public-private partnerships, as the Wannalancit complex demonstrates. In addition, because these spaces are usually in the downtown area of cities, their repopulation generates new foot traffic that almost instantly stimulates a host of service-related businesses including restaurants, cleaners, hair dressers, nail salons, coffeehouses, book stores, and bakeries. New job and business possibilities are also going to be in walking distance for a lot of residents, easing traffic congestion and making upward economic upward mobility more accessible than greenfields growth does. There is no question that creative and adaptive building reuse can breathe new life into urban spaces once given up for dead.

References and Short Reading List

Ariail, Kate D. 2000. "Old Buildings, New Uses.," *Independent Weekly Online*. www.indyweek.com/durham/2000-05-03/ae4.html.

Barnett, J. 1995. *The Fractured Metropolis: Improving the New City, Restoring the Old City, Reshaping the Region*. Boulder, CO: Westview.

Birch, Eugenie, and Douglass Roby. 1984. "The Planner and the Preservationist." *Journal of the American Planning Association*, 50 (2), 194–208.

Borseti, Teri. 2002. "Salem's Road to Renewal." *Boston Globe*, Sept. 21, F11.

Browne, Lynn E., and Steven Sass. 2000. "The Transition from a Mill-Based to a Knowledge-Based Economy: New England, 1940–2000." In Peter Temin, ed., *Engines of Enterprise: The Economic History of New England*. Cambridge: Harvard University Press, 201–249.

Chamberlain, Lisa. 2006. "Old Mills That Aren't Run of the Mill." *New York Times*, April 23, Sec. 8, 16.

Conaway, Carrie. 2002. "Preserving the Past: Who Should Bear the Cost of History?" *Regional Review*, 12 (2), 14–21.

Cumbler, John. 2001. *Reasonable Use: The People, the Environment, and the State, New England 179–1930*. New York: Oxford University Press.

Duany, Andres, Elizabeth Platter-Zyberk, and Jeff Speck. 2000. *Suburbanization: The Rise of Sprawl and the Decline of the American Dream*. New York: North Point Press.

Flint, Anthony, and Bill Dedman. 2002. "Urban Renaissance Eludes State's Mid-sized Cities.," *Boston Sunday Globe*, June 23, A1.

Foderaro, Lisa W. 2002. "Adding Life and Color to a Once-Faded River City." *New York Times*, July 29, A19.

Forrant, Robert, and Shawn Barry. 2001. "The Massachusetts High Tech Manufacturing Story," *Benchmarks,* 4 (3), 12–16.

Forrant, Robert, et al. 2001. *Approaches to Sustainable Development: The Public University in the Regional Economy*. Amherst: University of Massachusetts Press.

Gilkeson, John S., Jr. 1986. *Middle-Class Providence, 1820–1940*. Princeton: Princeton University Press.

Gratz, R., and N. Mintz. 1998. *Cities Back from the Edge: New Life for Downtown*. New York: John Wiley.

Groves, Nancy. 1999. "Fulton Cotton Mill: Not Your Typical Conversion." *Atlanta Constitution*, May 21.

Halpern, Robert. 1995. *Rebuilding the Inner City: A History of Neighborhood Initiatives to Address Poverty in the United States*. New York: Columbia University Press.

Holyoke. 1999. *The Holyoke Master Plan: The Agenda for Achieving Our Shared Vision of Holyoke's Future*. Holyoke: City Hall.

Kirchoff, Sue, and Bill Dedman. 2002. "'90s Boom Bypassed Many Mass. Regions, Census Show." *Boston Globe*, May 22, 1.

Kirk, William. 1909. *A Modern City: Providence, Rhode Island, and Its Activities*. Chicago: University of Chicago Press.

Malone, Hermione. 1999. "A Crowded Canvas: Providence Has Keyed Its Revival on Artists, but Some Fear the Cost of Success." *Boston Globe*, November 21, C8.

Manning, Joe. 2001. *Disappearing into North Adams*. Florence, MA: Flatiron Press.

Massachusetts Executive Office of Economic Affairs. 2002. *Toward a New Prosperity: Building Regional Competitiveness Across the Commonwealth*.

McQuaid, Cate. 2002. "Lowell's Lofty Goal." *Boston Globe*, July 19, D17.

Merrimack Valley Planning Commission. 2001. *Economic Development Strategy for the Merrimack Valley Final Report*. May.

Mira, Jim. 1997. "Historic Beverly Building Gets a New Life." *Boston Business Journal*, Oct. 17.

Mitchell, Jerry. 2001. "Business Improvement Districts and the 'New' Revitalization of Downtown." *Economic Development Quarterly*, 15, 115–23.

Moe, Richard, and Carter Wilkie. 1997. *Changing Places: Rebuilding Community in the Age of Sprawl*. New York: Henry Holt & Company.

Rodriguez, Cindy, and Bill Dedman. 2002. "Census Finds a World of Differences." *Boston Globe*, Aug. 27, 1.

Rome, Adam. 2001. *The Bulldozer in the Countryside: Suburban Sprawl and the Rise of American Environmentalism*. New York: Cambridge University Press.

Siegel, Beth, Barbara Baran, and Suzanne Teegarden. 2001. "Small Cities, Big Problems." *Commonwealth*, Spring, 15–20.

Traub, J. 1996. "Can Associations of Business Be True Community Builders?" *The Responsive Community*, 6, 28–32.

U.S. Department of Housing and Urban Development. 2000. *The State of the Cities 2000: Megaforces Shaping the Future of the Nation's Cities*. Washington, DC: HUD Office of Policy Development and Research.

U.S. Department of Housing and Urban Development. 1999. *Now Is the Time: Places Left Behind in the New Economy*. Washington, DC: HUD Office of Policy Development and Research.

Wadsworth, Kent. 1997. "Mills to Desks, Gurneys to Beds." *Journal of Property Management*, 62 (5), 26–32.

Wiewel, Wim, Michael Teitz, and Robert Giloth. 1993. "The Economic Development of Neighborhoods and Localities." In Richard Bingham and Robert Mier, eds., *Theories of Local Economic Development: Perspectives from Across Disciplines*. Thousand Oaks, CA: Sage Publications, 80–99.

Woodward, William, and Edward Sanderson. 1986. *Providence: A Citywide Survey of Historic Resources*. Providence: Rhode Island Historical Preservation Commission.

Other Resources

National Park Service, National Register of Historic Places. The register has been kept since the mid-1960s and now contains close to 75,000 historical places, many of them old mill buildings and mill complexes.

An important journal that deals with many of the theoretical aspects of development, yet does so in a very reader-friendly way, is *Economic Development Quarterly*. It is produced at Cleveland State University, and information can be found at www.sagepub .com.

An important journal that deals with a variety of planning issues from land reuse, to transportation, to parks and green space, and everything in between is the *Journal of the American Planning Association*.

Made in Brooklyn, a video, chronicles efforts to revitalize a large area of the old Brooklyn Navy Yard for mixed-use light industry and affordable housing. Distributed by New Day Films, Harriman, NY.

Photo: Jeffrey Blankenship

16

Historic Landscape Preservation
Saving Community Character

Annaliese Bischoff

Don't it always seem to go
That you don't know what you've got
'Till it's gone
They paved paradise
And put up a parking lot

> —JONI MITCHELL, "Big Yellow Taxi"

SO LAMENTS the popular songwriter from the sixties about the aftermath of insensitive development and poor planning. When my favorite radio station first played this song, I was a child living on an apple orchard soon fated to become a new parking lot for the Fine Arts Center at the University of Rhode Island in Kingston. At that age I felt quite powerless over the future land-use change that would take away my childhood stomping ground. To this day visiting the parking lot on the campus in Kingston evokes haunting memories of this personal loss. However, apple orchards can still evoke for me the precious memories of climbing a carefully selected tree, of sketching the gnarled limbs of an old friend, or of snacking on a freshly fallen apple.

The experience of losing an apple orchard to a parking lot helped direct me as a young adult to discover the process of landscape preservation within the profession of landscape architecture. From childhood through adulthood, the experience of place can shape our destinies and provide us with very powerful connections. The connection between who we are and where we are can help ground us within our communities. Looking after and guarding the valuable places near us contribute to our sense of well-being. Such stewarding of the land helps strengthen not only our sense of place, but also our sense of self.

In every community there are cherished places in the natural and the built environment. Children as well as adults form close attachments to outdoor places richly vested with memories. Sometimes the loss or threat of loss of such a beloved place can be a galvanizing experience for a community. Residents can rally together to preserve the fabric of these beloved places, and community members can initiate important conversations about the qualities they value and why they find them significant. Through the use of tools of historic preservation, the future of these places can be ensured. At the same time that preservation planning can provide care for the historic and cultural gems in a community, intelligent and creative planning can guide change and new development compatibly. Preservation and development need not be mutually exclusive.

This chapter showcases Sholan Farm, an apple orchard in the City of Leominster, Massachusetts, 40 miles west of Boston. The story of this orchard, recently rescued from the fate of becoming a residential subdivision, offers hope and direction for saving open space from development. Attained by means of creative solutions and strategies for protecting valued places, this success can inspire other initiatives. To this end every community should consider first: What are the threats to their valued places? What are the historic roots of the community? How are these expressed in the built environment? What are the opportunities to connect to those roots and celebrate them?

Through the search for answers to these questions, community members can also learn about the steps in the historic landscape preservation process. The relationship between the history of a site and a discussion of community needs can lead to a program of new uses for the site with a connection to the historic uses. Before we look at one specific apple orchard in detail, it is important to be able to identify all the resources within the broad range of landscape types that contribute to community character. Often when citizens first think about the features that make such a contribution, they identify historic buildings. An awareness of what can constitute a historic place can be expanded by a review of the broad range of resource types. The particular threats to these resources within a community can also be identified and discussed.

The Office of Historic Resources within the Massachusetts Department of Environment suggests a useful set of categories to help identify resources and what threatens them. This list certainly includes buildings as one category. However, other sorts of structures and objects also need to be considered. Canals, bridges, stone features, memorials, markers, gazebos, and fountains within a community may be important contributors to character. Downtowns in the form of village centers, formal town centers, streetscapes, or central business districts might also be considered. Under the category *landscapes*, river corridors, agricultural lands, municipal parks, formal gardens, cemeteries, and burial grounds are included. With *archeological sites*, historic, prehistoric, and traditional cultural places may be identified. With the category *historic roadways*, country roads, recreational paths, and designed roadways come to mind.

Landscape resources within a community can be threatened by either natural or human forces. Under natural forces untended vegetation can result in an overgrown landscape. This condition may indicate a derelict state detracting from character. Erosion may be another natural force. Human forces that can threaten a landscape resource include parking requirements, modern road standards, and deferred maintenance. Economic influences may bring demolition. And as with the featured case study here, new development may threaten the loss of landscapes. Awareness of the broad range of types of landscape resources and threats is key in a process to develop effective strategies for protection.

To begin the process of historic preservation, help is available through the National Park Service within the U.S. Department of the Interior. In addition to this federal source, help is also accessible from state preservation offices and environmental management departments or divisions. In Massachusetts the State Historical Commission offers a matching grant program for preservation projects. An innovative Historic Landscape Preservation Grant Program has been administered by the Department of Environmental Management. Help in thinking about the value of nominating a historic place to the National Register of Historic Places is readily obtainable. Help in developing a strategy to rescue and protect historic landscapes is available from both federal and state programs.

Valuing Your History

Losing an apple orchard can be sad for any community, as I personally experienced in my own childhood. However, the threat of losing the last active apple orchard in the very city where the famous "Johnny Appleseed," aka John Chapman, was born in 1774 seemed of much more than local significance in the millennium year of 2000. But after property owners Paul A. and Marjorie Possick of New Jersey filed a preliminary subdivision plan with the Leominster planning

Creating a Heritage Landscape Program in Your Community

The First Steps

Identifying heritage or historical landscapes in your own town is a process that can be quite simple—people meeting and agreeing which landscapes are really central to the meaning of the town. It can also be more rigorous and thorough. The publication *Reading the Land: Massachusetts Heritage Landscapes, A Guide to Identification and Protection,* prepared for the state Department of Environmental Management, lays out a clear process to follow when a full inventory of important landscapes is in order. Here we abstract from that publication to provide a sense of steps that can be taken to get started, and briefly describe what occurs after these initial steps.

Every community encompasses a variety of heritage landscapes; these landscapes are best known to local citizens. A heritage landscape program in your community will publicly recognize these special places and features of your surroundings. It will provide a basis for generating community support for the preservation of significant heritage landscapes. The first steps are to establish a Heritage Landscape Committee and prepare by learning about heritage landscapes. The next step, the inventory, which is the basis upon which you will build the advocacy and protection, has two distinct steps: the reconnaissance survey, followed by the intensive survey with evaluation. After the inventory has been completed, set priorities for preservation and disseminate the information to your fellow citizens and officials to build the high level of interest necessary to preserve the special places in your community . . . (p. 21).

Heritage Landscape Inventory Steps

- Learn about heritage landscapes and past inventories
- Establish a heritage landscape committee
- Build support from citizens and elected officials
- Explore possible funding and technical assistance options
- Consider engaging a consultant for the inventory
- Conduct the survey (reconnaissance, followed by intensive inventory)
- Evaluate the significance of the surveyed landscapes
- Establish goals for future inventory work
- Set priorities for preservation planning based on known or anticipated threats

- Share the information in the community, region, and state (p. 23).

Establish a Heritage Landscape Committee

The establishment of an effective Heritage Landscape Committee (Committee) and the ultimate success of the Heritage Landscape Inventory Program in your community will be related to the involvement of a broad representation of the community. The program is a local initiative; therefore, be sure to welcome anyone who wants to participate. Participants can involve a wide-ranging constituency with local, regional, and state representation. . . . Members of the Committee will become the ambassadors of the program. The experiences of the community, the types of heritage landscapes that represent the character of the community, the threats to the landscapes, and a general consensus of the features that are worthy of preservation will be determined by the Committee. For this reason, a balanced and broad-based Committee is an important ingredient for success.

The Committee may include representatives (staff and members) of municipal boards, commissions and committees, as well as delegates of local organizations such as historical societies, trusts, and neighborhood groups. Local residents knowledgeable about local history and ecology, or local professionals in a related field, should be identified. They can be an important addition to the Committee membership, or may provide volunteer services during the survey or review processes. It is helpful if at least one member of the committee is a municipal employee who has access to various municipal agencies, the rules and regulations governing the use of land, and materials such as assessors' maps and other records. Each Committee should assign a Local Project Coordinator (LPC). The LPC, in effect, heads the Committee and should be responsible for gathering input and organizing existing documentation about landscapes . . . (p. 22).

The Inventory

The Reconnaissance Survey is a broad-brush overview of the natural and historic features that make up the heritage landscapes of each community. It begins with the Committee developing or adapting a set of criteria for the landscapes they will include.

The Committee meets and, with the aid of maps and other background material, prepares a list of potential landscapes for investigation through discussion about why each landscape meets the criteria. Consider holding a public meeting to solicit input from the community at large. With this initial list in hand, visit each site or area, preferably as a Committee, and discuss what you see at each property or collection of properties. Although most data collection occurs in the intensive survey, the reconnaissance survey site visits are opportunities to make initial contact with owners and to take slides of landscapes, which can be used in any public informational programs you plan in the future. . . . The initial reconnaissance list should be prioritized or narrowed to perhaps 10–15 landscapes for the initial intensive surveys. You may want to rank the heritage landscapes in a matrix to reflect types, significance, imminence of threats, status of information, and visibility in the community. . . . Try to have a range of types and scales represented in the landscapes on your intensive survey (p. 25).

Reading the Land describes in detail the next steps to follow. Briefly, they include:

- Conduct an Intensive survey to decide which of the landscapes that are included on the reconnaisance survey are of the most importance and are the most feasible for protection.
- Evaluate the significance of the landscapes that have been identified to determine priorities for preservation
- Develop a preservation plan that identifies the most important landscapes to be protected, likely funding sources, and priorities for public funding.

An alternative publication that may helpful is the Preservation Brief 36 published by the National Park Service, *Protecting Cultural Landscapes: Planning, Treatment and Management*. It is an excellent guide to the landscape preservation process, and is available online at http://www2.cr.nps.gov/tps/briefs/brief36.htm.

Following a clear process in determining priorities and strategies will yield many benefits. The process itself is a way to build consensus and to establish the importance of historic landscapes in your particular town. Having undertaken a clear process provides a strong argument when going to town meeting or to city council for funds. It also establishes the community as a highly valued and knowledgeable partner for state agencies when they determine which projects to fund. It can also be fun! Finding the right pieces to save, along with the right locations for new building, is a key aspect of smart growth and community preservation. We wish you good luck with the process.

Source: *Reading the Land* was prepared by PAL Cultural Resource Management Consultants for the Massachusetts Department of Environmental Management and the Heritage Landscape Inventory Program, April 2003. Principal authors include Virginia K. Adams as the Senior Project Manager at PAL, Patrice Kish as the Director of the Department of Environmental Management Bureau of Project Planning, Design, and Development, and Jessica Rowcroft as the Preservation Planner at the Heritage Landscape Inventory Program. Copies are available at http://www.mass.gov/dem/programs/histland/publications.htm.

What You Can Do

Advice from the National Park Service

- Look at the land to understand who you are, where you have come from, and where you are going.
- Educate yourself about landscape preservation issues and techniques.
- Help young people to make the connection—enlighten them about the value of preserving and interpreting historic landscapes as a tangible way of understanding our place in our nation's history.
- Get involved locally by attending planning meetings to ensure that decision makers preserve and protect the unique character of the historic landscapes in which you live, work, and play.
- Join a landscape preservation group for a local park, farm, or garden, or even a historic site, such as a battlefield.
- Encourage your elected officials to support legislation that protects America's landscape legacy.
- Be vocal by supporting landscape preservation issues through newspaper editorials, newsletter publications, and the like.

Source: http://www.cr.nps.gov/hps/hli/hliwhat.htm.

board to construct 161 four-bedroom single-family homes (see Figure 16.1), the threat of losing this 167-acre parcel of land looked like a real possibility. Fortunately, the site was under the Massachusetts General Law Chapter 61A, granting agricultural tax status until June 2001. This protection required that the Possicks give the city the right of first refusal to buy the land. However, the city needed funds to purchase the land in order to save it from residential development.

While the historic roots of this site were not completely known, the immediate threat was in clear view. Susan Gardener, a member of the newly formed Friends of Sholan Farms, as well as of the Nashaway Genealogical Society, began to research the history of the site in more detail. Graduate students in my landscape preservation studio from the Department of Landscape Architecture & Regional Planning at the University of Massachusetts in Amherst, working with the planning department on a municipal preservation plan for the city, also looked into the history of this site. We found that in 1701 Chief Sholan, the leader of the Nashaway tribe, sold land to the municipality of Lancaster from which Leominster was later incorporated in 1740. What is noteworthy about this transaction is that the land was legally bought from the Native Americans. Because so few parcels were legally purchased, this land transaction offers an honorable history that can be proudly remembered. In 1912, when Paul Washburn bought close to 200 acres from Dennis Wheeler, he chose to name the land "Sholan Farm" after Chief Sholan. The Washburn family operated a dairy farm at the site until the 1920's, when it became an apple orchard, which it has since remained.

Developing Strategies and Solutions to Protect Historic Places

To begin the process of developing strategies to save places and protect community character, an overview of the options is useful. The importance of building supportive, creative constituencies and partnerships cannot be emphasized enough. Non-regulatory strategies can be useful on their own, but with the backing of strong partnerships and constituencies their effectiveness is greater. Strategies to consider include:

- Planning
- Land acquisition—fee, conservation restriction, preservation restriction

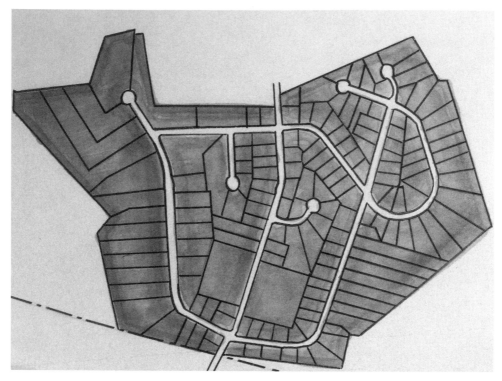

Figure 16.1. Subdivision plan for Sholan Farm.

- Education and recognition, and
- Interpretation

Regulatory strategies can offer more control. Two strong means include:

- Zoning
- Historic designation

At Sholan Farm several of these strategies were woven together to create a strong plan to save the property.

Preservation costs money and needs community support. In this instance the need for a plan to raise funds to purchase the land seemed clear. Early efforts to raise money, however, had more to do with rallying community support for the project than actually raising significant funds. These community-spirited initiatives included the sale of Sholan Farm apple candles, red marble apples, apple lapel pins, and Johnny Appleseed statues with cooperation from the Appleseed Advertising Company. With this visible community backing, Mayor Dean J. Mazzarella dedicated his support

to the project. The city council and several citizen interest groups engaged in discussion about the plight of the property. Raising the funds to save this parcel from development would take more than community spirit alone.

Following a two-year effort that drew national attention and some controversy along the way, a creative plan to save the property was signed into action by Mayor Mazzarella. Funds from the city, the Leominster Land Trust, the Trustees of Reservations, and private donations helped make this deal possible. But the deal was made reality through the leadership of State Secretary of Environmental Affairs Robert A. Durand with a $1.58 million contribution. By April 2001 the city was able to purchase the property for $4.75 million. As a condition of the state contribution of $1.58 million Durand negotiated an additional conservation restriction on 1,500 privately owned acres surrounding city watershed land that links directly to the Leominster State Forest and Wachusett Reservation. This restriction will ensure permanent protection of this valuable additional land while allowing public access for low-impact recreational uses such as hiking.

Figure 16.2. View of Sholan Farm.
The stunning vista through the apple orchard from Pleasant Street will now be preserved.
Photo: Annaliese Bischoff.

Figure 16.3. Apple orchard in spring.
Photo: Annaliese Bischoff.

Under city management Sholan Farm is now producing viable apple crops for public sale. As proprietor, the city appointed a Sholan Farm Post Purchase Use Committee to manage and implement plans and designs for the future of the site. The site's historic roots as an apple orchard will guide and inspire future uses. Three important management objectives include:

- Preserving a significant aspect of Leominster's heritage by preserving the last remaining active apple orchard in the city.
- Protecting the dramatic scenic vistas from Pleasant Street, which divides the property.
- Creating a fitting memorial to John Chapman, known best as "Johnny Appleseed," one of Leominster's favorite sons.

The committee continues to discuss and plan how these goals can best be developed. Through the innovative solution to save Sholan Farm the historic roots of the property are celebrated. An exciting new agricultural business venture for the city in managing this farm property assures the public a valued community asset (see Figures 16.2 and 16.3).

Designing with Your History

Whether the special places in your community include a farm, a park, a cemetery, gardens, riverways, canals, town centers, village greens, memorials, stone walls, buildings, scenic roads, or archaeological sites, strategies to guard these resources from threats need to be developed. Whether properties are threatened by human forces such as parking expansions, new development, or vandalism, or by natural forces such as erosion, steps to identify and protect the resources that contribute to the character of the community can be guided by a host of case studies. However, just as each community has its own unique character, each community also needs to uncover the best means of caring for its assets. The following lists of Web sources and suggested reading are intended as a guide to the process. Time to care for the historic and cultural resources within the community is time well invested for the vitality of our future. The richness of character from the past can inform and connect us to the future. Protecting the cherished character of the historic landscapes in our communities will spare us from both loss and regret. As Henry David Thoreau noted in *Walden* (1854):

The future inhabitants of this region, wherever they may place their houses, may be sure that they have been anticipated. An afternoon sufficed to lay out the land into orchard, wood-lot, and pasture, and to decide what fine oaks or pines should be left to stand before the door, and whence each blasted tree could be seen to the best advantage; and then I let it lie, fallow, perchance, for a man is rich in proportion to the number of things which he can afford to let alone.

Web Resources

National

Advisory Council on Historic Preservation: http://www.achp.gov/
Alliance for Historic Landscape Preservation: http://www.ahlp.org
American Association for State and Local History: http://www.aaslh.org
American Association of Botanical Gardens and Arboreta: http://www.aabga.org
American Farmland Trust: http://www.farmland.org/
American Institute of Architects: http://www.aia.org/
American Planning Association: http://www.planning.org
American Society of Landscape Architects: http://www.asla.org
Architects, Designers, and Planners for Social Responsibility: http://www.adpsr.org/
Association for Gravestone Studies: http://www.gravestonestudies.org
The Catalog of Landscape Records in the United States at Wave Hill: http://www.wavehill.org
Center for Excellence for Sustainable Development-Affordable Housing: http://www.sustainable.doe.gov/buildings/affhousing.shtml
The Cultural Landscape Foundation: http://www.tclf.org
Cultural Resource Management, National Park Service (NPS), Cultural Resources: http://www.cr.nps.gov/crm
Downtown Research and Development Center: http://www.downtowndevelopment.com/links.html
Frederick Law Olmsted National Historic Site, NPS: http://www.nps.gov/frla
The Garden Club of America: http://www.gcamerica.org
Heritage Preservation Services: http://www.achp.gov/
Historic American Buildings Survey, Historic American Landscapes Survey, National Park Service: http://www.cr.nps.gov/habshaer/habs/hals.htm
The Historic Landscape Initiative, National Park Service, Heritage Preservation Services: http://www2.cr.nps.gov/hli
The Land Trust Alliance: http://www.lta.org/

National Association for Olmsted Parks:
http://laz.uoregon.edu/~naop/
National Center for Preservation Technology:
http://www.ncptt.nps.gov/
National Main Street Center, National Trust:
http://www.mainstreet.org/
National Park Service: http://www.nps.gov
National Register of Historic Places, National Register Information
System Web: http://www.nr.nps.gov/nrishome.htm
National Trust for Historic Preservation: http://www.nthp.org
National Urban Forests: http://www.americanforests.org
Park Historic Structures and Cultural Landscapes Program, NPS:
http://www.cr.nps.gov/phscl
Society of Architectural Historians: http://www.sah.org/
Technical Preservation Services, National Park Service:
http://www.achp.gov/
United States Forest Service, Cultural Heritage Research:
http://www.fs.fed.us/research/rvur/recreation/cultural.htm
Vernacular Architecture Forum:
http://www.vernaculararchitecture.org/

State/Regional

Boston Women's Heritage Trail:
http://bps.boston.k12.ma/bwht/home.htm
Historic New England (formerly SPNEA):
http://www.historicnewengland.org/
Institute for Cultural Landscapes Studies, The Arnold Arboretum
of Harvard University: http://www.icls.harvard.edu/
Massachusetts Department of Environmental Management, Historic Landscape Preservation Program:
http://www.state.ma.us/dem/programs/histland/histland.htm
Massachusetts Historic Commission:
http://www.state.ma.us/sec/mhc/mhcpub/pubidx.htm
The Trustees of Reservations: http://www.thetrustees.org/

International

Association for Preservation Technology International:
http://www.apti.org

English Heritage: http://www.english-heritage.org.uk
Joint Strategic Planning and Transportation Unit:
http://www.jsptu-avon.gov.uk/
Royal Town Planning Institute: http://www.rtpi.org.uk/
UK Countryside Commission: http://www.countryside.gov.uk/

Recommended Reading

Birnbaum, Charles A. *Preservation Brief 36: Protecting Cultural Landscapes: Planning, Treatment and Management of Historic Landscapes.* Washington, DC: NPS Cultural Resources, Preservation Assistance, 1994.

Eliade, Mircea. *The Sacred and the Profane: The Nature of Religion.* New York: Harcourt Brace Jovanovich, 1959.

Hayden, Dolores. *The Power of Place.* Cambridge: MIT Press, 1995.

Hester, Randy. "Subconscious Landscapes of the Heart." *Places* 2 (3): 10–22, 1985.

Hiss, Tony. *The Experience of Place.* New York: Vintage, 1990.

Howett, Catherine. "Living Landscapes for the Dead." *Landscape* 21: 9–17, 1977.

Jackson, J. B. *A Sense of Place, a Sense of Time.* New Haven: Yale University Press, 1994.

Lippard, Lucy R. *The Lure of the Local.* New York: The New Press, 1997.

Massachusetts Department of Environmental Management. *Reading the Land: A Guide to Identification and Protection.* April 2003.

Meinig, D.W., ed. *The Interpretation of Ordinary Landscapes.* New York: Oxford University Press, 1979.

Page, Robert A., et al. *A Guide to Cultural Landscape Reports.* Washington, DC: National Park Service, 1998.

Schama, Simon. *Landscape and Memory.* New York: Knopf, 1995.

Stokes, Samuel N., et al. *Saving America's Countryside.* Baltimore: Johns Hopkins University Press, 1989.

Thoreau, Henry D. *Walden.* Boston: Houghton, Mifflin, 1854, 1882.

Venturi, Robert, et al. *Learning from Las Vegas.* Cambridge: MIT Press, 1977.

Photo: Samalid Hogan

17

Community Preservation

Residents, Municipalities, and the State Collaborating for Smarter Growth

Priscilla Geigis, Linda Silka, and Elisabeth M. Hamin

Massachusetts is widely known for its rich history, and also for its beautiful vernacular architecture and traditional town greens. Massachusetts is home to a population of 6 million people who share 5 million acres, with approximately two-thirds of that population inhabiting the eastern third of the state. But Massachusetts, like other states, is changing. Between 1950 and 1990, Massachusetts experienced a population increase of only 28 percent, yet land development increased by more than 188 percent. West of Boston, growth followed major highways, perpetuating patterns of sprawl development. In the state's less-developed western region, rural sprawl increased as homes on large lots proliferated on what had been prime farmland, increasing residents' driving times and reducing the congeniality and liveliness of small town centers.

Like other metropolitan and urban centers and urban regions across the country, the Boston metropolitan area has now come to include suburban communities as far as 35 miles away from the city center. At the same time many Massachusetts urban centers, including those outside the Boston area such as Springfield and Holyoke, lost residents to the surrounding suburbs. For example, the City of Worcester lost 15 percent of its population between 1950 and 1990, while the surrounding suburbs grew by more than 250 percent. The town centers that once defined the Massachusetts landscape are quickly disappearing as single-use development drains and obscures traditional growth centers. Massachusetts, like many other states, is now looking for opportunities to reverse these development patterns and revitalize the urban centers and traditional downtowns that were once the heart of our communities so that the unique characteristics of those communities can be maintained.

Planning and Zoning in Massachusetts Today

Ever since the colonists dumped tea into the Boston Harbor to protest taxation without representation, Massachusetts residents have boasted a strong independence in political decision-making.

This independence is reflected in Massachusetts' 351 separate and distinct cities and towns each governed by a city council or by a town meeting in which residents collectively make community decisions by a majority vote. The politics of local control is legislatively organized in Massachusetts and many other states as home rule, in which local communities can do pretty much what they want as long as it is not in conflict with existing state regulations (although the amount of actual municipal freedom created varies a great deal from state to state, based largely on how state land-use case law has developed). All land within the Commonwealth is contained in incorporated municipalities, whether towns or cities. Regional planning in the Commonwealth is currently limited to regional planning agencies that are largely consultancies, offering fee-for-service planning to smaller communities that cannot afford full-time planners and also collecting regional data and providing advice and some co-ordination for federal transportation investments. County government was abolished in 1997, further decentralizing local land-use decisions. These decisions are left to local leaders, and most often these leaders are citizen volunteers.

In Massachusetts, we have not passed a significant revision of land-use regulations at the state level since the Model Land Use codes were implemented back in the 1950s. The result of this, along with the incremental development of state case law, is many planning situations that planners consider less than ideal (to say the least). The lack of regional coordination among town plans is one of these, as is the lack of requirement for towns to even have a comprehensive plan. Similar issues include the fact that the state Supreme Court found that any zoning which requires lots bigger than about two acres was illegal (thus making real agricultural zoning virtually impossible), and that once granted, development permits are "grandfathered" pretty much indefinitely, in spite of any new municipal zoning or planning (meaning that creating real change through new plans and zoning is significantly hampered by old permits). Perhaps strangest of all, if a building lot has sufficient frontage on a road, a home can be built without municipal approval; this is called the "approval not required" or ANR regulation, and means that for many homes built in the state, the municipality has no say beyond building codes and set-back requirements. Thus, professional and citizen-planners struggle along in our state under less than ideal codes—but in this, Massachusetts is similar to many states in the nation. The good

news is that as this book goes to press a group of dedicated reformers have gotten legislators to consider a substantive revision to state land-use codes to address many of these issues, while retaining the strong local control tradition of land use in the state.

Building from the Best: Traditional Town Form in Massachusetts

The traditional and still visible town form in Massachusetts places the town's major public buildings, such as town hall and churches and schools, around a square, with the square a swath of green lawn used for farmers' markets and town festivals. The everyday businesses residents need—groceries, stationeries, etc.—were located in buildings surrounding or near the green. Large, medium, and small homes intermingle on relatively small lots on side streets leading away from the square. Town forests, open spaces, and public ways along rivers intermingled in the town's pattern of land use, providing recreation and the quality of life for which the state is famous. Just beyond town, the countryside began, and the local farms provided dairy, meat, and produce for the local markets. Even in the cities and suburbs, there tended to be a clear town center with density decreasing as one moved away from that center. The result is that even in most suburbs, there was a "there there," and most suburbs have their own identities and strong local allegiances.

This much-loved traditional urban form is under significant stress. The town centers can easily fall into disrepair as previous users move out and the space needs of new users don't match the old buildings. For many towns now the main street is home to some specialty retail, banks, and services, while the majority of the shopping occurs at a strip center on the periphery of town. While periphery big-box development clearly contributes to sprawl and makes the economics of town center businesses more difficult, this form does retain the aesthetics of the traditional town center while allowing the convenience of modern big-box retail. In more rural areas as well as cities and towns in the metropolitan areas, the clear division of countryside and town is eroding as homes on large lots eat up the land and eliminate local farms and orchards, thanks in large part to the approval-not-required provision mentioned above. Stream flows and aquifer recharge have become a major issue in the Boston metro area, as a lack of sufficient water capacity threatens to halt development. Residential development, and especially anything with more than two bedrooms, has become a dirty word in most towns and cities across the state, as fiscal impact analysis has demonstrated again and again that the municipal service costs for homes with school-age children far outpace the property taxes those homeowners pay. The only residential development that most communities seek is for groups like the elderly, who typically don't have children to educate. The result of this, along with market factors, has been an exponential rise in housing prices in the state, and particularly the Boston metro area, placing home ownership out of reach of many new households and putting significant stress on existing affordable housing stock.[1] A relatively moderate level of population growth along with strong local commitment to the traditional New England town form and land protection has meant that up until recently, the state has not suffered unduly even with these planning limitations. However, there is a sense that the limits to that situation are being reached.

The Community Preservation Initiative

From the state-level perspective, Massachusetts' political structure of independent entities in which individual cities and towns make most of their own land-use decisions has necessitated the development of a nontraditional approach to address sprawl. Rather than attempt a politically unlikely "top down" strategy in which planning decisions or actions are dictated to communities from regional or state-level agencies, the state has focused on enabling good planning within communities through a community-level-up approach. Under former Governors Paul Celluci and Jane Swift, this bottom-up approach became known as the Community Preservation Initiative. The term "community preservation" first appeared in legislation Bob Durand filed as a Massachusetts freshman legislator in 1985. The legislation was designed to enable communities to establish a dedicated fund for open space, affordable housing, and historic preservation funded through a surcharge on local property

taxes. This goal was eventually realized through the Community Preservation Act, which allows municipalities to vote to tax themselves to achieve local goals of community preservation, and provides state matching funds for municipalities that pass an act.

When Durand was appointed secretary of environmental affairs in Massachusetts in 1999, he adopted the term from the legislation to create a statewide planning program known as the Community Preservation Initiative. In creating the program, Durand expanded the definition of community preservation beyond open space, affordable housing, and historic preservation to include transportation, economic development, and other issues communities must balance as they continue to grow. Because of the program's approach—providing information and tools to local decision-makers to help them make informed decisions rather than dictating a particular outcome—the term "community preservation" also came to symbolize a grassroots, municipal-level-up, inclusive effort.

An Organizing Principle for an Integrated Future

Further defined, "community preservation" is an organizing principle designed to preserve and enhance the quality of life in Massachusetts, community by community, and watershed by watershed. The phrase "community by community" recognizes that, due to Massachusetts's political structure, local leaders are in the best position to make decisions about the future of their community. However, the phrase "watershed by watershed" recognizes that we must think beyond our jurisdictional boundaries and recognize that the decisions we make at the local level affect the larger community of which we are a part.

The concept behind "community preservation" is to encourage local leaders and residents to recognize and then work to preserve the unique aspects of their communities such as traditional housing stock, historic buildings, and open space, while at the same time balancing the diverse interests involved in community planning. Rather than isolate an interest such as natural resource protection and plan only for the desired protection of that resource, community preservation encourages communities to balance natural resource protection with affordable housing, economic development, historic preservation, and transportation so that an integrated vision of future growth can be achieved.

---

1. Many argue that this is a result of the way we fund schooling, where most of the cost of schooling local children comes from local property tax revenues. Under this argument, fundamental change to the situation can only come from having a greater share of school costs paid by the state, so that the costs of accommodating new children in a school system are widely distributed.

The Community Preservation Act

In December 2000, the Community Preservation Act became law in Massachusetts enabling communities to establish a local, dedicated fund for open space including recreation, historic preservation, and affordable housing. Funded through a surcharge on local property taxes, this landmark legislation is the first of its kind in the country to combine these three community interests and priorities. In the first election cycle, 31 communities passed the CPA, well beyond supporters' expectations. By June 2005, 141 communities had voted on a local CPA, 100 had passed it, and over $116.6 million in funding had been appropriated (Trust for Public Lands, http://www.tpl.org).

The evolution of the Community Preservation Act illustrates not only a responsiveness to meeting communities' priority needs as they continue to grow, but also political savvy in building successful coalitions, which later became a core tenet of its namesake—the Community Preservation Initiative.

In 1988, as a freshman legislator, then Representative Bob Durand filed the Community Preservation Act designed to help communities more easily acquire open space by establishing a dedicated fund for land acquisition. The legislation was patterned after similar land bank legislation adopted by Cape Cod communities and many states across the country. The bill remained unchanged for several years, never gaining legislative approval in both state branches.

While the bill languished in the House, Durand moved to the Senate and began to realize that community leaders needed to protect more than open space. Massachusetts was quickly changing, and the aspects that once defined our individual communities and our state were disappearing, especially in the eastern half of the state. In addition to land, community leaders wanted to preserve historic properties—whether buildings or landscapes—in order to showcase their community's traditional roots. They also wanted to provide affordable housing for low- and moderate-income individuals and families so municipal employees such as fire and police people and school teachers, the elderly, and adult children who grew up in the community could afford to live there.

Durand, working with his legislative colleagues, amended the bill to expand "community preservation" beyond land acquisition and, at the same time, broadened the coalition. The expanded bill with its three purposes—historic preservation, open space, and affordable housing—helped create a coalition of organizations that normally didn't work together. Bringing land protectionists together with historic preservationists and housing advocates was a first in Massachusetts and formed a powerful coalition that worked for years to pass the bill.

Creating partnerships reveals the core of community preservation because it takes a broad coalition to pass such legislation both statewide and in individual communities. The Community Preservation Coalition, composed of several hundred local and statewide organizations representing the three purposes of the act, formed to pass the legislation. Once passed, the coalition adopted a new role—that of educator and supporter—by helping communities understand the act and how to get it passed locally as well as how to implement it once passed.

As an incentive to pass the act on the local level, the legislature created a Community Preservation Trust Fund to provide cities and towns with state matching funds raised through a surcharge on transactions at the Registry of Deeds. Although residents from all communities who execute real estate transactions pay into the trust, the matching funds are available only to the communities that adopt the CPA. In the first year, $18 million in state funds was distributed to 30 communities, matching dollar for dollar the money raised on the local level. It is estimated that at the current rate of collection, the trust fund will provide a sizable match to CPA communities for the foreseeable future. Of particular note is that CPA has been passed by very large and urban communities, such as Cambridge, and also by some of the smallest, most rural communities in the Commonwealth. Additionally, much of the spending has been directed toward affordable housing, particularly in urban areas, with open space still receiving a good share of funds (Hamin et al., forthcoming). It is encouraging that the act has demonstrated the ability to meet the needs of a wide variety of communities.

The term "community preservation" requires some consideration here. It has not been free of controversy, particularly given the implications of the word "preservation." If we are "preserving," are we only looking back in time to some grander epoch, some golden community age, and trying to regain that?—is this an exercise in nostalgia? What are we "preserving" our communities from?—change? Does this mean putting a fence around our towns and saying "no" to the currents of the future? But change is inevitable, and often (although certainly not always) beneficial. Outsiders? That would be inappropriate in the American context, especially given the increasing percentages of minorities and immigrants in the culture. Is it only about historic preservation? Or natural land preservation? And what is a community, anyway?

Ultimately, as with the term "sustainable development" and other policy titles, the purpose of the words "community preservation" is to capture enough imagination, enough energy, enough shared purpose, in a catchy phrase so as to keep the interest of both legislators and the public. These are motivating myths, not precise explanations. That "preservation" was a persuasive, imageable enough word to serve this purpose well probably does reflect a certain sense held by New Englanders that there was a golden age for our towns, and that the physical manifestation of that golden age is the traditional town form, which needs to be protected from current forces of change. Given the beauty of many of the towns in Massachusetts as well as the challenges they face, this nostalgia does not seem ill placed, so the images, the emotions, suggested by the word "preservation" work here. The term "community" is also appropriate for the region. The flip side of the fierce local independence from regional or state bonds is an equally fierce loyalty to the municipality from its long-term residents. The long history of the town meeting and the denser settlement patterns compared to much of the country have created a culture that values local community—at least in principle.

We must be careful, however, that the use of those terms does not hide the contradictions and challenges of current planning. Even if we wanted to freeze our communities in time, recreating some golden era, change must occur. A certain unwillingness to accept change, in the form of new houses and apartments, has led to the drastic increases in housing value the region has experienced, and the stresses this causes for families are themselves a cause of change.

Even with a relatively slow pace of population growth, new development is necessary to house new families, whether those are the children of old-timers or immigrants into the state. Those new households require places to work and shop and transportation options. The new household members also require access to local government processes, which means that planning needs not just to preserve existing power balances, but also to engage newcomers of all ethnicities and orientations in the local civic culture. For the same reason community cannot be defined as the typical suspects, the long-term residents of a particular place, but must be defined to include all residents, whether new-comers or old-timers, U.S. citizens or not, of a particular town. Ultimately, to be successful community planning must balance preservation and change, seeking the best in both cases.

The Community Preservation Initiative seeks to empower local leaders to make sound, balanced growth decisions by providing the tools and technical assistance necessary to address growth issues in their community and region, and develop a vision for their future that complements rather than conflicts with their environment, history, culture, and quality of life. By creating GIS-based tools, hosting interactive statewide events, and making information more readily accessible, the education-oriented Initiative aims to inspire and empower local leaders and citizen/volunteer planners who are increasingly making the majority of Massachusetts's growth and planning decisions.

The Buildout Project

The community empowerment approach was best exemplified in the Initiative's first high-profile statewide project —the Buildout Project. Working closely with MassGIS and the state's regional planning agencies, the Initiative provided all 351 communities with a GIS-based map series illustrating each community's developed and undeveloped lands and how the community could be developed based on current zoning. The actual "buildout map" provided statistical data projecting the amount of residential, commercial, and industrial development as well as additional calculations including residential and school-child population and water use. The buildouts showed that the majority of Massachusetts's communities have zoned a disproportionate amount of commercial/industrial development that, if built, would not be residentially supported within the community and therefore would have an impact on surrounding areas. Rather than dictating zoning changes to community leaders, the Buildout Project visually showed them how their zoning decisions could affect their community as well as their neighbors. Since local decision-makers determine zoning within their communities, the message was: If you don't like the possible outcome at buildout, take steps now to change your zoning.

Since the community preservation approach encompasses a variety of disciplines, it also brings together a variety of partners to achieve a balance in decision-making. Early in the Initiative's creation, Environmental Affairs invited three sister state agencies to promote community preservation on a statewide basis by jointly hosting 26 regional public events each bringing together 10–50 communities. This venture was the first time that Environmental Affairs, the Department of Housing and Community Development (DHCD), the Department of Economic Development (DED), and the Executive Office of Transportation and Construction (EOTC) joined forces to provide a single state planning message to communities and offer united assistance in achieving growth goals. These Community Preservation Summits promoted the collective message that sound planning—whether at the state or local level—must involve the balancing of all interests. This holistic message became a model for integrated planning at the local level. Environmental Affairs also formed partnerships with the 13 regional planning agencies (RPA) in Massachusetts that are charged with helping communities address local and regional planning issues. The RPAs are critical to planning in Massachusetts, since over half of the state's communities do not have a professional planner on staff. Thus, the RPAs assist communities in developing individual master plans as well as regional plans that address intercommunity needs. The RPAs became an integral part of the Initiative since they could produce technical information using innovative GIS technology and provide on-the-ground assistance to communities, of which some were already familiar with the planning tools and techniques provided by the Initiative.

The partnership among the state agencies and RPAs, formed as a result of the Buildout Project, provided an excellent foundation for another collaborative effort—the Community Development Plan Program launched in September 2000. This program provided $30,000 worth of technical assistance to any Commonwealth community to develop a GIS-based map depicting the location, type, and quantity of open space and natural resource protection, housing, transportation, and economic development. Again, the program promoted community empowerment, as participation was voluntary. Two hundred and fifty communities of the possible 351 opted to participate.

The Commonwealth Partnership

In an effort to increase partnerships and expand outreach to communities, Environmental Affairs turned to the five campuses of the University of Massachusetts. In January 2000, Environmental Affairs Secretary Bob Durand and UMass President William Bulger established an ongoing partnership named the "Commonwealth Partnership" to develop opportunities for collaboration in teaching, research, and community-based outreach between the state and the university. While the Commonwealth Partnership involved collaboration in a variety of environmental disciplines, community preservation was a natural connection between the two entities.

The university and Environmental Affairs have similar missions—to use their resources and expertise to serve a wider community. Environmental Affairs, through its regulations, policies, and outreach programs, seeks to help communities protect precious environmental resources as they continue to grow and evolve. The university, through its curriculum, community-based projects, and outreach programs, seeks to help communities achieve their goals by providing technical assistance in a variety of disciplines.

The Partnership yielded several cooperative ventures with respect to community preservation. First, we established a ten-person Community Preservation Working Group composed of state leaders working within Environmental Affairs' Community Preservation Initiative and university professors and administrators working in community-based programs and in planning and landscape design departments at each of the university's five campuses. This Working Group provided a forum to examine collective human and financial resources and to discuss collaborative efforts.

The Community Preservation Institute

As a way of furthering the goals of the Initiative to aid local decision-makers, the Working Group created the Community

Preservation Institute, a nine-evening-session certificate program designed to help local leaders explore community preservation concepts and principles for planning and to apply them in their communities. Course topics reflect issues facing our communities and include water and land protection, historic preservation, affordable housing, transportation, and other areas, and are designed to help local leaders find solutions for their communities.

Through interactive classroom discussions, case studies, and team projects, the Institute uses a co-instructor team teaching model that combines the expertise of professional educators, government officials, and citizen group leaders, thereby embodying community preservation's partnership approach. Participants include elected, appointed, and volunteer community leaders from across Massachusetts. This book is an outgrowth of this collaborative effort.

Applicability to Other States

At its most fundamental level of principles for good planning, community preservation is widely relevant beyond Massachusetts, because it is about basic guidance of community growth to achieve better futures. Beautiful cities, towns, and countryside exist in many places. Small towns in Iowa share many of the same design characteristics, and the same desirability, as the town form in Massachusetts, for instance. In other places, the typical form of towns and cities is quite different, but still locally valued, economically functional, and aesthetically pleasing. Similarly, commitment to community is a shared value across the country. Even when an overall landscape speaks more of despair and disinvestment than of stability and care, that place will have loved spots and community strengths. Community preservation does not say that there is one best form. Instead, the point is to preserve and enhance what is best about particular places, creating more unique, more *real* communities. This happens most effectively and equitably when as many residents as possible are involved in the process, and when citizen leaders are as educated as possible about the wide variety of approaches now available in modern planning and zoning.

The question of relevance of the role for the state described by the set of initiatives discussed in this chapter is a bit more complicated. The balance of power between states, regions, and local municipalities varies from state to state

and region to region. In some states significant responsibility for and direction of the planning process has moved up to the state level by means of state-level growth management legislation. In these states, most notably in Oregon, community plans must meet certain criteria laid out by the state, so that local plans must achieve larger regional- and state-level goals. Even the newer "smart growth" approaches, while locally responsive, are much more determined by state-level policy than was the previous practice across the mainland of the country. In Massachusetts, as in many other states, this sort of state-level mandated planning conflicts with deeply held principles of local control, and state-mandated or managed planning appears highly unlikely. Indeed, this suggests the strength of support for property rights in Massachusetts's legislation—despite the state's reputation as a liberal bastion and history of community actions for shared good. Instead, what is feasible is state-led incentives and leadership, of which community preservation is a good example. We suspect that the overall approach will be most relevant to other states that also place a strong local value on local control, while recognizing that the state needs to take steps to encourage better local planning, in a politically realistic fashion. This happens to describe probably the majority of states in our nation.

Community Preservation as it has been enacted in Massachusetts is a collection of pieces, including the act which rewards municipalities for taxing themselves for community preservation projects, the citizen-education initiative, the buildout project, and the collaboration between the state government and the state university. While we hope that the whole is greater than the sum of the parts, states may well choose to adopt some of those pieces, and not others. For instance, in June 2002, the Maine State Legislature established, by statute, a Community Preservation Council to advise the legislature and the governor on community preservation matters and to recommend smart growth legislation. By borrowing the concept from Massachusetts, Maine has demonstrated that the state-level community preservation philosophy can be adopted beyond Massachusetts's borders.

Collaborative efforts between state government and state universities, such as the Community Preservation Institute, are also readily transferable. Many states continue to look for ways to engage their public universities in addressing issues of sprawl. The model that underlies the examples

The Community Preservation Institute

"I see issues in my community differently now. I understand that there are many stakeholders involved in a given project and therefore many interests which need to be addressed," explained Shannon Goleen, an architect in Dennis, Massachusetts, and member of the inaugural class at the Community Preservation Institute. " I feel better equipped to assist my community leaders to make educated decisions about growth," she added. Shannon is one of a growing number of over 250 alumni of the Community Preservation Institute, a joint venture between the Executive Office of Environmental Affairs (EOEA) and the University of Massachusetts (UMass).

In spring 2001, EOEA and UMass created the Community Preservation Institute to provide information and technical assistance to Massachusetts local leaders to help them address growth issues in their communities. Using case studies, team projects, and interactive learning techniques, the CPI exposes students to a broad range of issues including natural resource protection, housing, transportation, and economic development and encourages students to balance these interests when making decisions about future growth. The Institute is designed to help local leaders understand "community preservation" as an approach to thoughtful, balanced planning.

Through a team-teaching approach, involving instructors from UMass, state agencies, and citizen groups, students gain information as well as access to experts in a given field, enabling them to bring the best resources possible to their communities. Students also engage in team projects allowing them to focus on a real issue facing a community.

The Institute is a nine-week evening program available to any Massachusetts resident free of charge and has attracted both current and future community leaders. To encourage continued interaction beyond the Institute, EOEA created the On Line Learning Center to foster communication beyond the classroom. In spring 2003, the Partnership launched a pilot program that redesigned the Institute for high school students. *Community Preservation YouthVisions* is a one-day program that combines classroom curriculum with field-based learning to introduce students to a variety of planning and growth topics (see Figure 17.2). For more information about YouthVisions and the Community Preservation Institute, see Silka, Geigis, and Snyder (2006).

Figure 17.1. Secretary Durand with schoolchildren on Biodiversity Day.
Source: Mass EOEA.

presented throughout this book—in which policy-makers and university researchers work hand in hand—suggests how such engagement can be made effective. Such an approach overcomes the obstacles of different time schedules, different roles and responsibilities, and can result in a continuing exchange of fresh ideas between state government and public universities. The result can be a strengthening of strategies by which citizen leaders, students, public officials, and faculty solve the pressing challenges of community preservation. In addition, such collaborations can be a way to ensure that what our future community leaders—those who are now students at our public universities—are taught is not divorced from collaborative, interdisciplinary problem-solving that is furthering our understanding of community preservation.

Community preservation is not, of course, the end of the story for growth management and improved planning, even in home-rule states. Perhaps its greatest weakness arises from its very strength. This approach works within the confines of existing political reality, and requires perhaps the minimum of political engagement a state can undertake and still have some reform. As a result, it does not redress some of the significant underlying causes of inappropriate or inefficient growth in a state, or the lack of new housing. It does not change school funding and or fundamentally address the problem of cities' unwillingness to provide family housing; it does not address the approval-not-required conditions included in Massachusetts law, and thus cannot change conditions for many new houses. Problematically, while state activities encouraged some regional collaboration, core policies do not require regional action. In most cases, the only way to get significant regional cooperation on hard issues is through state legislation requiring it, and this approach does not address this pressing issue. A more ideal situation would bring state-level reform of building and zoning codes including requirements for regional cooperation and planning and broader sharing of education costs, while encouraging better local planning through such initiatives as those included within the Community Preservation Initiative. But planning, like politics, is the art of the possible. And so for strong local rule states where previously there has been little movement toward planning reform, community preservation suggests one way states can help communities out of the dilemma.

References

The best source for information on the Community Preservation Initiative both as a whole and in its constituent parts is its Web site, which can be linked to from the homepage of the Executive Office of Environmental Affairs, at: http://www.mass.gov/envir/. A second excellent source is the Web site for the Community Preservation Coalition, at: http://www.communitypreservation.org/index.cfm. Regarding the 2002 EPA award, see: http://www.epa.gov/smartgrowth/massachusetts.htm.

The Trust for Public Lands maintains a database on the status of local CPA votes and funding, as well as projects that cities and towns have undertaken, available at: http://www.tpl.org/tier3_cdl.cfm?content_item_id=1780&folder_id=1045. This same Web site lists the Commonwealth Act itself, at: http://www.tpl.org/tier3_cdl.cfm?content_item_id=1787&folder_id=1045.

An evaluation of the implementation of the CPA is available at E. M. Hamin, M. E. Ounsworth Steere, et al, 2006, "Implementing Growth Management: The Community Preservation Act," *Journal of Planning Education and Research* 25:1–13.

The Community Preservation Institute, which trained citizens to become local activists for good planning, developed an excellent curriculum and delivery method; while it is not currently being offered, archival information on the Institute is available through the Community Preservation Coalition at 33 Union Street, 5th Floor, Boston, MA 02108, (617)367-8998, (617)367-9885 fax.

Information on YouthVisions and the Community Preservation Institute is available in L. Silka, P. Geigis, and W. Snyder (2006), "Education for Sustainability: Preserve Good Ideas—Recycle Them," in R. Forrant and L. Silka, eds., *Inside and Out: Universities and Education for Sustainability Development* (Amityville, NY: Baywood).

Photo: Annaliese Bischoff

Appendix

Indicators of Community Preservation

Elisabeth M. Hamin

M ANY communities across the nation and world are instituting programs for indicators. Indicators, simply defined, are community-determined measurements of elements that are important to that particular place and those particular people. They are ways of seeing "how much" or "how many" or "to what extent" or "what size." Indicators are the best way communities can measure whether they are progressing in the right direction for their given goals and the more general goals of community preservation and enhancement. The indicators movement started with groups working toward sustainability at the community level, and therefore reflects the tenets of sustainability—that the best municipal policies achieve the intersection of improvements to the local and global ecology, economy, and equity. The best indicators are locally meaningful and effective measures of the topic at hand. As described by Maureen Hart of the group Sustainable Measures:

> An indicator is something that points to an issue or condition. Its purpose is to show you how well a system is working. If there is a problem, an indicator can help you determine what direction to take to address the issue. Indicators are as varied as the types of systems they monitor. However, there are certain characteristics that effective indicators have in common:
>
> Effective indicators are *relevant*; they show you something about the system that you need to know.

> Effective indicators are *easy to understand*, even by people who are not experts.
> Effective indicators are *reliable*; you can trust the information that the indicator is providing.
> Lastly, effective indicators are based on *accessible* data; the information is available or can be gathered while there is still time to act. (www.sustainablemeasures.com/Indicators/Characteristics.html, 2004)

Indicators are based on the awareness that what values we hold dear influence what data we collect, but also, what data we have at hand influences the policies we implement. A good example is economic data. If our primary local numbers tell us only how much property tax the economic activity in our town is creating, that is all we will be able to address. We will not be able to directly judge whether those businesses are creating jobs, whether they provide any money to other local businesses, how they affect the environment, and so on. Imagine instead if a community decides that the purpose of economic development is not just enlarging the tax base, but also encouraging local purchasing. This requires a different measure, one based on money that local businesses spend locally, and may suggest different targets for economic development activities. But if we have only the tax base data, we won't know which existing companies to target for support. For this reason, developing an appropriate set of indicators should be a matter undertaken with great citizen participation, and should be based on goals developed during a visioning process (Hart 1996; Kline 1997; Tyler Norris Associates et al. 1997).

A portfolio of indicators is used to benchmark, to measure, progress toward the goals identified in the comprehensive plan or other visioning document. The trends of specific indicators over time can suggest which policies are working, and which need to be adjusted, as the community evaluates its progress toward its goals. Indicators can suggest problems not foreseen in the comprehensive planning or visioning process, such as groups that are not being reached by local services. And the process itself requires a reevaluation of the goals of the comprehensive planning or visioning process, thereby creating a way to keep the process alive, to make adjustments along the way, and to test the validity of goals and programs over time. At their best, indicators projects draw the community together in efforts to measure and achieve community goals, and can publicize those efforts as well, thereby encouraging public support.

One of the challenges of creating indicators is balancing the scientific value of the chosen indicators against their accessibility and the ability of local residents to get involved in doing the actual measurement. Unfortunately, there is often an inverse relationship, in that the most widely accepted measures for scientific accuracy are the least accessible to the public and require the most expertise and equipment. On the other hand, these measurements that are the most scientifically valid may not have the public punch, the media interest, and the ability to generate local enthusiasm that more publicly oriented measures might. An example may help to make this more understandable.

In 1988, the town of Broomes Island, Maryland, was facing a challenge in getting public attention focused on the poor quality of the local Pawtuxent River. Old-timers who paid attention knew the river was getting more and more cloudy, carrying more and more sediment, but there appeared to be little interest in this local knowledge. Similarly, scientific warnings had had little impact. So, that year two sixth-grade science teachers and State Senator Bernie Fowler called the local media, put on white tennis shoes, and waded out into the river. When Senator Fowler could no longer see his shoes, he measured the distance he had gone. Then, in following years, on the same day every year, the senator did the same white-tennis-shoe test of the river's quality. In the meantime the town had taken steps to improve water quality, and thus each year they were able to record that Fowler got farther out into the stream before losing sight of his shoes. Though Fowler is no longer a senator, "the annual 'wade-in' is a big event, which is now promoted by the Maryland State Planning Office. And the indicator has inspired people throughout the bay area to act and measure as well. As of 1998, there were three other communities in the Chesapeake Bay Basin holding their own wade-ins" (Gasteyer and Flora 2000, 594). Clearly, this measure lacks scientific certainty—a storm the day before or failing eyesight on the part of the senator would change the results of the indicator for that year. But this approach succeeded wonderfully in highlighting the problem to the public, getting media attention, and validating local knowledge and thereby creating public support for action. However, it is not the sort of thing one could take to the Environmental Protection Agency to make a case for funding.

What this story illustrates is that there are essentially two kinds of indicators. The first kind are the more commonly known types of data, scientific but often complex, and requiring that experts in the field develop the knowledge. The second kind are more publicly oriented, perhaps less scientific, but able to be undertaken by regular residents or schoolkids, locally meaningful, easy to understand, and often associated with good opportunities for media coverage. I would recommend that a solid indicators portfolio should include some of both of these kinds of measures. To be sure, the scientific ones are generally easier to come up with, and are largely the ones included in our list below. The local knowledge measures require more creativity, and by definition respond to local issues, and thus are harder for a book like this to suggest. One way to go about beginning to identify some of these public indicators would be for a group to discuss what are key problems in the community and talk about how those problems affect their daily life and their perception of the local environment. Are there fewer "good" fish in the river? Have a fish-in and count what kinds are caught. How long does it take a pedestrian to cross a busy intersection? Have a walk-across on the same day each year and see if traffic measures are helping pedestrian access. How many native species of plants can someone count on a walk through the center of town or the local park? You guessed it, have a day when people walk and count native species.

Indicators need not be dry and dull; we all know that getting broad engagement in something is a whole lot easier when it is fun. Ultimately, engagement by the community in publicly measured and publicly interpreted indicators is much more likely to lead to action, as those who do the measurement also are invested in creating change to see the measure improve over time. I do not mean to suggest that only publicly oriented indicators should be used. It is also important to also generate scientific, replicable data, both for itself and for its use in verifying the results of more popularly oriented indicators and their usefulness in applying for funding from agencies and other groups. The best indicator portfolios will include some of both in each category.

In many ways, the indicator project is not new. First, planners and policy-makers have long collected lots of data, often in response to specific questions from legislators. What is different is the explicit recognition that the data we collect—our indicators—should respond to and support explicit community values and goals. Thus it is not just policy-makers who decide what data to collect or have access to that data. Instead it is as much of the community as is willing to get involved who both decide what is important to study, and also get the results and are thereby empowered to more effectively influence municipal policy. Second, because of the connection between the indicators movement and the sustainable communities movement, much of what is measured is different from what might be included in traditional community data measures. This reflects the broader concern of sustainability with quality of life rather than accumulation of goods.

The best indicators from a community preservation perspective will be those that address the connections between the built environment and social and/or environmental capacities and consequences. An example is a measure that calculates the amount of impervious surface—in other words, paved or built square footage where water cannot flow to underground aquifers—as a percent of lot size in new developments. Municipal regulations can encourage more paved surface through, for example, higher parking requirements or can discourage excessive paved surface through incentives for permeable paving or green roofs. Lack of aquifer recharge affects both local and regional watersheds, and more paving brings more stormwater runoff and so increases municipal costs to manage stormwater. So, improvements in this measure suggest that local regulations and practices are encouraging a better environmental and ultimately fiscal outcome from new buildings.

Care is always required in interpreting data, however. Increasing minimum lot sizes might achieve a reduction in the percent of impermeable surface for new developments, but have the negative consequences of fragmenting the landscape, requiring more driving and making non-auto transit choices more difficult, and potentially reducing levels of community interaction as people are more isolated in their homes. For this reason, while indicators are important information, changes in the numbers require explanation and interpretation to really connect policies and their community outcomes.

Listed below are some indicators which communities can consider, divided along the major chapter classifications of the book. As noted above, each community should develop its own set of indicators to reflect both the challenges and the values of that particular town. Nevertheless, it can be helpful to get a sense of what other places have included in their lists, and so for each chapter for which indicators are relevant, we include a few selected indicators for that topic. These are not intended to be a comprehensive list, and instead should suggest the types of measures a municipality may want to consider. We have grouped them together here, along with sources—for example, community indicators lists and how-to guides. When you are ready to begin an indicators project for your town, we recommend that you seek out the advice and examples available either through the Internet or through the sources included below.

This list likely includes too many indicators for any one community to track and interpret well, and also will exclude some indicators that would better reflect concerns and goals of that particular community. It is therefore a starting point, not an ending place. In addition, there are issues that communities need to address, and need indicators for, that this book does not focus upon. At the end of the table are some further areas for which indicators should be sought.

Overarching measure

Ecological footprint analysis (productive land appropriated to support average community lifestyle)[1]

---

1. For more on footprint analysis, see Mathis Wackernagel and William Rees, *Our Ecological Footprint* (Gabriola Island, BC: New Society Publishers, 1996).

Community Process

Chapters 1 & 2

Percentage of voting age population who are registered to vote

Percentage of registered voters who voted in local election

Number of people coming to any public hearing

Identifiable public-outreach consensus building efforts underway or forums undertaken

Evidence of interaction among cross-section of board members and stakeholders (meetings of board chairs or boards + stakeholders)

Number of NGOs active in community

Number of grant proposals filed by municipality and NGO, state, or federal agency partner. Number of letters issued by municipality to support grant proposals submitted by NGO, state, or federal agency partner. Number of these projects receiving funding.

Percent of municipal budget directed toward community development and environmental activities, including staff support for citizen boards

Diversity

Chapter 3

Graduation rate by race and ethnicity

Representativeness of community board members and elected officials by gender, ethnicity, and time living in community compared to community profile

Number of public hearings/notices held in predominant second languages of community

Comprehensive Planning & Zoning

Chapter 5 & 6

Proposed standard subdivisions

Proposed conservation or PUD subdivisions

Building permits issued for new construction

Building permits issued for renovations and additions

Overall average density (dwelling units/acre) of new projects compared to existing town density

Percent of infill versus periphery development

Months projects spent from initial application to permit approval

Public vs. private investment in infrastructure for new projects

Number of years since a comprehensive plan update

Number of years since a comprehensive update of zoning regulations

Number of zoning appeals total and percent approved

Number of hits on town planning Web site or visit to planning chatroom

Buildout/GIS

Chapter 7

Number of layers digitized and ready to use

Number of times GIS data was used by planning staff and boards

Number of times GIS Web site has been accessed by residents

Buildout analysis completed; number of times buildout analysis was referenced in local decision-making

Biodiversity

Chapter 8

Number of vernal pools (or other local issue) protected

Change in annual status reports of any state/federally listed rare or endangered species

Change in annual bird and other species counts

Number of volunteers for habitat projects

Number of days of ecology programming in local schools

Number of acres of wetland or forest (or other locally important habitat) lost or fragmented

Number of critical habitat sites with ecological management plans developed and being implemented

Watershed Planning

Chapter 9

Number of segments in watershed not meeting state water quality standards for bacteria, nutrient concentration, temperature, turbidity, conductivity, etc.

Deficit or excess of water in water budget (inflow minus outflow; goal is about zero); number of sub-watersheds showing deficits

Percent of aquifer recharge area protected through regulations or land purchase

Impervious surface percent in new developments and overall watershed

Number of projects/businesses with alternative water management elements approved (bio-swales, waste water reuse, etc.)

Percent of waterfront (river/lake/coast) with vegetated buffers adequate to protect water quality, quantity, and related habitat

Percent of unaccounted-for water (lost to leaks), or amount of old, leaky piping replaced per year

Liters or gallons of water per day per person used

Natural Lands

Chapter 10

Percentage of high biodiversity lands that are protected through purchase or easements

Acres of farm and forestlands protected through purchase or easements total

Acres of farm or forestland protected through zoning or other regulation (large-lot zoning like 1 house per 3 acres does not count)

Identifiable improvements in connections between existing protected areas

Number of Community Supported Agriculture farms or other "local hero" initiatives

Number of community gardens or number of people involved in community gardens

Percent of land that is unfragmented by roads or homes

Transportation

Chapter 11

Percent of subsidy spent on cars vs. mass transit vs. bikeways, etc.

Vehicles entering city by mode (bus, car, train, bike)

Number of pedestrian/bicycle traffic accidents

Miles of pedestrian-friendly roads

Percent of sidewalks accessible by persons with disabilities

Percent of people who live and work in the city

Automobile occupancy

Number of bike racks in city

Number of low-performing roads (highly congested)

Housing

Chapter 12

Waiting time for subsidized housing

Number of homeless or ill-housed

Population density/average acres used per new housing unit

Energy efficiency per building

Percent of adults that can afford median house price

Percent of adults that can afford median apartment rental price

Number of new units permitted per year

Number of units renovated per year or dollars invested in existing homes

Community Economic Development

Chapter 13

Retail sales per capita

Ratio of business start-ups to business failures

Total number of jobs

Percent of jobs paying a livable wage or enough to afford median house price

Number of adults participating in workforce training either in schools or on the job (if available)

Number of residents attending community college or four-year college

Average monthly percentage of population receiving food stamps

Estimated unemployed plus estimated discouraged potential workers, or change in workforce

Work hours required each month for basic needs

Children living in poverty

Percent of solid waste diverted to recycling

Pounds of toxics produced and released each year

Brownfields

Chapter 14

Number of acres reclaimed per year

Number of sites reclaimed per year

Federal/state/local/private investment in cleanup and reuse

Available listing for investors of property ready for purchase, cleanup, and reuse

Adaptive Reuse

Chapter 15

Building permits issued for new construction

Building permits issued for renovations and additions

Use of alternate building code for older/historic buildings

Historic Landscapes

Chapter 16

Number of landscapes identified as worth preserving

Local and private dollars invested in identifying or preserving landscapes

No. or size of existing historic districts

No. of listed historic buildings and landscapes

Grassroots actions to preserve buildings and landscapes

Beyond those discussed in this book, there are a variety of categories of indicators a community may wish to collect. Some of these include information on community schools, information on access to and use of childcare and preschools, community health statistics such as the percentage of kids getting all their recommended vaccinations, energy consumption, waste and recycling information, and public safety statistics. See the sources below for ideas on indicators for these categories, as well as other indicators that may be useful for your particular goals and community.

References

Gasteyer, S., and C. B. Flora. 2000. "Measuring PPM with Tennis Shoes: Science and Locally Meaningful Indicators of Environmental Quality." *Society & Natural Resources* 13 (6): 589–97.

Hart M. 1996. *Guide to Sustainable Community Indicators*. North Andover, MA.: Sustainable Measures. http://www.sustainablemeasures.com/.

Kline E. 1997. "Sustainable Community Indicators: How to Measure Progress." In *Eco-City Dimensions*, ed. M Roseland, pp. 152–66. Gabriola Island, BC: New Society Publishers.

Tyler Norris Associates, Redefining Progress, Sustainable Seattle. 1997. *The Community Indicators Handbook*. San Francisco: Redefining Progress. One Kearney Street, 4th Floor, San Francisco, CA 94108, or from the American Planning Association at www.apa.org.

Contributors

Jack Ahern is a professor of landscape architecture and head of the Department of Landscape Architecture and Regional Planning at the University of Massachusetts Amherst.

Arthur P. Bergeron, Esq., is a former assistant secretary of environmental affairs for the Commonwealth of Massachusetts and has a private law practice.

Annaliese Bischoff is an associate professor in the Department of Landscape Architecture and Regional Planning at the University of Massachusetts Amherst.

Andrea Cooper is the smart growth coordinator for both the Massachusetts Executive Office of Environmental Affairs and the Office of Coastal Zone Management, and chairs the Low Impact Development Group, a public-private partnership of over seventy-five organizations.

Veronica Eady is a senior staff attorney at New York Lawyers for the Public Interest, Inc. She is also an associate adjunct professor at Fordham University School of Law.

Robert Forrant is a professor in the Department of Regional Economic and Social Development at University of Massachusetts Lowell.

Kurt Gaertner is the director of sustainable development for the Massachusetts Executive Office of Environmental Affairs. From 1999 to 2003 he was engaged in the implementation of EOEA's Community Preservation Initiative.

Glenn Garber is the associate director of the Center for Rural Massachusetts at the University of Massachusetts Amherst, Extension land-use educator, and adjunct faculty in the Department of Landscape Architecture and Regional Planning.

Priscilla Geigis is the director of state parks and recreation for the Massachusetts Department of Conservation and Recreation. From January 1999 to April 2004, she was director of community preservation at the Massachusetts Executive Office of Environmental Affairs.

Toni Coyne Hall serves as associate deputy for community relations for the Office of Policy Development at the Massachusetts Department of Housing and Community Development.

Elisabeth M. Hamin is an associate professor of regional planning in the Department of Landscape Architecture and Regional Planning at the University of Massachusetts Amherst.

Brian Howes started the Coastal Systems Group at the Center for Marine Science and Technology at University of Massachusetts Dartmouth and is now program director for the School of Marine Science and Technology's Coastal Systems Program.

John Hultgren is currently enrolled at Northeastern University School of Law and worked for the Massachusetts

Executive Office of Environmental Affairs in the area of growth planning.

CHRISTIAN JACQZ has been director of the Office of Geographic and Environmental Information in the Massachusetts Executive Office of Environmental Affairs since 1992.

JOAN KIMBALL is the director of Riverways Programs, Massachusetts Department of Fish and Game.

ZENIA KOTVAL, AICP, is an associate professor of the Urban and Regional Planning Program at Michigan State University.

ROBERT H. KUEHN JR. was president of Keen Development Corporation and active in the New England real estate industry and civic groups for more than thirty-five years. He was also vice-chair of the Community Preservation Coalition.

KATHRYN LEAHY is director of Massachusetts Audubon Society North Shore Advocacy.

JEFF LEVINE is the director of planning and community development for the Town of Brookline and the former vice-chair of the Regional Transportation Advisory Committee of the Boston Metropolitan Planning Organization.

SHARON MCGREGOR recently served as assistant secretary for Biological Conservation and Ecosystem Protection in the Massachusetts Executive Office of Environmental Affairs. She currently consults for nonprofit organizations on biological conservation.

JOHN R. MULLIN, FAICP, is the dean of the Graduate School and director of the Center for Economic Development at the University of Massachusetts Amherst.

JANE PFISTER is a GIS/Web/graphics specialist for the Massachusetts Executive Office of Environmental Affairs. From 1999 to 2003 she was the GIS coordinator for EOEA's Community Preservation Initiative.

ROBERT L. RYAN is an associate professor at the Department of Landscape Architecture and Regional Planning, University of Massachusetts Amherst.

LINDA SILKA is a professor in the interdisciplinary Department of Regional Economic and Social Development, directs the Center for Family, Work, and Community, and is special assistant to the provost for community outreach and partnerships at the University of Massachusetts Lowell.

MARK P. SMITH is the director of the Eastern U.S. Freshwater Program for The Nature Conservancy (TNC) and previously was the director of water policy and programs at the Massachusetts Executive Office of Environmental Affairs.

STEVE SMITH is executive director of the Southeastern Regional Planning & Economic Development District, a regional planning agency serving twenty-seven cities and towns in southeastern Massachusetts.

RICHARD TAUPIER is the associate director of the Environmental Institute and a member of the graduate faculty in Regional Planning at the University of Massachusetts Amherst. He is a former (1984–94) assistant secretary of environmental affairs for Massachusetts.

JAY WICKERSHAM is a partner in the Cambridge, Massachusetts, law firm Noble & Wickersham LLP. From 1998 to 2002 he was assistant secretary of Environmental Affairs for Massachusetts and director of the statewide environmental impact review program. He is on the faculty of the Harvard Graduate School of Design.

JACK WIGGIN, AICP, is director of the Urban Harbors Institute and an adjunct faculty member of the Environmental, Earth, and Ocean Sciences Department at the University of Massachusetts Boston, where he teaches courses in urban and environmental planning.

Index

Page numbers in italics refer to illustrations. Page numbers followed by the letter "t" refer to textboxes. Color plates are indicated by plate number in italics (e.g., *pl. 1*).

agricultural protection zoning and, 80–81; amendments/rezoning and, 76, 86; bonus incentives for, 83, 85, 144; floor-to-area ratio and, 47t, 72–74; housing specifics and, 174–75; minimum requirements and, 82–83, 144; perception of, 46t–49t; special permits and, 76; zoning and, 44, 72–74

DEP. *See* Environmental Protection, Department of (DEP, Mass.)

Department of. *See individual departments*

desalination projects, 130

design guidelines, 83–84

design review boards, 84

developers, 49–52; activities of, 41, 43–44; backgrounds of, 40–41; definitions of, 39–40; exactions and, 76–77; lawsuits and, 14; open space valuations and, 146–48; public participation and, 12–14, 50–51; site selection and, 41–42, 50; thinking like, 51–52, 146; transportation systems and, 158–59, 161–62, 164; zoning/building permits and, 4, 44–45, 50, 186

development-oriented transit, 163n

dimensional/bulk zoning limits, 44, 72–73, 83t

diversity within communities, 3, 20, 27–36; case studies of, 27–28, 33–35; community preservation impact questions and, 32t; conflict and, 35; exploring opportunities in, 35–36; faces of, 28–30; indicators of, 244; information gathering about, 30–31; time for public participation and, 3, 29; using measures of, 31–33. *See also* environmental justice

Dixon, David, 174–75

Dolan v. City of Tigard, 77

Downcity Arts Project (R. I.), 213

down-zonings, 76, 86

Dracut, Mass., 29–30

droughts, 123, 124, 128

DuPage County, Ill., 117t

Durand, Robert A., 226, 233, 236, *238*

Durham, N. C., 210

easements, 145–46

East Cambridge, Mass., 159

Eastern Promenade Trail (Portland, Me.), 135t–136t

East Hampton, Mass., 215t

ecological footprints, 110, 243

ecological processes, 104t, 111

economic development, 183–92; adaptive reuse and, 216–17; brownfields redevelopment and, 198–99; case studies of, 189t; comprehensive strategies for, 187–88, 190–92; as core community preservation element, 32; EDICs and, 186; educational systems and, 184–85;

environmental justice and, 29t; financing of, 190; geographic information systems' role in, 93; housing and, 171–72; indicators and, 245; information gathering for, 187–88; land availability and, 184, 185; open space protection and, 138; public participation in, 187, 188, 190; sustainability and, 186; taxation and, 184, 191t; telecommunications services and, 185; transportation and, 156; trends in, 183–87; zoning for, 185–86

Economic Development, Department of (Mass.), 236

Economic Development and Industrial Corporations (EDICs), 186

ecoregions, 107t

ecosystems, 107t, 109, 110, 111. *See also* biodiversity

EDICs (Economic Development and Industrial Corporations), 186

Ellwood City, Penn., 198

e-mail newsletters, 19

eminent domain, 138

endangered species, 107t

Endangered Species Acts (federal and state), 78, 112

energy consumption, 246

Enterprise Zone designation program, 201

Environmental Affairs, Executive Office of (EOEA, Mass.), 22, 31–32, 33, 97, 179, 201, 236, 238t

environmental impact statements/reports, 161

environmental insurance, 42, 201

environmental justice, 29t, 30, 159, 198–99

Environmental Protection, Department of (DEP, Mass.), 18, *pls. 3–4*

Environmental Protection Agency, U. S. (EPA), 35, 196, 198, 201, 202, 217

environmental regulations, 42, 78–79

EOEA. *See* Environmental Affairs, Executive Office of (EOEA, Mass.)

EPA. *See* Environmental Protection Agency, U. S.

"Euclidean" zoning model. *See* zoning

European Union, 186

evolutionary processes, 104t

exactions, 75, 76–77

exclusive use zoning districts, 72

exercise opportunities. *See* active living

extinct species, 107t, 111, 112t

extirpated species, 107t, 111

fact sheets, 19

Fannie Mae Foundation Web site, 176, 179

Fan Pier (Boston, Mass.), 47, *49*

FAR. *See* floor-to-area ratio

farmland. *See* agricultural land protection

federal government: biodiversity protection and, 112; brownfields/Superfund sites and, 196, 201, 202; housing and, 170, 179; land use regulations and, 78–79; transportation planning and, 154, 158–61, 164; watershed planning and, 125; worker training programs and, 198–99

field surveys, 115

Fifth Amendment (U. S. Constitution), 70t, 77

filled empty niche species, 107t

floor-to-area ratio (FAR), 47t, 72–74, 82

Florida, 23–24, 158t

Florida Keys Marine Sanctuary, 23–24

Fowler, Bernie, 242

fragmentation: of habitat, 106, 114; of open space, 143–44

Friends of Sholan Farms, 225

funding: of affordable housing, 85, 179; of biodiversity conservation, 118; of brownfields redevelopment, 201–2; in comprehensive plans, 58; of economic development, 190; exactions as, 76–77; by grant programs, 118, 201–2, 222; of school systems, 50; of transportation, 154, 158–59

Garden Cities movement, 79

Gardener, Susan, 225

generalist species, 102

genetic diversity, 102t

gentrification, 175, 195, 199–200

geographic information systems (GIS), 31–33, 62–63, 91–98, 113, 115, 244

Georgia, 210

GIS. *See* geographic information systems

global climate change, 110, 154

global positioning satellite (GPS) units, 92

Gloucester, Mass., 98, 186

Goleen, Shannon, 238t

GPS (global positioning satellite) units, 92

"grandfathering" exceptions, 45, 74–75, 232

grant programs, 118, 201–2, 222

Greenbelt movement, 79

greenhouse gases, 110, 154

Green Neighborhoods Alliance (Mass.), 21–23

"green space," 134, 174. *See also* open space protection

greenways, 57, 138, 143. *See also* open space protection

growth rates, development, 85–86, 127, 130

Guide to Sustainable Community Indicators, 32

habitats, 106t, 114; loss of, 105–6, 108, 111

Hampshire College, 142t

Hanover, N. H., 143

Harlem neighborhood (New York City), 28, 199–200

Hart, Maureen, 241
Harvard University, 47t
health and well-being, 34t, 137, 246
hearings. *See* public hearings/meetings
heritage landscape programs, 223t–224t
Highway Department (Mass.), 157t
highways development, 153–54, 156
hillside ordinances, 144
Historical Landscape Preservation Grant
    Program (Mass.), 222
Historic Massachusetts, Inc., 178t
historic preservation, 221–29; adaptive reuse
    and, 215–16; case studies of, 157t, 222,
    225–28; comprehensive plans and, 66;
    constitutionality of, 70t; environmental
    justice and, 29t; getting started on, 222,
    225t; heritage landscape programs and,
    223t–224t; housing and, 176; indicators
    and, 245; open spaces and, 137–38, 143;
    overlay districts and, 74, 144; public
    participation in, 223t, 225t; regulation
    of, 78, 87, 226; strategies/solutions for,
    225–26
historic preservation/district commissions,
    11, 78, 84
Historic Resources, Office of (Mass.), 222
Hodges, Allan, 163n2
Holland, Mass., 98
Holyoke, Mass., 208, 214–15, 231
home rule, 70, 232
Hoover, Herbert, 70
Hopeworks 'N Camden, 93, *pl. 2*
Hopkinton, Mass., 96–97, *pls. 5–9*
housing, 167–81; adaptive reuse and, 176;
    in comprehensive plans, 57, 59t; as core
    community preservation element, 31,
    167–68, 170–75; costs for building/
    rehabilitation of, 179t; economic
    development and, 171–72; funding for, 179;
    indicators and, 245; information gathering
    on, 30–31, 168–69, 179–80; infrastructure
    and, 173; inventive solutions for, 172t,
    175–76, 179–80; open space protection
    and, 138, 174; shelter poverty and, 175–76;
    terminology of, 169–70; zoning and,
    172–73, 176. *See also* affordable housing;
    sprawl
Housing and Community Development,
    Department of (Mass.), 236
Housing and Urban Development,
    Department of (U. S.), 170, 179–80, 201

Illinois, 117t, 137, 173, 174–75
immigrants. *See* aliens, legal or
    undocumented
impact fees, 77
impervious surfaces, 125, 129, 134, 137
implementation strategies, 57, 58, 64t, 66

incubators, business, 190
indicators, 5, 32, 63, 148, 203–4, 241–46
Industrial Economics, Inc., 217
industrial parks, 184
industrial water-use plans, 127
informational meetings, 10
information gathering: from affected
    community members, 33; for biodiversity
    conservation, 113–14, 115; citizen guides
    and, 18; for comprehensive plans, 58,
    61–63; on diversity within communities,
    30–31; for economic development, 187–88;
    on housing, 30–31, 168–69, 179–80; from
    municipalities/planning staff, 12–13, 30–31;
    from state governments, 19, 30, 92, 94–95;
    for transportation planning, 164; Web
    sites and, 19, 30–31. *See also* geographic
    information systems (GIS)
infrastructure. *See* capital improvements/
    investments programs
institutional controls, 200–201
intensity restrictions. *See* density of
    development
intermodal centers, 164
Intermodal Surface Transportation Efficiency
    Act (ISTEA), 136t
Internet and public participation, 61
Interstate highways, 155, 156, 159
invasive species, 108–9
Iowa, 28
Ipswich River (Mass.), 130t
ISTEA (Intermodal Surface Transportation
    Efficiency Act), 136t

Johnson v. Edgartown, 80
joint-use easements, 146

Kentucky, 134
Kestral Trust, 142t

Lancaster County, Penn., 143
land acquisition strategies, 41–43, 145–46
land leases, 146
Landscape Architecture and Regional
    Planning, Department of (University of
    Mass.-Amherst), 57
landscape diversity, 102t
landscape preservation. *See* historic
    preservation; open space protection
land trades, 146
land trusts, 118, 145
land-use laws. *See* zoning
land-use studies, 56–57, 93, 94–95
language barriers, 3, 20, 33
large-lot zoning, 80, 143, 173
law-making. *See* legislative changes, initiating
lawns and landscapes, 118, 124, 128
Lawrence, Mass., 208, 210

lawsuits, 14
League of Women Voters, 18
leases, land, 146
Ledum Bog (Mass.), *108*
legislative changes, initiating, 18, 19–20
Leominster, Mass., 185, 222, 225–28
letterwriting campaigns, 19
level of service (LOS), 162t
Lewiston, Maine, 29
Lincoln, Mass., 50
Lindhult, Mark, 57–58
linkage laws, 77
Little, Charles, 138
Living Waters (Mass.), 113
loading areas. *See* parking standards
"local coordination" plans, 58
local planning boards: comprehensive plans
    and, 10, 58, 60; developers' plans review
    by, 44; special permit reviews and, 11, 76;
    subdivision planning/regulation and, 78;
    transportation planning and, 161–62
Longfellow Towers (Boston, Mass.), 46, *46*
Los Angeles, Calif., 134, 201
LOS (level of service), 162t
Louisville, Ky., 134
Lowell, Mass., 3, 28, 31, 33–35, 180, 208, 210
Lowenstein, David, 213
Lucas v. South Carolina Coastal Council, 70t
Lynn, Mass., 208

Maine, 27–28, 29, 134, 135t–136t, 148, 237
major residential development (MRD)
    zoning, 83t
MA:NS (Mass Audubon North Shore
    Conservation Advocacy), 21–23
maps, 58, 93, 115–16. *See also* geographic
    information systems
Maryland, 80, 242
Massachusetts: agricultural land protection
    in, 145; approach to planning in, 2, 5, 44,
    231–37; biodiversity conservation in, 105,
    113–14; brownfields redevelopment in, 42,
    196, 201; community development plans
    in, 97–98; diversity within communities
    in, 29, 35; geographic information systems
    use in, 94–98; growth rates in, 127; home
    rule in, 70, 232; housing in, 44, 56, 172,
    172t; land-use laws in, 44–45, 50, 77,
    232; open space development in, 134;
    state government role in planning, 5, 18,
    236–37; subdivision regulation in, 74;
    tax structures in, 138, 233; transferable
    development rights in, 86; transportation
    planning in, 160. *See also* names of specific
    municipalities
Massachusetts Audubon Society, 18, 19
Massachusetts Bay Transportation Authority
    (MBTA), 156, 159